Further praise for

"In *Human Givens* Griffin and Tyrrell offer innovative perspectives on promoting effective living. They have synthesized brain and social research in such a way that they provide new templates for understanding how to unlock the best in human nature."
Dr *Jeffrey K. Zeig, Director of the Milton H. Erickson Foundation*

"[This] approach offers a refreshing alternative to reams of expensive psychobabble." *The Big Issue*

"Real breakthroughs in the behavioural sciences are rare, and it's smart to beware of hype. But not all scientific progress is incremental. Sometimes, as in the germ theory of disease, it's exponential. Griffin and Tyrrell's contribution advances psychology as much as the introduction of the Arabic numeric system with its zero digit advanced mathematics." *Washington Times*

"While books are never a cure for what ails us in life, they are often a catalyst, a trigger that fires off those rare and profound 'aha!' moments that lead to deeper insights and understanding. *Human Givens* is such a catalyst." *Jack Davies*

"Important original work ... both aesthetically pleasing and of immense practical use... has great relevance to all areas of life... could save (tax payers) millions of pounds. A remarkable achievement which should attract the attention of any truly curious human being."
Dr *Farouk Okhai, Consultant Psychiatrist in Psychotherapy*

"*Human Givens* is the most practical and intuitive book I've read in years. People have been speculating about the utility of dreams for decades, but I think you guys have it hammered."
Charles Hayes, Autodidactic Press, USA

"Psychology doesn't have to be difficult and mystique has no part especially when the writers cross boundaries to take from all quarters and from there synthesize with such clarity. Some purists may not like it [*Human Givens*] but broken fences facilitate a wider view and allow one to see further." *Leo Kingdon*

HUMAN
GIVENS

HUMAN
GIVENS

A new approach to emotional
health and clear thinking

Joe Griffin and Ivan Tyrrell

HG

PUBLISHING

PUBLISHING

This paperback edition
first published in Great Britain 2004
Reprinted 2006, 2007

PRINTING HISTORY:
Hardback edition first published in Great Britain 2003
Reprinted 2003

Published by HG Publishing an imprint of
Human Givens Publishing Ltd, Chalvington,
East Sussex, BN27 3TD, United Kingdom.
www.humangivens.com

A catalogue record for this book is available from the British Library.

ISBN 1-899398-31-7
ISBN-13 978-1-899398-31-7

Typeset in Sabon and Franklin Gothic.
Printed and bound in Great Britain by Biddles Ltd.

CONTENTS

Acknowledgments

IN THE writing of this book, and evolving the ideas and teaching material that stem from it, we have relied greatly on the voluntary and involuntary, witting and unwitting, contributions from far too many people to individually acknowledge: wives, families, friends, colleagues and patients. We thank you all.

We have also had very direct help from Denise Winn and Jane Tyrrell with the organising, presentation and editing of the material.

Our thanks are also due to Elizabeth Abbott whose letter greatly illuminated the section on psychosis. And to Grahame Brown, Nicola and Keith Guy, Michael Hay, Jan Little and Andy Vass who all generously agreed to let us reprint articles that illustrate the importance of the human givens approach to their work. And to Farouk Okhai for reading the original manuscript and contributing such an encouraging foreword.

Special mention must also be made of Henri Bortoft and David Wade for spending the time to give us in-depth comments and invaluable advice as we struggled to clarify our thinking about consciousness and its relationship to matter.

We are additionally indebted to Henri for allowing us to quote from his book, *The Wholeness of Nature*.

Grateful thanks are also due to the estate of Idries Shah for allowing us to quote from his work, particularly the long passage on attention from his book, *Learning How to Learn*. He, more than anyone else, understood and appreciated the real significance of the givens of human nature.

Foreword

IT IS A general rule in medicine that, when there are a number of different theories purporting to explain a condition, one can be certain that all of them are wrong, though each may have certain facts right. There are over 400 different models of psychotherapy in the West today, with the proponents of each model competing with the others and laying claim to primacy. How is it possible to have so many different models when there is general agreement about how the brain works? Can you imagine having 400 different schools of physics or mathematics? By dint of clear thinking, Joe Griffin and Ivan Tyrrell lead us out of this muddle. They have assembled verifiable scientific information on how the brain works, including important original work of their own, and created a new organising idea – the human givens approach – that has the potential to transform the practice of psychiatry, psychotherapy and counselling. Although my interest is in psychiatry and psychotherapy, it is obvious to me that this big idea also has great relevance to other important areas of life, such as education, social work and personal relationships. Some of the information in this book will be new and startling to many, some, at first glance, will appear familiar. But Griffin and Tyrrell's assembly of it is unique in that the bits and pieces that stick out in other therapy models now fit together, and this fit is both aesthetically pleasing and of immense practical use.

For example, they succeed in making reading about depression exciting! This common, rapidly rising condition is costing Western society enormous pain; emotional and financial. It is also a major cause of premature death through suicide. Depressed mood, loss of interest and enjoyment, fatigue, poor concentration, guilt, suicidal thoughts, and disturbed sleep and appetite, are generally agreed criteria used to diagnose depression. Often a person with depression will complain of early morning wakening, with depressed mood and tiredness worst at that time. To overcome the fatigue he or she may try to sleep longer than usual but the tiredness persists. We also know that depressed people spend a greater proportion of sleep time in the REM (rapid eye movement) state, that artificially shortening the REM periods leads to a temporary lifting of the depression, and that anti-depressants, when effective, shorten the REM sleep time.

Griffin and Tyrrell link these findings in a way that makes sense of the facts and provides the basis for rational treatment which could save millions of pounds. The story begins with Griffin's findings from his research into dreams and REM sleep and makes a convincing case for the central importance of REM sleep in depression. A trigger or Activating agent (which may be a divorce, death, unemployment and so on) sends the brain on a search for similar Patterns (previous negative events) setting off a train of introspection which gives rise to the Emotion of depression with resultant Thoughts (such as "I am useless", "nothing ever goes right for me") that the depressed person gets locked into seeing as absolute truth. The prolonged REM sleep periods are attempts to deactivate this highly arousing chain of intro-spection, explaining the early morning wakening (in the more severely depressed) as a mechanism to limit the exhaustion caused by the intense REM activity.

If, when depressed, we are locked into ruminating on all that has gone wrong in our lives, it makes sense that treatment should aim at reversing this deepening spiral. Griffin and Tyrrell explain how the REM state can be accessed to lift the trance of depression quickly using inborn biological mechanisms. Their insight into depression makes sense of the unfortunate, but not uncommon, occurrence that will be familiar to many psychiatrists. Often a patient with depression is admitted to hospital or seen in a clinic, and put on antidepression medicine, but found to be even more depressed a few days or weeks later. Many such patients are often encouraged, by well-meaning staff, including counsellors and therapists, to "talk about their problems". In the light of the findings presented in this book, however, talking about problems and past failures can be seen to simply grind in a guilt-ridden, worthless, useless and unlovable self-narrative as 'the truth' from the patient's locked-in perspective.

In contrast to insight and 'getting to the root' therapies, cognitive and behavioural methods have been shown to be effective for depres-sion. We can now see that this is because they engage the cognitive or motor circuits of the brain, thus allowing the locked-in, highly aroused emotional brain to calm down, so enabling the patient to see alternative truths, possibilities and stories for his or her predicament. In addition to pointing out the erroneous assumption that thought precedes emotion, which forms the basis of the cognitive behaviour therapy model, the APET frame, which they introduce here, provides a much broader perspective. Just as significant, perhaps, as the introduction of the Arabic numerical system with its zero digit was to mathematics, providing as it did a much wider vista than the Roman number system (I–X).

People love stories and this book is illuminated with a number of these, including those known as case histories. Case histories, stories, metaphors, pictures and jokes make things much clearer than a linear argument. Imagine describing a rose to someone who has never seen one and then asking him to identify one at a florist's. But show him even a sketch (i.e. a pattern) of a rose and from then on he will recognise one regardless of the variety. Griffin and Tyrrell explain that we 'see' the world through such patterns, and run into problems when we use the wrong pattern to make sense of our predicaments.

Perception through pattern matching is of crucial importance in the development of post traumatic stress disorder (PTSD) and phobias. In both, the Activating agent (the trauma or phobic stimulus) is of such moment that it imbues a Pattern into the fast brain pathway (the limbic system) so that future experiences with even a fragment of that pattern evoke the terror (Emotion) of the original encounter. Again Griffin and Tyrrell explain how this can be reversed by accessing the REM state, with resolution of symptoms often in one or two sessions.

Another fascinating topic covered, and one of the human givens, is the attention factor. 'Attention-seeking' and 'manipulative' are often used pejorative descriptions of patients and clients, but if the importance of both giving and receiving attention as a normal human need was more widely recognised, the health systems of the world would be freed of an enormous burden. The 'thick notes (or thick chart) syndrome' is no doubt familiar to many hospital doctors: a patient is passed from one specialist to another with each doctor doing a set of investigations and often surgery to remove various organs, but the patient keeps coming back again and again! If their attention needs were met effectively in other ways these particular patients would not need to fulfil them through the ritual of history, examination, investigation, medication and surgery. On the flip side, if doctors and therapists were more aware of the attention factor, they would be better prepared for avoiding the trap of prolonging treatment in order to have their own attention needs met through their patients. As Griffin and Tyrrell relate, the evidence for the importance of the attention factor includes a shocking, ancient, but relatively unknown, experiment carried out by a European emperor.

And there are yet more treasures in this remarkable book including: why trance (focused attention) is a normal frequent everyday occurrence, during which suggestibility is heightened, and its role both in helping (the placebo effect, the transmission of culture and its morals) and harming (the nocebo effect, indoctrination); the conceptualisation of schizophrenia as waking reality processed through the dreaming brain; why autism may be the result of the genetic absence of mammalian templates; why unbridled anger makes you stupid and shortens your life; the therapeutic usefulness of seeing addictions as attempts to meet basic human needs; and why avoiding greed and helping others is good for your health.

The authors have put in a lot of work to show how knowledge of the way the brain works (gathered from a panorama of psychology, psychiatry, sociology, anthropology and neuroscience), can be used to help the distressed humanely. This book should be essential reading for all psychiatrists, psychologists, therapists and counsellors. For the general public, this knowledge is vital if they are to protect themselves, friends and relatives from the chicanery, often unwitting, which passes for much that is called counselling and psychotherapy.

But that is not all. In an intriguing afterword, using the new understandings about the REM state, Griffin and Tyrrell cast a new light on the nature of consciousness and why it might have evolved, a remarkable achievement which should attract the attention of any truly curious human being.

Farouk Okhai

MBCHB, MD (Texas), MRCGP, MRC PSYCH, FHGI

Consultant Psychiatrist in Psychotherapy

PART ONE

New Discoveries About Human Nature

Why we need to understand healthy minds

IT TOOK millions of years for the human mind to evolve to the point where we have the knowledge to direct our own development. We have reached a watershed. Exciting discoveries about how the mind/body system works show how human nature can unfold to create effective and fulfilled individuals. What will we do with this knowledge?

Science has discovered that nature endows each healthy human conception with a wonderful array of living 'templates' – an infinitely rich treasure-house of incomplete patterns that instinctively seek completion in the environment from the moment of birth, and that continue to do so as we grow and evolve throughout our lives. These patterns are expressed as physical and emotional needs and are in a state of continuous ebb and flow. If we are fortunate, and are born into a culture and environment that provides us with the means to get those needs met, we develop well. It is precisely the way needs are met, by the impact life has on them, that determines the individual nature, character and mental health of each person. Studying these innate patterns, and charting their unfolding, is the new science of human nature ... which is what this book is about.

Only by co-operating with these natural processes – the human givens – can children be educated and matured into independent, fully integrated and fulfilled adults. And, when things go wrong and people lose their way, only by working in alignment with the human givens can other people help them overcome emotional problems such as depression, anxiety, addictions, anger disorders and psychotic breakdowns.

And perhaps it is only by understanding these natural processes and overcoming the disadvantages we are also heir to – such as greed, vanity and the ease with which we can be conditioned – that we will be able to evolve further.

CHAPTER ONE

Seeking completion

WE SHARE in common with all living organisms – including plants and the most humble, single-celled, protozoan creature – the fact that we have an 'inner nature' which we have biologically inherited that is always seeking the right environmental stimuli to unfold properly. This truth is easily seen when we study other living things but is harder to grasp in ourselves because we are so wrapped up in the process every moment of our lives.

Every microclimate supports plants that cannot live elsewhere. The warmth and humidity of tropical South American jungles, for example, support over 8,200 orchid species, each with its own special requirements: the right soil conditions, nutriment, temperature, light and pollinating potential. The more unusual the microclimate, the more rare and exotic the plant.[1] The more common the plant, the less complex its environmental needs and the more resilient it is. Any gardener who sees that a plant is not flourishing will recognise immediately that a deficiency in the environment – too little or too much water, for example – is preventing healthy growth, or that the plant has a disease compromising its biological integrity.

At a basic level, all organisms seek nourishment to renew themselves and then give waste material back to the environment to be recycled again and again. Oxygen, the waste gas of plant life, for example, becomes an energy source for animal life.

If we look at human beings in the same way as a gardener studies plants, we can ask: what physical, psychological and social nutriment does this creature need for the successful bringing to fruition of its innate nature? We can also look for what might be preventing these inner templates from connecting to the greater world. But a person is not a plant and we need not just material but also mental, emotional and, some would say, spiritual nourishment if we are to flourish. And, while plants 'know' how to grow, children and adults need structured guidance to optimise their own self development.

The need for meaning

An important human given, the need for meaning, is driving us to write this book. This ancient natural human desire, the quest to understand, originally grew out of primitive creatures' evolving ability to move independently. Indeed, movement is fundamental to the very existence of brains, which developed primarily to control movement, to predict the outcome of movement and remember the result of past movements. Plants, by contrast, never evolved brains since they did not need to do this. (There is a tiny marine creature called the sea squirt which, in the earlier part of its life, swims around like a tadpole. It has a brain and a nerve cord to control its movements. But, when it matures, it attaches itself to a rock and stays in one place like a plant. Thereupon it digests its own brain and nerve cord because it no longer has a use for them.[2])

The mental faculty for controlling movement is crucial to daily life. It is involved in conceiving an idea about what to do, planning a response and then carrying it out. (Literally, when we think about getting a book down from a shelf, our brains mentally simulate the movement.) So important is it that the primary motor cortex and the premotor cortex are both located in the frontal lobe, which is one of the most advanced parts of the brain and determines not only where we direct our attention but also the relationship between short-term working memory and long-term memory.

It also appears to direct consciousness itself, which is why the frontal lobes have been termed the 'executive' function of the brain.[3] Movement and meaning are inextricably linked.

The contemporary search for meaning is infinitely more sophisticated than that of our primitive ancestors like the sea squirt. It now extends multi-dimensionally to the edge of the known universe and down to the sub-atomic level – even beyond space and time. For 35,000 years, since the beginning of cave art in the cultural explosion of the Upper Palaeolithic period, the search for meaning beyond day-to-day survival was spearheaded by remarkable individuals and groups who passed their knowledge on down through the ages.

Initially, through pre-gnostic ('pre-knowing') shamanistic traditions where sticks, stones and animals were worshipped, they explored both human nature and the reality around them, and they expressed and taught their findings through a framework that today is often called 'spiritual': a fluid mix of excitatory practices, beliefs, rituals and experiences all involved in achieving and using altered states of consciousness.[4] Freed as we are from the historical and ideological framework of those times, it is clear that these 'spiritual' researchers were on an evolutionary quest, investigating how to unfold our inner nature more effectively and, in the process, unlock the secrets of outer nature. This effort eventually resulted in the evolution of gnostic ('knowing') traditions. In essence, their *spiritual* quest was a *scientific* quest to understand more of reality by refining their perceptual apparatus in order to see more clearly into the heart of nature. The gnostic teachers among them, who always stood outside the ideologies of their time, always contended that within each human being there is the potential for a far richer personality, or perception. If this inner perception is to develop, it must first be conceived of as a possibility.[5] Its basis, therefore, must rest, in part, on refined imagination.

A person needs preparation (in other words, appropriate environmental input) in order to attain more intelligent perception. And an essential part of the preparation involves a calming down or diminishing of aspects of personality which hinder, or even destroy, the possibilities of refined perception. These include traits such as vanity, greed, self-obsession, etc. People driven by obsessions, for example, are unable to stand back and see beyond them. Likewise, people who are ruled by emotions cannot make progress, because strong emotions overwhelm finer perceptions, just as raucous shouting drowns out a gentle whisper.[6]

History shows that 'spiritual' knowledge, wherever it has appeared publicly, is quickly polluted by the greed in the world; the teachings of wiser people inevitably degenerate into dogma-driven cults, fossilise and become self-perpetuating power structures. Wars are fought, people are indoctrinated and ignorance is entrenched, causing terrible havoc around the world.[7] (Cult formation is not limited to extreme religious groups. It can be found in political parties, among academia, the arts, scientific laboratories, and business – in fact in any situation where people meet regularly, emotions are raised and charismatic personalities exert influence for their own ends.[8])

But the essential pattern of this ancient knowledge about human development is perfectly echoed by, and in tune with, the findings of modern science about not only the physical universe but human development at all levels. Neurobiology, psychology and sociology all show that there *are* inner patterns of perception that seek to connect with the greater world and, when they do, allow for greater refinement and progress as human beings. And it is clear that, when these developmental processes are blocked, we cannot move on.

For example, we cannot be mentally healthy if we are isolated. In her article, "What it feels like to be a child with no friends", Celia Brayfield wrote in the *Sunday Times*[9] about the effect of being brought up by a reclusive mother; "Friend was a word I didn't know when I went to primary school. We didn't do friends in our family. An old, dark leylandii hedge ended our garden and behind it we lived in complete isolation. My mother was content but I was suffocating with loneliness. When I got to school nobody wanted to play with me and quite a lot of children wanted to beat me up."

Little Celia drifted unhappily around, thinking, "I want to be your friend but I don't know how," and "… wondering why the other children were being so horrible. When people pick on you, you feel you must deserve it. I didn't know the rules and I certainly didn't know any of the songs or rhymes or skipping games a girl needs if she's going to be a social success in the playground.

"With no friends, I was also an easy victim for the bullies," she said. "On top of the normal day-to-day punching and kicking, the ringleader once threw me face first down a flight of stairs."

The article was inspired by a recent report on social skills teaching in British primary schools. The report estimated that one primary school child in five now has problems related to lack of social skills and mental health. It also highlighted the considerable body of research showing that, when small children have emotional difficulties, they can't learn anything.[10] Celia Brayfield wrote, "I was acting that out wonderfully [at school]. Although my mother made sure that I knew my letters and numbers before I started school, I lost them instantly and was soon lagging behind the rest of my class. The teachers thought I might never learn to read.

"I was saved by a teacher who took me aside in the playground and asked why I wasn't playing with my friends. Miss Potter was few people's favourite, a strict lady with fierce red lipstick, but her heart was surely in the right place. When I answered that I hadn't got any friends, she gave me a lecture on basic social skills. It began, 'To have a friend you must be a friend,' and, although I couldn't have been more than six, I've never forgotten it. Take the initiative, talk to people, smile, be nice and kind, do as you would be done by. It was probably the most useful thing I ever learnt in school.

"I went right out and did what Miss Potter had recommended and very soon had excellent friends."

Despite a successful career, missing the natural window of opportunity to learn essential social skills in the vital first years still left a shadow over her life. "I'm still not sure I'm doing life right," she says. "Often, I feel I'm lurching through relationships like young Frankenstein's monster trying to tap dance. I hear myself talking and my conversation sounds as appropriate as Eliza Doolittle on her outing to Ascot. I envy the dazzling creatures who draw a vast circle of friends around them like moths to a flame and I know I'll never be one of them. But I get by and I hate to think how my life would have worked out if Miss Potter hadn't intervened in it."

This example of what happens when just one need is not adequately met perfectly illustrates the principle behind the human givens approach. Here we see that, if the need to build rapport with others is not supported in the important first few years of life, it affects development and our lives as adults. Without meaningful connections to family, friends or colleagues, it's not easy to move our lives forward. In such circumstances anyone, however intelligent, can become emotionally overwrought and become stuck in the cycle of depression, unless such a lack is resolved.

With this modern needs-focused view of human nature, the old questions about the meaning of life can be put into sharper focus and we can develop a contemporary understanding about them. Just as one human given is that we are social creatures and need connection to a group of people who accept us, so too is it a given that we need meaning. But, just as its roots are in movement, meaning cannot be a static thing. It must, as in ancient times, be a 'stretching' process that continues to reveal new meanings by refining our perceptions and thus increasing our knowledge. There is always more to learn and understand. It is this stretching process, as our brains continually resculpt through new learnings, that makes us such an adaptable species.[11]

We can all feel a sense of flow, meaning and purpose when we challenge ourselves in some way: advancing a project, or developing a sport, skill, craft or art. As we stretch ourselves, something within us is seeking to fulfil an inner need through finding its completion in the environment[12] – a process that might be termed spiritual. Obviously, the challenges people face vary from person to person. It might be the process, for a businessman, of developing a new business or, for a musician, mastering difficult new music, and, as such, the process will be a spiritual one, because it serves to refine perceptions. And yet an activity that is initially stretching will soon become mechanical if, for instance, the business isn't developed once it is up and running or if the mastered music is simply repeated. To be stretched further, we need to seek new challenges. The brain always needs new challenges to keep it stretched, otherwise neurons (brain cells) start to atrophy. A busy brain is a healthy brain.

Mountaineers, for example, can spend years preparing to do something that to others might seem inherently pointless: to climb the sheer face of a huge mountain, at the top of which the rarefied air is difficult to breathe. Why would they want to do something as uncomfortable and dangerous as that? Well, for them, it is an intensely meaningful experience. They have more bliss in their hearts as a consequence of doing it. That is what draws them to climbing. Life *always* seems more significant when we stretch ourselves, in whatever way, because we are then more connected to reality. Many human needs, such as those for goal seeking, for physical agility, for endurance, for visual accuracy, for teamwork and for status, would find fulfilment in mountaineering, but this would satisfy climbers only for a limited duration. If mountaineering becomes too routine, and the climbers are no longer stretched, it ceases to be a spiritual activity for them because they no longer have to make a conscious effort to achieve mastery of it.

If we feel lonely, anxious, greedy, depressed or angry, there are clearly aspects of ourselves that are not being stretched. Parts of our nature have not developed properly, preventing the refinement and unfolding of other aspects of ourselves. We cannot develop more refined perceptions without fulfilling more basic human needs and appetites first and in a balanced way: just as alcoholics cannot develop and stretch their capacity for human relationships because of their drunken behaviour.

Pursuing this thinking, we can see that what a large part of this world mistakes for spirituality is nothing more than brainwashing by ideological organisations – from the extreme activities of fundamentalists like the Taliban in parts of Asia today, so reminiscent of the Christian Inquisition in medieval Europe, to the evangelical cults and happy-clappy new age religions that thrive in Western countries by gathering people together in groups to sing and emote. They sincerely believe that the feelings they generate in their practices are related to spirituality, whereas, however enjoyable they may be, they are manifestations of the 'herd instinct', which we share with rats, sheep and wildebeest. Whilst herding does indeed fulfil an inner need (safety in numbers), it is at a very primitive level.

From our point of view, spiritual activity is not simply the mouthing of ritualistic words and phrases and performance of formulaic movements, but the linking of the inner to the outer, the developing, stretching and refinement of human nature to fulfil a higher level of potential. To stop our search for meaning – our spiritual activity – at the level of the herd instinct and attention seeking, which is what seems to happen in many organised religions, is clearly not aiming very high. Perhaps now, with the new science of human nature, we can move beyond brainwashing and mindless repetition of old dogmas to realise that the continuing scientific quest for knowledge and meaning *is* one expression of contemporary spirituality and perhaps our most important undertaking. (Whether people choose to use or misuse the knowledge that is thus acquired is another issue.)

Nature gives each of us the potential to develop, but we have to be continually challenged to find proper fulfilment. There is a continuum. Getting our basic needs met is at one end, and the unadulterated search for truth, the most profound and difficult form of stretching for us, is at the other. So we can view the ongoing stretching of our capacities, as our inner templates try to find a match to relate to in the environment, as a developmental process. If this is what the spiritual quest is really about – connecting the inner to the outer – we can see it on a natural continuum, a scale built into the way matter and life has evolved.

The postmodernist fallacy

This idea is, of course, the opposite to the ubiquitous, some would say anarchic, postmodernist views that originated in modern art and design and have taken root and spread through all aspects of our culture like a virulent infection. Postmodernists believe that there are no absolute truths and therefore, because everybody's point of view can be deconstructed, all opinions are of equal value. They promote this with totalitarian ruthlessness, imposing institutionalised political correctness on the rest of us.[13] This may often seem harmless, as when someone can lie in bed all day claiming that this is a work of art simply because they say it is, and financially profit from their 'work'. Such behaviour gives people something silly to talk about. But some postmodernists do much more than exploit the gullible. They go so far as to say that all thought is equally relevant (that there are no boundaries, no rules, no hierarchies, no objective reality and all facts are just 'social constructs'), all species are of equal value, and a human being is no more important than an ant. This 'deconstructionalism', as it is termed, is a pseudo-scientific quest for negation.

But the postmodern concept is made redundant because we, *and nature*, can measure. The scaling question to ask is, to what degree does a plant or creature connect up its innate genetic templates to the environment and how complex are those templates, in terms of refinement of its perceptions? Clearly, a bat has access to an echo-sound location template that we do not possess. But, in overall complexity, its templates must be scaled lower than ours. In humans, for example, moral behaviour results from the ability to perceive and act on our shared interdependence and respect for other people's needs. To return to herding for a moment, we can see the herding instinct in a cloud of midges, birds, cows, and other animals; and we can see it in human beings, in any large gathering such as in football stadiums or churches. While getting together and singing from the same hymn sheet is clearly a low-grade activity, it is at a higher level than the swarming of midges because a human grouping contains more possibilities for learning, development and change.

There cannot *but* be measurable differences between human beings: some can run faster than others; some are less mathematically ignorant; some have more mechanical aptitude; some have more musical aptitude, etc. Clearly, different templates are differently refined in different people. It is the degree to which a species evolves more refined templates that determines how advanced it is. And, just as there are more highly evolved – adaptable – species, so will there be more highly evolved, adaptable, individual members of a species.

The growing knowledge that there is such a natural scale for gauging not only the development of a species but how individual members are flourishing will, hopefully, consign destructive postmodernist beliefs to curious footnotes of history.

The science of human nature

The ultimate aim of education (the word comes from the Latin *educare*, meaning to draw forth, bring out, develop from a latent condition) is to unfold and refine what is within. In real education (as opposed to conditioning people or training them to pass exams), the way we know that a young person or pupil is progressing is by observing how well he or she is learning to discern subtle distinctions in the meaning of observable phenomena as their perceptions become more refined. The process of successfully matching up inner patterns to the outer world is not experienced as a vague subjective feeling that could just as easily be generated by drugs. It is revealed objectively, in the ability of a person to perceive more of the richness of the patterns by which the world operates and therefore be more effectively engaged in it. This is why it is often said that a truly spiritual person is not a hermit sitting on a mountain contemplating his navel, but someone involved in the world.

Such an understanding removes the so-called conflict between science and spirituality – which is, in fact, only a conflict between fundamentalism in science and fundamentalism in religion. If spirituality is the search for meaning, the ultimate stretching of human potential, this must be the science of human nature and its unfolding.

Science and spirituality are therefore compatible, something the wisdom traditions down the millennia have always maintained. Once we realise that spirituality is about getting needs met, the complexity of relationships and connecting up patterns of understanding about how the world operates, we can see that it cannot be separated from the search for knowledge. Moreover, when a real understanding is present, it enables the possessor to be more effective in the world.

Approximately 35,000 years ago,[14] human beings became more than intelligent animals just instinctively reacting to promptings from the natural world all around. A great leap forward in human evolution occurred: we discovered how to access the dreaming brain, our own reality generator, so we could consciously daydream and use our imaginations, drawing on memories of the past, to visualise possible futures. The most talented individuals and groups who took this step and developed their imaginations quickly learned how to plan more successful hunting trips, solve problems, develop more specialised new tools, empathise and ask abstract questions (complex language, with a past and future tense, cannot develop without imagination), make music and entertain, decorate and clothe themselves, and educate children more efficiently. Some remarkable individuals seem to have elected to teach others, including children (as we know, from preserved footprints), how to access their imaginations by taking them deep into mountain tunnels and caves, sometimes two or three miles underground. Here, far away from the constant noisy distractions of the natural world, they taught them to use their brains in a novel way, to conjure up new thoughts and images. In such quiet subterranean centres, what we can only term 'psychological research' took place, and cave art began. Here were schools[15] for developing outward-focused imagination and speeding our ability to learn, directly connect with and understand, in greater depth, the natural world and a sense of invisible powers beyond it. People studied and thought about animal behaviour in new ways until eventually it was possible to domesticate, use and breed many formerly wild creatures. Fellow man also became infinitely more interesting to our ancestors, as, once possessed of imagination, they could not help but be aware that their lives were precarious and difficult, and began to realise that individual survival would be much better assured within social groupings. They could imagine how they might change their situation and stretch themselves in non-selfish ways for the long-term benefit of all.

About 10,000 years ago, in many regions of the world, we changed from being hunter-gatherers to farmers. Early farmers needed the ability to observe seasonal changes closely over long periods. They had to analyse information, perceive what was needed for a crop to develop its potential as food or medicine, learn how to plan long term and to find solutions to problems that arose, such as how to irrigate dry land and organise the manpower to harvest crops. They also needed a certain philosophical attitude towards the unpredictability of weather, blight and so on, and had to take account of the fact that skills were unevenly distributed in the tribe. Without access to imagination, none of these capacities could have come into being, and the development of farming, and the civilisations that arose as a result of it, would never have taken place.

Adapting to now

We nomadic hunters, farmers, villagers and small-town dwellers have reached the twenty-first century where most of us now live in urban conglomerations of great complexity. The wonderful boon of imagination we were given 35,000 years ago, as well as creating what is great in our culture, has also created an environment that seems out of control. We have the means to magnify our greeds and have made a world that whirls around us so fast, and in such disturbing ways, that we can no longer trust our culture to reliably provide the psychological nourishment for us to develop fully as human beings. When things go wrong and there are power cuts, transport system failures, wars, financial market crashes etc. – individuals feel helpless. The speed of change, and the carelessness with which governments instigate change, explains much of the massive increase in many forms of mental illness. The latest statistics show that half of all people in our culture will suffer from mental illness at some point in their lives and up to 20 per cent of the population is mentally ill at any one time. A fifth of all children are said to be seriously emotionally disturbed. The pressure is building rapidly.

To make another leap forward in our evolution, one every bit as significant as the great leap forward of 35,000 years ago, we urgently need to understand the inner processes that must be properly nourished for psychologically healthy human beings to mature, and nurture our children accordingly. That will involve a huge shift in perceptions for much of our species. Without such a shift, however, we can see that we are heading towards massive and unsustainable levels of mental illness, leading, perhaps, to our destruction. But human development grows out of necessity, and the pressure this puts on us generates fertile seeds of hope, waiting, hiding in strange places, for the right conditions to bring on the next phase in what will, we hope, be our continuing story.

CHAPTER TWO

Where does human nature come from?

IT IS A TRUISM that we come, as all matter must, from the stars. The basic elements, vast energies and great distances of deepest space that we measure with our sophisticated instruments and try to understand with our science and struggle to grasp in our imaginations, are where our consciousness originally came from. These fundamental physical elements and material processes in the universe may be our evolutionary parent, but to understand human nature we need first to pick up the story closer to home.

The unfolding growth of any living thing – plant or animal – can seem to the unsophisticated mind as if it is powered by some magical unearthly force. It is certainly an infinitely complex process. But we know that it relies on information transcribed from the genes, passed down through the ages. Genes provide the factual basis for the existence of any living thing. They are hereditary blueprints encapsulated in deoxyribonucleic acid (DNA), the chemical composition of which was discovered in 1953 by Watson and Crick.

But how do the genes insert their programmes, particularly for instinctive behaviour, into the brain? The answer, it seems, is that it happens in what is known as the rapid eye movement (REM) state of brain activity and, if you wish to understand how your mind works, there is perhaps no better place to start than by looking at the REM state,* an enormously important human given.

Curiously, it was also in 1953 that the REM state discovery was first

---

* In the early days of sleep research, various terms were employed to designate this active stage of sleep. Michel Jouvet, for example, called it paradoxical sleep: other researchers called it dream sleep. But the term REM sleep, although unsatisfactory in that it is only descriptive of one physical phenomenon associated with the state, is now widely used throughout the scientific community to designate it. So we use this term in this book.

published, by the American researchers Aserinsky and Kleitman.[1] They noticed that, for about three-quarters of our sleep, the brain was in a state of comparative rest. This state became known as slow wave sleep, the most recuperative part of any 24-hour period for any mammal, when the body is at its most efficient in fighting off infection and when tissue damage is repaired. But Aserinsky and Kleitman also observed that, for nearly a quarter of all sleep periods, the sleeping person exhibited darting, rapid eye movements behind the closed eyelids. They then soon established that the brain was highly active at this time, using as much energy as when awake. But it was several years before the connection between this state and programming instincts was made.

As we illustrate in this book, many mysteries of human psychology and mental health have been solved through studying the implications of the information that scientists painstakingly gathered as a result of Aserinsky and Kleitman's discovery. We now know, for example, why we evolved to dream; what dreaming is doing for us each night; why depressed people wake up exhausted (and how they get depressed in the first place); how the brain can become traumatised; how the brain learns; why we are so easy to condition, brainwash and manipulate; what psychosis is; how and why exchanging attention is so important; what hypnosis is – and much more.

The risk and the prize

To begin our exploration, we must ask some fundamental questions about the role of sleep. Why *do* mammals sleep? Day and night, in forests and fields, desert and tundra, caves and houses, creatures find the safest places in which to curl up and fall asleep. And, whilst asleep, why do they spend the majority of the time in slow wave sleep – the state in which the body and brain recuperate from the previous day's wear and tear – and some of the time in the REM state, completely paralysed, cut off from sensory contact with the world and all its dangers? What possible evolutionary advantage could there be for creatures to be so vulnerable for so much of the day – literally paralysed and at risk from hungry predators?

It was the French scientist Michel Jouvet who discovered that REM sleep was accompanied by muscle paralysis – specifically, the inhibition of antigravity muscles.[2] (The internationally agreed system for recording sleep phases now includes recording the signals coming from the muscles, as well as eye movements and brain waves.) And he was also the first to suggest that REM sleep may have evolved to permit more freedom in the expression of instinctive behaviours, pointing out that REM sleep, homeothermia (being warm-blooded) and the flexibility of instinctive behaviour are linked because being warm-blooded allowed the higher vertebrates more freedom of behaviour and was inevitably accompanied, as mammals continued to evolve, by increased complexity in brain development.[3]

In other words, once mammals and birds could keep a constant internal temperature, instead of their behaviour being governed, as in cold-blooded creatures, by simple set responses to changes in the environment, they became far more mobile with more options available to them.

There was a downside to achieving this increased mobility, however, and that was that the fivefold increase in the energy they needed to expend to achieve it had to be matched by a fivefold increase in energy intake.[4] It made no evolutionary sense for the increase in flexibility to be expended purely in increased time spent searching for food. Animals could save some energy by sleeping when they weren't hungry or when no food sources were available (and perhaps this is when slow wave sleep developed) but this alone wouldn't help generate the required extra energy.

What was also needed was a more highly developed and intelligent brain that would enable mammals to inhibit instinctive drives when they weren't required and to stimulate those actions that were likely to be more productive. This meant evolving a 'thinking cap', a higher cortex capable of suppressing, at least temporarily, some of the less vital instinctive responses whilst still able to direct behaviour to reach goals which the organism wants to achieve – the very role undertaken by the expanded neocortex in mammals. As the researcher Paul Maclean observed, "A remarkable feature of the neocortex is that it evolved primarily in relation to systems receiving and processing information from the external world, namely the exteroceptive, visual, auditory and somatic systems. It was as though the neocortex was designed to serve as a more objective intelligence in coping with the external environment."[5] For the instinctive brain to be able to respond to this new intelligent input, a new type of programming had to be developed. A type of programming that would make instinctive responses much more flexible and capable of being modified in their expression by this ongoing stream of information being processed by the cortex. The REM state, as we shall see, developed for this purpose.

The recognition of the importance of REM sleep as a programming state grew out of a crucial set of findings about when REM sleep occurs, gathered from information collected in sleep laboratories around the world. It soon became clear to scientists that REM sleep occurs most frequently when we are very young and less often when we get older. Also, it starts long before we are born. At between 27 and 40 weeks, human foetuses spend up to 80 per cent of their time in REM sleep. When they are born, 67 per cent of sleep time is REM sleep, a proportion that gradually reduces to 25 per cent by middle childhood. As healthy adults we spend about a quarter of our sleep in the REM state, until we reach old age, when the amount lessens. This clearly supports the idea that REM sleep is a programming state.

So too does the fascinating finding of William Dement and his colleagues in America. They noted that the amount of REM sleep an animal has depends upon how mature it is at birth.[6] Those species whose young are born capable of living almost fully independently, in terms of both mental and physical functions, have very little REM sleep at birth. Those species which are highly immature when born, however, show high levels of REM sleep. A baby guinea pig, for example, is born fully developed – a perfect miniature of its parents. At birth it needs to spend just 15 per cent of its sleep in the REM state. By contrast, the newborn rat is totally immature. It is born blind, naked and immobile, and spends 95 per cent of its sleep time in the REM state. But it doesn't stay immature for long and, within a month, REM sleep accounts for under a third of its sleep time.

The conclusion which Dement and his colleagues reached is that REM sleep is most important for the very young and clearly has something to do with the developing brain. Maybe, they thought, it provides stimulation for the developing cerebrum in an environment (the womb) where not a lot that is new and stimulating occurs. But meanwhile, back in France, Professor Michel Jouvet was suggesting a more plausible reason for the variations in length of REM sleep, one which fitted with the findings of Dement and his colleagues but improved upon their conclusions.

Jouvet suggested that REM sleep is concerned with programming the central nervous system to carry out instinctive behaviours.[7] He showed experimentally that REM sleep is controlled by a primitive part of the brain, and that, when a particular area of the midbrain is removed (the part which controls the inhibition of the antigravity muscles), cats seem to act out their dreams, which take the form of instinctive behaviours such as chasing or attacking (invisible aggressors), mating, drinking or grooming motions, and fear reactions.[8]

Other scientists' research findings supported his conclusions. It was observed, for example, that human babies also act out what appear to be sophisticated expressions of emotion during REM sleep – showing apparent perplexity, disdain, scepticism and amusement, etc. – and that they don't do this while awake.[9] Moreover, some of these emotions, scepticism and disdain for example, don't come into use until later in life. Another researcher noted that young babies smile in REM sleep, yet they don't do so when awake till they are several weeks old.[10] And yet another suggested that, because newborns can breathe, suckle and swallow as soon as they are born, none of which behaviours is required in the womb, they may learn this instinctive ability during REM sleep. (Observation of foetal lambs has shown breathing movements of the chest wall in REM sleep, regardless of the lack of air to breathe.[11])

Furthermore, babies born prematurely are seen to spend as much time in the REM state as they would have if they had remained in the womb for the normal 40-week term.

All this adds up to compelling evidence that the REM state serves to programme instinctive behaviours which the young of the species will need as they go through life. This endogenous source of stimulation sculpts the development of the brain. After an animal is born, the stimuli it encounters as it grows continually prompt the unfolding of more layers of this instinctive knowledge. Ever more complex neuronal connections are created in each stage of its life. When, as we reach sexual maturity, we set out to find a mate, fall in 'love' and produce children of our own, we are acting out the instincts laid down from our genes whilst asleep in the REM state many years before.

Now we come to another important question. If we just had straightforward, set, instinctive responses to everything we ever encountered in life we would be nothing more than mechanical robots. So, how exactly do these instinctive templates laid down in REM sleep make mammals more adaptable, flexible and intelligent?

Why the brain is a metaphorical pattern-matching organ

Clearly, animals we share the world with have instinctive responses that are the same throughout a species. Horses, for example, have their own way of communicating with one another, which has been studied in depth by many people. Monty Roberts, the original 'horse whisperer', is quite clear that this language is an ancient pattern of behaviour that *all* horses share. "The language of horses is universal. It has not even so much as an accent. So, if I go to Japan or Australia or Canada or Germany, wherever, it is exactly the same."[12] But we also know that horses and all other mammals have greater flexibility to adapt to changes in the environment than cold-blooded creatures, such as fish and reptiles, do.

This flexibility gives great advantages. Birds, for instance, which also exhibit REM sleep for short periods, instinctively set about building nests. But the diversity of shape, size, composition and location of nests built by birds, even of the same species, shows how great the variation can be in the execution of this seemingly simple piece of instinctive behaviour.[13] In effect, birds are programmed with an instinct to look for 'twig-like' things with which to build the nest and 'soft' materials with which to line it. This flexibility allows them to use straw, wire, plastic, etc., as well as twigs, to build a nest, and feathers, paper, foam, moss, scraps of cloth, etc., to line it. Similarly, many parent and baby mammals use the uniqueness of their voices to identify where the other is when they are out of sight. Humans might not be able to tell the sounds of baby animals apart but their parents clearly can. The instinct to respond to another's voice pattern is flexible enough to include the whole range of voice patterns that may be found within a species, from among which the individual can select the right voice as being 'like' the kind it is programmed to look for.

The more unspecified the parameters of genetically anticipated stimuli (and responses as well), the greater will be the flexibility in the animal's behaviour, and the greater the environmental learning component of the instinctive behaviour can be. In other words, the more patterns to match to that a creature has, the greater its metaphorical ability and the more flexibly it can operate and evolve. An example from studies of tool making by chimpanzees illustrates this. When they discover that their fingers are not long enough to get into the nests of the tasty (to them) ants and termites, chimpanzees will select a twig, strip it of leaves and push the thin end of the twig deep into the nest. They then wait patiently for the food to walk out along the twig, whereupon they gently pick it off and eat it.[14]

The more complex the life form, the more varied and rich are the instinctive patterns, or templates, laid down in it. Human beings are the most flexible of all mammals; therefore, our instinctive programming has the largest capacity for environmental input. By the time they are born, babies are already primed to look for human faces and build rapport. They can copy actions, sticking out their own tongues when an adult does likewise – yet how do they even know where their tongue is and how to move it to copy another's actions? As leading child development specialists say in *How Babies Think*, "[As babies] we know, quite directly, that we are like other people and they are like us."[15] This can only be as a result of instinctive programming.

To achieve this intelligence, instinctive programmes need to be sufficiently flexible to allow for a wide range of environmental variation. No baby can know in advance the exact shape or colour of its mother's face, nor the language that she speaks. Babies, like all mammals, need to know how to act in whatever environment they find themselves. This, it seems, is why instinctive *but incomplete* patterns of behaviour are programmed into the developing young of a species. The more incomplete or unspecified the 'programme' is, the greater the flexibility in a creature's behaviour, and the greater the opportunity to learn from the environment.

So we have partially answered why it is we need to sleep and go into the REM state. It has to do with the risky enterprise of evolving warm-bloodedness. That was the prize. For mobile life forms to become more flexible in their relationship with other creatures and inanimate matter – the plant kingdom and ever-changing weather and food supplies – they needed to develop the ability to exercise more choices. And the metaphorical abilities we evolved – to look for something important for our survival which is 'like' something we have been programmed to recognise (e.g., in the case of a baby, a nipple or the teat of a bottle or even, for a time, a finger tip), allow us to do that. It is these same metaphorical abilities that we use to learn language, build rapport, use imagination, question and analyse our own emotional responses and so on. And they are all programmed into us during REM sleep as metaphorical patterns. Since the patterns are never exact, they have to be held in an incomplete metaphorical form.

So, the brain is essentially a metaphorical pattern-matching organ, constantly seeking environmental stimuli to match up to the instinctive and learned responses amassed since conception. Not only does this give us the ability to recognise something we need (such as a nipple or teat) but it is the means by which we recognise something when we come across it again (we see a chair and can identify it by pattern matching, at the speed of light, to our knowledge of what chairs tend to look like). We use pattern-matching and metaphor to communicate with others ("it's like this" or "it's like that"), and to build on our understandings about the world (inventors often devise new ways of doing things by enlarging on or adapting the way something is achieved in nature). Our brains are constantly pattern matching, relating what is new to what we already know.

Metaphorical communication is an intrinsic part of the way all human beings understand and communicate experience. This is particularly important for therapists and teachers to understand because, just as we have the potential to identify appropriate metaphors, we may also make inappropriate metaphorical matches between two patterns. In fact, error is inevitable on some occasions because the capacity for analogy or metaphor *derives biologically from the programming of instinctive behaviour*. Instinctive templates for behaviour can only specify patterns to be identified in an approximate way. Many people have seen films of the ethologist Konrad Lorenz being followed around everywhere by a family of young goslings. Goslings are pre-programmed to attach themselves to the first large moving object they encounter after hatching because, normally, this would be their mother. Now, if that large moving object happens to be Konrad Lorenz's wellington boots and they attach to him and not the mother goose, clearly the wrong metaphorical patterns have been identified. The birds bonded with Lorenz: they followed him persistently; they became distressed when he left them and ran to him for support when they felt frightened.[16] Clearly this was a situation where the matching of an instinctive template to its environmental counterpart had gone awry.

Human beings have a far more sophisticated, creative capacity for identifying metaphor than do animals, but it stems directly from the metaphorical processes found throughout the animal kingdom. We have the ability to think analogically, that is, to think holistically, and to recognise how a pattern metaphorically matches another pattern. But we also have the ability to think logically, to break problems down and analyse them. Our conscious mind's preferred mode of operation is logical thought while that of our unconscious mind is analogical or 'association of ideas', as it is sometimes called. Unconscious thinking, therefore, represents by far the largest part of brain activity because everything of which we are not immediately conscious is, by definition, unconscious.

A great many mental problems are caused by these thinking processes going awry. When someone who has been sexually abused in a past relationship, for example, finds that they cannot bring themselves to have sex with a present partner whom they love, they are making a false analogical connection between the old abusive relationship and the new healthy one. It is a form of learned helplessness that the logical conscious mind seems powerless to overcome. Another example of false analogy matching is when a person is highly aroused early in their sexual life and makes associations between that arousal and particular objects, activities or situations. They then continue to be sexually 'turned on' by such connections (fetishism) which can seem inexplicably perverse to others. From this perspective, the goslings following Lorenz's wellington boots are 'perverts'.

When people unconsciously match present events to patterns established in the past that are inappropriate to the current situation, they need help to unhook themselves from those patterns. Such faulty conditioned responses get in the way of a normal response, preventing them from being fully in the present. (There are well-established techniques for doing this, which we explain in Chapter 11.) By contrast, the type of counselling that encourages the emotional re-experience of past problematic situations has the undesired effect of enhancing the mismatch – engraining the inappropriate patterns deeper – and thereby raising the emotional pitch, harming the patient and keeping them longer in therapy, or rather, as we prefer to call it, 'pseudotherapy'. (Of course some counsellors who encourage patients to review their pasts emotionally also go on to encourage their patients to take a more empowering view of their history, reframing it so as not to see themselves as victims. This can be highly beneficial.)

Without sleep, we warm-blooded creatures die

We know that REM sleep remains essential throughout life. The dramatic results from the first known experiments on sleep deprivation, conducted over a hundred years ago, found that it took between seven and ten days for puppies to die if they had no sleep. Why they died was unknown to the researchers at the time. Postmortem examinations showed no obvious changes in brain tissue or other vital organs.[17]

One of the great veterans of sleep research was Allan Rechtschaffen who, with enormous ingenuity, devised experiments with rats that enabled scientists to study the effects of 'net' sleep deprivation on test animals without other variables getting in the way. His control animals slept normally but in every other way were treated the same as those deprived of sleep. He found that there was no doubt sleep deprivation alone was responsible for the death of the test animals.[18]

Rechtschaffen and his colleagues searched and searched for explanations. At first they suspected a drop in body temperature might be the cause because all the test rats showed a decline in body temperature. But, when the experimental rats were kept warm with heaters, they still died. Breakdown in bodily tissues caused by accelerated metabolism or systemic infections was also ruled out in a series of elaborate experiments.[19]

Even though Rechtschaffen's studies failed to find out the direct cause of death in his sleep-deprived rats, they did provide us with new information. One consistent observation was that the test rats ate increased amounts of food while, at the same time, losing weight. These changes suggested that sleep-deprived animals have an increased metabolic rate, as though they have an increased need of energy. In fact, near death, the sleep-deprived animals showed an energy expenditure two to three times above normal. This could be caused only by excessive heat loss or by a dramatic change in the set point of the brain thermostat.

Rechtschaffen thought hard about this and went on to devise more ingenious experiments which showed that, indeed, the set point of the brain mechanism that keeps internal heat at a constant level was increased by sleep deprivation. Rats who had been deprived of sleep for two weeks preferred to remain in a 'heat corridor' where the ambient temperature was 50°C (122°F). The control rats found that unbearably hot and fled as fast as their legs could carry them to the part of the corridor where the ambient temperature was 30°C (86°F). Clearly, if the test rats preferred to be in a much hotter environment, their internal thermostats had been altered. Sleep deprivation disrupted the activity of the brain cells responsible for temperature regulation.

In further experiments, Rechtschaffen found that rats prevented from having REM sleep were unable to keep their body temperature stable. It became clear to him that REM sleep deprivation did not cause a change in the brain thermostat but did cause the disruption in heat conservation. The link between the evolution of warm-bloodedness and the REM state in the brain could not be more clear.

Interestingly, when sleep-deprived animals were near death and then allowed to sleep, all of these changes could be reversed. Most remarkable was that the animals showed large amounts of REM sleep rebound. They had to catch up on what they had missed. On the first day that they were allowed to sleep without interruption, overall length of REM sleep was five to ten times greater than normal. Rechtschaffen's conclusion was that "the need for paradoxical (REM) sleep may exceed the need for other sleep stages".

Other eminent researchers, building on even more recent work, go much further. "REM, it seems, is some sort of supersleep," said J. Allan Hobson.[20] He gives three reasons to support this. The first is that, "although it normally occupies only about 20 per cent of the total time we sleep each night, it takes only six weeks of deprivation of REM sleep alone to kill rats, compared with four weeks for complete sleep deprivation. Based on its relative duration of only 20 per cent of sleep time, we would predict that five times as long a deprivation period would be required if both states were equally life-enhancing." On these terms, one minute of REM sleep is worth five minutes of non-REM sleep.

The second reason he gives to support the idea of REM supersleep is one that will please catnappers around the world. Short naps are surprisingly beneficial "if they occur at times in the day when REM sleep probability is high. Daytime naps are different from night sleep in that we may fall directly into a REM period and stay there for the duration of the nap. Since the time of peak REM probability is greatest in the late morning, the tendency of naps to be composed of REM sleep is highest then and falls thereafter till the onset of night sleep (about twelve hours later)." The implication is that a little bit of sleep, at the right time of day, may be more useful than the same amount later on.

The third reason is that "following the deprivation of even small amounts of REM sleep, there is a prompt and complete repayment. The subject who has been denied REM sleep launches into extended REM periods as soon as he is allowed to sleep normally. In recent drug studies, when REM sleep was prevented the payback seemed to be made with interest. More REM sleep was paid back than was lost."

He then goes on to propose "a link between brain-mind states and genetics" which makes sense, given the evidence that our instincts are laid down from our genes in the REM state.

We would go further and suggest, from these findings, that, since babies show REM from about 10 weeks, it is the primary state of consciousness. As the sense organs start to receive inputs from the environment, the brain pattern matches to the instinctive templates programmed in during the REM state. Every time a new pattern-match is made it is preceded by a spark of consciousness, an alertness about what might be, followed by that 'ah ha!' moment as the pattern is recognised. After a baby's birth, this happens at an ever-accelerating rate, as templates for breathing, swallowing, seeing and connecting with human faces, responding to human touch, drawing milk from a mother's breasts, etc., are matched up to reality. As children grow and come across situations and things that they don't instinctively know how to deal with, the more conscious they become.

Waking consciousness is clearly a modification of the REM state. When the outside universe first gives feedback to the brain that it can pattern match up to, it is the templates programmed in during the REM state that generate a model of reality in us from which we operate. As we experience more, adding more memories, the reality we generate becomes ever more complex. Just as waking reality is a modification of the REM state, derived from input through our senses from the outside world, so our dream reality – when information from the outside world is cut off – also depends on the REM state, as we shall see.

But why, once we are programmed in early life with all of the instinctive behaviour patterns we require, do we need to continue to go into the REM state every night of our lives and, in a state of body paralysis, dream our dreams? To penetrate the secrets of nature requires great concentration and application. In the next chapter we will look at how the result of such effort, piecing together the implications of existing scientific knowledge about the REM state, and building upon it, has yielded the answer. This answer is having many surprising consequences and has enabled the development of key insights into, not only dreaming, but how we learn, depression, post traumatic stress disorder (PTSD), psychosis and autism, as well as giving us a richer understanding of consciousness itself. And all of these insights have huge practical applications.

CHAPTER THREE

The dreaming brain

WHEN WE wake up and remember our dreams, we are aware of a vivid quality that we totally believed in while dreaming. Sometimes we recall them as feeling more intensely real than waking reality. It is as if, while dreaming, we are 'locked' in our dream, removed from the outside world, engaged in something important. And that is exactly the case – as we will see.

Studying and interpreting dreams has a long history. The intensity and ubiquity of the dreaming experience made mankind certain that dreams were significant in some mysterious way. From ancient Sumeria we have written records from over 4,000 years ago that recount the oldest known heroic tale, *The Epic of Gilgamesh*. It is about the search for immortality and is full of dream accounts. In one dramatic dream, for example, Enkidu, the travelling companion of Gilgamesh, sees what the afterlife is like and this gives him a sense of certainty about the relationship between life and death that influences his whole view of the world.

To the ancient Greeks, dream interpretation was almost an industry. At one time there were about 420 sleep temples; these were dedicated to Asclepius, an acclaimed healer of eleventh century BC, and were where dream interpretation was practised to seek answers to problems and cures for illnesses. People would lie down on a *kline* (the Greek word used for a bed in these temples), whilst incubating dreams in which medicaments or other means to restore health in a sick person were said to be revealed to the dreamer. The influence of Asclepius continues to this day: from the names of his daughters, Panacea and Hygieia, we have the terms 'panacea' and 'hygiene', and the word *kline* is the root of the modern word 'clinic'.

So important were dreams to the Greeks in the ancient world that they had a god of dreams, Oneiros, who gave his name to *The Oneirocritica – the interpretation of dreams*, a series of five books by the Greek Artemidorus who lived in Italy in the second century. He held a sophisticated view of dream interpretation believing that the same type of dream could have a different meaning depending on the character and circumstances of the individual dreamer. *The Oneirocritica* was the second book to be printed in Europe on the Gothenburg Press and was still being used as a dream manual up until the 19th century.

Many Greeks believed that remembered dreams could influence waking action and that they were also channels of communication between man and his gods. They even had a means of accounting for why some dreams were based on reality and came true, while others didn't – true dreams came from the 'Gate of Horn' while false dreams came from the 'Gate of Ivory'.

But some Greeks took what is regarded today as a more modern view. For example, Petronius wrote: "It is neither the gods nor divine commandments that send the dreams down from the heavens, but each one of us makes them for himself." Plato noted that our higher reasoning faculties were absent in dreams leaving the way open to the expression of unbridled passion. He asserted that in all people there was a lawless wild beast whose presence is glimpsed in dreams of passion and anger. But he also thought it possible to have morally superior dreams when reasoning is appropriately stimulated and for knowledge, which we didn't know we had access to, to come into us in dreams.

Aristotle argued that so-called 'prophetic' dreams were simply coincidences, not heavenly messages, declaring that the most skilful interpreter of dreams is "he who has the faculty for absorbing resemblances", in other words, someone who can make metaphorical connections between waking events in the dreamer's life and the dream content. He also believed that dreams could in some way reflect the physical state of the dreamer and could therefore be used as a diagnostic tool, an idea also proposed by Asclepius and Hippocrates.

The Bible is full of significant dreams in which God imparts advice to individuals specially chosen to receive it. Early Christians adopted wholesale the beliefs about dreams and their significance from other religions, just as readily as they incorporated existing sacred sites, rituals and beliefs from earlier belief systems. This changed in the fifth century after the time of Saint Jerome, a Christian monk and celebrated 'Father of the Church'. We know from his writings that he was obsessed with sex. Consequently, he had frequent sexually explicit dreams (which, predictably, he denounced as the work of the devil). His view that dreams were from the devil spread throughout the Christian world, was actively promoted by the Inquisition, and didn't begin to fade until after the Renaissance. After Jerome, any revelation given to an individual in a dream was seen as satanic because only the Church had the right to interpret God's word and those interested in studying dreams, or pronouncing on the basis of them, were associated with the devil. Later, Martin Luther, the founder of Protestantism, endorsed this view. In his eyes, sin was "the confederate and father of foul dreams".

The learning and insights of the ancient cultures of Greece and Rome, as well as middle and central Asia, were collected, translated and preserved by Muslim scholars after the rise of Islam. Dreams and dream interpretation played a major role in Islamic cultures – the Koran itself is said to have been revealed to Mohammed largely in a series of dream visions – and dream 'interpreters' were once wide-spread.[1] But it wasn't until the nineteenth century that European scientists started to take an interest in the role of dreaming and made hypotheses about the connection of dreams with events experienced while awake and emotions insufficiently suppressed during sleep. It was Sigmund Freud who merged all this together with his theory of the unconscious, to create the first modern theory of dreaming.[2] In 1900, he published his mammoth work, *The Interpretation of Dreams*, a title borrowed from Artemidorus, the Greek scholar who had pub-lished five books on the subject over 1,700 years earlier.

Freud believed that dreams represented "the royal road to under-standing the unconscious". His theory was crucially informed by his understanding of neurosis, which he saw as an individual's unwitting expression of the inevitable conflict between conscious wishes and unconscious repressed ones. Dreams, he concluded, were the product of repressed wishes in the unconscious mind breaking through briefly into consciousness. (When an individual was awake, he reasoned, these wishes were 'censored' by some part of the conscious mind, whereas, during sleep, they could slip past if they were disguised in the form of a dream.) Freud thought that dreams were protective, enabling unconscious wishes to be expressed but without disturbing sleep. If the repressed wishes were not disguised sufficiently well in a dream, however, the 'censor' would be alerted and the dreamer would awaken, aware of having experienced what we call a nightmare.

Freud had many complex explanations for why dreams take the forms they do, seeing these as necessary distortions enabling repressed infantile wishes to be linked to an individual's active store of waking concerns and worries, or even insignificant thoughts and images, to get past the 'censor'. The deep meaning of the dream could only be reached, he believed, by means of free association to each of the elements recalled from the dreams – letting the mind roam freely, having taken as a starting point a dream element such as a fall or an erotic encounter with a dark-haired stranger. Freud was convinced that all dreams had a sexual concern at source.

Carl Gustav Jung, Freud's one time colleague, felt that, although free association might reveal a client's deep psychological concerns, it couldn't reveal the meaning of a dream. Nor did he feel happy with Freud's idea that dreams were disguised to slip past a 'censor'. He thought that dream symbols must be the unconscious mind's natural 'language'. He developed the idea of the 'collective unconscious', his term for an archaic consciousness of primitive people from which, he said, modern consciousness evolved. These archaic elements, he suggested, were sometimes expressed in dreams as archetypes, which could only be deciphered through a broad knowledge of myth and legend.[3]

Jung's theory, though never as popular or well known as that of Freud, informed the widely held modern view that dreams can help the conscious mind handle emotional problems more effectively. (This, however, is only indirectly the case, as will be explained shortly.)

Modern dream theories

In 1953, the researcher Calvin Hall put forward a cognitive theory for dreams being seen as a continuation of normal thinking processes about daily personal concerns.[4] He concluded this on the basis of findings from research that he was carrying out when the first atomic bomb was dropped in Japan. None of his subjects, he noted, had a dream whose content reflected this momentous event in any way. Hall thought that dreams were like works of art, through which ideas and concerns were transmuted into pictures. These images, once perceived by the conscious mind in a dream, would enable dreamers to develop a true sense of their self-conceptions, unadulterated by conscious distortions. He collected an impressive amount of evidence for his theory by recording other people's dreams, making careful content analyses and showing how often the content of the dreams correlated with the dreamers' known waking concerns. However, his basic tenet that dreams are personal communications does not really stand up. Why, after all, would nature devise such an intricate biological system to generate 'works of art' that – far from reliably communicating our preoccupations – are largely forgotten on waking?

This is where thinking about dreaming remained, until the uncovering of new and irrefutable scientific information made it possible to develop a whole new understanding. As we have seen, around the time that Hall was developing his cognitive theory, biological knowledge about the nature of sleep was progressing rapidly. Exciting new findings emerged from sleep research laboratories, following on from the discovery by Aserinsky and Kleitman that sleep occurs in different phases, including the phase of sleep that occurs every 90 minutes throughout sleep and is accompanied by rapid eye movements (REM)[5] It was quickly established that REM accounts for between one and a half and two hours of sleep time per night.[6] Moreover, people who volunteered their services to sleep research laboratories and who were awoken during REM sleep were found to remember their dreams 80 per cent of the time. Whereas, when they were awoken from what came to be called slow wave sleep, which had four phases of its own, they could recall their dreams only seven per cent of the time.

It was then found that REM sleep was experienced not only by humans. Nearly all mammals go into REM sleep, as we described in the last chapter. Even birds exhibit the REM state for short periods. For scientists, this finding alone put paid to the highly speculative Freudian and Jungian theories about dreaming because it was inconceivable that anyone could ascribe neuroses to cows, unresolved Oedipal complexes to kangaroos and archetypal myths to the parrot family.

Mental activity akin to dreaming, but usually of a more prosaic, recursive nature, has also been detected in about 60 per cent of non-REM awakenings. The mind is not by any means completely switched off during non-REM sleep. Mental activity, such as thinking, occurs at least some of the time, as do dreamlike processes. However, these are qualitatively different and can be separated out by sleep researchers. These non-REM dreams tend to be shorter, less complex, less visually and emotionally intense and less surreal: in short, less dreamlike. Their production involves very different parts of the brain. The dreamlike fragments which are most like REM are collected from Stage I onset sleep, which has a similar cortical arousal pattern to REM sleep.[7] An explanation of why dreams can occur at this stage will be particularly revealing, as we shall see later. For now though, we are noting that a partial engagement of the dream production system can be observed outside of the REM state proper.

The all-important PGO spikes

New information piled up. Michel Jouvet's discovery that REM sleep was accompanied by muscle paralysis – specifically, the inhibition of antigravity muscles – was also crucial, when linked to a different finding by Giuseppe Moruzzi. Moruzzi found that the REM state could be divided into 'tonic' and 'phasic' components. In the tonic phase, which lasts throughout REM sleep, the muscles are immobilised. However, periodically, bursts of sudden brief activity are imposed upon this underlying immobility, explaining not only the rapid eye movements but also the fine twitching of the muscles that also occurs.[8] This is the phasic stage. In this stage, changes in breathing and heart rate were also detected.[9]

All of these bursts of activity happen when electrical signals, called PGO spikes, occur in the brain. These signals arise at the bottom of the brain (in an area of the brainstem called the pons), move upwards into the midbrain (to a part called the geniculate body) and then to the occipital cortex in the higher brain. The signal gets its name PGO from its course – from pons (P) to geniculate body (G) to occipital cortex (O).

It soon became clear that the neurological system that generates the PGO spikes and the resultant phasic component of REM sleep is completely distinct from the system that causes the muscle immobility,[10] and can also be detected in other phases of sleep.[11] This would indicate that PGO spike activity may be linked to dreams, as these too occur outside of REM sleep. It may even explain why dreams occur in sleep phases other than REM and why the dreams are not so complete – because, as previously suggested, there is only partial rather than total engagement of the dream production system in hypnagogic dreaming (the twilight zone between wakefulness and sleep).[12]

We need, therefore, to think about the PGO spikes as a discrete but important aspect of REM sleep and dreaming. Studies into the effects of depriving humans of REM sleep for a night or more have shown that, on the first night that REM sleep is allowed again, there is an increase both in the amount of REM sleep experienced and in the amount of eye darting and muscle twitching that goes on – the PGO spike-generated phasic activity.[13,14] In an experiment in which a cat was aroused very gently at the point of entering REM sleep, the researcher, William Dement, found that, although the cat didn't re-enter the REM state when it went back to sleep, there was still a lot of PGO spike activity. Even when REM deprivation had occurred for a couple of days, the cat attempted no increase in REM sleep to compensate for all it had lost. But it did continue to show plenty of PGO spike activity. Importantly, this revealed that it is the phasic element which accompanies REM sleep that we can't do without, not the REM sleep stage itself, even though REM sleep is the most usual form in which we make up for the phasic deprivation. Clearly, something important is going on in the brain at these times of sudden PGO spike activity.

Dement also found that, when he deprived cats of REM sleep for any appreciable period, they started to show highly increased arousal patterns, becoming easily sexually aroused or easily tipped into aggression and rage. A few days after he gave them a drug which inhibits the synthesis of the brain chemical serotonin they started to produce PGO spike brain activity when awake. (It wasn't at that time known that PGO spikes could also ordinarily be produced when awake.) The cats showed hallucinatory behaviour and underwent dramatic personality changes – they were hypersexual, aggressive and constantly wanted to eat. Then, as time passed, and the PGO spike activity spread evenly throughout waking and sleeping, the cats became lethargic as if exhausted.

What was going on? Dement concluded that there are two systems via which animals, including humans, carry out, or discharge, instinctive impulses, and that we only have so much energy available to us with which to do so, after which our stores become depleted. Our instinctive behaviour is partly governed by the basic drives to drink, eat, reproduce, etc. The rest of it is governed by the PGO spikes, which do not operate when basic drives (for instance, to eat) are in operation. But what is the second drive system, governed by the PGO spikes during REM sleep, discharging? Although Dement came up with a suggestion, he was never really happy with it. As he put it himself, it seemed implausible to imagine that REM sleep exists to stop the nervous system from becoming overexcited. We can show, however, that the PGO spikes do indeed govern an important drive discharge system, a highly sophisticated one with vital consequences for our emotional and physical health.

Dement and others had been paying attention to the role of PGO spikes during sleep. In the 1980s, another team of researchers made the discovery, referred to above, that PGO spikes also show in the brain during normal waking behaviour, although this finding isn't widely known. PGO spikes, it appears, are part of the alerting system or 'orientation response' that draws our attention towards anything new and potentially threatening that is happening in our environment.[15,16] So the spikes are activated when there is a loud noise, and we turn towards it to see what caused it, or when a smell of burning leads us to the kitchen or when a sudden movement draws our eye. At the same time as the spikes are generated, we freeze momentarily (paralysis); signals start stimulating the cortex to let it know that something needs our attention, and other physiological reactions occur that are also characteristic of the REM state. In other words, the REM state is, effectively, one prolonged orientation response. The significance of this will be shown shortly.

The compelling evidence that REM sleep serves to programme instinctive behaviours which the young of the species will need to activate as they go through life might lead one to argue that, once the programming is done, the need for REM sleep should cease. Jouvet attempts an explanation for this. He suggests that programming instinctive behaviours on a continual basis enables more flexibility. Thus, according to an animal or human's individual experience in life, REM sleep might enable either the original programming to be reasserted (nature over nurture) or allow the effects of experience to modify the programming (nurture over nature). However, no analysis of dreams from REM sleep showed any consistent pattern of interaction between waking behaviour and the rehearsal of instinctive drives. Thus, although their discoveries added enormously to our understanding of REM sleep's early purpose, neither Dement, Jouvet or any of the other great researchers in the field were able to put a finger on why REM sleep is essential right through life for our survival. They had not answered the most fundamental question: why do we spend about a twelfth of our entire lives dreaming?

To answer this question it was necessary to look once more at the content of dreams, but in a light informed by the new biological discoveries. This is exactly what was done by one of the writers of this book, Joe Griffin. The full story of how he reached his findings is told in the book *The Origin of Dreams: how and why we evolved to dream*.[17] The following is a shorter account taken from an interview with him about his work.

Recording dreams

"My interest in studying why we dream began when I was a young psychologist. I woke up one morning and then drifted back to sleep and dreamed I was climbing a castle wall, which was starting to crumble, much to my alarm. When I awoke, with this image still vivid in my mind, I realised that just before I had gone back to sleep again, I had been thinking about a childhood experience when I had pulled myself up on a wall to retrieve a ball which had fallen on the other side. As I climbed the wall, I grasped a stone which loosened and fell away. I fell backwards on to the grass verge and the stone hit me on the forehead, making a gash large enough to require stitches. I still have the scar.

"I was already extremely interested in dreams and had read as much of the relevant scientific literature as I could find. So I knew about Calvin Hall's theory that dreams were 'works of art' which reflected the unvarnished personal concerns of the dreamer. It seemed clear to me that my dream was a graphic version of my earlier thoughts but with some significant changes. The roadside wall had become a castle wall and the single stone which came loose was replaced by an entire crumbling wall. Also, the dream seemed to reflect what just happened to have been in my mind after waking and before I dozed off again, which could hardly be considered to be a personal 'concern' of momentous proportions. So that was the moment I decided I would collect my dreams on a systematic basis and see whether I could link them with waking concerns or not.

"The problem I then faced was that I only rarely recalled my dreams. I knew from research findings that we all dream several times a night, even if we only rarely recall a dream. I also knew from personal experience that, when we do recall a dream, it is essential to tell somebody else about it immediately, or to write it down, otherwise we automatically seem to forget them. Certainly, whenever I go back to sleep again following recall of a vivid dream, I rarely remember it when I wake up. The solution, I decided, was to do as many before me had done and keep a pen and paper beside my bed so that, when I did remember a dream, I could commit it to paper straight away and not risk forgetting it.

"Over a period of time I became more and more proficient at recalling my dreams. I reached a point where I could automatically wake up after a dream sequence and record it there and then. What was more difficult was to recall and reflect on my thoughts and experiences of the previous day, which I hypothesised would be the subject of the dreams. Because of the metaphorical richness of the dream content, it was almost impossible for me to detach myself sufficiently, straight away, to identify what the elements of the dream might be standing for. I found it more fruitful to put the dream to one side and come back to it some time later, with a fresher mind. When I became more adept at doing this, I would almost invariably find myself recalling an experience or concern which showed a striking structural and symbolic similarity to the dream sequence. As I continued to collect and study my own and other people's dreams over the next nine months, I became convinced that dreams were representations of the most emotionally arousing experiences of the previous waking period. What's more, these experiences were *always* expressed in symbolic or metaphorical imagery.

"I recorded any dream, however insignificant it seemed, and was struck to notice that still all the dream elements were metaphorical. (It is accepted that dreams use metaphor but had not been known that *all* are cloaked in it.) I found that no one except the dreamer ever 'played' themselves in any ordinary way. If husbands, mothers or other relatives or friends featured in a dream as themselves, they were either out of 'shot' or were symbolically disguised in some way. Often relatives, friends or colleagues, even celebrities, appeared not as themselves but as relevant aspects of the dreamer's personality.

"This can be clearly demonstrated in a dream reported to me by Michael, an Irishman who came to see me for help with a personal problem. He had been a hospital porter but had recently begun training to become a psychiatric nurse, and was worried because he badly kept wanting to laugh at inappropriate moments when in the company of his fellow students. To relieve this need to laugh, he had developed the habit of making a jocular remark and then laughing heartily at it himself. This worked well enough with hospital porters but was not going down too well among his new student colleagues who, due to their training in psychology, had become more hypersensitive to odd traits in one another. I had suggested that his need to laugh was due not so much to his seeing humour in any given situation but more to his need to relieve the embarrassment he was experiencing in it.

"A few days later Michael reported a dream to me in which he was in a church which had a waist-high wall dividing the altar from the area where the congregation was sitting. In the dream he was on the other side of this wall from the congregation, and was urinating up against it. Standing on the altar was the chat show host Terry Wogan; he was the only one who could see what Michael was doing and was laughing. Everyone else started laughing too, assuming Michael had cracked a joke.

"In this dream, it seems clear that Terry Wogan (whom Michael had recently seen in person) stands for an aspect of Michael himself – the public image he thinks other people have of him: a witty and intelligent Irishman. People in the dream assume he has made a joke but in fact he is laughing at his own embarrassment. Even the urination is an interesting metaphor for his tension ('pissing' himself) and the uncontrollable need to laugh ('pissing himself' laughing). The wall dividing the altar from the congregation represents the barrier between his hidden self – the part that is anxious and embarrassed in company – and his public self, whom people see laughing.

"However, although the metaphorical pattern of this dream is extremely clear, I did not yet have an explanation for why dreams should so reliably take this form.

"At the end of nine months I felt confident that dreams were metaphorical expressions of waking concerns and presumed that the most important waking concerns were what the brain chose as the subjects for dreams. At this point, why we needed to dream, and why we dream in metaphor, still remained a mystery, but at least I could put the hypothesis that dreams were metaphorical translations of our most important waking concerns to a scientific test. If this theory was right, it should be possible to set up an experiment to predict the theme of dreams in advance. All one would have to do is to make a list of one's most important waking concerns in the day before dreaming, then compare this list of predicted dream themes to the actual dream themes recorded from the dream material collected during the night. If the theory was correct, the predicted dream themes should match those recorded.

"So as to have access to as many of my dreams as possible during the period of the experiment, I decided to set my alarm clock at two-hourly intervals every night for a week. Each evening I prepared my list of dream theme predictions, based on my most important emotional concerns of the day. To my utter dismay, the experimental results quickly showed that the theory could only be partly correct. Some of the predicted themes did appear in dreams but some of my most confident predictions failed to materialise. More disturbing still was the fact that often the dream themes reflected relatively trivial waking concerns whilst ignoring major ones. Clearly, some additional criteria besides emotional importance were being used by my brain to select the themes from waking experience to feature in my dreams. I decided to carry on collecting my dreams for another 12 months to see if I could identify what these criteria could be, but they continued to elude me.

"The breakthrough came when I had a row with my wife, Liz. She, a hard-working nurse, was, unsurprisingly, getting extremely fed up with being woken several times every night by my alarm, as I single-mindedly pursued my research. I was also suffering from tiredness and the stress of constant reflection on each previous day's happenings in order to explain dreams. This pressure resulted in an enormous row between us one night at bedtime. We both vented our feelings fully and turned away to sleep back to back, in a huff. As I was lying there it crossed my mind, before we eventually fell asleep, that this row was very likely to form the basis of a dream. So, I did what any self respecting experimenter would do: I risked further complaints from Liz, switched the light back on, and noted it.

"Yet, although I recorded five dreams that night, and my worries about the success of the experiment featured symbolically in a few of them, none contained anything that could be related to the row. It was while puzzling over this that the missing piece of the jigsaw suddenly fell into place: during the row with my wife I had *fully expressed* my anger, therefore completing the pattern of arousal, whereas my ongoing worries about the experiment were *not discharged*. What becomes the subject of dreams, I suddenly realised, is not *any* emotionally arousing events but *unexpressed* emotionally arousing concerns from the previous day that had not completed the arousal/discharge cycle. Far from supporting Freud's theory that dreams reflect subconscious infantile wishes, I confirmed, as I continued for several more years to collect and study dream content, that anything emotionally arousing, even television programmes, can become the subject matter of dreams if the arousal pattern is not completed – acted out – in the daytime.

"I concluded from this that dreaming is the acting out of uncompleted emotionally arousing introspections, all elements of which appear in the guise of sensory analogues – metaphorical representations. And this process would serve to free up the brain to deal with the emotionally arousing events of the following day, instead of having to maintain a readiness to continue responding to the emotionally arousing introspections of the day before.

"It follows that an important benefit of this REM process is that it serves to preserve the integrity of our instinctive personality – our underlying instinctive templates. This is because inhibitions placed upon the expression of an instinctive reaction pattern whilst we are awake are removed by acting out the completion of the pattern in the dream process.

"This does not, of course, mean that we can't learn to modify the expression of our instincts. On the contrary, because of our highly evolved higher cortex, we can, with practice over time, learn to control, for example, our anger and the expression of it, just as we can learn to postpone immediate satisfaction of our lusts and appetites. But dreaming maintains the *original* instinctive impulses at their original strength, as given to us by our genes. This is necessary because, although, thanks to our higher cortex, we can learn to control the expression of instinctive impulses, we may also need access to them in different circumstances. For example, anger is mostly not an appropriate reaction for normal minor irritations; the smooth running of social intercourse is more often better served when it is inhibited. But there are times when anger could be vital to our survival, to defend ourselves from physical attack, and we need access to it. Fortunately, the cortex is infinitely malleable and we can do that. It is a wonderfully flexible system whereby the instinctive core personality is kept intact but its expression can continually readapt to different circumstances. Our instincts are never closed down permanently in a specific direction. We can always go back to the original template.

"Just think what a disaster it would be if nature allowed us to be able to turn our instincts down permanently, with ease. We would be infinitely less flexible creatures. A child could quickly learn, say, that it is better to stay quiet and be non-assertive in certain situations. But later on, in situations where it was absolutely essential to survival to be assertive, he or she would effectively be crippled.

"So, one of the big advantages of dreaming is that it stops us becoming completely conditioned creatures. It is no accident that most totalitarian leaders sooner or later hit upon the effectiveness of sleep deprivation in order to torture and brainwash prisoners.[18] This is effective because, without REM sleep to re-mint the core templates and keep them in order, people quickly become unstable and more easily brainwashed and reprogrammed.

"If I was right about all this, I thought, this would be a very different matter from dreaming serving to solve problems or deal with concerns or even just to throw light on our worries, as others had suggested. It would mean that the dreaming process is, instead, a method of making 'space' in the brain. Without it we would need the most gigantic brains to contain all our unexpressed drives and concerns. Indeed, support for this idea came from research findings about one of the most primitive mammals: the duck-billed platypus. It has a huge neocortex, compared to what might be expected, and spends more time in REM sleep than any other creature – up to eight hours a day. This suggests that it is reprogramming entire instinctive programmes on a daily basis. Not only that, the evidence shows that the REM sleep of the platypus is the kind we see in the programming stage of the foetus.* The cortex is not stimulated and so dreaming cannot be taking place.[19]

"I further found that, if an issue is an ongoing concern, it will very likely be thought about again the next day and reappear in some form in next night's dream, hence repetitive dreams. This is all backed up by my experimental findings over twelve years of collecting dreams and by evolutionary explanations for the role of REM sleep, which help explain not only why the discharge of emotionally arousing events is needed, but also why dreams are metaphorical."

To dream, and let off steam

So, to recap, REM sleep continues into adulthood so that we can dream and thereby maintain the integrity of the instinctive templates that themselves were laid down in the REM state. It deactivates, once it has been stimulated, any undischarged emotional arousal that would be unproductive and consume unnecessarily high amounts of energy. We wouldn't survive very long if we all lashed out every time we got irritated or if we attempted to engage in sex every time a sexual thought crossed our minds. Bottling up such arousals and storing them would require much too much brain space. (Alas, we don't have a 'pensieve', the wonderful invention into which Albus Dumbledore, Harry Potter's headmaster at the Hogwarts School for Wizards, would

---

* Mammals, such as whales and dolphins, also have disproportionately large cortices. For a long time it was believed that they did not have REM sleep because they suffered the Ondine curse: they could only let one hemisphere sleep at a time because they might drown if they spent time paralysed in REM sleep. Hence the extra large cortex. But recent observations show that this genus seems to have evolved a highly specialised form of sleep that has the characteristic jerks of the head, neck and sometimes the whole body and the rapid eye movements typical of REM sleep in terrestrial animals. But these periods only last a very short time: the animal is paralysed, rolls over and begins to sink but then comes out of this sleep state to swim and breathe again. [Lyamain, O. I. et al (2000) Rest and activity states in a gray whale. *Journal of Sleep Research*, 9, 3, 261–267.]

siphon off all the thoughts and memories he didn't want to crowd his head with.[20]) So we have to have another way to deal with them.

Not only would storing patterns of arousal take up too much capacity in our brain, it would also cause another major problem. The repeated inhibition by the cortex of instinctive impulses would weaken or deactivate the instinctive impulses themselves. This would be a disaster for all mammals. To give another example of what might happen in such circumstances, if we were to punish children every time they got angry at home, they would soon learn never to get angry. We would have conditioned away their instinctive impulse towards anger as a defence mechanism. This might not cause problems at home, but what if they are bullied at school? They would be powerless victims.

Now we can see the brilliance of the REM state and how it circumvents these problems. By allowing, for example, a restrained anger impulse to be expressed in a dream, but not to be recorded by the higher cortex (we only recall a dream if it is immediately processed by the brain on waking), the aggressive instinct is maintained, and the cortex can restrain its expression in particular contexts. So the integrity of the instinctive (genetic) endowment is preserved, and we retain the learned ability to restrain it in certain circumstances. This makes for maximum flexibility, allowing us to modify instinctive impulses in certain circumstances and express them in others, when warranted.

Once all the findings from biological studies, scientific research into sleep patterns and Joe Griffin's experiments on dreams, are pieced together we can see that REM sleep remains concerned with instinctive drives throughout life but its later role is to deactivate them, leaving the neocortex free to deal with the emotionally arousing events of the following day. This is set in train by the firing of the PGO spikes (the orientation response), which lock the brain in the REM state (itself effectively one prolonged orientation response). As sensory information is inhibited when we sleep, the alert from the PGO spikes must be to something internal. And indeed, what is happening is that, during REM sleep, our attention is alerted to the presence of unexpressed emotional arousals from the day just gone. These are then deactivated in dreams. And, just as programming instincts involves creating a pattern or template for which an analogue can be found in the environment (twig-like materials, a friendly human face, etc.), so deactivation also uses sensory analogues or metaphors, enabling the brain to draw on images which *represent* the unexpressed emotional arousals of the day.

Because the right hemisphere is specialised for using metaphor and the left for using logic and language[21] we would expect that dreaming would primarily be a right hemisphere function. And this is so. REM sleep, as has been confirmed many times, is associated with brainstem arousal, right hemisphere activation, and low-level left hemisphere arousal.[22] This means that, while the right hemisphere dreams the dream, there can still be some left brain 'interior dialogue', puzzling over the dream sequence. However, such left hemisphere musings still accept the reality of the dream.

The REM state does not so much *simulate* a kind of reality in dreams as *generate* reality. What we experience in dreaming is an intensely real construction that we totally believe in at the time. It is a reality that in many ways is emotionally much richer than the reality of the waking state. We can illustrate this with a dream that was quoted in *The Origin of Dreams*. This is how the dreamer described her dream.

"We are going to a party. My family is there. I am walking along the road with my cousin and all our aunts and uncles. We call into a shop for sweets. My cousin gets served but the girl behind the counter does not seem to understand my instructions. She keeps getting the wrong bar of chocolate and seems very rude. We go into another shop and I get an old fashioned bag of Maltesers and we eat these small balls of honeycomb covered in milk chocolate. We then see my aunts, and my mother, walking up the road. All my aunts look as though they have been put through a chocolate machine; they all appear as different types of chocolate. I notice that my mother appears as my favourite chocolate, a packet of Maltesers. But she is falling some distance behind my aunts. I am annoyed that they are not waiting for her. My family are talking about a skirt that had been given to them by Granny. It is decided to give it to me try on. I do so and it fits me perfectly."

The dream was based on the following waking experiences:

1. The previous day a member of the dreamer's family had invited her

to a party. The anticipated party provides the setting for the dream.

2. The dreamer was a senior nurse and, on her ward round the previous day, she had been accompanied by an inexperienced junior nurse who seemed unable to carry out correctly the instructions she gave her and had been rather insolent. This analogy is represented in the dream by her difficulty in getting served by the rude shop assistant.

3. The old fashioned bag of chocolates relates to her weakness for eating chocolate (she had bought some on the way home from work the previous evening). The 'old fashioned' relates to her strongly held view that this weakness is handed down through the generations in her family.

4. The image of her aunts and mother as bars of chocolate relates to a conversation she had had a couple of days earlier with her boyfriend concerning her weight. He had said that, unless she was careful, she would continue to put on weight, just like the rest of her family, who were all overweight. These worries were restimulated by her guilty feelings at buying chocolate on her way home.

5. Another dream theme is the annoyance she feels when she sees her mother falling behind her aunts and her aunts not waiting for her. This reflects her concern for her mother, who had recently had heart trouble. She felt annoyed when she learned that her aunts were rushing to their doctors to have their hearts checked without waiting to see how her mother got on. Thinking about weight led her to recall her annoyance at her aunts' recent behaviour.

6. The final theme is that of the skirt, given by her grandmother, which fits her perfectly. Her aunts and her mother inherit their figure from her grandmother. The 'perfectly fitting' skirt is an analogy for inheriting the family 'figure', caused by a liking of sweet things, that she thinks she has inherited.

All dreams illustrate the rule that every element in them is an analogical representation of something else connected with a waking event. So it is that, in this dream, the dreamer's mother and her aunts don't appear as themselves but analogically manifest as different types of chocolate bar.

Clearly, this little dream vignette contains multiple levels of meaning. At the same time as expressing the dreamer's concern that her aunts were more bothered about their own health than her mother's, it also expresses her naturally greater affection for her mother than for her aunts, through the representation of her mother as her favourite chocolate. Further, the image of the aunts all being made out of chocolate succinctly conveys their having a common genetic pool, as does the skirt that fits. It also incorporates the dreamer's worries about eating too much chocolate and putting on weight herself, and about whether her mother's liking for chocolate was a contributory factor to her mother's heart disease.

All these sources of emotional arousal are represented in one brief dream and thereby deactivated. But in waking reality we can't handle images with multiple relationships *simultaneously* because it is too confusing and would keep us in a state where we could not make discriminations and make choices about how to act. The meanings of images in waking reality have to be selected from 'boxes' of separate meanings. We could all list a number of things that a chair could represent and be used for, for example, but we can only see a chair from a single point of view at a time – will we bump into it? Do we need to sit down in it? Is it comfortable? Is it an antique? Is it damaged? When functioning day to day, the brain has to cut down on the metaphorical richness available to us in the REM state that dreaming employs. We would be overwhelmed otherwise.

Anticipating reality

When we are awake, the brain is always trying to anticipate reality. Moment by moment, it is constructing a model of what it expects reality to be, by matching information it receives through the senses to pre-existing patterns already stored. So a tree is recognised to be a tree and a particular smell is recognised to signify a roast dinner cooking in the oven. It is only when what is expected *fails* to materialise that we get a sudden jolt of awareness, such as when we realise that a stick we see on the path ahead is not a stick, because it is starting to move, or when, as we start down a flight of steps in the dark, there isn't another step where we expect it to be. In such circumstances, the brain immediately fires the orientation response, focusing our attention on the discrepancy between the expected pattern (a stick, another step) and the new pattern that has been identified or matched (snake! no step!), so as to anticipate how important a survival issue it might be and set in train the appropriate reaction. In that split second of fear and unknowing, we draw on the REM state, with its huge library of metaphorical information, to attempt to make sense of what is happening: the moving stick is a snake (we get it right); we are falling to our deaths (we get it wrong – the distance between the steps is just a little deeper than we had expected).

So a prime function of the brain is always to anticipate the next moment of reality, second-guessing what the experience will be, so as to be ready to react appropriately. If you are walking down an unfamiliar, creepy lane one moonlit night and become aware of a strange lump ahead by the side of the road, your imagination might decide it looks like a dead body, filling you with apprehension. This emotionally arousing anticipated scenario is released to be pattern matched to incoming sensory patterns. But, when you draw up close, you find it is only a discarded bag of old clothes. The expected dead man 'reality' is disconfirmed.

In dreaming, of course, there are no incoming sensory patterns to match to. And, since we can only focus our attention if there is a pattern to focus on, real or imagined, the dreaming brain has no choice but to pattern match to incompleted expectations from waking (worries or concerns of the day that weren't resolved before bedtime), expressed metaphorically. This pattern-match will always be to an emotionally arousing but as yet unmanifested concern from when we were previously awake. In effect, even when dreaming, the brain is still trying to generate a model of reality. Dreams have to be about expectations because that is the way that the brain works 24 hours a day.

We can see the power of expectation in conversations. When somebody is describing something and making a point, trying to get their meaning across word by word, if the listener is paying attention they seem to receive the information in a holistic way and are often able to predict the speaker's next point. This is because, using the incoming information and previous patterns of memory, the listener is anticipating what is being said and modelling it in their mind. That is why so many conversations can almost appear telepathic. You know what the other person is about to say, or understand what they are getting at, so you can add to it.

Is dreaming connected to learning?

A currently popular theory to explain the function of REM sleep is that it is primarily involved in the consolidation of new learnings. The evidence used to support this comes from animal and human learning experiments.[23] When learning involves emotional arousal, it has been observed that REM sleep increases in the hours afterwards and recordings from individual brain cells in the hippocampus during REM sleep show that the nerve cells that were involved in the arousing experience fire again. The conclusion drawn is that the learning is being rehearsed and embedded in REM sleep.

However, it is not surprising if, after REM sleep, animals and people have an improvement in memory. This is because REM sleep is designed to reduce emotional interference in the brain from the previous day's uncompleted patterns of arousal arising from all the activation of anticipations that didn't work out. This would have the effect of improving performance anyway. The fact that the same nerve cells fire is also predicted by our theory, which holds that the *structure* of the waking experience that caused the autonomic (involuntary) arousal is maintained in the dream state. All that is different is that the *content* has changed into metaphors.

Of course, most learning situations cause autonomic arousal – even in experiments with rats, where much of the 'consolidation of new learning theory' originates. (Exploration of mazes is, for a rat, a highly autonomically arousing experience.) Whilst learning, we don't know what is going to happen; we are anticipating. Some of the time we get it right, some of the time we get it wrong. Some of the things we are anticipating may be dangerous, such as what might be round the corner in a maze for a rat; or distressing, such as the possibility of our failing an important exam. So the very essence of any learning situation is that we are generating expectations, some of which are confirmed and some of which are not confirmed. We would therefore anticipate that they would be manifested in a REM sleep and that the same nerve cells that fired during that learning experience would be re-fired in REM sleep. Indeed, research shows that the more emotionally arousing the learning experience, the more REM sleep follows[24] and that learning non-emotionally arousing material produces no increase in REM sleep.[25]

Clearly, too many facts are not accommodated by the 'REM sleep is memory consolidation' theory. It does not answer why it is that patients who are depressed have *excessive* REM sleep and their ability to concentrate, learn and memorise is impaired whilst depressed.[26] On the other hand, patients suffering from depression who are put on MAOI antidepressants, which totally block REM sleep, show a significant improvement in their ability to recall new information.[27] So, far from REM sleep consolidating learning and the recall of information, the elimination of REM sleep actually seems to facilitate the acquisition of learning and the recall of information in some situations.

Jouvet has reported several cases that confound the 'REM sleep consolidates learning' theory. He describes, for example, the case of a patient with syringomyelia, a painful disease of the spinal cord that, for more than three months, prevented him from sleeping, as verified by a continuous polygraph recording. This patient had no problems with learning or memory.[28]

Another famous case commented on by Jouvet concerned a lawyer in Israel who was a victim of a shrapnel lesion in his brainstem and had no REM sleep for several years. In spite of this he maintained his professional activity as a lawyer, which involved him in constant new learning as he prepared his cases. He would have been unable to carry out his job if he had had impaired memory.[29]

So, at best, the improvement in memory following REM sleep is a secondary consequence and the hypothesis that REM sleep evolved for consolidation of memory does not hold up. When the emotionally aroused expectations which failed to manifest in the learning situation are deactivated by the dream, it then becomes possible for the correct manifestations to be consolidated into long-term memory, without interference from the emotional arousal caused by the failed expectations. To return to the scenario of a rat exploring a maze: the rat may be anticipating the possibility of danger around every corner. In dream form that night, it will explore the maze again, but this time actually see the anticipated danger. This completes the activated circuit and switches it off, allowing the original memory trace to be consolidated and recalled without interference. In the case of the lawyer referred to above, the shrapnel wound in the brainstem that prevented REM sleep also prevented activation of the flight or fight impulse. Although clearly that would have brought problems of its own, one effect was lack of emotional arousal around learning, meaning that no arousals needed deactivating.

Why we evolved to dream

Dreaming is nature's solution to the problem that, once an instinct-driven pattern is activated, usually the only way to deactivate it is by carrying it out – which clearly does not give animals the flexibility they need to survive. Animals needed to evolve the ability to inhibit, when necessary, arousals such as anger or sexual urges, and deactivate them later, in a different way. Otherwise the arousal is unhealthily retained in the autonomic nervous system. That's why we evolved to dream. During REM sleep the activated instinct patterns 'left over' from waking are vicariously run out, thus deactivating them and releasing the data processing potential of the neocortex to deal with the emotionally arousing contingencies of the next day.

Thus we can see the beautiful economy of nature. The same process that programmes instinctive behaviour – the genetically anticipated patterns of stimulation – are also used to deactivate 'left over' anticipated patterns of stimulation from waking – the activated instinctive drive patterns. The instinctive frames of reference programmed in REM sleep don't have sensory content until they are matched up with their environmental counterparts. The anticipated or introspected stimulation which gives rise to dreaming, on the other hand, does have sensory content, hence its analogical processing in REM sleep – dreaming. Thus nature accomplishes two essential functions with the same process.

A dream collected by Ivan illustrates the metaphorical translation that occurs and gives a clear example of this process at work.

A dream ship

Ivan woke up one Monday morning, having dreamed that he was on a Norwegian cruise ship, which was odd because he had never been on a cruise. The ship had two decks, both of which were divided into a number of compartments, and had rails. The ship was extremely crowded and the passengers were moving very slowly, shuffling from one compartment to the next. Ivan, somewhat against his will, felt himself going with the flow. Every time he left a compartment he felt a sense of relief wash over him. There were several strange things about the ship. For one thing, he couldn't see the sea. For another, to his surprise and indignation, the crew of the ship seemed dirty and their manners inconsiderate: he had always thought of the Scandinavians as clean and polite people. In one compartment, he came upon the late Harry Worth, a comedian whose heyday was several decades ago and whom Ivan had never found very amusing. Harry Worth was trying to make the passengers laugh, but no one was taking any notice of him. He struck Ivan as a rather sad character.

This is how Ivan explained why he came to have this peculiar dream: "As I reflected on the dream after waking, I couldn't at first see what it was about. Then I asked myself what I had done the previous day that had got me aroused but which I had not expressed my feelings about and immediately the parallels with what had happened to me became clear. It was possible to read off the metaphorical translations my mind had made in the REM state.

"Sunday is normally a day I use to wind down after a busy week, which regularly involves a fair amount of travelling. But on this particular Sunday I had promised to go with my wife, Linda, to IKEA, the large Swedish (not Norwegian) 'warehouse' company that specialises in reasonably priced household items and self-assembly furniture. We had just moved to a new house and she wanted to buy some items for it. Since I often feel a bit guilty about being away so much, I had not only agreed to go to IKEA but actually pretended that I wanted to go! The feelings I didn't express were that, in fact, shopping on a Sunday is the last thing I ever want to do and I felt we couldn't afford to spend any money since we had just taken on a large mortgage.

"We drove forty miles up the motorway to the IKEA in Croydon, South London. It turned out to be a warehouse decked out on two floors with rails everywhere (like a ship). It was heaving with people, even though it was a Sunday. The staff (crew) all seemed to have dreadful, streaming colds and were coughing and sneezing. I clearly remember thinking it was disgusting that they were spreading their germs over so many people, crammed together in such a tight space. IKEA is set out in separate 'compartments', one for kitchen furniture, another for dining room furniture, another for living room furniture, and so on, through bathroom, bedroom, home office and garden furniture. We slowly moved with the crowd from compartment to compartment, with me pretending to be interested as my wife examined everything.

"In one 'compartment' a clown (represented in the dream by Harry Worth) was trying to entertain people with balloon tricks but nobody was taking any notice of him. I remember watching him for a while, thinking what a rotten job he had and feeling rather sorry for him. Although Linda looked at everything, she didn't in the end buy anything, so, every time we left a section, I felt relieved that she hadn't spent any money! (This was represented in the dream as relief on leaving each compartment.)"

This dream enacted Ivan's frustrating experience, but with even the most minor details changed (such as the ship being Norwegian instead of Swedish). The ease with which every aspect of it can be related to an observation he made or a feeling he experienced makes it a perfect illustration of how the deactivation process works during dream sleep.

Metaphors used in dreams are not necessarily very sophisticated. The brain tends to draw on whatever images are closest at hand or are most familiar, which is why some images recur again and again. (Also the dream may be deactivating the same concerns which are worried about day after day, and therefore uses the same repeat images.) Often a person seen on television the night before may appear in a dream, standing in for someone in real life because an aspect of their personality or story resonates with something of emotional significance in the dreamer's life. Completely banal images feature quite often. For instance, a woman who had been struggling with an essay she was writing for a college exam, uncertain she was getting the level right, had a dream in which she was a teacher. When she came to the front of the class to sit at the teacher's desk, she found two chairs side by side, one far too high for her and the other far too low. Although she pretty quickly saw the parallel with her concerns, she wondered why she had come up with the image of a chair, until she recalled her husband casually mentioning the evening before that the adjustable chair at their son's computer seemed too low for him, so he had raised it.

Some bitter juice

Any number of dreams demonstrate the validity of this explanation for the surreal content and vital function of dreams. Here are two examples from work in therapeutic settings.

Joe was demonstrating counselling skills to trainee addiction counsellors, working with a volunteer client who had been attending an addiction treatment centre. The client, a 60-year-old man called Kenneth, reported the following dream. He dreamed that he was squeezing juice from a grapefruit into his father's mouth as his father sat relaxing in a chair. While he was doing this, his father was complaining vociferously to his wife about her faults. Eventually Kenneth lost his temper and started shouting at his father for behaving in that way towards his mother.

In the counselling session, by enquiring about Kenneth's concerns of the previous day, Joe was able to help him sort out what the dream referred to.

Kenneth had been attending an addiction centre in an effort to control his drinking. He felt he had been getting on well with the senior therapist whom he had been seeing, and with whom he had shared a lot of painful material about his life. Then, on the day before the dream, he arrived for his session with his therapist, only to be told that he was going to be seeing someone new, an extremely young and, he assumed, inexperienced woman. Ill at ease because of her youth, he decided he didn't want to work with her, and walked out of the session. His previous therapist was then called, and she proceeded to tell him off for treating a member of staff in that way. Kenneth thought to himself, "I have co-operated fully with the senior therapist by telling her the bitter experiences of my life and she really shouldn't be telling me off." But he held back on the impulse to defend himself, and said nothing.

In the dream, the senior therapist was represented by his father, who was always a dominant character who regularly bawled at his wife. Kenneth felt he had given the therapist (in the dream, represented by his father) what she wanted (the bitter juice of the grapefruit representing the painful events in his life that he had shared). Yet here she was yelling at him (this, in the dream, taking the form of his father yelling at his mother). At the end of the dream, however, he finally stood up for himself, although he hadn't in real life. Joe was able to congratulate Kenneth for the assertive way he reacted in his dream; this raised Kenneth's self-esteem and gave him a strong sense of empowerment, which he took with him from the session.

In another instance, a psychiatric nurse used her knowledge of Joe's theory to help a Bosnian refugee who had come to England and begun to suffer terrible recurring nightmares about grenades going off in his mouth. As he had witnessed appalling atrocities in Bosnia, his psychiatrist was planning to treat him for post traumatic stress disorder. The nurse, however, mindful of the dream theory, decided to ask the man if he had anything on his mind in this country. It turned out that, because his English was so poor, he was very anxious that he would unintentionally say something wrong, which would set the authorities against him and he and his family would be forced to return to Bosnia. It was instantly clear – to him and to the nurse and the psychiatrist – that the grenades in his mouth symbolised his fear of destroying his and his family's chances with his inability to communicate clearly in English. Once he was reassured that he would not be sent back, whatever he said, the nightmares stopped entirely.

Using dreams intelligently

Dream metaphors that clients bring to counselling sessions can often have therapeutic value in this way. They may help clients to see more objectively what is troubling them, and may help the therapist realise how the client is feeling about the therapeutic relationship. Studying the content of one's dreams can also have the benefit of enabling us to stand back from our emotional concerns and look at them more dispassionately.

The finding that dream content always relates to waking concerns of the previous day is a crucially important understanding for any therapist tempted to act on the basis of a client's dream. It is never safe, for instance, to assume that dream content corresponds to something that has happened in a person's life, because the content is always a metaphorical representation of something else. Clinical experience indicates, for instance, that increasing numbers of children are seeing psychiatrists and psychotherapists with nightmares and flashbacks and other typical symptoms of post traumatic stress caused by frightening films seen on television and videos.[30] If they start to worry, "Could something like this be real/happen to me?" they are likely to have a dream relating to such anticipations.

Even an arousing thought is sufficient to generate a dream. For example, there are therapists who work on the (ill-advised) assumption that a client with an eating disorder almost certainly has a history of sexual abuse, recognised or not. Such a therapist may gently try to probe whether any such event did indeed occur at any stage in childhood, in the belief that memories of abuse are often pushed to the back of the mind and repressed, because they are so devastating. Having been asked a question of this nature about abuse, which may seem an extremely unexpected and shocking possibility to them, the patient is likely to introspect about their childhood after the session, trying to remember any ambiguous or suspicious events and feelings. This inevitably creates unresolved emotional arousals which would then translate into a dream, metaphorically involving abuse of some kind. When the dream is reported at the next therapy session, the therapist is likely to leap on it, seeing the dream as evidence confirming that abuse did occur and was repressed, and has now been triggered into consciousness. In such a way are uneasy spirals of misunderstandings begun. This has been a factor in cases of false memory syndrome, where parents protest that they are innocent of the 'abuse' apparently dredged up in therapy.[31]

It is quite possible that genuine, distressing events from long ago can be the subject of a dream – but *only* if the event was consciously thought about the previous day. If, for some reason, indignant emotions were aroused whilst reminiscing about the unjust bullying of a teacher long ago when you were at school, you could not act out and resolve the situation now because nothing can change the fact that it happened – so you would have to complete the pattern in a dream when you could supply a different outcome and deactivate the emotion. Likewise, if someone is currently being bullied at work, their dreams might draw upon childhood bullying memories as a metaphor for the present experience, but the dreams would be about the *current* bullying which evokes patterns from the past which are being used metaphorically.

It is important to emphasise that we use the terms 'conscious' and 'unconscious' differently from the way Freud, and the psychoanalytical and psychodynamic movement that followed in his powerful wake, used them. The conscious mind we talk about can only hold on to relatively few pieces of information at any one time as it tries to puzzle out something. Everything else is unconscious. Freud, of course, saw conscious activity as being censored, sanitised thoughts, and the unconscious as the repository of everything that was repressed. (And, whereas Freud considered dreams the cesspit of the unconscious, the dreaming that occurs in REM sleep can now be seen as nature's version of the flushed toilet!) One of Freud's notions that infected the twentieth century world was that therapy should endlessly dredge up the emotional history of patients and was, necessarily, a painful process. The effect of this was that for decades psychoanalytical therapists routinely undid the highly effective stress control work nature carried out for us each night, as it lowered emotional arousal in the dreaming process and preserved the integrity of our endowment of instincts. This is why it was often observed by ordinary folk that people having psychoanalysis seemed, if they stuck with it, to get madder and madder. The fact is that we don't even remember most of our dreams. Nature doesn't need us to. Dreaming is an automatic process that is performing a vital function outside of waking consciousness.

Alas, even without the interference of misguided therapists, we can regularly undo all the good work of the dream state just by thinking about the same worrying things day after day. This has an especial effect upon the REM sleep mechanism, which we will explain in the chapter on depression.

One of the most important implications of this new discovery about why we dream is that we can now see that the REM state is itself separate from the dream. Dreaming takes place *in* the REM state, which functions as a reality generator. The power and importance of the REM state in many key areas of mammalian life is only now just starting to be appreciated.

CHAPTER FOUR

The mind entranced:
sane and insane

THE MYSTERY of why we evolved to dream, and the puzzle about what dreaming does for us every night, is largely solved. If this insight – that the brain evolved to dream to deal with unresolved emotional arousals – is true, it should, as is often the case with a new discovery, throw more light on other mysteries, just as when one climbs a mountain and can see much further than from lower down. The new view we are going to explore now has many exotic and bizarre aspects but they all cohere and make sense in the light of this new knowledge.

Human beings in trance states clearly exhibit strange behaviours that have fascinated people since the dawn of self-awareness. It is these that we are going to examine first. Trance behaviours include: a massive increase in susceptibility to suggestion, great tolerance of painful procedures (skin piercing, burning), religious conversions, hallucinations, indoctrination, age regression, profound stillness, and the opposite – super physical performance. In trance, amnesia can be induced, creativity stimulated, blood flow altered, the immune system boosted, major operations – including amputations – undergone without pain, skin conditions (including ichthyosis, a deforming skin disease which causes the epidermis to become dry and horny like thick fish scales) cured and stigmata made to appear. Moods can be changed; depressed people can laugh again and overwhelming fears be faced and overcome. Also, in trance, strange transformations of character can occur: shy people may behave confidently, inhibited people turn into sexual exhibitionists and cowards discover bravery.

Trance can be induced by drugs, music, rhythmic dancing, rituals, shock, hypnotic language, touch, sexual activity, reflection, staring, recalling particular memories, stories, changing breathing patterns, any stimulus that arouses strong emotion and, paradoxically, any form of deep relaxation that lowers emotional arousal. It is therefore a common everyday experience. Yet it is still mysterious, and unrecognised by most people, who react just like the fish in the old story: these fish, as they swam in the ocean, kept puzzling over this thing they kept hearing about, called 'water', and what it could possibly be!

The history of hypnosis has had a rocky ride over thousands of years – accepted in some cultures, feared and banned in others. Down the ages its use has been associated with great therapeutic benefits (which it undoubtedly can confer), but also severe warnings about dangers that can arise from using hypnosis – for the hypnotic subject *and* the hypnotist – which we think are real. In all its long history, however, there has never been a clear scientific hypothesis about what hypnosis is and why it occurs. The enormous amount of literature the subject has generated, and still generates, is full of techniques, case histories, examples of strange phenomena associated with trance and hypnosis, and endless speculation, but no clear explanation for what it is that happens in trance.

How can a state so easy to induce in so many, often apparently contradictory, ways, and so easy to observe, be so little understood? Some scientists even go so far as to doubt that it even exists. An article published in the *New Scientist*[1] usefully summarises current debate about whether there is such a thing as a hypnotic trance state. On the one hand, there is increasing evidence that hypnosis is an altered state of consciousness. Its proponents nowadays produce dramatic PET scans showing that, when people are given suggestions under hypnosis that they are not experiencing pain or that they can see something that is not there (hallucination), brain activity is altered. It has been shown that, when people respond to such suggestions under hypnosis, the appropriate parts of the brain are activated, but that they are not activated in people who only pretend to be hypnotised.[2] On the other side of the debate, people who argue that hypnosis doesn't exist deny these studies are evidence of a trance state because all that they show is that people are responding to suggestions which people do out of trance just as easily. What is being measured is suggestibility, not an altered state of consciousness, they say.

So, what criteria would satisfy such people that hypnosis actually exists? The answer is, none. This is because they are looking for a state of consciousness that cannot be accessed by any means other than by hypnosis. And, if the brain is not behaving in an abnormal fashion specific only to hypnosis when someone is hypnotised, they will never bring themselves to agree that hypnosis is happening.

We will show that hypnosis *does* exist and that it is a naturally occurring state of mind that people dip in and out of, to varying extents, all the time. In that sense, it is not an altered state of consciousness, which is why its detractors have such difficulty identifying it, but a state which, whether we are aware of it or not, is utterly familiar to us all – just like the water that the fish were so oblivious of living in.

To unwrap and explore the implications of this – which extend even to our understanding of the evolution of consciousness – we need to start with a definition.

First things first – directing attention

We define a trance state, as do many others, as a focused state of attention during which wider environmental stimuli are ignored. The greatest innovative twentieth century influence on the clinical use of hypnosis was American psychiatrist Milton H. Erickson. "There are many ways of inducing a trance," he said. "What you do is ask patients primarily to give their attention to one particular idea. You get them to centre their attention on their own experiential learning ... to direct their attention to processes which are taking place within them. Thus you can induce a trance by directing patients' attention to experiences, to memories, to ideas, to concepts that belong to them. All you do is direct the patients' attention to those processes within themselves."[3]

It really is as simple as that. Anyone who can focus their attention, who has a good imagination or who can become emotionally aroused can be hypnotised (hypnosis is simply the art of getting people into the trance state). So it follows that a focused state of attention can be generated in thousands of ways, each with a direct bearing on the type and/or quality of trance state induced.

The most basic trance state (which we share with animals[4]) occurs when we become highly emotional. When the emotional brain takes over, it locks our attention on what has aroused us, to the increasing exclusion of other information from the environment. This focus means we are seeing reality from only one particular perspective because in this type of trance the higher cortex is less engaged in reality check-ing.[5] You can see this clearly when someone gets angry and you cannot reason with them. In anger a person is totally focused on their own view, incapable of seeing other points of view, and will appear stupid. We see this narrowed down focus in all instinct-driven emotional states, including anxiety, fear, disgust, greed, aggression, lust and elation.

Another way we enter trance is when we *voluntarily* choose to focus our attention on something that interests us. If we are intensely inter-ested in football, for example, and choose to watch a game, we become absorbed. Again, although voluntarily entered into, this state involves emotional arousal as the fortunes of the teams fluctuate. So this could also be described as an emotionally induced trance state – but deliberately engendered by oneself. Indeed, any good observer of their own and other people's behaviour will recognise that *any* form of absorbing activity entered into voluntarily is trance inducing: read-ing, music, drawing, enjoying a film or TV programme, athletic activ-ity, sexual behaviour, dancing, work, concentration on ideas, watch-ing something closely and so on.

But there is yet another trance state fundamental to our daily lives and behaviour – one produced when somebody *else* focuses our atten-tion. This, too, is one of nature's amazing solutions to a primary survival need we all share. Without it, we could not absorb family and cultural norms, relate to other people or live in interconnected groups. (Why this is so will become clear later.) Mentally healthy mothers are instinctively expert at focusing young children's attention. Good teachers focus the attention of children; the friendly raconteur in the pub focuses our attention, as does a good salesman and the leaders who arise in society. When this happens we can be deemed to be in a trance state. This is because, when our attention is guided, certain aspects of reality are left out and certain courses of action are made more compelling to us by the person organising the presentation of the evidence, story or plan of action that we are hearing. To the extent that they succeed in focusing our attention in a way that we accept, we are suggestible. So trance states can be created in us simply by another person focusing our attention.

Then there is the type of trance state that is the subject matter of the article in the *New Scientist* – the one that the hypnotist or hypnotherapist supposedly creates. Some people claim that there is something unusual about this trance state and others that it is no different from the state of suggestibility that occurs in everyday life – such as we have described above – or merely results from anxiety to please the hypnotist and so comply with whatever suggestions are made.

To some extent both parties are right. Whilst dreaming at night, for example, we might vividly experience ourselves in a field of snow, even though we are actually tucked up in our warm beds. There is nothing unusual about dreaming. We all do it. But when we dream, we are experiencing the creation of an alternative reality *in our imagination* – which can be thought of as the brain's own 'reality generator'. So going into a hypnotic trance is not really so extraordinary because every night, in our dream state, we unquestioningly believe in the alternative reality our brain presents to us – we can actually *feel* we are in a field of snow. Even when not in a dream state some people are quite good at visualising what it would be like to be in a field of snow – the whiteness, intense cold and so on.

It may be helpful to think in terms of two major types of trance states: posthypnotic trance states and programming trance states, both of which are seen in the REM state in animals and humans. We have earlier discussed at length how the foetus in the womb and the child in early life is pre-programmed in the REM state with the instinctive behaviours appropriate for different circumstances and stages of life.[6] However, the brain does not just rely on pre-programmed patterns; it can also learn new ones. New learning is always the result of existing patterns being added to or changed. In short, old patterns are enriched. Every new thing we learn is also learned in a programming trance state – we are absorbed, our attention locked.

However, whenever we act without thought or conscious effort – when we are on automatic, going about our routine daily affairs – we are pattern matching to an earlier time when we first learned such responses in the REM (trance) state. So whenever we repeat those actions or responses, we are, in effect, acting out posthypnotic suggestions. We have been programmed to act in whatever way it is that we have learned.

We most commonly associate posthypnotic suggestion with what occurs at public demonstrations by hypnotists to provide the audience with amusement. What happens is, however, no more mysterious than what we have just described. Suppose the hypnotist puts someone into trance (stage hypnotists always choose people who go into trance easily) and, before bringing them out of it, tells them that, whenever afterwards they hear a clock strike three, they will feel an itch on their forehead and scratch it. Whenever the clock strikes three, it activates that programming and they scratch. They are not aware of it when they are doing it but, nonetheless, their behaviour is being controlled by a posthypnotic programme.

Similarly when you get angry because you have a strong feeling that somebody is trespassing on your rights, you may suddenly strike out or hit them or say something aggressive in an involuntary way. When you calm down, you will say, "Why the hell did I do that ...? What made me say that! What came over me ...?" But, nonetheless, at the time you felt compelled to act as you did, just as a person is compelled to act from a posthypnotic suggestion given by a hypnotist. This is an important similarity. Indeed, you would be acting from posthypnotic suggestion. At some time in your past you would have learned to react with that behaviour when your fight or flight response was switched on under extreme provocation.

A considerable amount of human behaviour is the result of exposure to these kinds of posthypnotic suggestions, programmed during interactions with the family, peer groups and the wider culture. Some may be harmless in effect, as when we feel compelled to use a catch phrase from a popular TV programme. Others, we think, are not so benign. But the point we are making is that hypnotic phenomena are a given. And when we *deliberately* put a person who is a good hypnotic subject into a hypnotic state, we are activating the very processes that the brain itself activates during dream sleep, including the brain's astonishing and powerful reality generator.

The trance state of dreaming

Now we come to the connection between dreaming and hypnosis. Hypnosis is a way of accessing the REM state, the state of consciousness in which dreaming occurs. When the ramifications of this are understood, many of the mysteries and controversies surrounding hypnosis are resolved.

In dreaming we have an example of the trance state par excellence. It is the deepest trance state we know. When we dream, not only is our attention being directed in an involuntary fashion, but an alternative visionary reality is created that, ninety-nine per cent of the time, we totally accept whilst in the dream. This is so every night for all of us. (It can occasionally happen, of course, that a person becomes aware that they are dreaming – lucid dreaming).

Most of the people who say that trance states don't exist will agree that we all dream and that dreaming is a separate state from waking consciousness. They will also acknowledge (because there is so much evidence for it) that, in the dream state, the emotional brain is firing off on all cylinders and generating the dreams. This has repeatedly been demonstrated in sleep laboratories.[7] In dreaming the emotional brain is very much in control, and that gives us a strong clue as to how and why trance states evolved in the first place. They are connected to emotions. Another vital clue comes from the research we have already described which shows that the REM state during which dreaming takes place is involved with programming instinctive frames of references into our brain – instinctive activities that are based in our emotions.[8]

It is often observed that a deeply hypnotised person can hallucinate all kinds of realities, depending on their hypnotic ability and the skill of the hypnotist.[9] They hallucinate with the same intensity that occurs in the dream state and, whilst in the trance, have the same belief in its being real. It is only with the breakthrough in our understanding of the origin of dreams that we now understand why this is so.[10] We now know that the dream is like a script that is processed in metaphorical imagery by the reality generator in the REM state. In hypnosis we are directly accessing this reality generator and the hypnotist is providing the script. Even light trance, because it is a focusing of attention, taps into the same mechanism that salesmen, teachers, entertainers and others *inadvertently* use all the time to stimulate the imaginations of the people who are listening. Any close observer of people will have noticed rapid eye movements in those who are absorbed – the same movements that we see in dreaming. Clearly there is a connection.

But there is more to it than that. When the dream state naturally occurs, the person's body is normally paralysed, all muscle tone disappearing as the dreamer switches off outside perceptions of reality in order to focus on the inward reality. So there are physiological similarities between the dream state and what can be activated in the hypnotic state – and that *is* different from being absorbed by the salesman's hypnotic patter. Trance is clearly a matter of degree. Its characteristics change, just as water can change – solidify into ice or evaporate. What you can do with ice is quite different from what you can do with steam, but it is water all the same and retains its fundamental quality.

So, when a person has been put into a hypnotic state and they are imagining fields of snow or whatever, the skilled hypnotist can, in a good subject, evoke other physiological similarities with the REM state, such as paralysis of the body. These may even occur in some people spontaneously. And because the body in the REM state naturally shuts out sensory information it is easy, for example, to block out pain, alter sensory perceptions or, as some stage hypnotists do, convince people that intimate parts of their body are missing.

The trance state that the good salesman creates is hypnotic; the trance state in which someone is asked to imagine something, an alternative reality, is also hypnotic. But, with a good trance subject, you can alter their perceptions through changing their physiological state. In all these cases, what is happening is that the latent abilities that are naturally present in the REM state are being invoked: namely, shutting out certain physiological sensations and changing a person's perception so that one part of the brain takes in information while another part of the brain blocks it. This also occurs spontaneously during the dream state: a person can call or shout to you when you're dreaming, yet your brain may ignore it – though, sometimes, certain information does filter through and can affect the content of dreams. So there is a block, or partial block, against outside information getting into the dream state just as there is in hypnosis.

In hypnosis, subjects can be made to alter their blood pressure, stimulate their immune systems and other remarkable and well-documented things.[11] But even this has parallels with dreaming in the REM state. Who has not woken up, heart pounding, sweating and flushed from an arousing dream or a nightmare that has had strong physiological effects? And the immune system's healing response is known to be more highly active during periods of right hemispherical dominance during the day and night[12] and it is the right hemisphere that is dominant in dreaming and trance.[13]

So now we can see that many of the strange and seemingly bizarre phenomena evoked during hypnosis are quite normal when considered as REM state activity. Once it is understood that all we are doing in hypnosis is evoking the latent capacities of the REM state, the strange mystery of hypnosis – pain control, dissociation, hallucination, being absorbed, alterations of perception, paralysis etc. – no longer baffles. It's a puzzle solved.

Even the fact that we mostly forget our dreams, unless we make a conscious effort to fix them in our consciousness by telling them back to ourselves immediately on waking, is paralleled with the common experience of amnesia for hypnotic experiences.

Posthypnotic suggestions and the REM state

It's curious that we forget our dreams so easily when we wake up but that, later in the day, something can trigger a memory of a dream. The dream template only comes back when it recognises a pattern in the environment that relates closely to it. This may be connected to posthypnotic functions, because it is a misconception that sleep is the exclusive medium for the REM state. The REM state can be accessed in other ways, such as during the directing of attention in a hypnotic induction, or when having your attention directed to emotionally disturbing memories. As we have seen, in dreaming the REM state is activated spontaneously to deal with unresolved emotional arousals from the previous waking period.

Research by Erickson[14], for example, showed that, when a person who has been given a posthypnotic suggestion is carrying it out, if you interrupt them and give them another suggestion, they respond to the new suggestion too. In other words, they actually go back into the trance state whilst carrying out the first suggestion (and thus are in a state to be programmed to carry out the second one as well).

So, any time we become emotional or are acting through instinct, we are in a trance state where we are more easily programmed. At such times our attention can be diverted and somebody can take control over aspects of our behaviour. That is what all dictators, evangelists and salesmen do; they have learned how to raise people's emotional pitch so as to focus and lock their attention, making it easy to influence them to their own ends.

In charismatic 'religious' healing services, for example, the emotional temperature is first raised, automatically putting people into trance states. They are then more suggestible and it is quite an easy matter to invoke, for example, the blocking of pain through dissociation. Members of the congregation can feel their pain diminish and believe that cures are effected (as they *can* be with psychosomatic problems) and, if the leaders are unscrupulous, experience a compelling urge to part with lots of money.

Dr Graham Wagstaff, who has researched and written extensively on hypnosis, became interested in it in 1970 when, as a university student, he was hypnotised by the magician Kreskin and made to perform typical stage hypnosis activities, as people do on such occasions. After the show, he decided that he had done what he did by simulating trance and that hypnosis wasn't real. He has since devoted his academic career to proving that hypnosis as a separate state does not exist and is best explained as a form of social compliance.[15]

This brings to mind the story of the young man who went to a hypnotist and, when he was in a trance, the hypnotist talked to him about whales, for no reason that he could fathom. He then went off to university and studied whales, even earning a PhD for his work in this area, and continued to spend his whole career studying whales, without realising that he was responding to a posthypnotic suggestion. Equally, Wagstaff has spent much of his professional life studying hypnosis, so profound was its effect on him!

The compliance theory doesn't hold up. Other people's research gives a perfectly adequate explanation for Wagstaff's reaction. In one experiment, for example, Erickson gave a person a posthypnotic suggestion to open a window on a freezing cold day. His instructions were specific. When the clock struck at a certain time, he was to open the window. And when, indeed, the subject did so in response to the hypnotic suggestion, he was asked, "Why did you do that?" And he replied, "I am just so hot in here." This was despite the fact that everyone else was freezing. In other words, he made up his own reasons to justify his curious behaviour.

In another experiment, a woman was given the suggestion that she would take off her shoe and fill it with alcohol at a very posh dinner party. At the dinner she responded, filling her shoe with champagne. Again, when asked why she did this odd thing, she came up with a bizarre explanation, totally unaware that she was responding to a posthypnotic suggestion.

So, when Wagstaff, a highly intelligent man, finds himself doing bizarre things at a hypnosis show he has to create his own rationalisation for his behaviour, thereby creating the delusion that he was doing it through free choice. This rationalising behaviour has been shown time and time again to occur.

Quite often, very rational people are good hypnotic subjects. Joe is, to most people who know him, a very rational being. He remembered once responding to a posthypnotic suggestion to go and look for a certain book. After doing so, he remembered saying to himself, "I'm not really responding to a posthypnotic suggestion; I *know* that I'm doing this. It's my own free choice." Of course, if he really had free choice, he wouldn't have done it!

Hypnotherapists have even learned to exploit the intellectual, analytical thinking mode of sceptical patients by using a hypnotic confusional language technique. In a quiet, firm voice they will say something like, "*And sometimes a child makes the right mistakes for the wrong reasons, and sometimes a child makes the wrong mistakes for the right reasons, and some of those mistakes that are right now can be wrong at a later time, and some of the wrong mistakes now can be made right at a later time, and some of the understandings now that can be misunderstood at a later time can only be understood at a far later time ... and it all belongs to you ...*" and so on for some minutes.

After listening to a confusing monologue like this for a while, even the most intellectually resistant client invariably gives up trying to figure out all the meanings and just 'escapes' into trance.

Wagstaff's rationalisation has taken over much of his life because his mind is clearly unhappy with the rationalisation. He now has this compulsion to spend his life trying to prove his rationalisation is correct. People who have been controlled by hypnotic experiences can have the course of their whole lives dictated by it, which is one of the dangers inherent in 'playing around' with hypnosis.

It is because of this confusion between the idea of trance states, which are essentially posthypnotic – emotional states where we act from frames of reference in the emotional brain – and the physiological correlates of the trance state which can be activated in hypnosis, namely dissociation, amnesia, anaesthesia etc., that some people have the impression that hypnosis is an *unusual* altered state of consciousness. It is not. It is an essential, *everyday* part of our natural genetic inheritance of mind/body functioning.

When carrying out a posthypnotic suggestion, we are, effectively, in the dream state. Because we look perfectly normal, however, this may not be obvious to scientific observers. But we all know, from when we recall being in the dream state ourselves, that we experience an alternate reality in dreams and, *de facto*, are in an altered state of consciousness for the duration of the dream. If very few people actually remembered their dreams, it would be difficult to prove that the dream state existed. But, as it is, we can be quite certain that dreaming is a separate state of consciousness, even though the patterns of brain activity whilst dreaming are almost identical to those when we are wide awake.

Hypnosis and expectation

It is, of course, important for people to know that trances are states of focused attention that we all go in and out of all of the time. Those psychotherapists and counsellors who know how to make positive use of this to help people are generally more effective. (See Appendix I for details of a typical therapeutic trance induction using guided imagery.) But its use extends beyond psychology. In good subjects we can trigger the physiological equivalent of the REM state, namely shutting out pain and other physiological perceptions and causing disassociation. Some people still doubt that it is possible but, once experienced – e.g. having a pain-free major operation with hypnosis as the only anaesthesia, as Ivan has – it is impossible to deny.

To the degree that we have expectations (anticipations) about anything, our consciousness is shaped by those expectations. This means that in everyday life we are continuously in trance but to varying depths because our expectation is selectively focusing our attention, thus always preventing us from seeing the bigger picture – what's really there. We may see just what we expect to see, or what we are interested in seeing. And the more involved we are in our expectations, the more we are emotionally aroused. This is easy to observe when members of the public meet a famous person, such as the Queen, a pop star or a politician: they are in a trance; their attention is completely focused. This is why bizarre behaviour such as sycophancy so often occurs at such meetings.

It has long been observed that expectation can play an important role in hypnotic induction (although it is not an essential element, since people can unwittingly be hypnotised). When we observe the effect of expectation about what trance is, we can see highlighted the nature of trance state itself. This is because the REM state is a reality generator and will tend to fulfil the expectations that a person has about trance. If the person associates trance with relaxation, for example, then the REM state has the capacity to produce relaxation. In contrast, children don't tend to associate hypnosis with relaxation (or anything else), so they can be more active when in a trance.

Ernest Rossi, who has done much to publicise the work of Milton H. Erickson, once said at a seminar that one of the best ways to get people into a trance state is to have them observe someone else go into one first. By the process of observation, their expectations about going into trance are heightened and it is then much easier to work with them. This is as one would expect because, when attention is being focused and emotion aroused, people are already highly suggestible. By the time they sit in the therapist's chair to be hypnotised, they are already in a trance.

In Ireland there is an interesting phrase used to describe people who have had a lot to drink. They say, "He was really 'locked' last night!" What it means is that the drinker's consciousness was locked into a certain perspective. Once he started, all he wanted was to drink and drink and that (trance state) was the only reality that existed for him all evening. The outside world and outside responsibility did not exist at all.

The words 'your conscious mind is locked' are descriptive of what a trance state is. In trance, consciousness *is* locked because it is focused. Therapists are aware that a hypnotic subject's attention is locked, since an unexpected sudden bang or noise that makes the hypnotist jump has no effect on the person in trance.

We have no doubt that, as physiological monitoring instruments develop and are capable of even more subtle observations of brain activity, there will be even more physiological indices of the trance state of hypnosis. Already we can see from scanning the brains of people who are hypnotised to feel no pain, the parts of the brain that block out perceptions of pain are activated (something that doesn't happen when people are trying to fake being hypnotised[16]). It has also now been shown that "the same brain area deep in the middle of the frontal lobes that is racked up under hypnosis – the anterior cingulate – also increases its activity in REM sleep".[17] The anterior cingulate gyrus is part of the brain involved in focusing attention.

Scientific study of hypnosis

It is clear that an understanding of how emotions work, how genetic programming takes place and how the imaginative mind can be focused by other people, are prerequisites for understanding hypnosis. In other words, the trance state is a human given, and can be understood in terms of other important human givens – the emotional mind, the imaginative mind and the REM state. It is an intrinsic part of daily life: a reality that can quite easily be understood with the right organising idea.

Of course many scientists researching hypnosis naturally want to follow the traditional, ritualistic protocol that scientists working in other areas usually use. But these fixed and mechanistic tools of investigation are not always suitable for studying human consciousness and attention – as shown by what happened in the early days of clinical research into the subject. Absurd conclusions were reached about hypnosis because experimenters were using scripts to hypnotise people. Those who did not respond were described as unhypnotisable or bad hypnotic subjects. (Unfortunately many hypnotherapy training courses still encourage people to use scripts, which inhibits rapport building and is a limiting, inflexible way to offer suggestions in hypnosis.)

The crude nature of scientific research procedures in this area stops many scientists from thinking clearly. One of the mistakes that some of those who deny the reality of hypnosis make is that they define hypnosis as the state which is induced by a specific type of induction process they put people through. Then they find that other people who are good hypnotic subjects can be put into a similar state of consciousness without that induction and conclude therefore that induction is not necessary, so therefore hypnosis doesn't exist. They then go on to say the terms 'hypnosis' and 'trance' are redundant.[18]

We believe, however, that the words 'hypnosis' and 'trance' are useful and should not be entirely abandoned because scientists disagree as to how and when they should be used. (Nevertheless, as therapists, we find that so many people have been conditioned into a pejorative view of the word 'hypnosis' that we use the term 'guided imagery' instead, which evokes less negative reaction.) Outside of laboratory conditions, good therapists don't work with scripts. Although some people can be hypnotised by a mechanically read hypnotic script, more subtlety is usually required, as Erickson and others showed. Instead, an effective practitioner will take a flexible approach and use their subjects' own interests, creative imagination and behavioural traits to induce trance. Hypnotic ability varies enormously from individual to individual but, sooner or later, with enough time, *anyone* with normal brain functioning can be induced into a trance.

Lay people can accurately identify trance states in themselves and other people, and we know that hypnotic inductions and trance phenomena have been the subject of serious experiment for thousands of years in various cultures, resulting in highly sophisticated therapeutic effects.[19]

Focusing attention – inwards and outwards

We have a need for trance, as can be seen by our seeking out experiences that put us into it. For example, golfers will say, "I find it just so relaxing; that's why I play. I come out here and I can switch off everything else. Nothing exists for me then but the game." We feel more alive when focused on a task in a trance state.

It is as if, for all of us, our consciousness – the constant switching of attention that enables us to see reality in multi-dimensions as much as possible – is a real burden we carry around. Every time we switch attention we arouse, to some degree, the fight or flight response and activate a corresponding amount of stress hormones.[20] That creates tremendous wear and tear.[21] But, when we can go into a relaxed, absorbing trance state and our attention is kept focused, the fight or flight response is subdued.[22] Perhaps, without realising it, we are all looking for experiences where we can put the burden down and thereby avoid using energy for the emotionally arousing activity of constantly switching attention.

It is impossible to be anxious and relaxed at the same time. Relaxation is a lovely state to be in. It's entrancing! It's what a lot of people derive from many forms of alternative therapy or from drinking alcohol – their attention and consciousness get 'locked', so they don't need to make much effort. This temporarily filters out certain stress reactions that would otherwise affect their mind/body system. It's a temporary relief of course. You cannot escape reality for long.

Playing football or badminton will have the same effect. No matter what problems or what deadlines we have, once we start playing the game we are totally released – everything else just disappears for an hour. We become unconscious of our concerns for awhile. The only thing that matters is the game, nothing else. When the wider reality is temporarily forgotten, it is a refreshing release from day-to-day pressures. Whilst playing sport does involve physiological activation of the fight or flight response, there is an instinctive follow through, when one can play well, that switches off the arousal of the conscious decision making usually associated with it. That's why it seems so effortless – going into a state of 'flow' involves very little conscious decision making.

Depressed people stop doing things they used to enjoy, so they no longer have that release. Once trapped in a negative (unhelpful) trance state they lose the energy required to focus themselves on a wider horizon, one that has meaning and purpose.

The trance of depression[23] is quite unlike the trance of playing badminton for example which, by contrast, is an exhilarating state. That's because, when playing, we are totally focused *outwards*, not *inwards*. And what we are not doing, when in that outward focused trance, is carrying the burden of decisions to be made, deadlines to be met – all the things in life that require conscious choices and reality checking. We may also try to escape the burden through negative trance states. We become lazy, dreamy, depressed, anxious or angry. We abuse substances or excitement or relationships – do anything, in fact, except take up the burden willingly. When we focus outwards, as in sport, music, gardening and other activities requiring complete concentration, we are relieved of the burden for a while in a much less destructive manner.

We may not like the burden of daily life's demands. But, equally, getting caught up in a negative trance state also becomes a burden because, after a certain length of time, we start to get bored with it. We start to realise that there are all kinds of pleasures we are no longer enjoying and suddenly our life becomes meaningless. It's like becoming aware that we are dreaming the same dream over and over to a point where it becomes tedious. If we stay in a trance state, the rational part of the mind eventually becomes aware of how repetitive it is. We begin to think, "I'm not doing anything interesting in my life. My life is boring. I'm not enjoying my food as much as I used to. I have no energy. This is going to go on for ever." When such a trance state becomes a burden, we sink into depression.

Once we understand what a trance state is and the various ways it can be induced, we have a useful way of observing and explaining much of our behaviour. We love many types of positive trance experiences that externally focus our attention, precisely because they release us from the need to switch our attention continually from demand to demand, with all the associated physiological arousal and effort that requires. It *is* lovely to switch off.

Uses and abuses of hypnosis

To recap briefly: there is often confusion in the literature about the apparently weird occurrences (hallucination, loss of sensory feeling, paralysis, regression etc.) that can be associated with hypnotic states. These phenomena are easily understood, however, once it is realised that the hypnotist is activating the machinery of the dream state itself. Dreaming is concerned with our emotional and physical health, deactivating unresolved emotional arousals from the daytime. Whilst dreaming, we accept the often bizarre reality the brain presents us with, in the form of metaphorical representations of the concerns that are still arousing us. The contents of dreams are only strange because they are pure metaphor and, as we cannot reality check them, are accepted by us unquestioningly while dreaming, however odd they may be. This too can happen in stage hypnosis.[24] The most outrageous suggestions can be acted out by a subject, once the dream mechanism has been activated by the hypnotist, and can seem perfectly normal to the subject – until he 'wakes up'.

Just as dreams are always metaphorical[25] so using appropriate metaphors is central to good therapeutic practice, and many people's lives have been changed for the better just by hearing stories that reframe their experiences and give them a new unconscious mental map for charting their way through life's difficulties.[26]

Hypnosis not only helps us create alternative 'realities', as in dreams, it also makes it possible for us to bring about changes to our bodies. It can promote healing in skin and bones, reduce blood pressure, change the experience of pain, improve digestion and so on. There is nothing remarkable about all this when one sees the larger picture. When a hypnotist tells you, "You can't get out of your chair" and you say, "I'm stuck to the chair", it is not magic. We are all 'stuck' for about two hours every night, when we are paralysed during REM sleep.

Some people have a terrible fear that a hypnotist can take control from them with some magical power. It is not magical, but hypnotists *do* have power. This is because they are providing a dream script for your brain to work from, and this is a serious form of influence. Therefore, great caution is needed – power can be corrupting. For many hundreds of years Eastern psychologists have warned about the harm that can be done to human development by the ignorant or unscrupulous use of hypnosis.[27] We have seen the truth of this in tragic cases involving the generation of illusory memories of sexual abuse and multiple personalities by therapists, and the concern about the accidental triggering of schizophrenia by stage hypnotists.

We need to be clear about what is and what is not potentially harmful in the use of hypnosis. It is safe to evoke the natural anaesthesia that accompanies the REM state to carry out operations without chemical anaesthesia. It is safe to detraumatise a traumatic memory using hypnosis. It is safe to use guided imagery to suggest life-enhancing alterations to a hypnotised subject. However, if we use hypnosis so that, posthypnotically, a person experiences the integration of normal reality and an imaginary reality (as happens when stage hypnotists get people to hallucinate), then we are manipulating the very frames of reference through which that person's reality is experienced. This is potentially very harmful indeed. In a highly creative subject who has a predisposition to confuse 'normal' frames of reference and imagination, such an experience could precipitate a psychotic breakdown. Since the precursor to psychotic breakdown is excessive stress and depression, if the recollection of the hypnotically induced 'psychotic' experience were also stressful, then this would probably further damage the subject's ability to separate fantasy from reality. Such procedures are, of course, the very stuff of stage hypnosis and therefore carry a risk of triggering psychotic states in vulnerable individuals – the two per cent of the population genetically predisposed to schizophrenia. There are also potential dangers attached to suggesting symptoms away, which is of course possible in a good hypnotic subject. This is because certain symptoms may be fulfilling a particular function for us, which we haven't yet learned, or relearned, to fulfil in a more constructive way. So we need to teach a client an alternative way to meet a need currently being fulfilled by a symptom; or help someone to see their concerns from a different perspective. This more sophisticated approach is much more likely to have beneficial results.

It is perhaps not surprising that the dangers of hypnosis and the ways it can trigger psychosis are not widely recognised since, to recognise the dangers, one has to have specialised knowledge from several areas of study: psychiatrists specialising in psychosis usually study pharmacological approaches to treatment and don't study why we dream or hypnotic phenomena; while stage hypnotists do not feel that they need to understand psychosis. Indeed, until now, the experience of psychosis has been bewildering and profoundly inexplicable, not only for sufferers, but also for their families and for the caring professions. However, the insights from dream research that we have set out in this book throw new light on the experience of psychosis, and point the way towards more effective treatments.

Dreams, hypnosis and psychosis

One curious research finding confirmed by several major studies shows that, in five-year follow ups after a first schizophrenic breakdown, about 64 per cent of people in third world countries recover fully.[28,29] Yet the comparative figures for the developed world show that only about 18 per cent of schizophrenics recover.[30,31] There is something significant that we can deduce from this finding, when looking at it from the human givens perspective, as we shall see.

In third world countries, there is a much stronger tradition of emotional and family support, and greater tolerance for personal psychological crisis, which may therefore be less likely to spiral out of control. Also, there are more low-stress manual and handicraft jobs, and more meaningful tasks people need to perform for their subsistence, that facilitate recovery in a close-knit community. In these situations it is much easier for people to meet emotional needs for intimacy, support, status and validation than in the culture we have made for ourselves. Clearly, making sure the givens of our nature are fulfilled is a potent aid in helping people recover from psychological disorders, even ones as seriously incapacitating as schizophrenia.

An additional factor is that, in third world countries, the use of modern neuroleptic drugs to treat psychosis is minimal, whereas in the Western world they are the main treatment offered by the psychiatric profession, despite the strong evidence that these heavily promoted drugs hinder recovery, increase the rate of relapse and have a significant risk of causing severe brain damage.[32,33,34,35,36]

Psychiatric theorists are at a loss to explain schizophrenia. The various simplistic ideas that it was caused by specific deficiencies in brain chemistry, such as 'overactive dopamine systems', have not been supported by objective scientific research, despite the strident and misleading claims of some drug companies to the contrary.[37]

We have already described how the REM brain state, which underlies dreaming, is separate from the process of dreaming and dream content. It is also clear that the healthy brain is organised to keep the dream process separate from the waking state. We have shown how the behaviour of a person in a hypnotic state clearly mirrors phenomena of the REM state, such as muscle paralysis, dissociation, imperviousness to pain, and amnesia for the event after 'waking'. A psychotic breakdown is almost always preceded by an overload of stress and severe depression in a person's life, which, as we know, results in excessive REM sleep. We are now increasingly convinced that, when people are in psychosis, they are in fact trapped in the REM state, a separate state of consciousness with dreamlike qualities. In other words, schizophrenia is waking reality processed through the dreaming brain.

To illustrate this, we only have to look at a number of typical schizophrenic behaviours and experiences and see how they relate to the REM state.

Patients in a psychotic state often describe weird relationships with bodily feelings. One said that her legs felt empty: another that her arms didn't belong to her. This is a well-known REM state phenomenon and is also noted in hypnosis: patients may feel that their bodies are dissolving because, in the dream state, most sensory perceptions about the body are shut out.

It is also known that people with schizophrenia are unusually resistant to pain: even more so during severe psychotic episodes. One patient jumped out of a second storey window of a hospital, broke both his ankles, and walked to the shops oblivious of the damage he had done – damage that would have caused excruciating pain for any person in a normal state of mind. Again, this imperviousness to pain occurs in the REM state while dreaming, as we are cut off from sensory information. (Anyone who has woken up in agony because a limb, or ear, has been lain on in an unnatural way for a long period during dreaming will recognise this. The pain this causes is only noticed after you wake up.) It is this fact which is exploited when hypnosis is used for pain control or anaesthesia during surgery.

Psychotic patients may also talk about hearing voices. In the dream state, which is the province of the right hemisphere of the brain, people are not usually capable of independent thought, the province of the left hemisphere, because the mind is 'locked' into the metaphorical script of the dream. But if an individual is trapped in a waking REM state, with waking reality happening around them, there is still likely to be activity in the left hemisphere of the brain. We suggest that, because the REM state operates through metaphor, the only way it could make sense of these independent left brain thoughts would be to create the metaphor of hearing voices, or being watched, or spied upon by aliens – which easily becomes paranoia.

The visual illusions or delusions associated with schizophrenia are totally characteristic of the dream state, which generates hallucinatory realities that we believe in unquestioningly for the duration of the dream. Stage hypnotists make use of this when they put subjects into what is in effect a psychotic state, and induce them to believe that they are someone else or that non-existent people and objects exist.

Rapid eye movements are often seen to occur in psychotic states, which, of course, are the defining sign of the REM state. Psychotic patients also very quickly convert thought into sensory experience, with the result that they can become highly emotional almost instantly. When recalling a distressing memory, for example, they can be instantly transported right back into that memory and re-experience the emotions connected with it. That phenomenon, too, is a characteristic of the dream state, when arousals from the emotional brain trigger a thought pattern, in the cortex, which is immediately converted into a sensory metaphor – the dream. It is not surprising, then, that psychotic patients not only talk in metaphors but live them out, which explains their often bizarre speech and behaviour.

The REM state, as we have explained, is in effect a reality generator. It creates all kinds of perceptions in our dreams, but these are illusory perceptions – vivid metaphors. One psychotic patient actually described herself as "being trapped in the land of illusion".[38] Indeed, we know from talking to psychotic patients in their saner moments that they readily recognise that they are trapped in a dreaming state.

We suggest that we can use this insight to help people make sense of their psychotic experience. Ordinarily, there is ongoing interplay between the left and right hemispheres of the brain. We can help psychotic patients dip out of the dream state into the more analytical side of their brains by the type of questions we ask them and by talking about what is concerning them; and by connecting with their metaphors and attempting to change the meanings these have for them. They can then start to better understand what is happening to them and spend more time in normal, waking reality.

When we have made these sorts of observations about psychosis at MindFields College seminars, they have on occasion been heard by people who themselves have had a psychotic breakdown and recovered. These people have all responded extremely positively, even thankfully, to this understanding of their experience. The following remarkable letter, sent to us by someone who had heard these ideas discussed and then read an article about them in our journal, *Human Givens*, is a typical reaction.

> I was riveted by your article ... "Trapped in the land of illusion", which explored the connection between the dream state and psychosis – which might surely better be termed dream-walking.

In the same issue, psychologist Daniel Nettle discussed the link between psychosis and creative thinking – asserting that psychosis is a physical process (hardware, not a software, problem, to borrow a computer term) and that environmental influences have chemical consequences. I would like to relate some of the elements of my own experience of psychosis 17 years ago, which may have relevance to all this.

It was at a seminar this year, when Ivan Tyrrell first discussed the function of dreaming in the psychotic state, that I first 'came out' publicly about my own experience. I was so excited to find that someone else had noticed the similarity to dreaming that I wanted to contribute my own observations to support the idea. But I was also surprised to find I had an overwhelming surge of emotional reaction: heart pounding; a deafening ringing in my ears; my voice, barely audible, sounding far off as in a dream; words hard to form, just as in a dream. It was a ghastly flashback and insight into the high emotional state which was the (at the time) unperceived back-drop to the whole event. I am particularly interested in the notion that stress, anxiety, depression and psychosis may be on a contin-uum, and that a dreamlike state accounts for the altered thinking style of psychosis.

At the time of my original experience, I was suffering extreme anxiety, which made it impossible to sleep or eat. I was existing on coffee and cigarettes and, not surprisingly, although I would fall asleep exhausted, I would startle awake and find it impossible to get back to sleep till nearly time to get up again. After about a week of this I awoke one morning with a solid lump in my chest and totally bursting with energy. Something seemed to have happened, but what? I felt different; for the better: invincible, as if I had changed in some way. At first I thought it was just I who was different. But then I began to notice that people were looking at me strangely, meaningfully. I began to think they knew something about this too but weren't telling me what.

It was as if a veil had been peeled back to reveal a different world, like a dreamworld; one where everyone seemed to know what I was about and could see my inner thoughts. It was dark and frightening. There was nowhere to hide. People seemed to be in collusion, as if everyone was in telepathic communication with each other. Like secret agents. Dredging through memory banks for stories to explain this new order, suddenly I believed in magic, telepathy, and that this was a pilgrimage, a trial, some sort of test that I had to figure out for myself. Desperate for clues, I began to notice they were all around me, in overheard conversations, in supposedly casual gestures, even on the television.

My heightened emotional state was so intense and confused that no single emotion could be distinguished any longer. This condition, created by insoluble conflict and paradox in my life, created a chemical cocktail that overloaded my brain and sent it into a frenzy of activity. It reached a sort of white-hot pitch which I experienced as feeling 'high' with a solid fist in the centre of my chest.

In that heightened state I became hypervigilant: intensely sensitive and acutely perceptive of other people's responses to me. Observing people's minute micro-expressions as they observed me made me think that I could perceive their thoughts about me. The state had the self-centred character of depression. Add a little anxiety and you have paranoia. Seemingly being seen through by everyone you meet is terrifying, I assure you, as well as humiliating. Everything that happened seemed to add to the terror, making it more intense, and presumably exacerbating the condition.

It seems as if, at the time, thoughts were speeding so fast that they were not recognised as my own. (I have a mental picture of Winnie the Pooh circling an island and, coming upon his own footprints, thinking he had company.) It was as if thoughts were being 'picked up' from outside, because ideas seemed not to have been called up but just happened, unbidden. The suggestion, in the Griffin and Tyrrell article, that left brain activity during the REM states could account for the phenomenon of hearing voices could perhaps explain such 'imposed' thoughts as well.

Eventually I said something totally bizarre to my spouse, whose look of horror was so obviously not faked that I decided to confide in him. After listening to my tales and questions, he managed to reassure me that people could not in fact read my thoughts. So then I was able to relax a little, and begin the long job of sorting out the 'real' from the dreamlike, and deconstructing the 'nightmare' world. Even after I had learned to identify which was which, for quite a while, I was conscious of the two 'worlds': the ordinary one, where people are separate and there is some privacy; and the other ghastly, dreamlike one, where I was transparent, exposed, and there was nowhere to hide.

With support and protection I was able to resume normal sleeping and eating and was lucky enough to be able to recover my balance in the safety of my own home, without medical intervention.

My damage limitation strategy after this emotional rollercoaster was to aim for simplicity and calm and learn to ignore idle thoughts. The experience of having a stream of thoughts like so much tickertape just prattling away is something that I am still aware of when there is nothing more important to focus on, like being aware of the ticking of the clock once the telly is turned off. The fact that the brain consumes 20 per cent of our energy intake seems to support the imperative for appropriate fuel intake and is surely even more important where creativity is concerned.

If dreaming uses a huge amount of energy I hypothesise that consciously surfing one's imagination, as when writing poetry or music, designing, inventing or doing pure maths, also burns a lot of energy and can have an overheating effect because of the need to juggle ideas, hold lots of possibilities in the mind and employ different areas of the brain at once. Could it be that creative activity uses both sides of the brain, each interacting in harmony, but, in an emotionally 'overheated' state, the metaphorical mode is boosted, switched on persistently and the two modes become indistinguishable?

I also venture to suggest that, because of the speed and intensity of mental activity during the 'hot' phase, an abundance of new connections is made between brain areas not previously connected; and that, because of the circularity of thoughts, unhelpful circuits are created which remain forever tricky terrain. I have heard somewhere that it takes three goes to learn something but seven to unlearn it. So, if you learn a bad habit, it takes much more time and effort to undo it. I employed the tactic of starving it of attention and tried not to reuse those 'tangled' circuits.

I feel I now understand so much more about my own experience of psychosis. Pattern-matching explains the thinking style. The brain's propensity for narrative helps explain the desperate attempt to link unrelated events. The information that dreaming takes a huge amount of energy explains the sensation of the head getting overheated to bursting point. Learning that there is an emotional accompaniment to all perceptions has freed me from fearing I was the only one guilty of ideas with an emotional tag. And the dreaming mode of psychosis explains being so gullible!

The beauty of the human givens perspective is that it identifies the fundamental role of heightened emotion in all psychological disorders.

Pinpointing the anxiety at the root of a psychotic experience is like finding the end of Ariadne's thread: a beginning point from which to unravel all the terrifying confusion, and find a way out of the maze.[39]

In our preliminary investigations, using these concepts, we have found that psychotic patients calm down when they realise there is an explanation for what is happening to them. When calm, the psychotic phenomena become less threatening and less intense. Then we can start doing what third world countries traditionally do so much better – re-orientating people towards getting their emotional needs met and creating strong support structures for them.

Being unhappy, stressed and depressed is a strong predictor of later mental illness. This new understanding of what psychosis is means we can set out practical guidelines for treating it and thereby reduce the prevalence of severe breakdowns and increase the recovery rate dramatically when they do occur.

We are saying, then, that extreme stress, anxiety and depression lead to psychosis, where the patient's brain can no longer distinguish between the metaphorical reality of the dreaming process and the way a brain normally manages to order reality. If we are right, it follows that, if people were treated more effectively for stress overload and depression by properly trained (human givens) psychotherapists, the depression would lift in most cases and not degenerate into psychosis. Because psychotic people are so hypersensitive to metaphor, health workers need to be trained, when working with these patients, to use metaphorical language that encourages left hemisphere activity. They need to know how to reduce their patients' arousal levels with calming metaphors. Conversely, they need to consciously avoid metaphors that may remind patients of their predicament, flipping them back into their right neocortex and psychosis. This is a specialist skill that can be taught. They also need to consider that their psychotic patients' metaphorical language and behaviour represent emotional needs not being met, or that they are attempts to express what it feels like to process waking reality directly through the REM state.

In addition, the skills of occupational therapists need to be given much greater prominence in the treatment of these patients, who need to connect to reality in disciplined, concrete, purposeful ways: by gardening, cooking, making things, doing craftwork etc. Their daily routine also needs a clear structure and discipline.

But, above all, as a society we need to ensure these vulnerable people receive effective psychotherapy more quickly – before stress, anxiety and depression completely overload their dreaming mechanism and too much damage is done. Prevention is the better course wherever possible. Enormous savings could be made if those now doing so-called counselling and psychotherapy were trained so that they could act quickly to stop stress, anxiety and depression triggering major breakdowns in those genetically predisposed to developing psychosis. In other words, therapists need to work from the givens of human nature, not ideology, profit motives (drugs are not the only way to lower the arousal that puts pressure on the dreaming brain), or bureaucratic convenience. We predict that, with such an approach, people in the West, as well as in the East, could have fewer psychotic breakdowns and higher recovery rates from schizophrenia.

The observing self

Some people may wonder why nature has made our brains so susceptible to influence. After all, scientists keep telling us that it is the most intelligent and complex organ that exists in the universe, but, if other people can influence it so easily and alter its functioning, surely this is a major defect? However, with the organising idea that hypnosis is accessing the programming state of the brain (REM) *which is absolutely vital for life itself* – for programming our instinctive knowledge and the acting out of it through posthypnotic suggestion – then you realise that hypnosis is tapping into the most basic programme of all. A programme without which we couldn't exist. So potent is this mechanism that our highest achievements, and civilization itself, grew out of it.

All of us *need* to have and retain a propensity to be programmed by other people and by the wider culture. All of us are conditioned by the values and belief systems we are immersed in.[40] Our politics, religion and moral values are an accident of birth and none of us chooses the bed we are born in. But, whilst programming instinctive templates (and the facility of being conditionable so we can add to them) are essential processes that enable us to adapt and survive wherever in the world we are born, there are also great dangers associated with them. This is because it seems natural to us to act out that programming. It's the most natural thing in the world to believe in the value system and the religious or cultural ideals we are brought up in and surrounded by.

One obvious danger is that we easily end up not being able to stand back and realise that we *are* programmed and therefore never question those values and see beyond the 'truth' of our own culture. In other words, if the conditioning is too rigid, we lose flexibility of thought and behaviour. All cultures are relative and see reality differently and are biased or prejudiced in favour of certain aspects of reality, while omitting others. This allows people to deny the rights and values of other cultures and makes it easier to commit atrocities against them. The process conditions us, limits our options, and, in addition, allows certain elements in society to take advantage of us – unscrupulous salesmen, politicians, dictators, cult leaders, cynical entertainers, trivialisers – who, by preoccupying us, waste our time, exploit or even enslave us. And, by denying other people's reality, we can be taken to war. People in all cultures need to be more aware of this.[41]

The fact that we are so easily conditioned explains why so many people need psychotherapy. They accept the models they have been conditioned into by their family and, where their family is dysfunctional, it's difficult for them to spot the maladaptive patterns that they are operating from without the help of a therapist. It is important to remember that the chains by which conditioning enslaves us need not be all that strong. The integrity of our core instinctive personality is kept intact by the REM state. If we are willing to take a step back we can alter the distorting patterns installed by our environment and install more adaptive ones to express our instinctive impulses.

Fortunately therapists have an ally in nature which has provided us with a mechanism for making it possible to step outside our conditioning. It is variously called 'the observing self', 'the transparent centre', and 'that which is aware'.[42] Our observing self is the natural opposite of the trance state. When our observing self is activated, we have stepped back from our trance state and thus widened the focus of our attention so that we can see from more than one viewpoint.

Traditional Eastern psychology has long taught the art of flexible disengagement from emotional trance states so that the world can be seen more objectively. It is only when we are in our observing self that we can actually question our own conditioning. This is because the observing self is a more fundamental part of us than even our thinking and feeling selves. It is our awareness that everything else feeds into. A person could lose arms, legs, sight, hearing and yet still have that sense of 'I am', and being a centre of experience of reality – 'I am aware'. The observing self supersedes thought, feeling and action *because it experiences these functions*. As the psychiatrist, Dr Arthur Deikman, who coined the term, says, "No matter what takes place, no matter what we experience, nothing is as central as the self that observes ... It is incapable of being objectified; whatever you can notice or conceptualise is already an object of awareness, not awareness itself. Unlike every other aspect of experience – thoughts, emotions, desires and functions – the observing self can be known but not located, known but not 'seen'."

As Deikman further points out, "The observing self is not part of the object world formed by our thoughts and sensory perceptions because, literally, it has no limits; everything else does. Thus, everyday consciousness contains a transcendent element that we seldom notice because that element is the very ground of our experience. The word *transcendent* is justified because, if subjective consciousness – the observing self – cannot itself be observed but remains forever apart from the contents of consciousness, it is likely to be of a different order from everything else. Its fundamentally different nature becomes evident when we realise that the observing self is featureless; it cannot be affected by the world any more than a mirror can be affected by the images it reflects."[43]

The evolution of the observing self in human beings is possibly the most important distinction between us and the rest of the animal kingdom. This was first recognised by Eastern psychology but only in the last two decades is it beginning to be incorporated into Western psychology. All good therapists have the skill to help a client step back into their observing self (even if they don't call it by that name) to identify the patterns of conditioning that need to change.

Hypnotic ability

Going in and out of trance stays with us as a necessary function throughout our lives. When we give attention to people, and receive attention, we are going in and out of trance – internal focus, external focus, back and forth – and this serves a valuable need for us. It enables us to stay constantly in sync with the people around us, in our family, our society, our culture. If we didn't keep doing this, a process that paradoxically gives us flexibility, our own thought processes would become so bizarre that we would end up unable to operate within our culture. This is what happens to people with various types of mental disorders. The thinking of lonely, isolated people becomes more unstable and bizarre. Normal people's thinking is stabilised and kept congruent with the models of our culture by going in and out of trance on a regular basis in the company of those around us. Whilst this is a great aid to keeping us sane it is also our greatest weakness because the process limits our options.

This means that all the arguments about whether some people are hypnotisable or not are irrelevant because *every* undamaged person is hypnotisable. (Of course not everybody will believe this, however much evidence you give them. At a dinner party, Ivan was once sitting next to a psychologist who had authoritatively declared earlier that there was no such thing as hypnotic trance states. Late in the evening, it became clear that the man had gone into a profound trance whilst staring at a candle. After observing this for a few minutes Ivan slowly passed his hand back and forth between the psychologist's eyes and the candle. It took several passes before the psychologist 'came back to the room'. Nevertheless, when challenged, he declared he had not been in trance!) We are all pre-programmed with instinctive templates and are activated by them – going in and out of trance – all day long. We hypnotise each other to varying degrees many times on a daily basis. Erickson showed that you could eventually hypnotise everybody. Sometimes he would take days over it but he did it. And somebody other than Erickson might have been able to put that 'difficult' person into a trance straight away – perhaps the boss barking an order, for example. (Of course, psychotics are already largely in a trance state, experiencing waking reality through the REM state, and what they need is help to engage more effectively with reality outside of that state.)

It is easy to hypnotise people when you understand the principle that it is simply a question of either mimicking the stages of relaxation before sleep, or any other part of the slide into the REM state. This can be done by inducing rapid eye movements through tracking a moving hand or pendulum, or getting subjects to focus their attention in some way, with all the creativity at your disposal. People can be hypnotised using their imagination, following a train of thought that they are intensively interested in, or by physical stimulus, sudden sound or shock. All have the common denominator of focusing attention. You just have to be flexible enough to find out what works with each individual.

Here is an example from Joe who recently had a stressed man come to see him for therapy. "He was clearly embarrassed, so when I started talking about relaxing, and he felt himself relaxing, he began to giggle. Of course, as Erickson would have done, I said immediately that, 'one of the best ways to relax is to giggle. In fact, the more you giggle the more deeply relaxed you go, and if you try to stop it now you will find yourself compelled to giggle even more ...' and he started shaking with mirth! And I said, 'I wouldn't be at all surprised now if you find that the shaking and giggling gets so intense that the shaking and giggling goes right down to your toes.' And it did! It was wonderful. Nevertheless, I was holding his attention. The more he laughed, the more he was allowing me to hold his attention. And that's all you need to do. If you can hold that attention mechanism for a minute or two minutes, the brain just assumes it is in some kind of a dream state and the neocortex surrenders power to you, just as it surrenders two hours every night to allow itself to be directed by unresolved emotional arousals and dream them away.

"In the case of the giggling man I went from there into talking about his business and what he was doing in his business, because that was also something that was intensely interesting to him. As I talked about that, I was keeping his attention even more focused. Once I had his attention focused for several minutes, he was in quite a profound, deep hypnotic state. In other words, his brain had actually allowed me to take over its attention-directing mechanism and I could evoke all kinds of phenomena in him. After about half an hour, when he came out of trance, he had amnesia about everything that happened after the giggling. It was as remote to him as most dreams are and dreams are notoriously difficult to remember.

"I am quite certain that, if he was being worked with in an experimental laboratory situation, many scientists would have concluded that he was unhypnotisable because he couldn't stop giggling, and the approach I used didn't conform to a standard procedure. If I were following a script, it wouldn't have worked. You have to work with what is there."

It needs to be understood that there are people who more easily surrender their ability to focus their attention than others. This is due partly to biological and partly to environmental factors. People who allow their attention to be focused easily *don't even need a trance induction*. You can say to them, "I want you to close your hand and when you try to open your hand you won't be able to open it", and they will respond to the suggestion. That's how some stage hypnotists select the people they are going to work with. Commonly, they might say, "I want you all to put your hands tight together and when I count to three your hands will be stuck together". Then they pick out of the audience those who immediately respond to the suggestion – none of whom has had any form of induction. So if someone wants to prove that hypnosis doesn't exist, they will always be able to find people who will respond to a suggestion easily, and be able to assume that hypnosis is only suggestion. Conversely, there are people who are so psychically defensive or left brain dominant, that reassurance, flexibility and creativity are required on the part of the hypnotist in order to encourage them into a trance. We can only hope we have made it clear why we put hypnosis and hypnotic phenomena where they belong, right at the centre of human psychology and our understanding of what it means to be human.

PART TWO

Appreciating Our Biological Inheritance

CHAPTER FIVE

The human givens

WHAT, IN everyday terms, are the physical and emotional needs programmed into us from our genes? And how does nature set about helping us to meet those needs? Some possible answers to these questions are what we will now put before you.

Above all, as animals of the genus Mammalia, we are born into a material world where we need air to breathe, water, nutritious food and sleep enough to dream. These are the paramount physical needs. Without them, we quickly die. We also need the freedom to stimulate our senses and exercise our muscles. In addition, we instinctively seek sufficient and secure shelter where we can grow and reproduce ourselves and bring up our young. These physical needs are intimately bound up with our emotional needs – the main focus of this book.

There is widespread agreement as to the nature of our emotional needs. We can list some of the main ones, along with some of the resources nature gave us to help us meet these needs:

Emotional needs include:

- security – safe territory and an environment which allows us to develop fully
- attention (to give and receive it)
- sense of autonomy and control
- being emotionally connected to others
- being part of a wider community
- friendship and intimacy
- sense of status within social groupings
- sense of competence and achievement
- meaning and purpose – which come from being stretched in what we do (create) and think.

The resources nature gave us to help us meet these needs include:

- The ability to develop complex long-term memory, which

enables us to add to our innate knowledge and learn.

- The ability to build rapport, empathise and connect with others.
- Imagination, which enables us to focus our attention *away* from our emotions and problem solve more creatively and objectively.
- A conscious, rational mind that can check out emotions, question, analyse and plan (left hemisphere).
- The ability to 'know' – understand the world unconsciously through metaphorical pattern matching (right hemisphere).
- An observing self – that part of us which can step back, be more objective and recognise itself as a unique centre of awareness, apart from intellect, emotion and conditioning (frontal lobes).
- A dreaming brain that preserves the integrity of our genetic inheritance every night by metaphorically defusing emotionally arousing expectations not acted out the previous day.

It is such needs and tools together that are the human givens, nature's genetic endowment to us. Over enormous stretches of time, they underwent continuous refinement as they drove our evolution on. They are best thought of as inbuilt patterns – biological templates – that continually interact with one another and (in undamaged people) seek their natural fulfilment in the world in ways that allow us to survive, live together as many-faceted individuals in a great variety of different social groupings, and flourish. It is the way those needs are met, and the way we use the resources that nature has given us, that determine the physical, mental and moral health of an individual. As such, the human givens are the benchmark position to which we must all refer – in education, mental and physical health, and the way we organise and run our lives. When we feel emotionally fulfilled and are operating effectively within society, we are more likely to be mentally healthy and stable. But when too many of our physical and emotional needs are not met or when our resources are used incorrectly – unwittingly or otherwise – we suffer considerable distress. And so do those around us.

We have already said much about our most important resources: the REM state and our ability to pattern match; our emotional intelligence; our creativity, imagination and problem solving skills; and our ability to stand back and take a wider view. These have become vital tools in enabling us to negotiate our way through life and make a positive impact upon our environment. Now we want to take a closer look at some of the most important of our emotional needs.

The need for security

At birth, like most mammals, we have a need for security, and we are dependent upon the protection of our parents and other older members of the species until we are old enough to look after ourselves. Our survival depends on their supplying warmth, safety and appropriate nutriment, including attention, so that we can develop well. This is a 'given' and the innate knowledge that dramatically increases the chances of our needs being met is also a given. Newborns, for example, know immediately how to develop rapport with the adults on whom they depend for food, warmth, safety and comfort. They know instinctively how to draw noisy attention to themselves to make sure they are fed and kept comfortable.

Scientists have used many ingenious experimental techniques to find out what babies already know when they are born. For example, it was discovered that they know from birth to look for human facial features and imitate what they see. If a mother looks at her newborn and sticks out her tongue, the baby will stick out its own tongue while looking back at her. It quickly moves on from this to recognise different emotional expressions and other people's faces.[1] In other words, all babies have innate communication skills that they put to use immediately to 'pattern match' to parents' behaviour.

Three specialists in infant development have this to say, about this particular human given: "At first glance this ability to imitate might seem curious and cute but not deeply significant. But if you think about it a minute, it is actually amazing. There are no mirrors in the womb: newborns have never seen their own face. So how do they know whether their tongue is inside or outside their mouth? There is another way of knowing what your face is like. As you read this, you probably have a good idea of your facial expression (we hope intense concentration leavened by the occasional smile). Try sticking out your tongue (in a suitably private setting). The way you know you've succeeded is through kinaesthesia, your internal feeling of your own body.

"In order to imitate, newborn babies must somehow understand the similarity between that internal feeling and the external face they see, a round shape with a long pink thing at the bottom moving back and forth. Newborn babies not only distinguish and prefer faces, but they also seem to recognise that those faces are like their own face. They recognise that people are 'like me'. There is nothing more personal, more part of you, than this internal sense you have of your own body, your expressions and movements, your aches and tickles. And yet from the time we're born, we seem to link this deeply personal self to the bodily movements we can only see and not feel. Nature ingeniously gives us a jump-start on the 'Other Minds' problem. We know, quite directly, that we are like other people and they are like us."[2]

These researchers also came to the conclusion that, "Trying to understand human nature is part of human nature".[3] Each individual human journey of discovery – our quest to understand other people and ourselves – begins as we struggle to connect, through this imitation process, with others like ourselves. So it follows that this given to imitate, triggered at birth by our need for security, is the beginning of the growth of rapport-building skills. If we do not learn how to build rapport early, our chances of being looked after and developing friendships in those first vital years are diminished.

Building rapport only begins with mother and baby; it is the basic requirement in the formation of all future relationships. At its most fundamental level, it is created through a dance of matching movements, including body orientation, body moves, eye contact, facial expression and tone of voice.

All normal babies are pre-primed to listen out for human language patterns and pay attention to them, and this quickly extends to more sophisticated levels of pattern matching; to intonation, naming words, abstract words, etc. The genetic basis for the acquisition of language is a given but, because the process is a metaphorical one, it gives infants the flexibility to acquire the specific language of the country where they are raised. A child may be born of English parents but, if the family then moves to Japan and the child is brought up surrounded by Japanese speakers, that child will have no difficulty in becoming fluent in that language as well as the mother tongue. This innate ability to acquire language is therefore an analogical process. The instinctive template for language acquisition is metaphorically matched up to whatever form of language the environment offers. Thus the pattern is completed.

As language develops, the speed, volume of word delivery, and range of words, phrases and descriptive images a person uses become incorporated into the rapport-building process, alongside body language. It is like a dance routine that gets more complicated as the music progresses.

Children who learn this dance of empathy in the first months of life – as their mothers, fathers and siblings match their tone of voice, degree of arousal, and expressed emotion – grow up more confident and better at establishing rapport with others.[4] The pattern for rapport building, genetically laid down in the child, has matched up with a pattern in the environment to complete itself. That this is a process of fulfilling a template becomes obvious when we study the behaviour of children where the pattern has *not* matched up as nature intended. When parents continually under- or over-respond to their children's emotional behaviour, perhaps by failing to listen to or hug them when they are upset, or by becoming angry when they are timid or too smothering when they are loving, it causes a distress reaction in the children and they learn to repress their natural responses.

Emotional uncertainty about the relationship with one's parents can have knock-on effects, even when a family is by no means uncaring or neglectful. The greater the matching of behaviours between two people, the more likely they are to feel themselves in emotional rapport, to like each other and be interested in what each other is saying. Studies show that the greater the degree of co-ordination between students' and teachers' movements, for example, the more friendly, happy and enthusiastic they feel during their encounters.

Couples have been video-taped discussing a contentious issue and, when the tape is played back and each partner is asked to identify what the other was feeling during the heated discussion, the most empathic accuracy is always shown by those whose non-verbal behaviour matches that of their spouses whilst watching the video. If, whilst watching the video, they react in the same way as when they were making it, they showed poor ability to surmise what their partners were feeling. Only when body movements are in sync – often known as 'pacing' – is there empathy.

Each human given interacts with all the others in an increasingly complex, multilayered way which develops as we grow older. The need for security changes in quality the more we learn. It begins to derive, not from our parents, childhood home, or even the familiar geography around our home, but from the knowledge that we can manipulate what is going on around us and have some considerable control over events. Our sense of security therefore is in part generated from our knowledge that we are competent to deal with whatever situation we find ourselves in. In addition, we also know that, wherever we are, security can be found in close relationships. This brings us on to the next important human given that we would like to examine.

The need for intimacy

The need for intimate emotional, physical and sexual closeness to others is a strong one. We may not always recognise this pattern, and even consciously or unconsciously deny it, but, when the world conspires against the proper enactment of this element of the genetic blueprint, emotional disturbance results. This is well illustrated in the case of a 25-year-old farmer, referred by his GP to Ivan for help because he was having suicidal thoughts. He had, until recently, lived with his parents and his much older brother on the family farm where they were all born, and which he and his brother now owned and worked. When asked what was troubling him, this strapping young man launched into a lengthy description of his day-to-day problems on the farm: how his brother dealt with the arable farming and he handled the cows; how his brother tended to interfere, as did his parents who still lived in the main farmhouse. It was because he had become so fed up that he had moved to the nearby village to get away from them all, although he wanted to continue working on the farm and had no intention of leaving.

As the story went on and on, Ivan found himself struggling to get a clear picture of anything concrete to work on, and sensed that the young man was skirting around his real concerns. So he suddenly slammed his hand down loudly on the table (which focused the young man's orientation response) and then quickly and loudly asked, "What's the problem?!" The man jumped with the shock of it and instantly blurted out, "I haven't got a girlfriend!"

Not only, it turned out, had he never had a girlfriend, he was still a virgin and spent much of his waking time thinking about women and sex, and fantasising about falling in love. Deep inside, he felt sad, unfulfilled, lonely – and desperate. These strong emotions locked his attention and prevented him from establishing normal social relations with the opposite sex. So strong were his feelings that he literally lost his voice whenever he tried to talk to any girl he was interested in. He was deeply depressed. He found life without intimacy unbearable, which he expressed by telling people he was thinking of killing himself. With the problem in the open, it could be broken down and solved. Therapy was short term, targeted at increasing his social and rapport-building skills, and had a positive outcome.

The drive for intimacy with another person is powerful – so powerful that most people call it love. When we feel loved by someone else, it has a measurable effect upon our health, as various studies have shown. It has a particularly positive effect upon – appropriately perhaps – the heart. High risk factors for heart problems, such as cholesterol levels, diet, smoking, taking exercise and family history of heart disease – have far less bearing on the outcome of heart disease than whether or not one feels emotionally supported by another person.[5]

Strong intimate attachments normally form when a baby is about six or seven months old, and this has been observed across cultures, regardless of child-rearing practices. Before this time, a baby tends not to mind who cuddles it. But, at around seven months, a normal baby easily becomes disturbed or upset if separated for even a short while from its primary carer. Animal studies, and evidence of the outcome for children in orphanages left with little stimulation or human contact, indicate that the period between six months and three years is the sensitive time during which attachments optimally form. (After that time, it has been observed, there may be increasing withdrawal from social contact.) All living things require time to grow and develop and biologists have discovered that neurons in the human brain regions concerned with emotions, particularly fear and anxiety, are not sufficiently myelinised (sheathed in a material which allows more rapid conduction of nerve impulses) before six months of age.[6]

Much attention has been paid to 'attachment' over the last 50 years and 'attachment theory', as it became known, prompted countless psychological studies. Infants who are securely attached, so observations from some studies show, are happy, as they grow, to explore their surroundings and put their burgeoning independence to the test, confident that their caregiver will be there for them to 'return' to. They are more likely to grow into popular, co-operative and competent children whereas insecurely attached youngsters, who are far less certain that their caregiver will be there for them, either at all or in any positive way, are less likely to be comfortable with themselves and other people.[7]

But attachment theory is just that, a theory. Taken to its extremes, it has been used to induce guilt in dual income families, whose infants spend their weekdays being cared for in nurseries or by nannies, and not by their intended primary caregivers. Though there are plenty of research findings to link an apparent failure to attach securely in infancy to emotional and social problems in adulthood, the findings by no means clearly show cause and effect, and often there are other different, perfectly reasonable explanations.

There are also many reasons for the different degrees of emotional bonding that occur between mothers/carers and babies, which can have significant effects on emotional development. For instance, whether present all the time or not, the way a mother behaves towards her baby and the way the baby behaves towards the mother may be the crucial element in whether or not a baby becomes emotionally responsive. When a mother smiles, a baby responds, making a mother more likely to smile more, and so on. Each is responsive to each other's positive actions. Having a depressed mother, who doesn't engage in such behaviours, can severely affect a child's emotional and cognitive development. But, conversely, a baby's own difficult temperament can have a bearing on whether a new mother becomes depressed, and therefore less likely to bond. Where a baby's motor control is rated as poor (the baby thus, perhaps, being less able to make and sustain eye contact with carers), the mother is at almost five times the normal risk of developing postnatal depression. When a baby is classed as 'irritable' (highly sensitive to slight stimulation, quick to become distressed and requiring a lot of help to become calm again), the mother's risk for depression is raised more than three and a half times.[8]

As Nancy Thomas, an internationally known specialist in therapeutic parenting, has eloquently put it, "It is by looking into each other's eyes that we learn to connect with other human beings. And it is as we connect and start to care about others that we start to develop conscience. So the children who scream when mum picks them up and become calm when put down need more holding, not less."[9]

If this crucial early need for intimate sharing is not met, an individual may fail to develop the emotional skills of empathy, or emotional literacy, as Daniel Goleman has termed it.[10] This is what enables us to sense other people's moods and take them into account, and to act and react appropriately and sensitively. People who lack a developed sense of empathy have great difficulty in forming close relationships. This is particularly easy to see in people who fall within the autistic spectrum, where the templates for empathy have not been laid down correctly from the genetic 'bank', or are damaged in some way. But, even in a healthy baby, the development of good empathy skills is drastically inhibited when the template is not matched up in the environment.

Love and resilience

The ability to love and receive love – to care and be cared for – by at least one other individual has an important part to play in the development of a healthy emotional life. This is *not* to say that everyone must seek a mate, and that only with a mate can one find fulfilment, but that the experience of loving and being cared for has a beneficial impact upon self-development and our sense of self-worth, whatever our chosen path.

For one thing, being loved makes us more resilient. The human brain is pliable and adaptable enough for people to be able to alter the future course of their life positively, even after a bad start.[11] This has been demonstrated in one particularly famous study. Researcher Emmy Werner and colleagues attempted to discover why only some children living in stressful or highly difficult circumstances appear to pay a lasting emotional price. They looked at around 600 children on an Hawaiian island, 200 of whom were deemed to be at high risk of developing psychological problems because of childhood difficulties, such as complicated birth, poverty, unstable family life and having parents who were mentally disordered. They studied them at ages two, ten, 18 and 32, and found that, despite the odds, a third of these high-risk children became competent and confident adults.

When the researchers tried to account for this difference in outcome, they identified a number of discrepancies between the children who grew up emotionally healthy and those who did not. Those in the emotionally healthy group were easier as babies (and thus were easier for a parent figure to bond with). They were more loving, kind and affectionate, and ate and slept well. They achieved well at school, had diverse interests and were more popular and independent. All these children also had a close positive relationship with at least one parent or caregiver, and received emotional support from someone outside the family, such as a teacher or family friend. Having at least one strong, caring and supportive relationship was the key factor that enabled children to develop resilience to hardship in their early lives. The findings of this study speak volumes.[12]

Moreover, affectionate touching and stroking have many positive effects on the body and the psyche. This has always been known instinctively but was first explored scientifically as a result of chance observations made in the 1920s by an anatomist. As part of his work he removed rats' thyroid and parathyroid glands. He didn't expect the rats to survive the operation but, to his surprise, most of them did. On further investigation, it turned out that this was because the survivors had been regularly handled and petted by their keepers all through their lives. They were less nervous and less stressed than unpetted rats and more able to recover from the trauma of the operation.[13]

In another study carried out much later, rats removed from physical contact with their mothers slowed in growth, but when researchers stroked those rats with a wet brush (as a substitute for a mother's licking), the animals started to thrive and grow normally again.[14] Regular gentle stroking of rats' backs with a wet brush encourages their brains to develop differently from those of unstroked rats and, as a result, as adults, they are mentally more able.[15] (The process works both ways. Many people get their need for intimacy met by owning a pet.[16])

We now know, of course, that touch is absolutely life giving. Massage of premature babies, for example, significantly increases their chances of survival, encouraging their metabolism and speeding weight gain. Since the importance for their development of touching and holding them has been recognised, they are no longer left in incubators attached only to tubes and apparatus.[17]

In adults, massage has been shown to reduce stress and anxiety and help lift depression. It can banish tension headaches, and help ease abdominal complaints, joint conditions, and back pain. By lowering emotional arousal, it causes a lessening of pain in various conditions such as cancer and heart disease, and can generally lift the spirit. Just as a mother's touch can distract a child from the pain of a grazed knee or a bumped toe, the comforting touch of another's hand can slow a speeding pulse rate, and reduce anxiety.[18]

The effects of touch can also be more subtle. In one famous experiment carried out by the head of anaesthetics at Harvard Medical School, a number of patients with similar symptoms, about to undergo the same operation, received a preparatory visit the night before by the anaesthetist who would be present the next day. For half of the patients, he provided just the usual brief information and checked that all was well. But, for the others, he varied his normal routine. He sat on their beds, held their hands, and was warm and sympathetic, spending five to ten minutes longer with each patient. After the operation, the patients who had received the warm approach asked for only half the amount of post-operative pain relief that the rest requested, and they were sufficiently well recovered to leave the hospital three days earlier than the 'untouched' patients.[19]

The need to give and receive attention

Without nutriment we die. Western psychologists only discovered that attention is a vital nutriment about eighty years ago. However most adults today are still largely unaware of the significance of giving and receiving attention, and how that affects their own and other people's behaviour.

We all know that people draw attention to themselves in myriad ways – by being the most stylish, fashionable or expensively dressed, or the noisiest and most noticed at social gatherings. Some exhibit eccentric behaviours, wear garish clothes, sport deliberately odd hairstyles, boast about their achievements, pepper their conversation with swear words or swagger and strut, and so on. But the lure of attention seeking can be far more subtle than that. People are attracted, far more often than they realise, to *situations* that provide opportunities for getting attention. This might be so when someone publicly performs good deeds or carries out a job that requires the wearing of a uniform. The uniform ensures them attention, either in the wearing of it or for what they are doing in it, and this applies regardless of whether the wearer is a policeman, nurse, traffic warden or vicar. Likewise, when individuals act as spokespeople for particular organisations or happily give a professional opinion whenever a relevant event is in the news, they enjoy the attention that brings. Some bask so much in such attention that they may even be happy to supply an opinion on a topic entirely unrelated to their professional expertise. The craving for attention easily overrides common sense about the limits of expertise, though few of us realise that it is our attention needs we are attempting to satisfy at the time.

Everyone wants to be the centre of attention at some time. It is normal to want to shine and be acknowledged when we do well or put a lot of effort into something. Children flourish when they are praised and made to feel special when they perform well at any task. Even shy children, who back away from being the centre of attention, desperately wish that they could have it and enjoy it.

In modern times, the first breakthrough into recognising the importance of attention was made back in 1927 when, at the Western Electric Company's plant in Hawthorne, near Chicago, a remarkable experiment into productivity was carried out. Researchers wanted to know whether they could up productivity by simple measures such as introducing different systems of breaks or organising working hours differently. Six women were chosen to be the subjects for this experiment and, for its duration, they were installed in a separate workroom away from the rest of their colleagues. The researchers then systematically altered the women's working arrangements in one way after another and monitored the effects this had on productivity. They introduced short rest periods twice a day, then increased the length of the rest periods, then tried no rest periods but a shorter working day, and so on. After each innovation, the women had to report what they thought about the new working condition.

A year later, productivity was much improved. At first, however, there was no clear reason that the researchers could identify to explain the success, as each innovation seemed to have the same level of beneficial effect. The explanation came when they realised that the only difference that was consistent throughout their experiment was the *attention* that they were giving the women. It was attention, not five-minute rest breaks or going home at 4pm, which was having a positive impact on productivity.[20] This finding, consequently known as the Hawthorne Effect, led the researchers to suggest that, if supervisors also gave workers due attention, and expressed interest in their work and their wellbeing, this in itself could promote an increase in motivation, and a corresponding increase in output – and so it proved.

The need for attention is an important given. That without it we cannot survive was shown in an horrific experiment carried out in the Middle Ages at the behest of the German emperor, Frederick II. He had newborn babies removed from their parents and cared for by nurses who fed and cleaned them and then left them isolated. The nurses were strictly forbidden to touch, talk or give them any attention whatsoever, in an attempt to satisfy the emperor's curiosity as to what language the children would speak if they didn't hear a native tongue. He never found out, because the children all died before they ever reached the age when children attempt language – they perished from attention starvation.[21]

Despite this thirteenth century experiment, and the discovery of the Hawthorne Effect in the twentieth century, the concept of attention did not itself receive much attention from Western psychologists until relatively recently. (Indeed, the main thrust of the Hawthorne finding, as far as most psychologists were concerned, was that the act of being observed changes the way an individual normally behaves, and the consequences of this for experimental design.) It is, however, a phenomenon that has been well understood in Eastern psychology for a long time.

Idries Shah, who spent many years studying and exemplifying the Eastern heritage of Sufi knowledge and relating it to contemporary Western science, formulated a theory of attention from that tradition in which he made clear that many social and commercial transactions are in fact disguised attention situations. He also pointed out that, if individuals are unaware that what is driving them in certain circumstances is the demanding, extending or exchange of attention, believing they are engaged in something else – such as learning, informing, helping, buying or selling – they are likely to be less efficient in achieving their ends (both those they think they are serving and their genuine attention needs) and will be less able to act and react in ways that are appropriate to a situation, whatever it is.[22]

When asked to define the characteristics of attention, he suggested that humanity could benefit enormously by "studying the attracting, extending and reception, as well as the interchange, of attention".

He proposed that it is important for individuals to realise:

- That this attention-factor is operating in virtually all transactions;
- That the apparent motivation of transactions may be other than it really is. And that it is often generated by the need or desire for attention-activity (giving, receiving, exchanging);
- That attention-activity, like any other demand for food, warmth, etc., when placed under volitional control, must result in increased scope for the human being who would then not be at the mercy of random sources of attention – or even more confused than usual if things do not pan out as they expect.

This is a profoundly more subtle understanding of the importance of attention than found in Western psychology till now. Shah also went on to enumerate principles that follow from this, which we quote in full:

1. Too much attention can be bad, (inefficient).

2. Too little attention can be bad.

3. Attention may be 'hostile' or 'friendly' and still fulfil the appetite for attention. This is confused by the moral aspect.

4. When people need a great deal of attention they are vulnerable to the message which too often accompanies the exercise of attention towards them. E.g. someone wanting attention might be able to get it only from some person or organisation which might thereafter exercise (as 'its price') an undue influence upon the attention-starved individual's mind.

5. Present beliefs have often been inculcated at a time and under circumstances connected with attention-demand, and not arrived at by the method attributed to them.

6. Many paradoxical reversals of opinion, or of associates and commitments, may be seen as due to the change in a source of attention.

7. People are almost always stimulated by an offer of attention, since most people are frequently attention-deprived. This is one reason why new friends, or circumstances, for instance, may be preferred to old ones.

8. If people could learn to assuage attention-hunger, they would be in a better position, than most present cultures allow them, to attend to other things. They could extend the effectiveness of their learning capacity.

9. Among the things which unstarved people (in the sense of attention) could investigate, is the comparative attraction of ideas, individuals, etc., apart from their purely attention-supplying function.

10. The desire for attention starts at an early stage of infancy. It is, of course, at that point linked with feeding and protection. This is not to say that this desire has no further nor future development value. But it can be adapted beyond its ordinary adult usage of mere satisfaction.

11. Even a cursory survey of human communities shows that, while the random eating tendency, possessiveness and other undifferentiated characteristics are very early trained or diverted – weaned – the attention-factor does not get the same treatment. The consequence is that the adult human being, deprived of any method of handling his desire for attention, continues to be confused by it: as it usually remains primitive throughout life.

12. Very numerous individual observations of human transactions have been made. They show that an interchange between two people always has an attention-factor.

13. Observation shows that people's desires for attention ebb and flow. When in an ebb or flow of attention-desire, the human being, not realising that this is his condition, attributes his actions and feelings to other factors, e.g. the hostility or pleasantness of others. He may even say that it is a 'lucky day', when his attention needs have been quickly and adequately met. Re-examination of such situations has shown that such experiences are best accounted for by the attention-theory.

14. Objections based upon the supposed pleasure of attention being strongest when it is randomly achieved do not stand up when

carefully examined. 'I prefer to be surprised by attention' can be paraphrased by saying, 'I prefer not to know where my next meal is coming from'. It simply underlines a primitive stage of feeling and thinking on this subject.

15. Situations that seem different when viewed from an oversimplified perspective (which is the usual one) are seen to be the same by the application of attention-theory. E.g. People following an authority-figure may be exercising the desire for attention or the desire to give it. The interchange between people and their authority-figure may be explained by mutual-attention behaviour. Some gain only attention from this interchange. Some can gain more.

16. Another confusion is caused by the fact that the object of attention may be a person, a cult, an object, an idea, interest, etc. Because the foci of attention can be so diverse, people in general have not yet identified the common factor – the desire for attention.

17. One of the advantages of this theory is that it allows the human mind to link in a coherent and easily understood way many things which it has always (wrongly) been taught are very different, not susceptible to comparison, etc. This incorrect training has, of course, impaired the possible efficiency in functioning of the brain, though only culturally, not permanently.

18. The inability to feel when attention is extended, and also to encourage or to prevent its being called forth, makes man almost uniquely vulnerable to being influenced, especially in having ideas implanted in his brain, and being indoctrinated.

19. Raising the emotional pitch is the most primitive method of increasing attention towards the instrument which increased the emotion. It is the prelude to, or accompaniment of, almost every form of indoctrination.

20. Traditional philosophical and other teachings have been used to prescribe exercises in the control and focusing of attention. Their value, however, has been to a great measure lost because the individual exercises, prescribed for people in need of exercise, have been written down and repeated as unique truths and practised in a manner, with people and at a rate and under circumstances which, by their very randomness, have not been able to effect any

change in the attention-training. This treatment has, however, produced obsession. It continues to do so.

21. Here and there proverbs and other pieces of literary material indicate that there has been at one time a widespread knowledge of attention on the lines now being described. Deprived, however, of context, these indications survive as fossil indicators rather than being a useful guide to attention-exercise for contemporary man.[23]

So one consequence of an excessive or inadequately met need for attention, as Shah points out, is a willingness to embrace behaviours or views which were anathema to an individual before. We may affect a deep desire to learn about whatever it is that the person from whom we seek attention enjoys or is knowledgeable about. We see this, for instance, when a young woman, besotted with a new partner, willingly accompanies him to football matches, motor racing tracks or treasure hunting with metal detectors, even professing interest – something she would never have done before. And, likewise, a young man may also, at least temporarily, develop a tolerance for shopping expeditions with *his* new beloved, because he is enjoying the attention she is giving him.

Indeed, as Shah says, many sudden major changes of opinion, commitments or even the company one keeps, are unconsciously instigated as a result of a change in a source of attention. So individuals who are desperate to be liked by another person, and to whom the offer of attention is being held out, are the more likely to embrace the ideals of that person, even if that means rejecting beliefs and tenets that they have never before questioned. So people who join political parties and religious groups, even terrorist organisations, may do so because a need for attention has drawn them to the organisation, or, initially, to an individual member of it, rather than because of any driving belief in the cause. That belief, or apparent belief, may follow but, tellingly, may last only as long as the organisation can fully satisfy the individual's need for attention.

In the case of cults, there is a high price to be paid for having one's attention needs met by them. Lonely individuals are commonly sucked into a group's midst, enticed by promises of being loved and accepted, both by the creator and by those already in the group. To retain that good feeling, they must (and usually all too willingly do) embrace the beliefs and perform the practices the cult espouses. Attention needs are then being met on a mutual basis.

If attention is nutrition, what exactly is the nutriment we get from it? And why is it so important? One clue comes from a comment Shah made after listing the above 21 principles. He was referring to the difference between real teaching and the pseudoteaching found in many cults but what he said applies equally to any situation where people give up volition to others and sycophantic behaviour predominates. "Attention upon oneself, or upon a teacher, without the exercise of securing what is being offered from beyond the immediate surroundings, is a sort of short-circuit. As Rumi said: 'Do not look at me, but take what is in my hand'." Where we focus our attention is, of course, critical in learning. If we are attention starved we may focus on the person rather than the meaning of what they are saying. This is especially so in a real learning encounter, rather than in a cult-like situation. Invariably, in cults people are encouraged to focus on the personalities of those who are indoctrinating them with simplistic beliefs, rather than emphasising content which students really need.

All this is true, we need attention, and how we get it can make us vulnerable to indoctrination, but there is more.

Clearly, in the attention exchange, we suspend our critical faculty. But, although this makes us vulnerable, it is also something that we *have* to do if we are to consider new patterns of information – the nutriment. To really understand new ideas, information and other people's perceptions, the brain first has to absorb them, and this is best done in a safe environment when in a receptive, open, uncritical state. Then, once patterns are absorbed and understood, we need to disengage from them. We need to step back into the observing self and consciously consider them, analyse them and 'check them out', as it were. Whether one does this or not is the difference between learning and conditioning. (One of the drawbacks of modern media is that, whenever new ideas or policies are proposed, plans presented or discoveries announced, they are *immediately* placed in the firing line of confrontational criticism – this is more emotionally arousing and therefore presumably considered to be 'good TV'. But the problem with this is that the absorption stage is bypassed. This is why, for example, debating programmes on TV or radio are so often unmemorable and unsatisfying and political debates in parliament seem so childish and lacking in depth.)

When attention is focused and we grasp what someone is telling us in an uncritical way, we have absorbed a pattern at an unconscious level. Its full meaning and ramifications may not become apparent at once but, once the pattern is in the brain, it will affect future actions and add to the sum total of our knowledge. Knowledge only becomes real in action, when it is experienced. This is how we learn.

As said, we need to learn the skill of disengaging from patterns and considering them critically, once they have been absorbed. Unfortunately, in our exchanges of attention within our immediate family or tribe, we often uncritically adopt their lifestyles and values and so can easily be conditioned into harmful behaviour and beliefs.

This is why, for example, therapists need to be very much aware of the role played by attention in the maintenance of their patients' symptoms. Patients often derive a massive amount of attention from having their symptoms, and the very act of focusing their attention on the symptoms helps to maintain them – whether they are manifested as anorexia, anxiety, anger disorder or anything else. Joe had a woman patient who maintained a belief that her husband was set upon murdering her. She kept this belief for seven years, in spite of having extensive counselling and continual reassurance from her husband and family. She freely admitted that part of her mind knew her husband was loving and supportive and that all her family was there for her – and yet she maintained this apparently psychotic belief. To make progress, the attention had to be withdrawn from the symptom. The family was taught how to withdraw attention by ignoring her whenever she made these delusionary remarks about her husband being set on killing her. Instead, they were required to pay her attention only when she behaved and thought normally. The symptom then became unrewarding and faded away because her attention needs were now being met in healthy ways. We have to realise that people do have a need for attention but the attention has to be given to normalcy. Typically, what we focus on is what we get. So, what a patient is encouraged to focus on – through receiving attention for kindness or humour or demonstrating cooking or computer skills – is more likely to be maintained.

Therapists also need to be aware that they themselves are highly vulnerable when exchanging attention with their patients. This is because, by continuously focusing on their patients' pathological models of reality, they are at risk of absorbing them uncritically, unless they take counter-measures to reduce the danger. This can be done in a few ways. Firstly, therapists need to be trained in how not to be passive recipients of patients' neuroticisms but to listen with a more objective enquiring mind as they search to see what function the patient's disturbed thinking has for them. What emotional needs are not being met? What innate resources are being misused? What kind of language is the patient favouring that might endanger the therapist? (Use of abstractions or 'nominalisations', such as 'depression', 'misery', 'anger' and 'hopeless' etc., have no intrinsic or sensory meaning, and thus necessarily send therapists on an inner search as their brain pattern matches to what depression, misery or anger means to them in their own life experience. Inevitably, this generates emotional arousal and thus increases the risk of early burnout.) Taking a step outside of the situation as described enables therapists to challenge continuously their patients' unrealistic models of reality – first in their own minds, and then in that of their patients.

Secondly, for therapists to ensure that they are not conditioned by their patients' neuroticism, they need to have a life outside of therapy where they mix and exchange attention with people who are mentally healthy.

Thirdly, the recommended practice of brief therapy is itself a form of protection, focusing as it does on swift behaviour change and thus reducing both the time for, and likelihood of, adopting any unhealthy models of reality.

No culture can develop without attention exchange, but the quality of attention is critical because a culture, of any kind, amounts to the sum of the shared perceptions of its members as to what is collectively regarded as important and meaningful. Perceptions are shared in society partly through conditioning and partly through the refining of shared perceptions, so that they become more objective and more complex. Whereas dysfunctional individuals and families cause chaos all around them, as do dysfunctional business organisations, governments, bureaucracies and cultures, the more developed and mature a family, culture or organisation is, the more refined are the perceptions the majority of its members share.

This is ultimately why we need to study "the attracting, extending and reception, as well as the interchange, of attention". Our species' very future may depend on it.

The search for social support

All needs are interrelated and nowhere is this more easily seen than in the powerful force that underlies and promotes the sharing of perceptions. This programme drives us to connect with *groups* of people – the wider social world beyond our immediate family. The individual brain only really thrives when in complex co-operation with a community of other brains. We wouldn't be where we are today if we had not evolved as social beings – tribal creatures – because meeting this need provides the optimum conditions for survival, thus perpetuating our genes through our children.

All networks, institutions and systems of education and government down the ages are extensions of the original means by which people ensured an effectively functioning society within which each individual could play a pertinent role. (Thus the disaffection, anger and despair of those who feel left out, and see no chance of attaining gainful employment or the wherewithal to acquire a decent home and build a fulfilling family life. The end result of emotional needs not being met in large numbers of the population is always civil strife. Good government is invisible. This is because it is getting on with making everything run smoothly for the benefit of those it serves who consequently feel more fulfilled. You are only aware of government when it is noisily blustering about its failures.)

Because we are evolving far beyond other animals, our brains take approximately 20 years to develop fully and so, as we grow, we depend on the support of our family. Finely tuned social antennae are thus essential, if we are to learn the rules of survival.

The first interactions between a mother and her baby are, in effect, the beginnings of social orienting – the baby to the mother, then to the family and then to the outside world. Even though, as the years pass, we become physically independent, our social dependence never disappears. The more complex societies become, the more this is so.

We need the contribution of other people to make and operate, to give just one example, various means of transport: cars, trains, buses and aeroplanes. None of these 'artificial mobility enhancers' (as zimmer frames and walking sticks are called in NHS hospitals!) would be possible without complex co-operation. An individual could not manufacture a jet plane, or the high tech communication system needed to fly it, from scratch. The importance of our social functioning is also illustrated by the fact that humans are, on occasion, prepared to accept the risk of being killed, by fighting for the advantage of family, tribe or the country to which we belong.

Our brains evolved to respond to other people, to empathise and engage with them. Neuroscientists have recently realised that even those parts of the brain originally assumed only to be concerned with 'lower' functions such as motor control, also have a vital part to play in our social development. Even the brain itself is intrinsically social: "The newest neurological findings suggest that the brain itself is a social organ; in the womb, neurons in the developing brain become functional only if they connect with other neurons. The brain's most primitive regions – the cerebellum and the amygdala – are the very ones involved in the brain's social processing. Indeed, the amygdala has neurons within it that only fire in response to other people's reactions. Furthermore, evolution shows that the brain has changed itself to survive, adapt and improve the success of its host person in a group of people."[24]

Because we are not 'closed systems' we can be impinged upon in a deep way by the warmth and friendship of others – and also be profoundly responsive to it. People with strong support networks of family, friends or community are happier and emotionally and physically healthier than people who feel isolated and unable to make connections with others. Feeling isolated and unable to make connections are operative words, here. It is an individual's perception of being unloved and out of things that affects health and wellbeing, as many studies clearly show.[25,26,27]

Like a retreating tide leaving fish stranded on the shore, the withdrawal of social support is disastrous for the individual concerned. And, alas, it is increasingly common as more people live apart from close family or friends and find themselves floundering. Some, for example, go where their job or career takes them, which may be far from any established social support structures. Others, young single mothers living on benefits, may be placed in council housing wherever it is available, which all too often is some distance from the help and support of families. Or the family unit itself may have disintegrated. Some lonely individuals' social world may shrink to the size of the computer in the bedroom, offering its seductive link to the inanimate and ultimately highly limited world of the internet where 'friends' are people they have never met face to face.

Thus it is that so many people lose contact with others who care enough for them to support them through the inevitable uncertainties and heartbreaks of life. Increasingly, lonely people succumb to physical and mental illnesses and feel the need to turn to 'experts' for help in the art of living. Where once they would automatically have turned to relatives and friends for help, they now seek out counsellors or therapists. But, in modern living, we are less attuned to coping with other people's distress.

An article in the *Sunday Times*, written by our colleague Denise Winn, illustrated all too clearly this inability often either to hold out a helping hand or even just say the right words. One woman, widowed after 40 years of happy marriage, reported, for instance: "People I knew well would cross the road if they saw me coming, and if they did have to speak and ask me how I was, I learned to my cost that I mustn't really tell. They wanted me just to say, 'I'm fine'." Another woman, who had cancer and lived alone, said: "People tend to avoid coming to the house to help because it means acknowledging that I am ill. If I say, 'I have to go in [to hospital] again, could you feed the cat?', they are likely to start talking about some nice jumper they saw in Woolworths."[28]

Another writer, Dr James Lynch, described this situation thus: "What emerges from the eyes of a bereaved individual is grief; what emerges from the eyes of those recently divorced is anxiety; what emerges from the eyes of those who live alone is loneliness; what emerges from the eyes of the unloved adolescent is frightened anger ... The dialogue of pain, anxiety, anger and loneliness is also part of life but it is a dialogue that can be both frightening and painful. How convenient to label these as scientific-medical problems, and therefore have others look into their eyes."[29]

The threats to community life

One of the unfortunate trends of the 1970s and 1980s in Britain was the propagation of a philosophy that community does not exist. It was famously promoted by former prime minister Margaret Thatcher, who declared that "there is no such thing as society". According to this belief, we are just a collection of individuals who happen to be involved in a race for the survival of the fittest (a nineteenth century explanation for the force that drove evolution). A brutal consequence of this trend was the rapid spread of the notion that how 'fit' you are can be measured; and that performance targets can be set and meeting such targets should take precedence over other, less measurable, considerations. Because common sense and decency had no measurable value, they counted for little in this new scheme of things. Numbers suddenly mattered more than people. Market forces determined everything. Naked materialism triumphed – evolution in action. But, by ignoring our innate need to feel part of the wider society, tremendous damage was done to the social infrastructure of Britain and other Western countries. Over the coming decades we will have to deal with the result of putting that inane philosophy into practice.

The proposition that evolution works through the survival of the fittest still appears to have the support of modern science behind it. That is certainly how the public sees it, thanks to the way the media simplifies scientific endeavours. For example, one of the most disempowering beliefs of recent years, from the mental health point of view, is the notion that evolution is propelled by 'selfish genes'. This catchy phrase was coined and vigorously promoted by the scientist Richard Dawkins. It is an attention grabber, just like a memorable advertising slogan. It could almost have been designed as a rallying cry for the 'me' generation. Our genes fight for power, and nature allows only the most dominating selfish genes to survive and rule.

In essence, selfish gene theory assigns to DNA the central role in the development of life. Our bodies are merely temporary hosts, enabling the survival and propagation of DNA, and most human behaviour is dominated by the selfish genes. In his book, *The Selfish Gene*, Dawkins asks us, "What on earth do you think you are, if not a robot, albeit a very complicated one?"[30] Fortunately this somewhat simplistic extension of the fundamentalist Darwinian viewpoint is not generally accepted in the scientific world, although it certainly caught the popular imagination.

Nature always selects an *organism* that survives – not a *gene* that survives.[31] A gene can only survive by being part of an organism – part of a larger context. DNA cannot survive outside of a cell. It is not DNA on its own that passes from one generation to the next but the living cell of which DNA is but a part. This is vividly illustrated by examining the basic unit of biology in plants and animals: the cell. The cell itself evolved from the fusion of free-living bacteria. When these bacteria fused together, their combined abilities formed the basis for the living cell from which all plant and animal life arose. For example, mitochondria, the energy powerhouses of cells, evolved from free-living, oxygen breathing bacteria that symbiotically integrated with other types of bacteria to form a more efficient complex cell.

This means that the very basic unit of life, the cell, came about through the co-operation, or the development of interdependence, between independent creatures.[32] It would seem to us far more likely, therefore, that evolution is not driven by selection of single genes, but works in a holistic way, increasing co-operation. This co-operation in a more complex environment furthers the survival chances of the individual creatures in it. In this case, the selfish gene theory, which seems to non-scientists to legitimise the idea that we are born to be cruel and tyrannical, hurting others if necessary to achieve our own ends, is based on a false premise. We can see the holistic setting of co-operation and interdependence everywhere we look in nature. It occurs all over the animal kingdom between different species. All animals depend on other creatures for various needs, such as maintaining their sources of food, keeping their skin clean, etc. Plants depend on insects for pollination. And so on, throughout nature. We contend that the principle of co-operation and increasing interdependence is equally as fundamental to nature as any principle based on greed and individual striving for dominance.

The drive for co-operation may in fact be behind what has been termed reciprocal altruism, as a means of explaining how altruistic gestures can be linked with survival needs. Doing something helpful for someone else, the theory goes, commonly results in someone doing something helpful for us in return, which eases our load. Quite simply, reciprocity oils the wheels of society. This truth is recognised and transmitted throughout the world in folk tales and stories where acts of kindness and co-operation play a part in the overcoming of apparently insurmountable obstacles.

Keeping greed in check

From the human givens perspective we recognise that all organisms, including humans, have different needs and that, if the needs are met pretty well, they will mature in a fully rounded way.

Greed tends to dominate an individual or group when needs are not met in balance, and feeds the ubiquitous confusion between needs and wants. If our need for attention is not met, for example, we become attention seekers, which can become destructive to relationships. We can become greedy for comfort, turn to food and overeat and become lazy. We can be greedy for status, if status has been denied us in childhood and adolescence, and this can develop into an aggressive drive to dominate others in order to extract status through power. Any healthy human need, if unnurtured, can swell into a destructive want. In a mature society, the process of getting people's needs met provides a natural rhythm of checks and balances to ensure no one becomes excessively greedy or cruel.

But greed draws its strength from the fact that, in a fundamental way, like all basic emotions, it is directly linked to survival. Every living thing *has* to take from the environment around it to stay alive. This is why our greeds can become overwhelmingly powerful. Like all emotional states, a greed for something, whatever it is, focuses and locks our attention so we are unable to see the bigger picture – what's really happening.

Greed, however, like an evil master of disguise, is not always easy to see in ourselves or in others. It sneakily pops up in a variety of ways – invariably causing havoc. For example: we can be greedy to have a problem solved or a difficulty 'lifted from our shoulders' and, at first sight, this doesn't seem too serious. However, the strength of emotion around wanting a solution to a problem can prevent us from stepping back and seeing that the first solution that presents is not necessarily the best one. It may, in fact, contain aspects that will make the problem worse, and therefore be a disastrous course to follow. Thus it is that people can take out a loan to pay off a fairly small debt but then be saddled with an exorbitant interest rate that incurs a much larger debt in the long run. Similarly, when we are greedy for attention, we are blinded to the motives of the person giving us that attention and can be manipulated, deceived or coerced against our interests. This is why con men and flatterers will always thrive.

In short, greed prevents us from standing back and taking the time to have a long, cool look at an issue – because greed, driven by the emotional brain, needs 'instant' satisfaction (the 'I want it now' syndrome). When we become greedy for emotional stimulation, for example, it makes us emotionally 'bloated'. The more we have of something, the more we want until we can no longer see, through the emotional smokescreen we have erected, any other options or connections we could develop. This is how many religions continue to exert a hold over mankind long after they have lost contact with the inner truth behind their teachings. The religious institutions that provide emotional stimulation, calling this 'spirituality', have simply discovered that, because such stimulation is addictive, people keep coming back for more. With too much emotional stimulation, of course, we effectively suffocate our potential for developing more refined perceptions.

So greed plays a role in stopping us thinking for ourselves and becoming more objective. It steers us towards 'authorities' to tell us what to do and to putting 'heroes' on pedestals to guide us or allowing 'father-figures' to think for us, reassure us and tell us what to believe. This is why people so easily accept the tyranny of corrupt authority (authority is often corrupt because of the calibre of person attracted to – and greedy for – power). It is easier. Everything is simplified. Our greed always draws us towards what appears to be easy to get, even if this leads to immense complications later.

But nature, as always, performs a balancing act. To meet the needs of the individual and the wider group, natural regulation occurs, when given the chance. For instance, individuals will only have their own needs for intimacy met if they are not too greedy for attention for themselves: too much attention seeking detracts from the ability to give due attention to others, thereby preventing the desired intimacy from developing. In the same way, a corrective to selfishness exists in parts of the world where cultures require people to treat strangers well, automatically to come to their aid if necessary, share their last crust of bread with them and do such things for no material reward whatsoever. In this respect, perhaps our own successful culture, technologically advanced and sophisticated as it is in many ways, is psychologically and socially still immature by comparison.

Until it is more widely recognised that the need to be connected within the community is a human given, there will still be people who miss developing their potential because of the environment they find themselves in, fail to fit well into society, commit crimes and exploit or abuse themselves and others. The rise in serious social problems is the inevitable consequence of our collective ignorance.

In addition, the way we go about helping disturbed people will continue to be far less effective than is possible. Much counselling and therapy training, for example, is founded upon the magical assumption that people can 'self-actualise' and 'find themselves' through endless talking and introspecting long and deeply, and thereby overcome their neuroses. (Trainee psychotherapists are even encouraged to undergo many sessions of 'psychotherapy' or 'counselling' as part of their training, despite research that shows this does not make people more effective in such work.[33]) This flies in the face of all the research findings which clearly show that mental health is connected to focusing outwards, caring for other people and getting our needs met by being active members of a community, helping meet the needs of others.

The too many tribes problem

When 'tribes' first developed, it was in the interests of social evolution that individuals uncritically absorbed the moral laws, social habits and culture of their own tribes in order to maintain their membership of it. The ability to do this is bound up with the need for attention – giving and receiving it. As we have seen, the interchange of attention is nature's mechanism for enabling us to remain in tune with the mores of our family and the tribe and culture to which we belong. This ability also enables us to absorb uncritically the role models, morals, habits and culture of our tribe so that we can maintain our place as a member of it. This was a very necessary evolutionary development for our survival as social animals. But the downside of this necessary mechanism is that each culture is relative, omitting or distorting certain value systems.

This relativity is clearly seen when we look back over the history of past cultures – the preoccupations of an ancient Roman emperor were not the same as those of a Chinese emperor of the Han dynasty or a South Sea islander before the coming of Europeans – but it is equally applicable today, and not only between countries, religions and races. The values and culture of a London lawyer are not the same as those of a London taxi driver, Northumberland hill farmer, Welsh business-man, Scottish actress or motorway maintenance worker from the Midlands. Although we each inhabit a primary 'tribe' in our own country, often defined by our career, job or peer group, we are members of many other tribes, each with its own jargon, rituals and beliefs. Living like this, tribe piling on top of tribe, loosely co-existing but often incomprehending of each other's reality, creates many opportunities for misunderstanding and conflict. It suggests that the need for greater adaptability is becoming ever more critical in a world where technology is forcing us to become one global village. Where once whole civilisations could exist without being aware of another, now each nation and tribe impinges ever more intrusively on the rest, putting ever greater demands on our collective tolerance and under-standing. For many this creates a stress overload, which is why, despite our material wealth and the efforts of hugely expensive health services, mental illness is on the increase worldwide.

In traditional small, cohesive tribes – and only a few still survive – depression was virtually unknown. This is because the characteristic appearance and behaviour of depression is intended to convey a message to those around the depressed individual: "I am stuck, I am blocked, I don't know where to go from here". In a small society, such a message is readily heard and acted upon. Help and guidance becomes available. Studies of traditional New Guinea tribes and the Amish and Hutterite communities, for example, which still adhere to a slower, more human, seventeenth century lifestyle, show that, if a hut or barn burns down, everyone rallies round to rebuild it straight away. Out of disaster come closer human ties and social benefits, even pleasures. There is community support for individuals, balanced by an understanding that the individual has a responsibility to the commu-nity. In such societies, depression and suicide are almost unknown.[34] But in our modern, technological society, where the world comes into our living room but we are increasingly separated from family and friends, a person can send out an emotional message that they are depressed for months or even years and nobody may actually notice.[35]

The law of 150

The loosening of traditional networks disturbs another ancient biological pattern – the 'law of 150'. The resultant disruption is negatively affecting communities around the world and raising the anxiety levels of millions of individuals.

The larger the neocortex of any kind of primate, the bigger the social group they live in.[36] *Our* brains evolved to enable us to be more social – and the more complex the social arrangements we have to cope with, the more evolved our brains need to be. All primates, including monkeys, apes and humans have an *optimum* size of social group which each can cope with. In the case of humans, it appears to be 150.

In surviving hunter-gatherer societies the average number of people in each group is around 149. In military organisations the basic unit of 'the company' is no more than 150, suggesting that, regardless of developments in modern technology, there is no genuine substitute for the small functional unit that can be effectively controlled in a personal manner. Larger organisations are usually dependent on hierarchies and rules in order to keep everyone marching to the same drumbeat, whereas, in smaller groups, peer pressure and personal loyalties to one's commander can create what faceless authority cannot: a sense of belonging and involvement, and of having a particular place within the whole.[37]

There is a similar cohesion to religious groups that keep their communities small. The Hutterites, a religious group which, for hundreds of years, lived in self-sufficient agricultural communities, first in Europe and now also in North America, have had a policy of splitting each colony in two, when the number of inhabitants reaches 150. "Keeping things under 150 just seems to be the best and more efficient way to manage a group of people," one Hutterite leader said. The obvious deduction from this is that anyone wishing, for instance, to develop schools in disadvantaged areas, with the aim of creating a positive ethos and motivation to do well, would do better to establish several little schools, rather than one or two big ones. Similarly, commercial organisations that keep their basic units small are likely to be highly successful, because of their cohesiveness. Gore Associates, a multimillion-dollar high tech firm in Delaware, USA, with very low staff turnover, has no titles (everyone is an 'associate'), no bosses and no elaborate strategic plans, but is known as one of the best-managed companies in America. The founder, Wilbert Gore, discovered by trial and error that things were more likely to go pear shaped if more than 150 people were working together. He decided to build small plants, which comfortably had room only for 150 people, and, if the business grew, to split, keeping each new venture within the 150-unit size.

In this age of technology and globalization, and without knowing anything about the law of 150, individuals still instinctively find it important to create a sense of community by founding small groups that better enable co-operation. Often it is projects set up to help others that are most successful at bringing people together. So charities set up soup kitchens; housing estates form tenants' committees; schools set up peer group mentoring schemes and social services departments initiate family group conferencing – all designed to reassert the positive caring aspects of traditional support networks and fulfil this biological given of our nature.

By helping others we help ourselves

As organisms we evolved to co-operate, and nature so arranges it that co-operation leads to benefits for all parties concerned. Indeed, there is growing evidence to show that we can only fully enjoy true well-being when we are concerned with matters beyond our own needs and interests. People with strong social ties, for example, are less likely to die from disease of any kind than are those with few or no such ties. And men who give time to voluntary work for charities are two and a half times less likely to die from disease (of any kind) than men who didn't do voluntary work.[38] Interestingly, there was no equivalent effect for women. Researchers hypothesised, probably correctly, that, as women tend to take the major caring role for dependants, they don't need additional voluntary work to reap the apparent health benefits.

Another study showed that those whose voluntary work involved them in personal contact with the people they were helping were healthier than those who carried out only voluntary administrative tasks. (But even the administrators did better than those who did nothing at all.) As Drs Robert Ornstein and David Sobel, the authors who cited this research, commented: "We need to meet the people we help, see their lives, connect with them".[39] It may assuage our consciences to send money to good causes, but that, it would seem, is only half the story.

In another study, this time of over 700 elderly people, those who contributed the most enthusiastically to their social network showed fewer of the effects of ageing. The more they gave, the more they themselves benefited.[40]

Why should it help us to help others? There have been many hypotheses. When we help others, we take our minds off ourselves (nothing deepens depression like dwelling on it). We briefly enter the world of another person or group of people we may not otherwise have met, and participate in a needier life, as they live it, thus gaining a new appreciation of our own competencies and talents, with a corresponding boost in mood. We may also feel nourished by the genuine gratitude and appreciation of others, and this metaphorical mental nourishment may be transduced by the brain into real physical nourishment of the immune system (in the same way that people have survived starvation in concentration camps by endlessly discussing wonderful meals they have eaten prior to their incarceration).

There is massive evidence to show that helping others has a direct effect on the immune system. In one much quoted study, a group of students at Harvard University were asked to watch a documentary about nuns working with the poor and dying in Calcutta. Antibody levels in the students' saliva were measured before and after the film, and a significant increase in antibodies was found post viewing, compared with the levels of other students who watched a straightforward film. However, not all of those who watched the Calcutta film increased their immunity in this way. So, to gain more insight into their reactions, the students were shown a photo of a couple sitting by a river and were asked to write a story based on what they saw. Those who wrote positively of the couple, imagining that they had good feelings for each other and stayed happily together, showed the largest increase in protective antibody levels. However, those who imagined bad outcomes, with one partner deceiving or hurting the other and the pair splitting up, actually showed decreased antibody levels and reported more illness over the year.[41] Clearly how we perceive the world, and our own and others' positions in it, affects our health in a powerful way.

So, from the human givens perspective, we can say that anything that improves social support should be encouraged, particularly when directed at distressed people. (Alas, many such interventions become bureaucratised and complicated, and, as a consequence, lose their power.) Simple instruction and rigorous practice are often all that is needed to transform a sad social outcast into an accepted member of the group. As psychotherapists working from the human givens, we have found that simple steps, such as engaging in more activities or practising social skills, often provide the quickest and most successful means of meeting important unmet needs and helping people to connect more fully and joyously with life.

In no common condition is our view of the world as distorted as it is in depression. The depressed person tends to think everything is wrong, will always be wrong, and it is all their fault. The world has it in for them and there's nothing that can be done about it. Just how dramatically this tunnel vision view can be turned around is vividly shown in Milton H. Erickson's account of the African violet lady.[42] One of Erickson's patients had asked him to visit his aunt, a middle-aged woman who had never married and who lived in Milwaukee. She had a private income and a housekeeper, maid and gardener to take care of her every need. But she had fallen out with her family and for the previous nine months had become deeply withdrawn and depressed.

When Erickson called upon her, telling her he was a doctor and that the nephew had asked him to visit, she expressed no interest. Her behaviour was very passive so, to attempt to get at least some sense of her and her life, Erickson asked her for a guided tour of her house. "She led me from room to room," he said. "I looked around very carefully at everything. In the sun room I saw three beautiful African violets of different colours in full bloom, and a potting shed in which she was propagating another African violet. African violets are very delicate plants. They are easily killed by the slightest amount of neglect."

Erickson also deduced from the presence of a large open bible and several church magazines that she had a keen interest in the church. He then challenged the true depth of her faith on the grounds that she wasn't using her God-given gifts in the way that she should. Although she had had no interest in anything he had said up till that point, this comment grabbed her attention.

Erickson said, "I am going to give you some medical orders and I want them carried out. Do you understand that? Will you agree that you will carry them out?" She passively agreed. So he continued, "Tomorrow you send your housekeeper to a nursery or florist and you get African violets of all different hues. Those will be *your* African violets and you are going to take good care of them. That's a medical order. [This was in the days when doctors' orders were much more likely to be respected and obeyed.]

"Then you tell your housekeeper to purchase 200 gift pots and 50 potting pots and enough potting soil. I want you to break off a leaf from each of your African violets and plant it in a potting pot, and grow additional African violets until they are mature. [These particular flowers propagate when the leaf is planted.] And when you have an adequate supply of African violets, I want you to send one to every baby that's born in any family in your church. I want you to be a good Christian and send an African violet to the family of every baby christened in your church. I want you to send a gift of an African violet to everyone who is sick in your church. When a girl announces her engagement, I want you to send her an African violet. When people get married, I want you to send them African violets. In cases of death, you send a condolence card with an African violet. And to the church bazaars – contribute a dozen or a score of African violets for sale."

With that Erickson left. It was soon reported that her depression had lifted. As Erickson said years later, "Anybody that takes care of that many African violets is too busy to be depressed. She died in her seventies and I have a newspaper cutting recording the fact that, 'The African Violet Queen of Milwaukee has died'. I saw her only once."

This case history illustrates clearly many of the human givens principles of therapy. First Erickson quickly assessed what needs were unfulfilled in the woman's life. Then he focused her attention and made her promise to do something that he knew would re-engage her with the community. He creatively drew on her own belief system and resources. In this case it was her skill with African violets that he cleverly linked with the universal appreciation the human community has for flowers. By precisely describing what he wanted her to do, he employed her imagination to rehearse success. He gave her enough work to do to ensure that her negative introspections would stop and her depression would lift. In other words he devised a therapy specifically for her: one that she could keep up independently.

This last point is particularly important. Therapists have to help depressed people use whatever skills they already possess to reconnect them to the community, so that their needs can be met autonomously. Erickson called this the utilisation principle – whatever the patient brings to the situation is made use of to help them to move on. It doesn't matter whether traits are positive or negative. If someone is obsessive, positive use can still be made of that – perhaps, for instance, by asking the individual to keep careful records of how, when and where they carried out any tasks the therapist sets them. If they love travel, they might be required to take a journey for a particular purpose. Someone who believes their workaholic behaviour makes them more effective can be helped to see they are more effective if they conscientiously build periods of relaxation into their schedule. If they have a strong belief system, a therapist can work from that. If they grow African violets and are part of a Christian community, that can be made very good use of! Of course, some people may not have a particular skill they can use to help get needs met; they might be shy or poor at socialising, for example. Then the counsellor has to teach them social skills, or make sure that *someone* does.

It is important to make use of aspects of individuals' own personalities or the resources they have already developed, so that they can build on, or move on from, what they already know and feel comfortable with, and therefore adapt more easily to a positive change in circumstances. Imposing ways of being or doing from the outside does not help people to develop autonomy and make the most of who they already are.

The need for control

Human beings need to feel a good measure of control over their own lives. All children, unless thwarted, move inexorably towards their own independence, first just gradually trying out what it is like to do things for themselves and eventually becoming fully self-sufficient. It is human nature to want our own corner of things to control as we like – whether the way we live, the way we arrange our living space or just having a drawer at the office in which to keep our personal effects and a surface to carry a photograph of our loved ones. One of the reasons for the unpopularity of hotdesking, the practice of using whichever desk is free when one is in the office, is that it depersonalises and removes individual control over space.

Despite the widespread belief that too much responsibility and overwork are damaging to health, research has shown that having too little responsibility and control over one's work can be just as stressful. A study of 10,000 London civil servants found that those with low control over their work were more likely to become ill and die than were those in higher status jobs with more autonomy.[43] Anxiety disorders often begin when individuals feel that control of some aspect of their lives is being removed from them. Then increasingly they come to fear that they cannot stop terrible things of any kind happening to them.[44]

When people are ill and in pain, anxiety about the outcome has been shown to increase the experience of pain. One of the world's leading authorities on pain, British professor Patrick Wall, has lucidly described the process: "Fear generates anxiety and anxiety focuses the attention. The more the attention is locked, the worse the pain. There is therefore a marked correlation between pain and anxiety. The anxiety here is not the free floating variety with a feeling of general disquiet that something is wrong but cannot be identified. The anxiety of pain is generated by the unknown, and grows worse as the pain persists and short-term expectations of relief fail to be fulfilled."[45]

The anxiety of pain is generated by the unknown. In other words, we are fearful because we are not in control of the outcome. If we are told that we have done nothing seriously damaging to ourselves, that the pain will diminish shortly and we'll be as right as rain, the pain instantly lessens. Its meaning becomes different. We are no longer in the hands of an indifferent Fate.

In psychologist Martin Seligman's theory of learned helplessness, acute depression can arise as a consequence of perceiving oneself to have no control over situations. He and colleagues hit on this discovery when they were testing a learning theory on dogs. The test involved administering mild electric shocks to the dogs that were strapped down and thus could not escape them. When the dogs were later placed in cages from which they could escape if they tried, and were given electric shocks, the dogs initially ran around trying to get out and then quickly gave up and whined quietly as they received the electric shocks.

The researchers were extremely surprised by this reaction, until they realised that the dogs were responding as if still in their previous condition, where they couldn't escape the shocks. They had, in effect, learned that their best efforts achieved nothing and that therefore they were helpless.[46]

Seligman then went on to test his theory with people. Students who had volunteered to carry out an experimental task, for which they were required to wear headphones, were subjected to a loud un-pleasant noise through the headphones which they couldn't turn off, even though pressing a particular button was supposed to be able to stop it. They soon stopped trying to control the noise, and on another occasion didn't even bother to try. Later in the experiment, the students were asked to solve a difficult problem. Although they were all capable of solving it, the students who had been subjected to the interminable noise and were powerless to control it quickly gave up on the problem.

It is an accepted fact that feeling helpless can help generate depression. As depression may then itself increase feelings of helplessness, an individual can be trapped in a vicious cycle. Trying to give people back an interest in and sense of control over their own lives is an important part of treatment for depression.

Coping with change

One major cause of both depression and anxiety, stemming in both cases from loss of control, is the rate at which change is occurring in our world. Our biology has not changed for tens of thousands of years, yet the changes that have been made over a very short time in our environment and how we live our lives have been nothing short of dramatic. For very many people alive today, television had not even been invented when they were young. Now we have 24-hour coverage on countless channels; the whole world is computerised; and, increasingly, one is 'out of it' if lacking email or perhaps even a website.

Technological development and the ease with which capital investment in industry and commerce can be moved around the world in
search of the most favourable deal has created job insecurity, even in
professions where it was once the norm to expect a job 'for life'.
Unfortunately, our incredible ability to create always leaps ahead of
our ability to adapt, and it may feel as if we are forever locked into a
cycle of attempting to adjust to unprecedented situations.[47] This difficulty may be coupled with the anxiety that even our creativeness is out
of control: and that outcomes such as global warming, increased
pollution and dwindling natural reserves may be the unwanted and ill
considered consequences of human advances.

While it isn't possible to turn back the clock, it is certainly possible
and desirable to do what we can to ensure, where possible, that we
exert some degree of control over our lives. It has been shown, for
instance, that a brief talk with the anaesthetist before an operation
significantly reduces the need for post-operative pain relief.[48] The
magic ingredient here is information. By telling a patient exactly what
is going to happen, what pain to expect and what the stages of recovery will be, the disabling element of uncertainty is removed, and the
need for anxiety lessened.

The trend generally in health care nowadays is towards offering
patients full information about their conditions, creating in effect a
partnership in care, rather than expecting them to sit quietly and just
take the pills. Not all patients welcome a plethora of information but
most cite benefits to feeling more in control. It was rejection of
enforced passivity which spurred the revolution in maternity services
brought about over the last couple of decades by disaffected mothers
who wanted choice in how and where they gave birth, rather than the
artificially medicalised procedures then on offer.

Many people diagnosed with cancer have found comfort and
strength in seeking out their own sources of information and complementary treatments. Increasingly, people turn to the internet to find
out what they need to know, to arm themselves with choices. Visits to
health sites are second only to visits to sex sites, in terms of popularity, we are told.

The converse of learned helplessness, feeling positively about our
ability to cope with life's adversities can have a significant impact on

our actual ability to cope. Such beliefs are linked with what psychologists term 'locus of control'.[49,50,51] Those who feel that they can make an impact on events in a positive way and are responsible for much of what happens to them (taking the view, for instance, that hard work brings rewards) are said to have an internal locus of control, while those who think that what happens to them is largely determined by forces outside their control ("people pick on me for no reason") and abdicate responsibility are said to have an external locus of control. While patently we aren't responsible for, and can't control, everything that happens to us, believing that most things are beyond our control is disadvantageous for health. Belief in one's own ability to influence recovery is always advantageous, whether it is a case of speeding discharge from hospital, speeding recovery from an injury or adding a few more precious days to a terminal illness.

Symptom control

Sometimes very simple procedures can enable us to take or regain control over aspects of our lives. For instance, the introduction of patient-controlled anaesthesia, a painkiller delivery system that allows post-operative patients to administer their own pain relief, up to a safe maximum level, has *lessened* the amount of analgesia generally required after surgery. Being in control of when pain relief can be given removes anxiety and fear of pain, both of which, of course, increase pain. Learning an effective relaxation technique and knowing how to put it quickly into practice, wherever one is, can take the power out of an overwhelming fear of panic attacks. Simple cognitive techniques whereby an individual is taught to question their automatic reactions (for instance, countering thoughts such as "I'm going to die if I stay in this room!" with thoughts such as "I've been in this situation before. If I breathe slowly, it will pass") are also powerfully effective.

Taking responsibility

Giving people responsibility is an effective means of restoring an individual's sense of control – not in terms of control over others but in the sense of being able to do whatever is required. Sufferers from mental illness have found the need to care for others, such as children or elderly relatives, a helpful aspect of their own recovery. In one nursing home for elderly people, a wild-bird feeder was placed outside one of the windows. Those residents who were given the responsibility for keeping the feeder stocked with food reported being happier and more satisfied with their lives than those who could only watch the birds feeding.[52] Similarly, in another study, elderly residents in a home were given control over simple matters such as what meals they ate and how the furniture was arranged in their rooms. They were also asked to choose a houseplant to take care of. These simple changes, which increased their control over and responsibility for elements of their own lives, not only had the effect of keeping them happier, more active and alert, but also kept them alive longer, compared with residents who did not have a say in their care.[53]

Control does not have to be absolute to be positive for mental health. It was once found that people who best survived torture were those who had a cast of mind that enabled them to retain a modicum of control over what was happening to them, even to the limited extent of counting to ten before screaming. The case has been described of a man who was tortured by the Gestapo during interrogation. The man knew that the point would come during the torture when he would lose consciousness and so, when he felt that point approaching, he would make the effort to last out for an additional sixty seconds.[54] In one account of the case, the comment was made that he didn't crack during several months of intense interrogation because he remained, in his own mind, "acting rather than acted upon".[55]

We can none of us escape from the fact that we all have to live with uncertainty. In the personal sphere, we cannot rely on jobs being there forever; we cannot rely on a marriage lasting. Whereas once a marriage might have been given a longer chance, or even have been seen as duty to uphold, increasingly individuals look for personal fulfilment and walk out on a relationship that has ceased to provide it. It has been argued that the current preoccupation in our society with health, diet and fitness reflects an attempt to take back, in some small way, a sense of control in this increasingly uncertain and insecure personal world. People may feel less able to control, or rely on, events and agencies outside of themselves, but they can control how much they eat and how much they exercise.[56,57]

But we also cannot live our lives worrying day by day whether a disaster may befall our family or a comet may hit the earth. No human being has ever known what is around the corner and we all live a transient life while pretending that life is constant. Living with uncertainty is complementary to our need for control. It puts it in perspective. Some things we can control, and are beneficial for us to control. Others we can't. Being prepared for change is a positive attribute, minimising the risk of suffering stress reactions, anxiety, ill health and worse when inevitable changes happen. Being able to tolerate ambiguity is an important aspect of mental health. Fortunately, the more we discover about the brain, the more we learn of its amazing ability to adapt to even the most trying of circumstances.

CHAPTER SIX

The gendered brain

THE OPPOSITE sex to oneself fascinates, confuses and exasperates everyone. Sex is inescapably part of being human and sexual differences are endlessly explored; yet their implications are rarely thought through. Debate about whether differing male and female behaviours are the result of nature or nurture has gone on since Darwin's time. Is it instinctive for males to protect females or have we just been socialised into thinking that that is what men ought to do? Do men take less interest in domestic life because of their genes – or because they can get away with it? Are women really better with babies than men are? Are they more in touch with their emotions than men, or is it only because men have been taught that it is unmanly to show what they feel? And so on ...

Clearly, all behaviour is a mix of both genetic and environmental influences but – and it is a big but – certain important aspects of male and female behaviours *are* biologically based. While it is only possible to speak in general terms, because there will always be exceptions, we believe these biological bases and their consequences for male/female relationships need to be acknowledged. Alas, because of widespread intolerance of behaviour different from our own, and the emotional arousal this produces, we often have disharmony between the sexes. Yet, if the neurobiological reasons for differences were better understood and taken into account, or even celebrated, men and women's behavioural styles could be complementary, as perhaps intended by nature.

We imagine that only the most diehard extremists would now claim that there are no natural differences at all in the behaviour of the sexes, although it was once believed that a boy could, if necessary, successfully be brought up as a girl and vice versa. In a classic and now celebrated tragic story, an attempt was made to do just this in the case of a baby boy who lost his penis when a circumcision operation –

undergone for medical reasons – went badly wrong. The parents of the boy (who – to protect his identity – was always referred to as John in the book that told his story[1]) sought the help of a psychologist called Dr John Money, who worked at the Johns Hopkins medical centre in Baltimore, USA. They had seen him on the television, talking about his success in reassigning sex in cases of ambiguity caused by hormonal and genetic disturbances, and about his resultant conviction that 'gender identity', a term which he coined, only emerged as a consequence of how a child is brought up. If children believed themselves male, they would comfortably be male and identify with maleness; if they believed they were female, they would identify with femaleness, he said.

This seemed the best hope to the devastated parents of John who had a twin brother whose circumcision had been successful. Dr Money was only too keen to have a chance to prove his theory. He advised that John should be surgically castrated and undergo construction of 'female' external genitalia before the age of two (after the age of two, gender reassignment was less likely to be successful, he believed). After the operation, the parents were told never to treat John as anything other than female and to let no doubts or concerns enter their own minds, in case these were somehow picked up on by John.

So John became Joan and, to all intents and purposes, had no reason ever to question that he had not been born the twin sister of his little brother. Dr Money saw the family each year and, mindful of his instructions, they reported only positive consequences of the gender reassignment. This gave Dr Money an unnaturally rosy impression of events, which he didn't see fit to question. Five years later, in 1972, he proudly reported to the American Association for the Advancement of Science that the operation had been an unqualified success. This caused an enormous stir at the time, and led to worldwide acceptance of the practice in such circumstances.

But Joan's life was in fact one of misery, and this only came to light because of endocrinologist Dr Milton Diamond's determination to find 'her' and encourage 'her' to tell the truth. Diamond had always questioned Money's stance about gender identity. In fact, by the time Diamond did find the by then grown-up twin, Joan had been John again for many years. It became clear that John had never felt like a girl. He had always wanted to play with his brother's 'boyish' toys, was intrigued to watch his father shave (but had no interest in his mother's make-up) and was noted at school to have "strongly masculine" interests. John even walked and sat like a boy, legs apart. By seven, he could not be persuaded any more that he was truly a girl, regardless of what he was told by any adult. This is clearly an enormously strong position for such a young child to take. By 13, John had stopped dressing as a girl and even started to urinate from the position that felt most natural – standing up. He endured much teasing from other children because treatment with female hormones was giving him elements of a female form, yet he walked and acted like a boy. When eventually it was realised by his endocrinologist that the gender reassignment had dismally failed, John was told the devastating truth by his father. He was then able to have corrective surgery and reinstate himself fully as John. This tragic tale fortunately had a happy end, as John eventually married and became a devoted stepfather to his wife's three children.

So what do we know of the innate differences between males and females, besides the obviously sex-related ones? The first thing is that babies are born male or female; their brains develop differently and at different rates and, even before birth, males are more vulnerable. More than 120 male embryos are conceived for every 100 girl embryos, yet only 105 males per 100 girls reach term.[2] Males are more at risk of death or damage from perinatal brain damage, cerebral palsy, congenital deformities of the genitalia and limbs, premature birth and stillbirth and, at birth, a male baby is physiologically four to six weeks behind a baby girl, according to a review of male fragility in the *British Medical Journal*. Its author commented, "A typical attitude to boys is that they are, or must be made, more resilient than girls. This adds social insult to biological injury."[3]

It has been noted that baby boys are more emotionally reactive than girls, paying more attention to, and demanding more attention from, their mother than baby girls do – perhaps because of greater immaturity at birth and therefore even greater dependence.[4] By the age of three, however, there is a marked difference in reaction to emotion shown by boys and girls. Psychologist Erin McClure of Emory University in Atlanta analysed the findings of 58 published studies that had looked at the ability of adults and children to interpret emotion conveyed by expression or tone of voice. From infancy, girls outperformed boys in their ability to interpret facial expression of emotions, and the difference was found to persist right through childhood and adolescence to adulthood. McClure concluded that ability to interpret emotion is not just the result of gender stereotypes and expectations but that "sex-specific, neurological maturation patterns [could be] potential sources of sex differences in facial emotion processing".[5]

Boys appear also to be less sensitive to the distress of others. In one study, quoted in the *British Medical Journal* review, a group of six-year-old boys and girls could hear on a baby monitor the sound of a baby crying. They thought the baby was real, when the crying in fact came from a recording. Girls were much more likely to speak soothingly to the baby, while boys more often turned the speaker off. But it wasn't that they were unconcerned. Their heart rates showed greater anxiety than that experienced by the girls. They couldn't tolerate the baby's distress – nor their own, concluded the author of the review, consultant child and adolescent psychiatrist Dr Sebastian Kraemer. Boys are more likely than girls to dismiss bereavement or separation of parents as of little concern – although it is known that boys are affected even more strongly by marriage break-up than girls are.[6]

Might all this indicate a lower emotional threshold in boys? Could the apparent uncertainty about how to handle emotions be caused by genetic factors or by the different values placed upon the expression of emotions by males?

Clearly, the differences between men and women are not just the obvious physical ones. Fifty years' research by male and female scientists conclusively confirm that their thinking strategies and the way they handle emotions are different too. Men, on average, perform better at spatial tasks that involve mentally rotating objects and, in imagination, manipulating them in some fashion, which is why men, on average, find map reading easier and why women very often have to turn the map around in the direction they are going before they can make sense of it. Men are also more accurate at target-directed motor skills, such as guiding or intercepting projectiles. Given the fact that, for most of human evolution, men were primarily the hunters and the defenders, we would expect this skill to be more advanced in the male. On the other hand, women tend to perform better than men on tests involving fine motor skills and perceptual speed, in which the subject must rapidly identify matching patterns. They also easily outperform men on tasks involving verbal fluency: when they read a story, a paragraph or a list of unrelated words, they demonstrate better recall.[7] More of the female brain is set aside for verbal activity.[8] The right hemisphere, as well as the left hemisphere, is generally more active, whereas, in people less verbally dextrous, most involvement is in the left hemisphere.[9] (It is the right hemisphere that is more directly responsive to emotions arising from the limbic system.) In higher mathematical and abstract reasoning, however, it is men who excel. At the top end of the ability scale, there are thirteen mathematically gifted males to every female. This is why the physical sciences are so male dominated. Men simply find them easier.[10,11] On the other hand, female inclinations guide them away from such subjects towards those that are more amenable to their innate skills.[12] Even girls with high mathematical abilities will often choose to study something that appeals to them more.[13]

In general, men talk to *give* information or to report on events and establish their status. They talk about things – cars, work, politics, ideas, research, sport, food, drink – rather than people. They are more interested in conveying facts, not emotional responses. They are goal oriented. They focus on solving problems and find it more productive to concentrate on one task at a time. They are less likely to ask for help or directions. Men compete.

Women, on the other hand, talk to *get* information and to get into rapport and connect with other people. They talk about *people* rather than *things*. They convey feelings and details and are relationship oriented. Who they know and what they know about other people is more interesting to them. They are better at multi-tasking and quicker to ask for, and accept, help or directions. Women co-operate.[14]

But, although the thinking strategies differ between the sexes, they don't differ nearly so much as the emotional strategies we use.

Because women, on average, are more in touch with their feelings, they are generally regarded as being more sensitive, *warmer* and, as the current phrase has it, emotionally intelligent. Indeed, the acts of reading the subtleties in children's mood changes, and comforting and nurturing them, are in all cultures, better done (on the whole) by mothers. The father's role *is* nurturing but in a different way. As their children grow, men play with them in a more physical and adventurous way, with emphasis on risk taking predominating, rather than female concerns for security and safety. The male interaction with offspring has the quality of apprenticeship about it. Consequently, for this and other reasons, men are typically characterised as being *colder* and less emotional than women. Research, however, reveals a more complex picture.

From a very young age boys are *more* emotional than girls. This is easy to confirm from personal experience. In supermarkets, it is little boys who throw the biggest and longest lasting tantrums. And, in families breaking up, it is boys who are most emotionally disturbed by arguing parents and divorce – and boys are more distressed by a family bereavement. In all kinds of situations, it is boys and men who feel the most intense emotions and are more physically damaged by them – heart rate increases, blood pressure rises, immune system falters etc. This difference seems to occur because the male autonomic nervous system, which largely controls the body's stress response, is more sensitive than the female's and takes far longer to recover from emotional upset. Because of this, males have evolved ways to suppress or override emotions. And in this they are encouraged by parents and wider society, which bring to bear social pressure to encourage restraint, thus keeping their attention off their emotions and focused outwards.

Girls, on the other hand, because they are less emotionally intense at a young age, are allowed, and indeed encouraged, to express their emotions. This difference between the sexes, with men on the whole more skilled in controlling and holding back emotions and women more skilled at expressing and putting emotions into words, is at the root of much contemporary marital conflict.[15]

The fact that, in arguments, male blood pressure and heart rates rise significantly higher than rates in females, and stay higher for much longer is at the root of why a man typically prefers to stonewall or withdraw when his female partner is upset about something. Men stay silent or leave the room because they are trying desperately to keep a lid on emotional arousal. They have learned that, if they were to verbalise their feelings and get angry, they would lose control of the ability to think straight; their blood pressure would go up even more; and they would put themselves in danger of having a heart attack or even becoming violent in a crude attempt to resolve their distress. But, because women have an equal need to do exactly the opposite and so want to vent their feelings, this typical male behaviour winds them up and a spiral of misunderstanding can easily develop.

In Richmal Compton's popular *Just William* stories, much amusement is derived from the female ability to manipulate males and get what they want by raising the emotional temperature. The lisping, tyrannical, six-year-old Violet Elizabeth Bott only has to say to William and his gang of 11-year-old 'outlaws', "I'll scweam and scweam, 'til I'm sick" and the boys cave in and do whatever she wants them to. Only slightly more sophisticated variations of this pattern are seen time and again among adults – which is why we laugh at William's predicament, if perhaps a little ruefully, because we recognise it.

A few years ago, there was a fashion for encouraging men to get more in touch with their feelings and express them; in other words, adopt the innate female strategy. If this had succeeded it would have been a disaster, undoing tens of thousands of years of human evolution that gave the human species distinct advantages. What both sexes need is not more *expression* of emotion but more *understanding* of it – what it does and its role in the way we perceive people and events. In this, both sexes are equal.

So, whilst there were, and are, good reasons for males to develop skills of emotional restraint, at the same time it must be recognised that females need to express their feelings in order to communicate and build rapport. Women are mentally damaged by holding back on expressing emotions, as men are mentally damaged by expressing them, and this has to be accommodated. To have a meaningful relationship with *anybody* information has to be exchanged about how we feel. But in the relationship between the sexes, as in all things, a balance has to be struck so that emotions are expressed sufficiently to satisfy female needs, but not so strongly as to over-arouse male anxiety or anger. She must feel understood and empathised with, and he must not feel that emotions are running so high that the situation is escalating dangerously out of control. This takes practice. Spreading knowledge about the differences in the way that men and women naturally handle emotions is crucially important in education, work, personal relationships and therapy. Individuals are less likely to feel personally attacked if they have more of an insight into how their partner perceives things. In fact, many find this discovery extremely liberating. Their expectations of one another become far more realistic, and satisfaction with the relationship correspondingly increases.

Rough and tumble

An aspect of male behaviour that is constantly put under the microscope is the male tendency to be more pushy, noisy, competitive and aggressive. Does such rumbustious behaviour occur in boys because it is a learned behaviour – expected, and therefore receiving reinforcement from the adult acceptance or approval that greets it? Or is there something more basic involved here? Even the most 'equality'-minded individual is hard pushed to say that boys and girls don't behave differently from each other from a very young age. Sex difference researchers have consistently found that boys like rough play more than girls do, take up more space and make more noise[16]; they have shorter attention spans, going from one activity to another more quickly; and they are less sociable than girls.[17] In other words, the priorities of the sexes are quite different.

People who work in nursery settings are highly aware of these differences between boy and girl play. But it has been common practice to discourage the more rough and tumble male play style – particularly any kind of game which involves war, weapons or super heroes. Ivan was discussing this male/female play difference once with a neighbour who runs a nursery near where he lives. She commented, "It is always just so noticeable that boys want to play with guns or swords. Even though we tried to stop this, because the thinking was that we shouldn't be glorifying violence, the boys always found ways to play what they wanted, using pretend guns and swords and spears instead."

Cracking down on such 'war' games is in line with the common American and European policy of zero tolerance of violence in nursery settings. Penny Holland, senior lecturer in early childhood education at the University of North London, used to be a strong supporter of that policy. She has now reversed her position completely. "Far from viewing zero tolerance as protective of children by conveying the message that violence and aggression is never okay, I believe that it is possibly detrimental to the development of both boys and girls," she says. "Increasingly, adult perceptions of the potentially dangerous male include naturally boisterous young boys, who now often become labelled as potentially aggressive and violent even at nursery stage. Apart from the high likelihood of self-fulfilling prophecy then coming into play, boys are at further risk of such labels, as a result of the early start to formal education in the UK. ... Our unrealistic early expectations of boys and our rejection of their noisy play fighting can introduce a different edge to their behaviour at this stage: it becomes resistant behaviour."[18]

She is convinced that demonising boys' bold behaviour and excessively valuing quiet behaviour, usually demonstrated by girls, has led to a deeper fixing of the aggressor/victim stereotype. In her review of others' research in the last decade, and from her own, she has found that relaxing zero tolerance has had positive effects on children's behaviour – enabling more co-operative than antagonistic play, greater responsibility for behaviour and more opportunities to help children direct imaginative play.

Children are clear about the boundaries between play fighting and real fighting, studies show, whereas it is often teachers, particularly females, who are uncertain. Research shows that just one per cent of play fighting degenerates into real fighting (except among children who have pre-existing problems with aggressive or antisocial tendencies), whereas teachers dramatically overestimate, and expect about a third of play fighting to get violent.[19]

Holland suggests that an over-zealousness in breaking up 'fights' may be counterproductive in that it prevents children from developing their own rules and strategies to keep the game safe and therefore deprives them of an important opportunity to manage their own behaviour. Her own interest in the impact of zero tolerance stemmed from a different concern, however. She had noticed in the nursery where she worked a few boys who had no interest in anything other than super hero or war play. Deprived of every drumstick which they tried to use as a sword or guns made out of plastic linking blocks, they wandered aimlessly. What, she began to wonder, could all this rejection be doing to their self-esteem? When it was decided to relax the zero tolerance rule, and allow constructed weapons (construction being a creative act which could fire the imagination) rather than reproduction toys (which only allow imitative play), these boys instantly made themselves into super heroes. But it was quickly clear that they had no idea where to go with this play. By entering the game and suggesting imaginative scenarios, Holland was able to help them learn to be more creative about their own play. She says, "I now firmly believe that we can use play fighting and super hero games to open certain children up to options other than violence. When we reject this type of play, we are going against a child's reality, and emerging sense of self-esteem and belonging." She also found that, once super hero play was not taboo, the boys quickly moved on from it, using it just as a springboard into other, more imaginative games. Their determination to engage in super hero play when such play was out of bounds was a mark of their resistance against what they perceived as personal rejection, rather than any deep need to play war games.

The way boys play follows a natural innate drive. If they don't go through this phase they are going against nature. Ivan remembers as a small boy being given a cowboy hat, gun and holster for a birthday present by an uncle, and being ecstatic. But overnight the gun and holster disappeared – thrown out by his mother who strongly disapproved of gunplay. The feeling of disbelief, helplessness and injustice was physical, and overwhelmed him for days. By frustrating the acting out of this template, his mother achieved the opposite effect because Ivan went on to spend an inordinate amount of time making bows and arrows, powerful catapults, cannons, bombs and, in his teens, unbeknown to his mother but condoned by his father, a beautifully engineered, fully working matchlock rifle that fired ball-bearings hundreds of yards. He was only cured of this violent and dangerous obsession with weapons by a traumatic incident when the matchlock rifle blew up in his face and nearly killed him and two friends.

As any male or parents of boys will know from their own experience, playing with guns or other weapons as a child doesn't usually lead to an unhealthy interest in them as adults. They serve a vital, natural play purpose and then cease to be of interest at all. The only children who become aggressive during play fights, it has been shown, are those who, sadly, have had real life experiences of witnessing or being on the receiving end of aggression themselves.[20]

Equally interestingly, however, it emerged from Holland's work with super hero play that, once it was given the OK, girls were willing to join in too. She claims that, just as it is not natural for boys, neither is it natural for girls always to play quiet games involving the dressing up box or the home corner. They do these things because they are better than boys at learning which behaviours receive social approval. Because quiet games also fit with their more naturally co-operative and quieter natures, they have been happy to comply and play them. But, once noisy play was given approval, and the nursery staff joined in, girls were keen to participate too. Holland suggests that, by keeping the boisterous side of girls subdued, adults are teaching them to suppress their physicality, and their sense of personal power – "sanctioning the passivity which is the corollary of male violence".[21]

What is needed, then, is more maleness and male values in nursery settings, not the token contribution of males who have been successfully assimilated into the largely female culture of early years education. It has been noted in other research that one of the special contributions of fathers' involvement with their families is their propensity for 'lively play'. Family expert Susan Golombok has pointed out that, whereas mothers have a caretaking role, it is often through play, particularly rough and tumble, that fathers and children (of both sexes) build their relationship.[22]

It is known that children whose fathers play-fight with them grow up more well-adjusted, friendly and popular. By contrast, children who are mollycoddled at home and discouraged from rough behaviour are more likely to turn into bullies, or become their victims. The innate instinct that fathers have to play rough and tumble games somehow helps children to learn self-control and become secure in their identity.

And that is the nub. By going against nature, in whatever way, we rob people of confidence in their sense of self – just as surely as John was robbed of his identity when made to live as Joan. We may also be building up a pile of problems of our own making. It almost always seems to be little boys who are disruptive at primary school, race around the classroom, refuse to settle, and interrupt activities that others are engaged in. By the time they are at secondary school, many of them aren't even bothering to turn up regularly. Far more boys than girls are excluded from schools each year, both at primary and secondary level. This is an alarming consequence of the feminised teaching patterns prevalent in so many homes and schools today.

Educating facts

It has at last started to be realised that the way we currently organise education favours girls, not boys. Five-year-old boys do not take easily to sitting in groups at tables and getting on quietly with reading or writing. They want to be rushing about, doing active things, and being stimulated. The reason appears to have its root in the brain, most particularly in an area known as the reticular activating system. This is a system of nerve pathways in the brain that regulates levels of consciousness, right through from deep sleep to drowsiness to relaxed state to full alert and undivided attention. It integrates the information received from all of the five senses as well as from other areas of the brain and determines the overall activity level of the brain. It alerts us to whatever warrants attention, be that an emergency or just something interesting, by initiating brain production of the neurotransmitter dopamine. In so doing, it involves the frontal lobes of the neocortex, which, on injection with dopamine, can bring reasoning to bear upon the situation. It is in the frontal lobes that the decision is reached that the dark lumpy thing on the ground is an empty black sack and not a crouching attacker. In other words, the reticular activating system activates responses from both the emotional and the conscious brain, and enables the conscious brain to reach its intelligent conclusions.

We now know that the reticular activating system in the male is less sensitive than that in the female, with women paying much faster attention to flashing lights or loud noises delivered in laboratory tests.[23] This is probably why women tend to wake at the first whimper from the baby in the next room while men sleep contentedly through. But it also means that it takes more to capture the attention of a male than it does a female, and this has been linked to the higher levels of antisocial behaviour found in boys and the increased levels of attention deficit hyperactivity disorder.[24]

In the classroom, girls are more likely to have their interest captured and maintained than boys. Generally speaking, boys need something more highly stimulating than low key activities to engage their involvement. Unfortunately, because the reticular activating system has to stimulate the neocortex before the thinking part of the brain can contribute its two pennyworth, bored boys are often left at the mercy of their emotional minds; this produces frustration and causes them to become disruptive. Boys with hyperactivity disorders have a particularly high alert threshold, meaning that it takes considerable stimulation to get their attention at all! And, once captured, it can only be briefly retained, unless caught by yet another high stimulus activity, perhaps involving status or competition.

The male need for higher stimulation also explains why boys and men commonly enjoy risky activities, such as snowboarding and climbing and parachuting, more than women do. They are more likely in adolescence to experiment dangerously with drugs and alcohol and other substances. More young men than young women between the ages of 15 and 24 die from accidents.

Because boys' brains need higher levels of stimulation to engage their attention and modern methods of teaching don't allow for this, it is now far harder for boys to flourish in schools. In infant classes, they are expected to write and colour neatly, when the fine motor control areas of their brains mature later than those of girls.[25] While there are many arguments about the exact contribution of testosterone to male non-sexual characteristics,[26] it appears to be accepted that testosterone levels and competitiveness are linked – dominance having evolutionary advantage when males were in competition with other males.[27] Testosterone rises in athletes before races and matches, and in chess players before tournaments.[28] In school, it is natural for boys to want to compete, but this is largely frowned upon in the modern education system, certainly at primary school level, where co-opera-tion, not competition, is valued. Education now favours the female way of learning, accenting the verbal skills that girls develop earlier than boys,[29] and emphasising co-operative activities with no outright winners. But boys need to compete, or support teams that compete. They thrive on challenge. One only has to look at the deadly serious-ness with which many men treat the viewing of league and interna-tional football – they are elated when they win and in despair when they lose. Winning *and* losing are both par for the course.

In schools and many colleges, however, there is increased emphasis on continuous assessment, rather than exams. And, in some schools, competition of any kind is studiously avoided, because the teachers are wedded to the modern myth that losing impinges badly upon self-esteem.

In a strangely backhanded way of promoting the idea that everyone is equal, one school we were told of came up with an original way to deal with the problem of winners and losers. Some 30 of its pupils were involved in an educational TV series that involved a maths quiz in each 'episode'. Children had to be in two teams of two, per pro-gramme, competing against each other. One team had to win and one to lose each time, so that the winners could go on to the next stage of the quiz. Fearing that losing might damage children's self-esteem, each pair of teams had to toss a coin to see who would 'win' the quiz. Those who lost the toss were forced to give a wrong answer, even if they knew the right one. On one farcical occasion, the 'winning' team kept getting answers wrong and re-shooting had to take place, while the 'losing' team knew all the answers. This supposedly egalitarian approach was designed to save everyone's face – the children were, in effect, only acting. But that was not how it felt to the children who knew the answers and were forced to act as if they didn't, on a quiz game that would be watched by their own and other schools, by chil-dren who wouldn't know they were acting! One boy was so upset that he refused to give the wrong answer and had to be removed from the set. As he said, "It's not like being the bad guy or playing dumb in a TV drama. That's obviously acting. But in the quiz, it just looked like we didn't know the answers." As the best in maths in his year, he couldn't handle that.

It is excellent that girls' abilities are now fully recognised and that they are given all the educational opportunities which boys have always received. Our concern is that the current teaching style, from a mainly female teaching staff, now only suits girls, not boys. On average, males have superior abilities in mathematical reasoning and problem solving aptitude tests, yet girls generally now do better in maths at school than boys. Girls do better generally, outperforming boys at A levels as well as at GCSEs and National Tests (colloquially but incorrectly known as SATs) taken at seven, 11 and 14.

Girls are able to sit quietly at tables with several other children, and get on with their work while a teacher assists children on another table. Boys, if left to get on with work in such a setting, are more likely to start messing about. Because they require more stimulation and are more active and noisy, they need more attention. But high quality attention is not always a strong feature of modern educational methods. As one mother said about the secondary school that her son attends, "The school will support in every way they can those who want to work. But if children show a disinclination to bother, they don't push them at all, nor seem to have any expectations of them. Yet all adolescents, particularly boys, go through phases when they are more interested in other things than schoolwork. A child's future can depend upon how that is handled."[30]

Interestingly, men are still ahead of women in the attainment of first class degrees from Oxford University. Researchers found that women revised for longer, while men took greater risks. Lead researcher Dr Jane Mellanby commented, "Men may benefit from a more confident style which produces answers which are deemed worthier of a first than the slightly more tentative, balanced answers produced by many women."[31] As we know, males are in general keener to take risks than females and, in the traditional examination system, this clearly can pay off, leaving women this time the losers.

The education system would serve both males and females better if it could be geared to take account of each sex's strengths, as was the case in the past. The way boys and girls were educated, from the earliest times, was through mentorship, starting with hunter-gatherers taking their children out on the hunt over 100,000 years ago, through the teaching of crafts, how to make things, and how to prepare food, all the way on up to the teaching methods employed at the earliest (Islamic) teaching centres and later European and American universities and every village school. Teachers and students got to know one another. They interacted constantly throughout the day. The teacher knew each child, had a clear vision of each child's understanding of the work in hand, and worked with each child (or encouraged working in pairs) until the teacher was satisfied that they had absorbed and understood the material ... or were hopelessly incapable of being educated. Because this latter was virtually an admission of failure on the part of the teacher, it happened rarely. Such was the success of this method that it was also the basis of the apprenticeship system. It is, of course, closely akin to the way parents bring up children. It is natural, in tune with the givens of human nature.

Brain differences

Although supporters of the biological bases for sex differences in behaviour have been as vociferous as those who claim all differences are learned, the actual biological differences are not as far reaching as originally suggested. Doreen Kimura, professor of psychology at Simon Fraser University in Canada, has spent years replicating most of the original research and has been able to ascertain which findings are reliable and which are not.[32] Males *are* better at targeting abilities, such as throwing a ball or a dart, whereas women have more agile finger movements. This would fit with the standard sex roles in the hunter-gatherer societies in which we have lived for most of our existence: the males tended to hunt while the females collected berries, etc., and made pottery and clothes.[33] Men have superior spatial abilities and, as we have already said, better mathematical skills overall. Females learn verbal skills earlier but do not have greater verbal intelligence as adults, although they are better spellers. The largest area of consensus among sex-difference researchers is in the area of hemispheric differences. There is greater communication between the left and right brain hemispheres in women. This may facilitate the female's greater awareness of non-verbal modes of communication, such as body language and tones of voice. The disadvantage of increased communication between the hemispheres is that it may impede performance on tasks that require highly focused activity – for instance, motor skills such as football and golf. As some commentators put it, "She has a floodlight, he has a spotlight".[34] We have already discussed some of the ramifications of such differences for male/female communication, in respect of emotional understanding. They also help explain why males tend to get more totally absorbed in activities and find it more difficult to break concentration – a fact which women may find extremely irritating when trying to get their attention.

Men's lesser ability to spread their attention and manage several things at once may go some way to explain why most men avoid all aspects of home management if they possibly can. Running a home and family requires ten pairs of hands, as everyone knows, yet women seem to manage it admirably with one. They can keep an eye on the stew, do the ironing, put a plaster on a cut knee, answer the phone and make complicated arrangements almost without losing a beat. Remember the Peggy Lee song with the refrain, "Because I'm a wo-o-man" which, tongue-in-cheek, describes something of the same? When men do take a share in the household tasks, they may not complete them in the manner their womenfolk expect, because they do not notice or register detail in the same way that women do.[35] Cups lying around the room are not noticed and picked up. Dirt may not be cleaned away properly, and so on.

Of course there are men who like to keep a tidy, spotless house and of course there are women who loathe, and are poor at, cleaning. But, in general, men are less attuned to domestic chores – or to any chores that require considerably split attention. That doesn't mean they should never have to do them and women always should. It does mean that life might be more harmonious if, in equal- or partial-share households, women could lower their standards of acceptability for the tasks done by their partners – or come to an arrangement over a division of tasks which would play to the strengths of each.

Violent men and violent women

The big problem in the area of sex differences is sorting out which are biologically based and which are cultural or societal. Biologists have long thought, for instance, that the amounts of testosterone coursing through the male's body are responsible for male aggressiveness and violence. This view came about as a result of experiments in which, for instance, mice exposed as foetuses to high levels of male sex hormones grow up to be more aggressive.[36] But it is not so simple. A mass of evidence has now been marshalled to make the case that administering testosterone to human males makes them no more aggressive than they were before.[37] These studies show that, while men are unquestionably more violent than women, there is nothing innately male about violence. American psychologist Erich Fromm distinguished between benign-defensive and malignant-destructive aggression, the former genetically programmed and aiming to remove threat, the latter a maladaptive behaviour than is not genetically programmed and is characteristic only of man.[38] There is plenty of evidence to back up that view, showing that it is disempowered men whose lives lack love or meaning who are most likely to be violent. Aggression most often arises in the context of harsh parenting, under-privilege and abuse, poor supervision, parental loss etc. As the human givens approach would predict, biology is only a small aspect of such outcomes.[39]

While men's violence has erroneously been laid at the door of their genes, the equally erroneous belief persists that women are less violent than men. While they clearly inflict, in general, less damage on men than men do on women, many women do resort to violence to vent their feelings. Melanie Phillips, in her book *The Sex-Change Society*, cited considerable evidence to show that women can also inflict serious harm and initiate *more* domestic violence than men.[40] For in-stance, in one New Zealand study, 18.6 per cent of young women said they had perpetrated serious physical violence against their partners, compared with 5.7 per cent of young men.[41] Canadian researchers found twice as much severe violence by wives against husbands as vice versa.[42] Although the general public tends to think of child abusers, particularly sex abusers, as men, this is by no means always the case, as we know from our dealings with many workers in this field. Many children have suffered in silence or been disbelieved because those who hurt them were women. No doubt such aggression in women derives from the same sources as those we discussed above, when we were talking about violent men. Mentally undamaged men who are getting their emotional needs reasonably well met appear to have a strong template *not* to attack females and children. It is this fact that women who attack men rely on. Most men just take the attack, with-draw from the environment if they can and wait for the woman to calm down. But if the male inhibition to attack women is breached, which happens particularly if a man has had a lot to drink, the conse-quences are often dreadful.

It is to the credit of the early feminists that women can now take their true place in society and make the most of their potential. Alas, however, it seems we have come full circle and the price of the eman-cipation of women is the emasculation of men. Extreme feminists argue hotly for sameness, claiming no biological differences between male and female behaviours. So everything which can be done by a man can also be done by a woman, and vice versa, bar pregnancy and childbirth. Such a stance helps neither sex, but adversely affects males more. Phillips has argued that it is easier for women to take on additional 'male' roles and qualities (breadwinning, ambition, action) than it is for men to assume traditional 'female' roles (homemaking and childrearing). "The explanation for this is that, far from the monstrous image of all-powerful patriarchy conjured by feminism, masculinity is so fragile that men feel compelled to demonstrate their differences from women if they are not to lose their identity altogether. It is men, not women, who are the vulnerable sex."[43]

She cites, in support of her case, evidence that unemployed men spend even less time with their children than employed fathers do, and that either type spends far less time on childcare or household management than employed or unemployed women.

"Feminists used to be angry that biology was seen as women's destiny," she said, in an interview for *The New Therapist*. "Alas, the problem for men is that biology plainly isn't their destiny. They have to construct it. I think that an important part of masculinity is that it's not femininity. ... Assuming that the father can play the same role as the mother is to misunderstand a key feature of masculinity itself. The father's role has to be different from the mother's because men have a terror of being swallowed up by femininity and losing their very gender identity."[44]

Professor Anthony Clare addressed this issue of male identity when he wrote, "What price all that brute strength, might and energy now, when more people are employed making Indian curries than mining coal? .... Men can go on defining themselves in terms of what they do but it has become a great fraud, a confidence trick they persist in playing on themselves. When it comes to work, women can do it too. There is nothing uniquely male about any of it. If work used to define masculinity, it does not do so any more. A revolution has occurred."[45]

And this, of course, is the reality we now live with in Western countries, although work for very many women is an economic necessity and, given the choice, they would prefer their partners to have it.[46] As women are encouraged back into work by politicians, there are increasing numbers of unemployed and never-employed disaffected men, looking desperately for identity. We also have rising numbers of single parent families headed by women. It has been observed, in fact, that male unemployment is the most important factor in female lone parenthood.[47]

But fathers are by no means dispensable. The outcome is best for children of single mothers when the mother is financially secure, has a supportive network of family and friends and the children are given the chance to maintain close contact with their father.[48] No surprises there.

It is not our aim – nor do we have the expertise – to tackle such social issues here, but we strongly believe that their true sources must be identified and acknowledged if we are to recover a fully functional family life within which children can flourish. We accept that it isn't always easy to separate behaviour that is innate from behaviour that is culturally determined. But if, in this age of striving for equality between the sexes, we try to deny natural differences between males and females and defy their individual strengths and weaknesses, we will be losing valuable knowledge and understanding, and ultimately be less able to meet the needs of either sex.

CHAPTER SEVEN

The body-linked mind

IF SOMEONE says, "My psoriasis has flared up again. I've been under terrible stress lately," it seems a perfectly reasonable supposition. Yet until at least three-quarters of the way through the last century, the idea that our attitudes and reactions to events in our lives could have an impact on our body defence systems was anathema to most main-stream physicians. The Russian scientist Pavlov had discovered in the 1920s that the immune system could be conditioned by experience. Fifty years later an American scientist made a similar discovery[1] – rats given immune system suppressing drugs with saccharine flavoured water continued to experience a lowering of immunity when given the saccharine flavoured water alone. And suddenly there was an explosion in interest in the understanding that the healing response is a rich system of mind/body connections.

The field is now inelegantly known as psychoneuroimmunology, but is none the less exciting for that. Whereas once it was thought that the brain and the immune system carried out their separate businesses, unable to influence each other, what psychoneuroimmunologists revealed is that there are strong interconnections, enabling our thoughts and our feelings to play an important part in our physical health. The hormones which course through our bodies when we are under chronic stress can impair immune function. And emotional reactions, by equally complex routes, can impair the functioning of specific organs. A meta-analysis of about 100 smaller studies confirmed that certain emotional 'attitudes' (i.e. emotions experienced long term, almost as a character trait, such as chronic anxiety, prolonged grief, tension, hostility, suspicion and pessimism) could double the risk of a whole range of diseases, including heart disease, headache, asthma, arthritis, peptic ulcers and skin disorders.[2]

Many books have been written about this fascinating subject, and indeed we have been covering it ourselves in this book – we have looked, for instance, in some depth at the impact on health of having close relationships and strong social support systems, and the ability of the mind to enhance its own health and healing powers. Indeed it is impossible to write a book about mental health without extensive references to mind and body links. Here is just a taster of the research findings so far.

The stress and anxiety factor

Since the laboratory finding about the rats' immune systems' reaction to stress, it has been impossible to ignore the impact on the body of chronic stress and anxiety. While our bodies are designed to handle brief bursts of stress to help us handle difficult situations (that is what the fight and flight response is all about), if all the energy which is generated is not expressed in appropriate physical action (in our evolutionary past, either fighting or fleeing), it doesn't quickly disperse. If we remain on the equivalent of constant alert, through anxious worrying, the chemical cocktail of stress hormones that maintain the ongoing arousal weakens our immune system.

Excessive anxiety compromises the immune system to the point where it can speed development of cancer, increase vulnerability to viral infections, exacerbate plaque formation leading to atherosclerosis, and blood clotting which may in turn lead to myocardial infarction. Stress overload can accelerate the onset of insulin dependent diabetes and influence the course of non-insulin dependent diabetes. It can lead to ulceration of the gastrointestinal tract and trigger symptoms of ulcerative colitis (inflammatory bowel disease). Even the brain is susceptible to the effects of long-sustained stress. Damage can be caused to the hippocampus and therefore to memory.[3,4]

There have been many studies that show the adverse effects of stress on the body's ability to fight infections. In one particularly famous one, carried out at the (now defunct) Common Cold Unit in Wiltshire, people were asked in detail about the amount and nature of stress in their lives and were then exposed to the common cold virus. Those who saw themselves as being under the greater stress were the more likely to catch the colds. People with fewer social supports were also more likely to catch colds.[5] Similarly, people are more susceptible to outbreaks of the herpes virus when they are under stress,[6] and to the onset of symptoms, if HIV-positive.[7]

Other recent research studies show that people under stress have a poorer response to vaccines and that wounds are slower to heal when people are stressed. When small wounds were inflicted on the arms of (willing) carers of spouses with Alzheimer's disease, for example, these took longer to heal than those inflicted on non-carers. The same effect was found in students taking exams. Oral wounds healed 40 per cent more quickly when the students were on vacation than when they were taking exams. The slower healing effect persisted after the exam as well. This could be a relevant finding for surgeons because anxiety commonly persists after surgery, as well as being rampant before it.[8]

One study revealed just how important it is to have a sense of being able to 'cope' with one's life and have an element of control over it. Rats which were exposed to electric shocks experienced a lowering in immunity if they couldn't escape those shocks, whereas this didn't happen if they could escape the shocks. When they were injected with tumour preparations, those that could escape shocks were more often able to reject the tumours, whereas those that couldn't more often developed cancer.[9]

Of course, not everyone who is under stress, even extreme stress, develops serious illness and it may well be the coping mechanisms that they use which play an important part in their maintaining health. It is also important not to rush to the conclusion that getting suppressed emotions 'out' is the health-giving ingredient in cases where poor handling of emotion seems to lead to physical illnesses such as stomach ulcers.

In one very telling study carried out in the 1950s, American gastro-enterologist Dr Arthur Mirsky and psychoanalyst colleagues came up with a hypothesis to explain why only some patients secreting high levels of pepsinogen developed peptic ulcers. They decided that high levels of pepsinogen plus high 'dependency needs' determined who developed ulcers, and Mirsky was given the chance to prove this by studying over 2,000 recently drafted members of the US army – 18-year-olds and 19-year-olds living away from home for the first time, thus presumably suffering the dependency conflicts which the analysts had in mind. Mirsky found, from a very small number of men (ten) who were identified as having intense dependency conflicts, that seven of them developed ulcers. This Mirsky saw as significant,[10] although his methods and findings would probably have been questioned by other scientists.

The point we want to make is that, as a consequence of his findings, analysts decided that treating dependency conflicts seemingly associated with ulcers would help the ulcers heal. But the ulcers actually *worsened* in patients who underwent psychoanalysis. Quite clearly, the added stress of having to revisit the real or imagined traumas of their youth on the analyst's couch exacerbated the ulcers. Some decades later, it was sensibly shown that helping patients to understand the link between emotions and ulcers, to find better ways to handle stress and to think more flexibly led to cessation of symptoms in 30 out of 32 ulcer patients.[11]

All the rage

Once it used to be thought that the highly stressed individual, always rushing to get everything done, always needing to achieve, impatient, aggressive and competitive (dubbed Type A) was at highest risk for heart attacks, while the laid-back, easy-going individual (Type B) would be more protected. It is now known, however, that it is not the motivation and desire to achieve that is the problem. It is allowing oneself to be made angry that hurts the heart.

When we get angry, we are activating the body's fight or flight mechanism as effectively as anxiety does. The whole process of stress hormones being released, heart rate rising, blood pressure shooting up, etc. gets into gear. And, as part of this process, cholesterol levels rise. As with anxiety, all this is all right if it happens only every so often. It was what we were designed to do. But when it keeps happening, the raised cholesterol levels can clog the arteries, narrowing them so that blood flow is restricted, and eventually maybe causing a heart attack.

People who rush about busily doing a lot of things and taking on lots of responsibilities are not necessarily at higher risk of heart attacks, if they enjoy the pressure. Those at risk are the people who are quick to be roused to anger a great deal of the time or who are almost permanently harbouring feelings of hostility – "Why should he have a better job and a bigger house than me? Why didn't I get that promotion? Who does she think she is, telling me what I should be doing? How dare they keep taking off more and more trains!" Many people become addicted to being angry. It is a very seductive, apparently uncomplicated response: "I am right. You are wrong!"

Numerous studies confirm that the anger response is a likely component in the development of heart disease. In one, which had considerable impact upon research in the field, heart patients at Stanford University Medical School were asked to recall incidents that had made them angry. While they were doing so, their hearts starting pumping at least five per cent less efficiently – cardiologists view a drop in pumping efficiency of seven per cent as serious enough to cause a heart attack. Even more importantly, the patients admitted that the anger they were experiencing on retelling the tale was only half as strong as the anger they had felt at the time.[12]

But hostility could only ever be part of the story, of course, in the development of heart disease. Dr Robert Ornstein and Dr David Sobel, in their book *Healthy Pleasures*, lucidly suggest how hostility ties in with social isolation and lack of connection with the community. "There is a strong sense of self involvement underlying hostility. A person who thinks of himself or herself as better than others in many ways is vulnerable to anyone who confronts such claims. Hostility may be a strategy for coping with such challenges by saying, 'Who do you think you are to challenge me like this!' To the self involved, almost any event can be viewed as a personal threat: the turn of the stock market, the prospects for one's company, and the daily difficulties in a marriage. Individuals who think that everything is theirs – my wife, my kids, my company, my car, my neighbourhood, my church – have a lot of territory to defend.

"Those who are hostile use more self-references in conversation; they use the words 'me', 'my', 'mine' and 'I' more frequently. The 'mine' expression is the aspect of the self that claims ownership – 'that's my money!' When we begin to look at the world through these eyes, a viewpoint usually considered egocentric, there are consequences within the brain and the heart. Heart attack survivors are usually less self-involved than those who die from a heart attack. Blood pressure reactions to challenges are higher, too, in self-involved individuals. The self-centred, hostile person tears his heart out because he or she is likely to have intense reactions to stress. Such a person responds to everything as challenge and mobilises to face it.

"Self-centred, hostile people set themselves apart from the world rather than see themselves as a part of it. They have seceded from the social union, and cut themselves off from the life sustaining give-and-take of social intercourse. The result may literally break their hearts."[13]

Anger, or course, is an emotion and like all emotions it is a tool given to us by nature. It is neither good nor bad in itself. It is how we use it that needs looking at. Anger is there to tell us that our emotional brain thinks that our rights are being trespassed upon in some way. The emotion of anger alerts us to this perception.

The emotional brain comes to its conclusion as a result of matching a pattern from what is happening now to a past experience. Now, that pattern-match may be close enough and the threat to you real. Or, from another point of view, it may not be real. The person you are angry with may not realise they are upsetting you. So it is the job of the higher cortex to take a wider view to see whether the feeling of anger is justified and your rights are being trespassed upon, and, if so, to decide the best way to assert your rights. If, for example, someone much stronger than you, with the ability to annihilate you, is trespassing on your rights, it is the job of the higher cortex to tell you to bide your time. Survival comes first in this instance.

People who frequently get angry not only damage their hearts and increase their chances of developing cancer, but also severely affect others around them. (Anger is hugely damaging to relationships, of course.) Such people need to learn anger management skills (see page 212).

Why depression is linked to disease

Depression also suppresses the immune system. We saw earlier how rats who had no chance to escape from electric shocks were more vulnerable to cancer tumours. Depressed people commonly perceive themselves as having no options, no way out of their depressed thinking. People who are already ill with serious conditions and who are depressed about their illness or their chances of recovery are more likely not to recover. This has been shown in patients receiving bone marrow transplants[14] and in dialysis patients[15]: depression was a good predictor of which patients would not come through the treatments.

In a study carried out in Wales, researchers assessed the states of mind of 37 people who had had a first heart attack and also elicited their beliefs and intentions about adopting healthier behaviours such as better diets, taking more exercise or stopping smoking. Those who didn't believe in their own ability to change were, unsurprisingly, the least likely to have made any changes three months later. Depressed people were the least likely to take charge of their health.[16] People who are depressed after a first heart attack also react more poorly to minor day-to-day stresses; blood pressure rises more than that of non-depressed patients who have had a heart attack.[17]

Depression is itself a powerful predictor of who will suffer heart problems: in one study, it was more reliable as a prognostic tool than severity of artery damage, cigarette smoking or high cholesterol levels.[18] That there is a direct connection between the depression and the heart disease has been shown by Dr Dominque Musselman from Emory University in Atlanta, Georgia. She found that depressed people have 41 per cent more sticky platelets in their blood (increasing the likelihood of clots) than non-depressed people. Getting rid of the depression was sufficient to return their blood almost to normal. Interestingly, when she gave them an antidepressant, the recovery effect on the blood only occurred if the individuals felt happier on taking the medication. Similarly, those who responded to a placebo drug by becoming happier also experienced the anti-clotting effect.[19] Those who did not respond to either drug or placebo continued to have sticky blood.

Even relatively minor conditions may be affected by depression. Outbreaks of herpes are found to be more common when people who already have the virus are feeling down. Depressed people also get sick more often than others, have more colds and have more sleep problems.[20]

When people are depressed, they are in a negative trance state, trapped in the tunnel vision of black and white thinking. Just having this sort of mindset itself increases risk of illness. In a recent study, head teachers were interviewed and classified as 'absolutist' or 'non-absolutist', according to the way they handled two work problems set as a test. Absolutist head teachers, those who saw life in terms of rights and wrongs and viewed the opinions and actions of others as acceptable or unacceptable, were less satisfied with their jobs and had poorer mental and physical health. Non-absolutist head teachers, who were more flexible in their approaches, found problem solving easier and enjoyed better health.[21]

The great addiction mystery

Even addictions are not diseases with neat physical causes, despite the finding of genetic elements to conditions such as alcoholism. Any successful ex-smoker, for instance, will know that the most uncomfortable aspect of giving up smoking is psychological, not physical. This is so, even with such drugs as heroin.

We all know people who drink or take drugs too much during a bad phase in their lives; we may even have done so ourselves – after a divorce, a redundancy or other major upset. We are most vulnerable at those times when we lose our moorings. The phase in life where people most commonly lose their moorings, drift and feel rudderless – willing to try anything – is when they are young. For some groups of adolescents and young adults, drug or alcohol abuse is almost an obligatory rite of passage. But in most cases, no matter how bad the addiction seems at the time, people recover from such a phase without too much difficulty when they move on to the next stage in their lives and get their needs met in more natural ways. They mature out of it.

A remarkable discovery about the dynamics of addiction came about as a result of the Vietnam War. American soldiers in Vietnam frequently took narcotics, and nearly all those who did became addicted. The authorities were worried about the social consequences for American life when tens of thousands of young heroin addicts returned home. They charged a group of medical epidemiologists to study these soldiers and follow them up for a long period. To their amazement, the researchers found that most of the soldiers gave up their drug addiction when they returned to normal life. Only a small percentage of these former addicts became re-addicted.[22] Life for the soldiers in Vietnam epitomised the kind of barren, stressful, and out-of-control situation that encourages addiction. When they came home and could lead a fulfilling life among friends, family and colleagues, the soldiers didn't need drugs.[23]

The puzzling question is: why does nature, which clearly applied so much intelligence to the evolution of human beings, enabling us to become the most creative and adaptive of any species on this planet, also make us so vulnerable to addiction? Why do so many people wilfully indulge in self-destructive behaviour, and risk damaging their relationships, their children and their work prospects? Why do they let addictions make them behave immorally, against all principles that they may have held prior to the addiction – resorting to stealing, prostituting themselves, and so on. At first sight it seems incredible that this could happen to such 'advanced' creatures as ourselves.

The answer lies in a highly adaptive mechanism, the 'carrot and stick effect', which is built in to all life forms and which is nature's way of motivating us to seek meaningful activities and thereby learn. Alas, however, it is a mechanism that can be 'hijacked' by addictive behaviour, as we will explain.

The mechanism works like this: when we engage in any experience or activity that is challenging and that we learn from, the brain provides the experience of pleasure. This reward, the 'carrot', spurs us on to repeat and become more proficient at whatever it is, giving enjoyment to what we are learning and encouraging mastery through practice. In this way, we are helped to meet one of our fundamental needs – the need for purpose or meaning. However, the brain doesn't continue to provide the same amount of pleasure every time we repeat that experience or activity, otherwise, we would not move on to seek yet more challenging experiences or learning situations. We would just keep doing what we can do well. For the sake of evolution, there has to be a way to encourage creatures to keep stretching themselves – to explore, experience differences, learn, develop new skills, etc. – so that they can adapt to environmental changes. So, once we have mastered some new experience, the brain turns down the reward and the pleasure begins to lessen. But we miss that pleasure and crave to experience it again – suffering, in effect, withdrawal symptoms. We can stop feeling the pain, and start feeling the pleasure again, if we proceed to challenge ourselves further – in the same or a different field. So the withdrawal symptoms serve, in effect, as a stick to drive us on.

Whenever we need to keep on doing whatever it is we have learned to do, even if it is no longer so pleasurable: then the withdrawal symptoms serve as the stick, if we stop. For instance, if an overweight man decides to start taking regular exercise for the sake of his health, he may start walking a mile each evening and initially derive enormous pleasure from becoming more fit. After a while, though, it starts to become a boring routine experience – he doesn't get quite the same pleasure out of doing it. On wet nights, he is tempted to stay in front of the television. And yet, if he does, something feels wrong. He feels guilty and uncomfortable slobbing about in the evening, knowing how much better it will be for his body if he takes his usual walk.

Feeling bad or empty or that something is missing is the stick that the brain uses to goad us into maintaining worthwhile behaviours. Different brain chemicals help us to maintain what we have achieved (with the stick of painful withdrawal symptoms), while at the same time motivating us to stretch ourselves in ways that further our development (with the carrot of pleasure). It is a wonderful mechanism that enables all life forms, from single-celled organisms upwards, to progress.

However, in addiction, this process goes disastrously wrong. This is because, when we ingest a pleasure-inducing addictive chemical, it hijacks the receptors designed for the chemicals that the brain uses for rewarding us and making us feel good. When we pump them in from outside, the same pleasurable feelings are released in the brain. However, if we keep taking the drug, in the search to re-experience the 'high', the mechanism that we have just described kicks in and cancels out that pleasure. Then, if we want more pleasure, we have to increase the dosage of the drug. But, if we then stop taking the drug at any point, the 'stick' comes into use – we suffer withdrawal symptoms, which can only be assuaged (we think) by taking more and more of the drug. However, in keeping with the valuable principle of 'utilisation', we can actually make effective use of this very same human given – the brain mechanism of the carrot and stick effect – in curing people of addictions (see page 214).

Using the mind to help the body

It should now be clear that what people believe about themselves plays a large part in helping them conquer pain or worsen it, recover from disease or succumb to it. Belief and attitude also appear to have an impact on our susceptibility to illness. These are strong cards to work with in a therapeutic setting, the personnel office, the staffroom in schools or anywhere else that is concerned with human resources and the nurturing and care of others. What could be more empowering than being helped to see just how much control we can have over our own health, whether in preventing illness or speeding recovery?

Small things also make a big difference. For instance, small pleasures are not a luxury but a gateway to better health: little enjoyments – such as stopping to really savour a cup of aromatic coffee or the taste of country-fresh vegetables, having flowers on the kitchen table to admire, taking an early evening stroll or having a leisurely bath perfumed with an exotic bath oil – all serve to help empower our immune systems. People may need 'permission' to relax and encouragement or motivation to take up exercise, both of which work wonders for mind and body too, so the more that is disseminated about the mind/body link in health, the better it is for all.

In therapy it is our job, we believe, to do whatever is needed to help people develop a more positive outlook and re-engage with life at all levels. Creativity may be needed to enable this to happen. This is exactly what Milton H. Erickson did when he helped the 'African violet queen' reconnect with friends and community, from whom she had withdrawn, by the task he set her of growing and distributing African violets.

Psychotherapists, while concerned with mental health, need to make use of the resources of both mind and body to achieve it. Unfortunately there is still dualism, whether intended or not, in some professionals' approaches to psychological problems.

After a major abdominal operation recently, Ivan had to stay in hospital to recover. In the bed next to him, another man was also recovering from a similar operation. Over the following few days, it became clear to Ivan that this man's problem had been misdiagnosed. Apparently the man had had an operation as a result of many months of irritable bowel syndrome, severe abdominal pains, constipation, etc. In the end, it was decided, (after all sorts of laxative treatments had been tried) to open him up and examine his bowels and other organs to see if there was some blockage or tumour that wasn't showing up on scans. The operation turned up nothing abnormal. There was absolutely nothing physically wrong with him. So he was put back on laxatives.

Ivan couldn't help overhearing this man's conversations with his family, when they visited, and with nurses and doctors. It became apparent that he was a highly anxious individual. His anxiety had been exacerbated on learning that his wife needed a new heart, and she was waiting for a heart transplant. Moreover, the stomach problem started after he had been told by a doctor that his wife could literally drop dead at any moment. This was his biggest concern, and a constant one. Whilst in hospital, he became highly anxious about whether or not his wife was well enough to keep visiting him and whether or not she was well enough to have him at home whilst he recovered from his operation. Clearly, his alarm response was permanently activated, with all the consequent bowel problems caused when the body is on high alert. He needed psychotherapy, not surgery.

But when Ivan asked staff in the hospital whether they took account of the psychological profile of patients with these kinds of conditions, the answer was a resounding 'no'. They said that the surgeons who operated on this man had not even considered that there might be a psychological component to his symptoms. And, to be fair, even if it crossed their minds, they did not have ready access to anyone who would be competent in using psychological techniques to help him.

The mind affects the body and the body affects the mind. Exercise, as we know, lifts mood by stimulating the production of brain chemicals called endorphins, helps provide an outlet for high circulating levels of adrenaline caused by chronic anxiety, and also turns the attention outward – away from the constant negative and harmful introspections that characterise depression. It is a perfect example of the physical impinging upon the mental. Yet it isn't likely to be recommended by clinical psychologists when they work with clients suffering from anxiety and depression. Researchers who interviewed directors and teachers of clinical psychology doctoral training programmes found that by no means all were aware that exercise has been found beneficial in the treatment of mental disorders, and even those who were aware of it would not prescribe exercise to clients. Prescribing exercise was not only felt to be incompatible with the normal treatment regimes of clinical psychologists but also just too simple. As the researchers suggested, many were unable to accept that what they could offer, after years of training, could sometimes be achieved by an enjoyable game of tennis or an invigorating country walk![24]

Effective therapies work only to the degree that they are in tune with the human givens and the fulfilment of those givens in the environment. Being able to see the patterns connecting all behaviour allows the provision of a much more powerful and creative form of therapy than any single approach taken on its own. Everything that science is finding out about the impact of mind and body systems upon each other urges us to take a more holistic approach to mental and physical health. In the final part of this book, we will be looking at how the APET model, and its practical application, makes it much easier to do this. But first, we wish to examine a puzzling condition, which we believe a better understanding of our genetic inheritance can explain: autism.

CHAPTER EIGHT

Water babies
and our distant aquatic past

MARIE IS Joe's autistic sister. "I remember, as a little boy," he says, "that, whenever my mother went out with my little sister, people stopped to admire her golden ringlets and beautiful face. She was about two years old. My mother felt very proud. But it soon became apparent that Marie had problems. She spoke of herself always in the third person, then gradually lost her speech altogether and began making strange, ritualistic movements, continually whirling and turning. She was also endlessly fascinated by water. At every opportunity she made for the stream that ran close to our home and my mother was terrified she would drown. Back then, in the 1950s, we were given no name for Marie's condition. It was only a quarter of a century later, when I became a psychologist, that I recognised Marie was autistic. Even her outstanding beauty was a classic feature."

In this chapter we look at what can happen when mammalian templates are not fully developed in a human child, and present a new theory of autism.[1]

Autism is still viewed as a mysterious condition. The National Autistic Society describes it as "a lifelong developmental disability that affects the way a person communicates and relates to people around them".[2] The many different symptoms can occur by themselves or in combination with other conditions and, because children with autism – like all children – vary widely in their abilities and behaviour, each symptom may manifest differently in each child. Autism is four times more common among boys than girls.

In the past 20 years of extensive research into autism, no insights have been developed to explain the full range of strange, ritualistic, self-obsessed and sometimes very destructive behaviours associated with the condition. Joe's theory, for the first time, does explain them, and also suggests which approaches to treatment are most likely to be successful. Furthermore, it explains the origin of many normal human gestures, feelings and emotional expressions. The theory is ethological but we can also cite support for it on biological grounds, reached totally independently and from a completely different route by neuro-physiologists at the University of Maryland. It has become known as the 'water babies' theory.

The central argument is that childhood autism results from a human infant's failure to develop mammalian behavioural response patterns, specifically the human responses that orientate children in their environment and form the basis for all subsequent learning. In the absence of these, autistic children have to rely on an earlier system of orientations that are present in normal development but usually play a very minor part.

To explain this, we need to go back to the enormous shift that occurred between our aquatic beginnings and our becoming land creatures. En route, we progressed from having a primitive brain (often called the reptilian brain) to a mammalian brain. It is in the part of the mammalian brain known as the limbic system that the emotions, appetites and urges that direct our behaviour and ensure our survival are generated.

As we have seen, one of the greatest achievements of mammalian evolution was the development of social life – in other words, the development of communication and co-operation between members of the group, which afforded greater protection to the group as a whole and allowed a longer period of development for the group's young. This, in turn, enabled more learning to take place during the lengthier maturing period, resulting in greater flexibility and potential for further evolution. The neocortex, the last and most sophisticated part of the brain to evolve, is especially concerned with reasoning, analysing incoming information, thinking, memories, planning and consciousness.

In the transition state between fish and reptiles, which subsequently allowed evolution into mammals, there was an amphibious phase. The amphibians, of course, needed two sets of responses: those appropriate for land and those appropriate for water. As mammals evolved more and more responses appropriate for the land, those responses became ever more dominant. But they did not lose entirely the earlier responses that were suited for the sea. Instead, these more primitive responses continued to play an important role in evolution, in many cases providing the initial behavioural response on which adaptations could be built. Evolution does not start from scratch to construct each new species. Rather it builds on, and holds on to, whatever was found useful in the ancestral life force. This is an important point.

Fishy features

One obvious example of fishlike behaviour, which almost all mammals seem to perform without learning, is swimming. Most mammals' spines, and therefore their bodily bulk, are parallel to the ground when walking – the natural position for swimming. Primates are among the least successful at swimming because they have evolved to stand upright. Very young children, however, show a swimming reflex up till the age of six months, at which point it is repressed to allow walking to develop.

There are some features of the human embryo and foetus that are also present in other mammals and in fish. The gill arches, for example, which appear at a certain stage of foetal development, support breathing in a fish but go on to become the bones of the inner ear in humans. The arteries of the human embryo are at first very similar to those of fish and the human embryo also has a tail.[3] By stroking the sole of a 14-week-old foetus's foot with a hair, it is possible to elicit quite complex and co-ordinated movements. These include bending of the big toe, slight bending of the sole of the foot, fanning of the other toes (creating a lobe-like shape typical of the fish that mammals descended from) and stretching of the leg.[4] This is exactly the movement a fish would make if it wanted to move its pelvic fin away from something dangerous or unpleasant.

Interestingly, young children make a similar movement and shape with their hands when they want to be rejecting. The renowned ethologist Niko Tinbergen published a photograph that showed how a very young child showing displeasure with his mother adopted the same unusual posture commonly used by autistic children – hands raised in front of the head with fingers fanned out, one palm facing inwards, the other outwards, the end fingers slightly bent and the child's head leaning towards the outward pointing hand.[5] Tinbergen's point was that behaviours typical of autistic children can also be seen in normal children when they are under stress. The position described, however, is exactly that which we would expect if the hands were fins and the child were in water and wanted to swim away. Again, the hands are held in a lobe shape, characteristic of our fish ancestors' fins.

Adults, particularly from cultures given to gesticulation, often adopt a similar gesture as a non-verbal signal of disagreement during conversation. One palm is brought up to the face, palm outwards, with the head turned sideways from the other person, while the other hand makes a swift downward movement, often ending by striking a desk or some other object. The effect of these movements in water would be movement away from the speaker.

Adults may use this sort of gesticulation when they are agreeing with each other too; they lean forwards and make circular flicking movements of their hands towards the speaker. If sitting down, the gesture may finish with the slapping of a thigh. Waving in greeting or farewell, the ritualised way we show our warm feelings towards the person approaching or departing, is also based on the instinctive fishlike movement of the fins which in water would bring us closer to them.

Although these gestures are clearly communication signals, they are nevertheless built upon the instinctive response of that ancient part of our brain which automatically reacted by moving towards or away from different stimuli. Fish use either bodily movements or movements of their fins to propel themselves through water. The former is their main method of movement, although the fins are in constant use because they act as brakes and aerofoils as well. While we humans can consciously inhibit gesticulatory movements if we wish, and express our reactions with words, the ancient part of our brain still urges us towards some form of movement. We may not physically move away from someone when we disagree, but we may still do the equivalent of moving our fins, because we are not consciously aware of what such actions mean any more.

If autism results from a baby's failure to develop the mammalian behavioural response patterns (templates) appropriate for it, then, it could be that the aquatic response patterns, which are always present but peripheral in a normal baby, will come to the fore and provide the basis of the child's perception of reality and its place within it. It would follow that such an outcome must be due to a failure in the programming of the instinctive basis of these patterns into the child. Michel Jouvet's findings[6] that the role of rapid eye movement (REM) sleep state in the foetus, newborn and young is to programme the central nervous system to organise instinctive behaviour is, therefore, crucial to understanding why these mammalian patterns are missing in autism.

As we have explained at length, the REM state is not only concerned with the programming of genetic knowledge in the brain before birth and in early life. It also plays an important role throughout our lives, when we dream each night, in maintaining our instinctual mammalian integrity. We would therefore expect children with autism to have primitive patterns of REM sleep compared with those of normal children of the same age. This is exactly what has been found.[7]

We have shown that instincts are programmed in the form of analogues, such as the instinctive template for language, for example, which has to be matched to the languages spoken in a particular culture. But when this programming is compromised or damaged in some way, as it is with autistic children who are missing normal social and perceptual orientations, they are obliged to fall back on whatever instinctive templates or orientations are available to them as a means to connect to reality. These will necessarily be non-mammalian. And if those templates are suited to a water environment, then autistic children are going to show behaviour that appears to be puzzling and bizarre to the rest of the human race. They are likely to feel as though they are living in a totally alien world. Indeed, if we read the self-descriptions of those exceptionally talented autistic people that have been able to communicate something of their experience to us, it is obvious that this is so.

Jim Sinclair, an autistic adult, has said: "Being autistic does not mean being inhuman. But it does mean being alien. It means that what is normal for other people is not normal for me and what is normal for me is not normal for other people. In some ways, I am terribly ill equipped to survive in this world, like an extraterrestrial stranded without an orientation model."[8]

Temple Grandin, acknowledged superstar among autistic people, described herself as "an anthropologist on Mars", providing Oliver

Sachs with the title of his bestselling book on autism.[9]

The five areas of disturbance that are recognised as typical characteristic symptoms of autism are: motility, perception, relating, speech and language, and developmental rate.[10] It is possible to look at the typical behaviours of an autistic child and relate them very closely to behaviours that would have been typical of our aquatic ancestors.

Autistic fishlike behaviours

Motility disturbances are characterised by both excitable and inhibited behaviours that have been described as follows: "The motor excitation involves hand flapping, excited whirling and circling, darting and lunging movements and toe walking. In contrast, motor inhibition is manifested by posturing and prolonged inhibition."[11] A better description of fishlike behaviour is hard to imagine. Toe walking makes sense, as the feet have evolved from fishes' fins, which were unbent. There would consequently be a desire to have feet bent as little as possible – or at least not more than that required for a lobe shape, the shape of the fins in our fish ancestors.

Descriptions of autistic children's behaviours almost always include a fascination with spinning, flicking and rocking movements. They are not interested in the real purpose of different objects and toys but in the role something might play in their own ritualistic, stereotyped movements. A toy car may, for instance, be used solely for spinning its wheels. Autistic children often become extremely dextrous at manipulating objects so that they spin. Plates, boxes and assorted other objects will be sent twirling across the floor to the evident delight of the child. Not only will autistic children spin objects, but they will also spin themselves around for long periods and without any apparent dizziness.

The tail fin of a fish works a bit like a propeller but with the tail being swept from side to side instead of being on a rotary screw. It would seem highly plausible that the spinning dance of autistic children is an attempt to replicate this movement. Their pleasure in spinning objects may spring from an innate pleasure in the perception of spinning movements similar to that of fins. This can clearly be seen in the following description of an autistic child's behaviour: "As Raum leaned over the objects he set in motion, he would rock as if one with them. His hands and fingers responded with erratic and jerky patterns of movement."[12]

The flicking movement which autistic children often make when holding string or other suitable objects can be seen as an effort to replicate the snakelike undulating movements of a fish as it courses through water. The next description of an autistic child's behaviour illustrates this vividly: "She sits with a long chain in her hand. Snaking it up and down, up and down for 20 minutes, half an hour – until someone comes, moves her or feeds her."[13]

Some autistic children learn to stimulate themselves with only partly circular movements, for instance by rapidly turning the pages of a book – reflecting, perhaps, the fins' only partly circular motions. Some, before they have even learned to stand, perform a circular dance on their knees; "circling round and round a spot on the floor in mysterious self-absorbed delight," as the same author described it.[14]

Unusual movements of the hands are often most noticeable when autistic children become excited; they may flap their hands and arms, jump up and down and make facial grimaces. (This sort of behaviour is also seen in normal children when they are intensely excited while watching an event they cannot participate in.) When fish get excited, they gulp in more water to obtain more oxygen, appearing, as they do so, to make facial grimaces. They flap their fins more too, to create more speed. Interestingly, excited hand flapping, posturing and twirling have been noted as the usual reactions of an autistic child to spinning objects; as a result, they are often presented by experts as an aid to diagnosis of the condition.[15]

Autistic children usually withdraw from human contact, failing to raise their arms when they are about to be picked up and frequently showing an aversion to physical contact.[16] Yet they love certain types of rough games that involve contact; these include being thrown into the air, bounced on someone's knee and being tickled. The movement of the fish's tail fin, which repeatedly kicks the fish forward, must be a bit like being bounced on a knee. Fish have most of their sense organs running along the side of the body and it may be that, for the autistic child, being tickled along the sides of the body and under the arms represents an innate anticipated source of stimulation.

Autistic children's love of rocking back and forth may be seen as a gross attempt to replicate the fish's primary body movement when swimming. The fact that they frequently make a backwards and forwards movement, as well as the side to side swaying movement of fish, can be explained by evolutionary changes: our main muscles are now in front and behind the spinal column rather than laterally sited as in fish, and therefore forward and backward rocking may provide more powerful stimulation than sideways movement.

The sudden lunging and darting movements of autistic children are clearly characteristic of fish behaviour and the position in which many hold their arms when unoccupied is very similar to that of the lobe-shaped pectoral fins of our fish ancestors. The following description illustrates this vividly: "Many of these children hold their arms in a special way when unoccupied. They have their elbows bent and their hands near together in front of them, dropping at the wrists with fingers slightly curled."[17]

Autistic children are fascinated by surfaces; they love to feel cool, smooth plastic, smooth wood and soft fur (sometimes rubbing their faces against someone's fur coat while ignoring the wearer). The cool, smooth textureless sensations which they evoke may resemble the sensation we experience when we place our faces or hands in water. Autistic children are highly fascinated by water too. They like to pour it endlessly through their fingers or, sometimes, from one container to another. Their love of water is so pronounced that they may without thought take off their clothes in public so that they may sit in an inviting pool of water.

When, as an adult, Joe went to visit his sister Marie, she didn't recognise him as her brother but she was keen to persuade him to follow her, which she achieved by staring at the door knobs of doors they arrived at, to encourage him to open them for her. In this way they progressed down many dark corridors until eventually they came to a little room, empty except for a sink and a single tap. She indicated that she wanted Joe to turn on the tap (neither in the opening of doors or turning on of taps was it natural for her to use her own hands as tools). When the water was running, she was deliriously happy.

Autistic children commonly refuse to eat any but two or three specific foods.[18] Young fish also eat only certain foods and continue to seek these foods out from an abundant supply of food items.[19]

Difficulties in getting autistic children to eat solid food have frequently been reported[20] and one father has described how his son nearly choked to death when he was given solid food at an age when normal children can chew without difficulty.[21] Interestingly, a classic book on Palaeozoic fish[22] states that rhipidistian fish, believed to be our ancestors, were predators that swallowed their food whole, without chewing.

An insensitivity to pain is common in autistic children. They may happily run out of doors in winter with no clothes on. Fish, of course, are cold-blooded creatures not as sensitive to cold as warm-blooded animals. Further, autistic children often ignore knocks and bumps and injuries that would cause great distress to a normal child. Fish may also feel little pain. It has been noted that trout or pike, which have managed to escape, with lacerated mouths, from a fishhook, have immediately turned and taken the tempting bait again.

Autistic children may indulge in self mutilation, biting or picking at parts of their own bodies or bashing their heads against walls or floors. Such self-destructive behaviours are usually performed as a form of aggression, designed to keep others away and prevent interference from them. In this respect, their behaviour is similar to that of fish, which, in normal circumstances, rarely fight another fish. Instead they put on aggressive displays by beating the water with their tail fins, after which one or other withdraws. (One researcher has pointed out that autistic children may begin the action of striking someone who has aroused their anger but can never actually go through with it.[23])

Not surprisingly, then, the best way of treating self-destructive behaviour is to leave the child alone.[24] When mild electric shocks were applied by one researcher as a deterrent,[25] the undesirable activity increased – which is explained in this theory as an increase in aggressive display in the face of increased 'aggression' from the researcher.

The parallels between aggressive behaviour in autistic children and aggressive displays in fish may not be so obvious when it comes to other forms of self-abuse, such as pulling out their own hair and biting their own hands. However, if the 'water babies' theory is right, these could be attempts to provide the kind of stimulation usually provided by being in water – for instance, the experience of resistance and of water being taken in by mouth (and exhaled through the gills).

A summary of motility disturbances compiled in the 1970s for the National Society for Autistic Children (now National Autistic Society) cited the following habits common to autistic children: rocking; head banging; jumping; twisting, flapping and writhing of arms and legs, especially when excited; spinning; facial grimaces of all kinds; odd ways of walking, especially on tiptoe; unusual hand movements, e.g. turning hand with outstretched fingers in front of the face; and extreme pleasure in bodily movement such as swinging, rocking, riding in cars, etc. We suggest that all these behaviours are well explained by Joe's 'water babies' theory.

The second category of disturbance identified is autistic children's disturbances of perception. These children are frequently thought to be deaf because they show no response to loud noises such as the sound of plates crashing to the floor, yet turn sharply at the slight rustle of a favourite sweet being unwrapped behind them.[26] (Curiously, scientists at one time thought fish were deaf.)

The explanation for the autistic child's apparent deafness may lie in a characteristic that is common to all of their behaviour – that is, their responses do not seem to generalise. For example, they may readily grasp an object that they can spin but will let fall most other objects that are handed to them, as if they lacked the ability to hold on to them. Many writers have commented on the autistic child's reluctance to grasp an object firmly to use it as a tool (clearly, Marie demonstrated that behaviour). So hearing and grasping may only occur when there is something the child particularly wants to do with an object. (In Marie's case, even though the doors and taps served as means to an end, it was only the water she was interested in.) There is no generalised reflex to use hand dexterity to explore or interact with the environment. Fish don't use their fins to explore their environment, nor do they use them as tools. It may therefore be that autistic children's reluctance to explore the environment may be due to the absence of an instinct to use limbs for that purpose.

They may also lack the mammalian-developed ability to localise sound, responding only to associations that have been conditioned. Fish have a very poor ability to locate sound but do have sensitivity to frequency vibrations. An increase in vibrations would very likely mean the fast approach of another fish, therefore one likely to be a predator. Similarly, sounds an autistic child enjoys at a lower level often cause distress when increased. Autistic children love various types of music, responding particularly to the rhythm and vibration. So, it seems, do fish. On an edition of the BBC's *That's Life* programme many years ago, a variety of music was played through a microphone placed in an aquarium. The fish huddled excitedly round the microphone for the most rhythmic, vibrating music and showed little interest in other types.

Autistic children also appear to have problems seeing, and are sometimes thought to be shortsighted or even blind. They very commonly give the impression of looking through people and may show no reaction to new people or new things. They often also walk or even ride a bicycle without looking where they are going, bumping into objects as if they didn't see them. Contrary to the impression given, however, they do not actively avoid looking at people and in fact look at them longer than they look at objects.[27] The mistaken impression is due to their habit of darting glances and then looking away. This is quite alien to the way normally developed people use sight when relating to others.

What autistic children are particularly sensitive to is movement and outline, which is how they tend to recognise objects.[28] Fish, in an ever-moving environment, are of course especially sensitive to movement, and a sensitivity to outline helps in a fish's fantastic ability to find its way and recognise other fish and food in an environment where it is frequently difficult to see. When autistic children are spun round in a chair, they, unlike normal children, do not show nystagmus (involuntary jerky movements of the eye), unless the spinning is being done in the dark. This accords with the 'water babies' theory, whereby autistic children would naturally use their eyes to observe movement and outline, which would not be possible in the dark.

Autistic children also pay more attention to what they can touch, taste and smell, rather than to what they can hear or see.[29] One pair of researchers found that: "if a buzzer was sounded and simultaneously a small tug was given on a piece of string tied around the child's ankle, autistic children, unlike other children tested, were more likely to attend to the thing they felt rather than the thing they heard".[30]

Autistic children's fascination with anything that shines or twinkles, such as silver or shiny paper, may be explained by a predisposition to encounter the patterning of light refracted in water. Fish view the world through a medium that has very different optical properties from those of the atmosphere. Light rays entering the water are refracted. Our fish ancestors had a pineal opening on the top of their heads which was sensitive to light and which possibly helped protect them from overhead attack, in that an approaching predator would block out some of that light. Interestingly, autistic children often react to sudden changes in illumination with great fear.[31]

Autistic children are endlessly fascinated by their own hands and feet, looking at them as if they are strange and puzzling. They frequently, as already described, place their hands under their faces in the position and shape of the pectoral fins of our fish ancestors. It might well be, then, that they are confounded by their hands' ability to appear in places other than those in which they expect them to be permanently located. Similarly, their legs can do so much more than instinctively they expect them to be able to do. Their fascination may be rather akin to what our own would be if we found our limbs could suddenly detach themselves and perform actions some distance away from us.

As might be expected, autistic children usually lack the mammalian reflex of lifting the arms in anticipation of being picked up. Their aversion to human contact, other than in tickling and rough play, has its counterpart in fish behaviour. Fish avoid physical contact except in the spawning season.[32]

It would be surprising, in terms of the 'water babies' theory, if language, that most recent of evolutionary acquisitions and one uniquely geared to social interaction, should have its development unimpeded in autistic children. Fish have a limited sound production capability, which has been shown to have some communication value for some species. The sounds are made by such means as the expulsion of air and the grinding of teeth.[33] Some autistic children never learn to speak, while about a half learn to say a few words or phrases, often tending to repeat these at random (echolalia). Repetitious sound, such as that induced by the fish's body moving through water, may be innately satisfying. In children who do progress from this stage of speech, most continue to show severe disturbance in their pattern of language acquisition, compared with normal children.

Disturbed rate of development, the fifth and final category identified as symptomatic of autism, shows itself in deviations from the normal sequences in motor, social and language milestones. For instance, an autistic child can sit without support very early on but shows delay in being able to pull up to a stand. This makes sense in terms of the theory: the autistic child usually shows no orientation to use hands as tools or legs to stand upright on.

Spatial intelligence can be precocious, with autistic children able to do jigsaws upside down – in other words, paying attention only to the shapes, not the clues in the pattern and picture. Many fish species have an excellent ability to recognise a variety of shapes.[34] Autistic children have a remarkable ability to find their way back to places after just one visit or to locate objects they haven't seen for years. This calls to mind the equally remarkable ability of some species of fish to return to their spawning ground after crossing many thousands of miles.

Oceanic feelings of transcendence

In descriptions of autism, there are frequent references to the Buddha-like serenity which autistic children show during their periods of self-absorption. One parent said of his son: "In almost every way his contentment and solitude seem to suggest a profound and inner peace. He was a 17-month-old Buddha contemplating another dimension."[35] The meditation practices of the East could easily have been inspired by autistic behaviour. The whirling dervishes, for instance, induced trance by spinning themselves. Certain types of meditation involve staring at a certain object for a long period of time or the repetition of a mantra. The state that these practices induce has been described as a state of thoughtless awareness in which the emotions have been stilled – an apt description of much of the autistic child's reality. In *Ecstasy*,[36] a cult book in the 1960s, the phrase "oceanic feeling" was used to describe the feelings of transcendence which adherents of these techniques claim to induce, and identified walking by water as one of the triggers.

Aldous Huxley's thesis that there is a functional similarity between certain transcendental experiences and the effects of certain hallucinogenic drugs is also relevant, and would fit with the water babies hypothesis that the part of the brain stimulated is the evolutionary ancient part which, though normally inhibited, is sensitive to the interrelationship between rhythm and form. Autistic children often flap their hands up and down and make lunging or jumping movements while standing on their toes. In our remote evolutionary past, such movements may have been associated with swimming. Some particularly sensitive people may, under the influence of hallucinogenic drugs, have an overwhelming desire to carry out such movements. Unaware that these movements were evolved for free passage through water, they may conclude they can fly. This might explain why some people, under the influence of these drugs, have tragically leapt to their deaths.

Support for the 'water babies' theory

Since Joe devised this theory we have been fascinated to read the research of Dr Stephen Porges, a neurophysiologist at the University of Maryland who has noted that the polyvagal nerves in the human brainstem, which are involved in the regulation of body movements, facial expressions, muscle movements for hearing and speech and the expression of emotion, are co-opted from an ancient system of nerves that regulated movement of the gills and body muscles in fish, as well as many of their sensory inputs.[37,38] He has suggested that, as autism clearly involves deficits associated with this system of nerves, the cause could be problems with tuning in these nerves for mammalian orientation. He has applied his hypothesis in a technique that he has developed for helping people with autism listen to speech.

So it may well be true that autistic children are almost inhabiting another world, one unfortunately that leaves them very uncomfortable, like a fish out of water, and handicapped in this one. How much an autistic child can be helped may depend upon whether the mammalian templates aren't present at all or whether they are present but the ability to read them has been blocked by some insult to the brain experienced before or after birth. If it is only the ability to read the templates which is blocked, then it should sometimes be possible to stimulate those templates and create normal functioning. A successful therapeutic approach must therefore involve making behaviours that are rewarding to the normal child, because of instinctive mammalian orientations, also rewarding to the autistic child. To do this we must build a bridge between the autistic child's world and the normal human world. In other words, the therapist or parent must enter the autistic child's world, using whatever orientations the child has access to, in order to connect them to our world.

Spinning alongside an autistic child, for instance, encourages them to notice you. That can be the first step towards building rapport and leading them, in their turn, to mirror more normal behaviours.

In another graphic example of this technique, a mother involved herself in the activity of a two-year-old autistic child who spent hours staring into space while rubbing the pile on a particular spot of carpet. "We had the girl's mother place her hand next to her, right on the favourite stretch of floor. The child pushed it away but her mother gently pushed it back. Again she pushed, again the hand returned. A cat and mouse game ensued and, by the third day of this rudimentary interaction, the little girl was smiling while pushing her mother's hand away. From this tiny beginning grew emotional connection and relationship."[39]

Methods which concentrate on the systematic application of conditioning techniques to produce in sequence those orientations necessary for the natural development of intelligence and emotional behaviour have, in some cases, resulted in normal behaviour, including intellectual, emotional and linguistic ability comparable to or higher than that of normal children. The Lovaas technique is the most coercive of this kind of approach. A gentler approach, known as the Option Method, adapts many of behaviour therapy's techniques and makes particular use of imitating the child's behaviour. [40]

Some approaches concentrate on only one of the deficits experienced by autistic children. Holding therapy was developed in 1983 as a means of combating the autistic child's tendency to avoid physical contact. The parent or carer is encouraged to hold the child on their lap, wrapping their arms firmly around them and gazing at them in a positive loving way. If the child struggles, even this is praised. Stephen Porges, who developed the polyvagal theory, has reported success in increasing facial expressiveness, range of voice tones and social behaviour in autistic children by exercising and stimulating middle ear function specifically to extract human voice sounds – which autistic children usually tune out.[41]

As we have seen, tantrums and self-mutilation can most effectively be dealt with by removing the child and placing him or her somewhere on their own. Similarly, stereotyped behaviour in young children is most likely to decrease if ignored, as the child finds increasing satisfaction in normal human behaviours.

Older autistic children often develop bizarre fears and behaviours acquired as a result of associations with some experience they find unpleasant. In such cases, the technique of 'flooding' can work. One little girl, for instance, was terrified of the colour red and threw a screaming fit if ever she was put on a red bus. It is possible the fear developed on an occasion when she heard a red bus revving up, a sound many autistic children find frightening. Her parents cured her of her fear by saturating their house with red, despite her protestations, so that it became a major and unavoidable factor in her life.

All these approaches help induce the orientations that the autistic child is missing and, in turn, may stimulate the interactions necessary for the normal mental and emotional development of the child.

Autism is a continuum disorder and we can learn a lot from people at the high end like Temple Grandin who function in some ways very well indeed. Such people are usually said to have Asperger's syndrome.

Casualties of evolutionary pressure

A major part of our evolution was achieved by slowing down the growth process, keeping us infantile for longer. It takes much longer for us to mature than it did our primate cousins. Why, unless to allow us more time to learn? The longer the growth period, the greater the environmental input to the completion of instinctive behaviour patterns. In other words, we developed the ability to evolve culture, to learn new and more demanding skills, to think, plan, organise and be creative. To successfully play our parts within civilisation, the old mammalian instincts, mostly concerned with the emotions, have had to be damped down. A society has to be governed by reason, not emotion. But if nature veers too much in that direction, the price is loss of contact with the instinctive basis for understanding and making relationships. Autistic children are, perhaps, the tragic casualties of evolution a step too far.

A highly eloquent and knowledgeable colleague and friend of ours at MindFields College, Tim Jacobs, has Asperger's syndrome and wrote an article for the journal *Human Givens* about what living with the syndrome is like.[42] (This led to his appearance on a BBC radio programme on the subject.)

He has told us that one of the chief limitations he experiences is 'straight-line thinking', a term he coined. He had gradually become aware that his mind leaps from one thing to another without any moderating influence. This, of course, has a significant impact on his behaviour. Everyone who works with him knows this to be true, merely by observation. He finds it almost impossible to hold two or more lines of thought in his mind at the same time and appraise and prioritise them to see how one thought or perception might be affecting the other. This 'straight-line thinking' is a pale reflection of what we see in deeper levels of autism, where obsessional thinking keeps individuals stuck on one particular behaviour and they resist any disruption of it.

An example of straight-line thinking was given to us by the wife of a man with Asperger's syndrome. She was in the passenger seat when her husband was driving and, as he was slowing down for a red traffic light, she pointed out he was in the wrong lane. He immediately started to pull over, completely forgetting the red light, and overshot, to the consternation of other drivers. Once the thought came into his mind that he should change lanes, he was off on that track and had to do it at once.

An autistic or Asperger baby does not have the template programmed in for reading other people's non-verbal behaviour, nor the template to keep monitoring what impact their behaviour has on other people – templates which enable us to adjust our own behaviour in the light of what we perceive. This ability is now often called 'interpersonal emotional intelligence' – the instinct to hold two or more lines of thought (perceptions) in the mind simultaneously, so that we can relate our behaviour to other people's behaviour. It is this ability, this given, that enables us to connect with each other fully, to make the meaningful relationships that enable us to thrive.

PART THREE

Emotional Health
And Clear Thinking

CHAPTER NINE

The APET model:
the key to effective psychotherapy

WHEN emotional needs are not met, for whatever reason, anyone can suffer distress. If the situation persists, more serious emotional disorders are easily triggered: anxiety, obsessional or addictive behaviour, depression, bipolar disorder (manic depression), psychosis etc. At this point, people often decide to seek help to alleviate the emotional pain they are suffering. That brings a new problem: where to go for effective treatment.

Psychiatry tends to medicalise all conditions and predominantly relies on drug treatments, with all their attendant risks – not least that taking drugs is disempowering psychologically. This 'medical model' ideology is under attack as evidence mounts about the harmful side effects of drugs.[1] The often confusing world of psychotherapy and counselling – which is only slowly emerging into the light of scientific enquiry – is also under attack.[2,3] Periodically, new studies show that neither does much good and both often do more harm than good.[4] There are also ongoing arguments within the profession as to the difference, if any, between counselling and psychotherapy and who should be considered qualified, and on what grounds, to practise. Rarely do counselling tutors work with real patients in front of students, to demonstrate the techniques they espouse. There are no standardised assessment criteria for counsellors and psychotherapists across the different schools of therapy and few courses assess students' effectiveness with real patients before qualifying them to practise.

Estimates vary but currently there are at least 400 different 'therapy' models on offer throughout the world[5] – which in itself indicates the general lack of shared perceptions about how best to help people. In other words, psychiatry and psychotherapy are still at a primitive level of development.

This situation is clearly chaotic and bewildering for all concerned:

members of the general public seeking help and those sincerely trying to provide it. It also bothers neuroscientists such as Professor Ian Robertson who said recently, "I am dismayed at how counselling and psychotherapy practice in many areas has become wilfully divorced from evidence and science to the extent of becoming self-perpetuating cults in some cases. No one has the right to pick and choose a theory as a matter of personal preference and then offer it as a service to someone when there is a possibility that that service might do harm. We have to move towards evidence-based practice and away from cults and ideologies."[6]

Just as the human givens are holistically interconnected and interact with one another, allowing us to live together as many-faceted individuals, it seems that different therapy approaches also need to interact if they are to be capable of addressing the different elements of who and what we are. Yet, as each new therapy for dealing with human distress is launched upon the world, it immediately begins a process of entrenchment, digging itself into a rut by developing a systematic philosophy to be applied mechanically to every person with a problem.

All major therapies seemed wonderful to some people in their heyday. Perhaps the most valuable aspect of Sigmund Freud's psychoanalytical therapy, for example, at the beginning of the twentieth century, was to draw the attention of the Western world to the ancient insight that many of our everyday behaviours are largely controlled by unconscious processes. However, the value of incorporating this simple but important truth into our culture was then largely undermined by Freud himself. Driven as he was by messianic ambition and paranoia, and working from invented, unrealistic models of human functioning and psychology, based largely upon the mechanistic nineteenth century understanding of biology, he mounted a propaganda campaign for his bizarre ideas. Thus he effectively muddied the waters of psychiatry, psychotherapy and counselling for the remainder of the last century. The development of complex psychoanalytical theories (which were never scientifically tested by Freud or his followers, only asserted as true) had their roots in just six case histories – which were all that Freud ever published, and all of which were disasters from the point of view of his patients.[7] The legacy of psychoanalysis and its offshoots is a disturbing story of misguided, often harmful, treatment.[8]

Behaviour therapy, which developed partly in reaction against the absurdities of psychoanalysis, also contained a profound insight. While others were still grappling with the 'deep unconscious', behaviourists discovered that changing behaviour was often able to help people resolve problems. They made use of the knowledge that there are innate pleasure circuits in the brain that can be stimulated by certain behaviours. When people were shown how to replace destructive behaviours with the more rewarding positive behaviours, they found it easier to make healthy changes. The method often worked because any counsellor who clearly targets the elimination of behaviours that are stopping a person's needs being met, while fostering behaviours that increase the likelihood they will be met, is bound to have success. Encouraging depressed people to become more physically and socially active, for example, stimulates an increase in serotonin production and thus helps to lift clinical depression. That is powerful therapy.

Unfortunately, behaviourism soon swelled into a total philosophy that would brook no dissenters. Students were told: *there is no such thing as consciousness. There is no such thing as mind. What you think has no effect upon you. You are your behaviour and nothing else.* Pure behaviourism became a gross distortion of what humanity is about. It undermined values and meaning in life and took away people's personal autonomy.[9]

Then came the growth of client-centred therapy ('active listening') developed by Carl Rogers. His idea was that, if you truly listen to somebody with a problem, and let them know that you *are* really listening, by feeding back your understanding of what their problem is, people can move forward from a stuck position. Patients do need to have their stories heard in a respectful, non-judgemental atmosphere. Sometimes, when a person is temporarily emotionally overloaded, just being heard in a supportive way is all it takes for them to calm down, view their situation from a wider perspective and chart a way forward. Most people coming to therapy, however, need more than support. They have to borrow someone else's brain for a while to help them lower their emotional arousal and think clearly and learn, so that they can move on. Their counselling may involve social skills training, learning anxiety or anger management skills, getting help with an addiction, or being detraumatised from terrible past experiences that are influencing their present behaviour. So, although active listening is an important component of therapy, it is usually only a small part. But, with person-centred counselling, again the inevitable happened. Active listening expanded into a philosophy which said: *all anybody needs is for someone to really listen to them and a 'self-actualising principle' inside them will then manifest itself and sort all their problems out.*[10]

This is beautiful idealism but, as we have seen, painfully wrong. Someone with depression can be listened to sympathetically for ever and a day, and still they may not come out of it – in fact, they are more likely to become even more deeply depressed. (This is why psycho-dynamic 'insight' therapy is contraindicated for treating depression – the depressive trance state has to be broken, not deepened.[11]) One of the main reasons for counselling being found, in studies, to be ineffective for helping people[12] could well be that counselling training is still largely based on this active listening/self-actualisation philosophy. Of course, knowing how to listen is a vitally important skill, but much more is needed to provide effective help for people with emotional problems.

Cognitive therapy, a more recent and somewhat more successful approach, is clearly going the same way. Cognitive therapy is based on the straightforward idea that, if people can be helped to use their rational minds and question the evidence for their damaging negative belief systems, they can change. Helping people to make more realis-tic assessments of their life *is* powerfully effective, especially if they suffer from depression or anxiety. But in cognitive therapy we already see the same degenerative process at work. The original brilliant insight, which could be grasped at a single workshop and generated an enthusiastic following, attracted pedants who then made it the subject of complex books. Even more complex books followed, each analysing the complex books that had gone before. Now they all litter psychology bookshelves, and people have come to believe that several years' training is required to discover what cognitive therapy is all about before they can practise it on the public.[13]

This mental thickening process seems to happen with every school of therapy – psychodynamic, Rogerian, behavioural, biomedical, gestalt, cognitive, etc. Many of them began with a useful insight but then became closed systems of thought, unable to incorporate the totality of what it is to function as a human being. Cognitive therapy, for instance, focuses primarily on the rational aspect of the human mind as a means of lifting depression or anxiety. We could equally accurately say that problems are caused by a misuse of imagination and that a solution is to help people use their imagination more effectively.[14]

As therapies become complex, so they develop jargon that makes them incomprehensible to outsiders. As Hakim Jami said, commenting back in the fifteenth century on this perennial tendency: "If the scissors are not used daily on the beard, it will not be long before the beard, by its luxuriant growth, begins to think it's the head".

As a rule, when an approach starts getting really complex, you can be certain it is going wrong – it is trying to make up for what it lacks by inventing ever more complex jargon to explain away its failure to get results. An organic integration of the insights contained in each school then becomes impossible. That is why the human givens approach puts its emphasis on helping therapists to see how all these elements interrelate.

People coming from a psychoanalytical perspective have said that the human givens approach only deals with symptoms, not the underlying problem. But research and experience does not support them. When time is spent digging up everything you can remember about what went wrong in your life, and exploring problematic past relationships in an effort to 'understand', it does not improve confidence or give you the skills to deal with life today. And yet such psychological archaeology was the dominant approach in therapy for a long time. It still lingers on in many quarters and is often the basis for the way psychotherapy is portrayed in literature and the media, and by the entertainment industry, who don't yet seem to realise that Freud and Jung have little practical relevance to modern psychotherapeutic practice. Indeed, they are more often now seen as having held it back from developing more quickly.

So what is effective therapy? Until the 1970s, studies seemed to find that all therapies were roughly as good or bad as each other at solving human problems.[15] This was because, for the most part, therapists were rating their own effectiveness. More objective research has overturned that view. We now know that certain approaches are hugely effective in helping people, and others are much less so – some are even harmful. For example, when many hundreds of efficacy studies were looked at together, in a meta-analysis, brief, solution focused therapy was proved more effective for the treatment of anxiety disorders, depression, phobias, trauma and addictive behaviour than any long-term psychoanalytic style of therapy or drug treatments.[16,17,18]

When we considered how we could teach psychiatrists, clinical psychologists, psychotherapists and counsellors to work within the givens of human nature we puzzled over how to find ways that could encompass all the new discoveries about brain functioning in a model that had clarity, was true to the new knowledge and could draw on the work of the more effective therapists. How could we get across the fundamental flaw in cognitive therapy – that thought comes before emotion – and stress the pattern-matching nature of the brain and the way this produces emotional arousal, but without throwing away the positive aspects of it?

We knew cognitive therapy took a long time to work and that research seemed to show it was one of the more successful approaches for helping people suffering various forms of mental distress. Indeed, cognitive behavioural therapy (CBT) is now a preferred treatment for many forms of mental disturbance in many health services around the world. This didn't make sense to us because, although the cognitive approach acknowledges the reciprocal interaction between cognition and emotion, it holds that changing thinking processes is the best way to change inappropriate behaviour and emotions. We knew that this was not right. Indeed, our observations were confirmed by recent research that shows that, over a 12-month period, neither CBT nor non-directive counselling is more effective as a treatment for depression than a few short visits to a GP.[19]

The cognitive model was first formulated some decades ago. While it signified a brilliant step forward in therapeutic treatment, compared with the psychodynamic approaches predominant at the time, it is clearly not in alignment with what we now know about how the mind/body system works. This, we felt, explained why it can seem so slow and cumbersome. Typically patients are expected to learn the language of the model, monitor their thoughts and moods, fill in complex forms and perform various prescribed homework tasks. It's an unnatural way to carry on and the therapeutic relationship is very much one of patient seeing expert rather than a collaborative experience. Not surprisingly, up to 20 sessions are often needed to make an improvement, and that's only if people can take to that way of working in the first place. Many people find it difficult to do (as emotional arousal makes it hard for them to concentrate) and drop out disappointed.

By understanding the thinking behind the cognitive model we can see the importance of the new knowledge more clearly. Albert Ellis, the originator of rational emotive behaviour therapy, which was the first form of cognitive therapy, set out the structure of his 'thoughts cause emotional consequences' idea in his ABC model. **A** stands for the activating agent, the trigger event or stimulus in the environment that is reacted to. **B** stands for the beliefs or thoughts we have about that event. **C** stands for the emotional consequences of those thoughts. So, the reasoning goes, something happens, we interpret it through our thoughts and core beliefs, and we have an emotion. In other words, our beliefs and thoughts give rise to our emotions. The cognitive model states simply that, if therapists change their patients' thoughts and irrational beliefs, "shift their perceptions from those that are unrealistic and harmful to those that are more rational and useful",[20] then patients' emotional lives will be improved.

Another pioneer in this field was Aaron Beck, who founded cognitive restructuring therapy. He concentrated primarily upon classifying and identifying what he regarded as the thought distortions that gave rise to all psychological disorders.[21] Over the decades, cognitive therapists have continued to add to and further refine these thought styles and belief systems, which include, for instance, catastrophic thinking, overgeneralisation, personalising, sensationalising, fault-finding, 'musterbation', nominalising, self-righteousness and disqualifying positive life experiences.[22] We could see that most, if not all, of these thought distortions have one thing in common. They are all sub-categories of the black and white, polarised thinking style – fight or flight – that originates in the emotional brain. This key insight is missing from cognitive therapy.

Ellis, Beck and other writers on cognitive approaches state or imply in their writings that, when problems occur, it is thinking that is defective. We would say that this is not a helpful stance because, when thinking is driven by the emotional brain, it is *always* operating out of the all or nothing, black or white, fight or flight mode. The more emotionally aroused the brain becomes, the more it reverts to the primitive logic of either/or thinking.

So the basic error in cognitive therapy is the idea that it is thoughts and beliefs that causes emotion. The methods may sometimes work, because there *is* an important connection between thought and emotion (and because cognitive therapists concentrate on concrete difficulties experienced in the here and now, not the past, which is the key to solving problems). But, by focusing on the idea that irrational thinking causes emotional disturbance, cognitive therapists are less likely to be as effective as those who take the human givens perspective, which fully takes into account current knowledge about the way the brain works. It is a given that any form of emotional arousal makes us more single-minded – and hence more simple-minded.

But how to get all this across? One morning, as we set off to the Redhill Hospital Post Graduate Centre to teach our approach to the first pioneering group of aspiring human givens therapists, Joe announced that he had hardly slept all night from thinking about this problem. As a consequence, when he woke up he had found the answer and planned to lecture on it that very morning.

His inspired talk was electric. Everyone in the room knew this was a significant moment. For the first time, he described the APET model, a more psychologically and physiologically accurate view of mind/body functioning that people could work from.

The **A** in APET stands for the activating agent, a stimulus from the environment, just as in the cognitive model. Information about that stimulus, taken in through our senses, is first pattern matched by the mind to innate knowledge and past learnings, hence the **P**, which in turn gives rise to an emotion, **E**. This, in turn may inspire certain thoughts, represented by the **T** (though thought is not an inevitable consequence of emotional arousal).

Now we had a model that was much more in tune with reality and that anyone could understand. It would not only help therapists be more effective, but throw light on numerous other phenomena: how a virtuoso violinist performs the immense complexities of a concerto – the ethereal harmonies, melodies, tones, changing rhythms and moods

– and thereby transports an audience to more subtle realms; how we recognise an old friend we haven't seen for twenty years; why there are not millions more car crashes every day, as motorised populations around the world negotiate complex urban road systems at speed; how a farmer knows exactly the right moment to begin harvesting; how we learn; why placebos work; what happens in our minds when we start to laugh *before* something funny happens; how a craftsman knows when a work of fine art is finally complete; how we pick up what someone else is feeling, and why we sometimes feel anxious without a conscious reason for it. The key to it all is pattern-matching – the process of matching up innate or learned templates that is constantly occurring as we interact with our environment.

The importance of perception

Good therapy and counselling *always* centre around meaning – changing meaning from negative to positive, from harmful to helpful, is what effective counsellors do. To change the meaning is to change the template through which we experience reality. When we do this, it literally changes consciousness. So the APET model is a way of reminding us of this because it symbolises the order in which the brain perceives meaning and reacts to what it perceives. Perception, and the way we react to our perceptions, always depends on pattern matching to innate and learned knowledge. The inborn patterns – templates – are so fundamental that no reality can exist without nature pre-setting them into organisms in the first place. Although we talk about pattern-matching, in a way it is more accurate to talk about pattern *perception*. This is because it is not so much that we actually hold a template and seek the match of it; *we actually perceive reality through the template*. In other words, what we perceive are the *meanings* that we attribute to certain stimuli.

This was demonstrated startlingly clearly in cases where cataracts were removed from people blind from birth. Arthur Zajonc describes the outcome of one such operation: "In 1910, the surgeons Moreau and LePrince wrote about their successful operation on an eight-year-old boy who had been blind since birth because of cataracts. Following the operation, they were anxious to discover how well the child could see. When the boy's eyes were healed, they removed the bandages. Waving a hand in front of the child's physically perfect eyes, they asked him what he saw. He replied weakly, 'I don't know.' 'Don't you see it moving?' they asked. 'I don't know,' was his only reply. The boy's eyes were clearly not following the slowly moving hand. What he saw was only a varying brightness in front of him. He was then allowed to touch the hand as it began to move; he cried out in a voice of triumph: 'It's moving!' He could feel it move, and even, as he said, 'hear it move,' but he still needed laboriously to learn to see it move. Light and eyes were not enough to grant him sight. Passing through the now clear black pupil of the child's eye, that first light called forth no echoing image from within. The child's sight began as a hollow, silent, dark and frightening kind of seeing. The light of day beckoned, but no light of mind replied within the boy's anxious, open eyes.

"The lights of nature and of mind entwine within the eye and call forth vision. Yet separately, each light is mysterious and dark. Even the brightest light can escape our sight."[23]

It is always easiest to see such effects when illness or disability prevents a normal reaction. So, again, we can see the fundamental significance of meaning illustrated in the actions of people with ideo-motor apraxia (IMA), a condition that occurs as a result of certain diseases of the central nervous system and affects a person's ability to grasp or use objects. Research has shown that, if people with IMA are asked to pick up a cylinder the size of a cup and pretend to drink, they cannot do it. If, however, they are asked to make this same imitative movement while actually eating a meal, they are much better able to grasp and raise the cylinder. Suddenly the task is more meaningful. It has a context.

For everything we become aware of, there is a pre-existing, partially completed, inner template, innate or learned, through which we literally organise the incoming stimuli and complete it in a way that gives it meaning. These metaphorical templates are the basis of all animal and human perception. Without them no world would exist for us. They organise our reality. (This idea is explored more fully in our Afterword.)

With this understanding we can see how crucial *meaning* is when helping people who are using inappropriate patterns through which to understand their reality. Obviously, if people's attention is locked by strong emotions – depression, anxiety, lust, anger, awe, greed, etc. –

those emotions frame the meaning of life for them. That is why lowering emotional arousal is so important and needs to be done *before* attempting to adjust the patterns to bring them closer to reality. If a person has the belief or template that the world owes them a living, for example, they need an input to correct that; otherwise they will always see their interactions with other people through this parasitic viewpoint and fall foul of the people around them. Likewise, someone who idealises the opposite sex is doomed to disappointment until a more realistic template is set in place.

Emotions before thought

Patterns of perception in our brain always seek completion in the environment and each perception is 'tagged' with emotion. Emotions are feelings that create distinctive psychobiological states, a propensity for action and simplified thinking styles.[24] They originate in the limbic system and it is here and in the thalamus that all basic patterns are co-ordinated.[25] This system is continually on the lookout for physical danger, monitoring information coming through our senses from the environment. It does all this prior to consciousness. There is an emergency short cut or fast track in the brain via which signals of potential threat sent by our senses reach a small structure in the limbic system, called the amygdala, before they reach the neocortex, the 'thinking' brain. This allows the 'emotional' brain to respond instantly to threat by triggering the fight or flight response, and this happens before the conscious brain knows anything about it.[26] In other words, we first unconsciously interpret each new stimulus in terms of, "Does it represent a danger, or is it safe?" Perhaps even more fundamentally, "Is this something I can eat, or is it something that can eat me?" or, "Is it something I can approach or something I should get away from?" The conscious mind is presented with the end result of this analysis – what the emotional brain considers the significant highlights.

The information that comes into conscious awareness arrives up to half a second after the reality has been experienced unconsciously.[27] In other words, human beings experience conscious reality *after* it has actually occurred. It is what happens in that half second that is significant. Information, processed subconsciously at enormous speed, is compared to patterns already existing in the brain derived from previous experiences. On this basis, the emotional brain decides whether what is happening now is threatening or non-threatening. Only after this filtering process has occurred is information sent 'up', if necessary, into consciousness.

Our conscious reality is always accompanied by emotions, ranging from very subtle to extremely strong. Emotions exist at a stage prior to language. They are the only language available to the subconscious mind for communicating the significance of patterns. It is the emotions that propel the higher cortex towards deciding an appropriate reaction to a particular situation. We become conscious of a feeling of anxiety, distrust, anger or attraction, and the higher neocortex then has the choice of ratifying or questioning it. That is when thoughts come into play.

In summary, if an emotion is strong, the signal will take the fast-track route and trigger a response before the neocortex has had time to get involved. This is what happens when someone suddenly feels anxiety in a dark alley and runs away from a possible attacker in the shadows. It is also what happens in non-emergency situations that certain individuals respond to *as if* they were emergencies, because they haven't learned to adjust an inappropriate pattern from the past: for instance, when aggressive men automatically hit out at others before they have even had time to think what they are doing and why.

When the emotional arousal isn't quite so strong, the information can take the 'slow' track, which involves the neocortex. In such circumstances, in the dark alley, it is the neocortex that may decide that the shadows are in fact empty and that the feelings and thoughts that they have prompted need modifying. At this point the conscious mind is acting as part of a feedback loop to the pattern-matching part of the mind, sending the message, "I think this pattern needs adjustment. I'm imagining things. Calm down."

It is the job of the conscious mind to discriminate, fill in the detail and offer a more intelligent analysis of the patterns offered up to it by the emotional brain. The 'either/or' logic of the emotional brain is its most basic pattern – one that goes right the way back to earliest life forms, unicellular creatures – and this, crucially, is the foundation on which much of our behaviour and thinking rests.

The fact that all emotions operate from a black and white, good or bad, perspective has had huge consequences for human evolution and history. The emotional brain is necessarily crude in its perceptions and the degree to which the fight or flight response is activated is the degree to which our thinking becomes polarised – more black or more white. As the emotional temperature rises, the emotional brain 'hijacks' the higher, more recently evolved, cortex and very quickly begins to blank out the more subtle distinctions between individual stimuli. (When one is in danger of losing one's life, the ability to make fine discriminations must be shut off, so that we can act instinctively to take the decisive action needed to save ourselves.) So, with emotional arousal there is only a right or a wrong, all or nothing, black or white perception. Everything operates out of these two extremes.

If we look around the world today, wherever we see prejudice, discrimination, conflict, violence, torture and inhumane behaviour it is invariably accompanied by high levels of emotional arousal. The people doing these things are not different from the rest of us. Even the most intelligent person can behave like an ignoramus when emotionally aroused. And an atmosphere of continuous emotional arousal maintains ignorance because, when the higher neocortex is inhibited, no one can see the bigger picture. Black and white, emotional logic eliminates fine discrimination. As the old saying goes, "The coarse drives out the fine". Or, to put it more colloquially, high emotional arousal makes us stupid.

The higher neocortex evolved partly as a means to discriminate the thousands of shades of grey that exist between black and white. It has the capacity to modulate emotional responses – stand back and explore subtle implications and complexities, look at bigger contexts, analyse – but to do that it has to be able to interact with the emotional brain, *which is only possible if the emotional brain isn't too highly aroused*.

It is impossible to communicate normally with people who are too highly aroused. This is because, in their aroused state, they cannot process data contradictory to their black and white thinking. They cannot give attention to another viewpoint. As we've seen, high emotional arousal locks the attention mechanism, effectively putting the person into a trance state where they are confined to viewing the world through an inappropriate pattern or template, limiting their perception of reality. The best tactic when trying to communicate with a highly aroused person is to buy time and do whatever is necessary to bring their arousal level down first.

There is one important proviso. Some people need to be in a state of high emotion to perform specific tasks well. For them, emotional arousal itself is an essential tool because it is focusing their attention on the task in hand. For example, at a great sporting event, athletes rise to the occasion and give a better performance than ever before. These are people who need the extra emotional arousal (caused by the big occasion) to focus their attention to help them to go into a state of flow. Getting the degree of arousal right has to be learned because it is normal to be more anxious at such times and emotional arousal (put in place by the big occasion) can rise to such an extent that performance disintegrates. That is what happens to anxious individuals when taking an exam; however intelligent they are, their minds go blank. (The solution is to use relaxation and guided imagery techniques, several times before the event, to rehearse being more relaxed on such occasions. The more often we can experience positive rather than disabling levels of arousal and associate them with exam taking, the more likely it is that this state can be achieved in the exam room.)

Nearly all great actors say that they feel nervous before a public performance. Yet, they also say that, without that nervousness they don't produce their best; the anxiety they have prior to going on stage enables them to focus their minds more intensely and produce their best work. But it's a fine line. At the height of his powers Sir Lawrence Olivier once spent almost an entire performance with his back to the audience because he was so nervous. He couldn't get into flow. So it is always a question of the right amount of arousal for the job in hand.

Even in learning, a certain amount of emotion is involved. A good teacher has to focus their pupils' attention and, as we know, what focuses attention better than anything is emotion. But the teacher doesn't over-arouse the pupils, instead he or she will present the subject matter in a way that is so intrinsically interesting it causes sufficient emotional arousal in the pupils to focus their attention.

Some pupils by nature need an awful lot of stimulation. And boys, on average, need more stimulation than girls. Pupils who suffer from ADD (Attention Deficit Disorder), sometimes referred to as ADHD (Attention Deficit Hyperactivity Disorder) need an enormous amount.

These children and adults need regular amounts of intense stimulation to feel alive. Research shows that if ADD children (in the main these are boys, though some girls have the condition) are given regular and frequent breaks where they can be intensely physically active and receive sufficient stimulus from exciting activities, they can calm down enough to focus their attention for a period of time in the classroom, provided the teacher makes the subject matter interesting enough to keep their attention.[28]

So, emotional arousal should by no means be viewed as negative or destructive. That would be black or white thinking in itself. It is always a question of the *right* degree of emotional arousal for the task in hand.

Counsellors and psychotherapists who recognise that people with emotional problems are locked into tunnel vision know that their key role is to open up that view. An effective counsellor has the skills to disengage the templates that 'lock' individuals into disabling view-points and help them access ones that widen their vision. This is known as reframing.

When we take account of brain physiology, we can see that the fastest way to begin helping distressed people is to calm them down first, thus releasing the higher cortex from the mental paralysis caused by excessive emotional arousal. Clients are then more able to help themselves escape from their predicament.

Three vital principles

From what has been explained so far about brain function, we suggest that we can draw out three principles that are vital for therapists and counsellors to understand if they are to deal effectively with the most common emotional disorders, such as phobias, post-traumatic stress, anxiety, anger, clinical depression and addictions:

- the brain works principally through an infinitely rich pattern-matching process;
- emotion comes before thought – all perceptions and all thought are 'tagged' with emotion;
- the higher the emotional arousal, the more primitive the emotional/mental pattern that is engaged.

By studying therapy models with these fundamental principles in mind, we can more easily see their strengths and weaknesses. Any therapy that encourages emotional introspection, for example, is unlikely to be helpful for most common problems. This explains why efficacy studies repeatedly show that psychodynamic and person-centred approaches to treating depression or anxiety tend to prolong or worsen the condition while any form of therapy that focuses on distraction will lift it.[29,30,31]

That there is emotional accompaniment to *all* perceptions may not seem obvious. It is now known that emotions are not neatly restricted to one area of the brain but are mixed up with both cognitive and bodily processes. However, we may only notice the emotional element when it stands out in bizarre ways. For example, Capgras' syndrome, which results from brain damage to connections between the temporal lobes and the amygdala, has the effect of making sufferers think that people they love and care about are impostors.[32,33] Although the parts of the brain that pattern match and recognise familiar people are still working, the damage prevents the integration of the emotional responses, feelings and meanings associated with, for instance, one's parents or spouse. Because these are not activated, someone who suffers from the syndrome jumps to the conclusion that "This person *can't* be my father/mother/husband/wife!"

Normally, people don't give a second thought to the feelings that accompany seeing their parents or partners. The feelings are normal, routine, and so the brain doesn't bring them into consciousness. All unremarkable emotions are neutralised in this way – a fact that makes the phenomenon difficult to observe until an exception demonstrates it. So, even though the most common of perceptions have feelings associated with them, we only become aware of feelings, and our thoughts about feelings, when they are somehow unexpected – surprising. Surprise is the common element.

The power of thought

Finally, the T in the APET model, that refers to thought: when the neocortex is not over-emotionally aroused it can employ ever more subtle evaluation procedures. The neocortex is in a state of continual flux from second to second, minute to minute and hour to hour.[34] This has to be so. We would not be the adaptable creatures we are otherwise. The neocortex is nature's solution to the need for adaptable responses to an ever-changing environment. By gifting us with innate instinctive patterns that are not totally programmed, and giving us the ability to add to these patterns almost infinitely, nature made us into the remarkably flexible, talented creatures we are, able to explore ever deeper into the nature of our world.

Every researcher and writer on the subject describes this incredibly complex organ, the neocortex, in awed tones. It has literally billions of potential neuronal connections and the almost inconceivable ability to remodel itself according to the richness of input coming in through the senses from the environment. It continually makes new connections, strengthening valuable ones and withering old ones that it no longer finds useful. It can hold on to and store whatever information is pertinent to its current reality and use that store of connections to modify the emotional responses received from the emotional brain – a complex fine-tuning operation. It is this continual refining of the metaphorical pattern-matching process that allows us to discriminate ever more accurately between the polarised extremes of the emotional brain's black and white responses.

We shall look next at how we can make best use of all these in-built mechanisms of brain functioning.

Using the APET model

Using the APET approach (activating stimulus processed through the pattern-matching part of the mind, giving rise to emotion, giving rise to thought) provides therapists with many more points of intervention than simply helping distressed people to challenge their belief systems directly, as in cognitive therapy.

Human givens therapists are acutely aware, for example, of how influencing the activating agent (the A in APET) can in itself dramatically improve people's lives. If someone is depressed because of being bullied at work, a therapist can encourage the discussion of options, such as changing jobs.

One young married woman suffered vomiting fits during her critical and somewhat interfering mother-in-law's all too frequent visits to her home. The young woman was encouraged (by Joe) to be sick on the kitchen floor in front of her mother-in-law (instead of running to the bathroom), and then rush to her room, leaving her mother-in-law to clear up. This had the effect of reducing the frequency of the mother-in-law's visits (the activating agent) and gave the younger woman back control in her own home. The vomiting stopped.

The powerful effect of changing the activating agent can also be seen at work in social contexts. Social workers may particularly need to work with the activating agent that causes distress, with one of their roles being to ensure that people who are poor or ill have a roof over their heads, warmth, clothing and sufficient food.

A highly dramatic example of its use in a social context was the initiation of a remarkable project, in 1980, to clean up New York's subway system. The thinking behind it was that the impetus to engage in certain kinds of antisocial behaviour comes not from particular types of people but from the nature of the environment. Billions of dollars were invested in cleaning and rebuilding the subway stations, removing all graffiti from trains and replacing trains that were beyond recovery with shiny new, *clean* ones. The instant any graffiti appeared on a surface, it was removed – whatever the cost. If a train was defaced, it was taken out of service and returned to its pristine state. Within six years the clean up was complete. The same zero tolerance policy was then enacted on crime. Even minor misdemeanours were prosecuted. The crime rate in New York, even for serious offences, fell dramatically, all because, when a signal goes out from the environment that 'this is not a place to behave in a criminal way', the brain pattern to behave antisocially is not elicited.[35] In other words, changing the activating agent activates different patterns.

Human givens therapists pay considerable attention to changing inappropriate patterns that cause individuals distress. This can be done in a variety of ways. For instance, when someone is stuck in some way, a time honoured way to change the patterns in their mind is through telling stories, using metaphors and appropriate humour. In this way, their imagination can be stimulated and experiences reframed. This is why highly effective counsellors and psychotherapists tend to be natural storytellers.

Indeed, the benefits of this essential skill extend even further. When a more useful metaphorical pattern is offered to clients, for instance, they have the capacity, through the brain's own pattern-matching process, to decipher the metaphor for themselves, with the result that their solution is 'owned' by them rather than imposed on them by the therapist. Because it is the clients themselves who have made the connection, the connections are all the more 'hard-wired' and more firmly established. The method also enables rapport to be maintained because, if a client doesn't feel that a particular story or metaphor is relevant to them, they can just let it go past them, without feeling they have rejected 'advice' from the therapist. (Often, however, the meaning of a pertinent story will penetrate at a later date.)

Human givens therapists are particularly aware of the pattern-matching process in the phenomenon known once by philosophers as 'reification' and by linguists as 'nominalisation'. This is the act of turning a verb or adjective into an abstract noun. A politician, for example, might change the verb *to modernise* into the noun *modernisation*, claiming that "what we need is *modernisation*", as though the process of modernisation were something concrete that you could buy, see or touch. Similarly, we might be told that "we need to deliver *innovations*" as if they were parcels. The problem with these words is that they contain no sensory information – nothing specific such as who should be doing precisely what to whom. They are content free, which is why they hypnotise both the listener *and* the speaker. To make sense of them, we have to go on an inner search to find a pattern-match for what such words mean *to us* before we can give meaning to them. Consequently, they always mean something different to every listener while simultaneously giving each the feeling that they understand what the speaker means. That is why they are the stock-in-trade words of politicians, preachers and gurus.

For example, if a political leader says, "I am going to put more *resources* into *education*", everyone may applaud and be supportive. ('Education, education, education' was a recent New Labour party slogan.) But 'putting *resources* into *education*' means something quite different to every teacher, child or parent. And, to assign a personal meaning to these abstractions, they are forced to search inwards for a corresponding pattern. Because this happens unconsciously, they don't notice the con trick being played on them. One person might think the politician is going to instigate research into what exactly is the best way to educate a child. Another might think teachers are going to be paid more, or better schools will be built, or class sizes reduced, or schools made safer, or that there will be **more** exams, or that there will be **fewer** exams, or that the curriculum will be widened, or teachers trained better, and so on. The politician is trying to get support and credit by using these abstract terms to appeal to the different individual concerns of all those listening. This is an illusion. THE POLITICIAN HAS NOT PROMISED ANYTHING SPECIFIC AT ALL. You do not 'supply', 'give' or 'input' an abstract noun like *education*. You **educate**. And what people are educated about, why, how, where and by whom, are the questions that must be asked. So it is our duty to make politicians define exactly what they mean and to not let them off the hook until they do.

Likewise, a guru might say to his congregation, "We are gathered here today because we all share the same *values* and seek eternal *happiness*, which is to be found only by following the path of *truth* and *love* to *enlightenment*". When a guru or preacher keeps up this hypnotic language for any length of time, it makes his listeners feel as if he is addressing his remarks directly to their 'heart' – in other words, he is arousing emotions in them.

So, because there are no precise, commonly shared perceptions about the meaning of such abstract words, they readily confuse people and make us vulnerable to self-deception and manipulation by others.

The only way to prevent this is, firstly, to learn to spot nominalisations. (You can tell if a word is an abstract noun by asking yourself, "Can I pick this up and carry it away?" or "Can I buy this off the shelf?" If you can't, it is a nominalisation.) Secondly, we need to learn how to challenge them, which is easily done by turning them back into verbs and asking people to be more precise.

For instance, if someone says, "My *expectations* must come first", we might respond by asking, "What exactly do you **expect?**"

If someone says they have *anger* in them, we should ask "What exactly is making you **angry?**" (People do not have *anger*. It is not a substance in them like blood. In the same way, people do not have *depression* or *fear*. They are depressed **by** something or afraid **of** something.)

If politicians claim they are going to put more *resources* into the health services or transport or whatever, they should be challenged as to precisely how much they are planning to spend, on what, why and when. Similarly, if they say they are going to take *responsibility* we need to know what exactly they are going to be responsible for, how this will be measured and what the penalties are if they fail.

The point we are making here is that operating through metaphor and generalisations, as we all must, is a vulnerability as well as an advantage. People use this kind of abstract language to hide ignorance, protect territory and deceive and manipulate people. Jargon, psychobabble and 'culty' language is almost entirely made up of it. It is important to be aware of this because we are social creatures and, unless we have perceptions more or less in common with those around us, it is difficult to co-operate with one another and our interactions at all levels become cruder. That makes it harder to ensure our proper needs are met and makes selfish, unethical behaviour more likely.

One of the first to emphasise the importance of recognising nominalisations in psychotherapy was the psycholinguist John Grinder, one of the founders of Neurolinguistic Programming (NLP).[36] Patients very commonly use nominalisations because they can't think straight and are ignorant about why this is so. They throw out nominalisations as a cry for help. It is the counsellor's job to dispel the ignorance so that they can be more realistic about their situation. Examples of negative abstractions that patients might use include: *anger, black cloud, evil, misery, despair, depression, worthless, useless, hopeless, fear, gloom, low self-esteem*. If therapists are not aware of the pattern-matching process, such words can lead them to identify closely with the misery of their clients. Again, the way to deal with them is to challenge them. When a patient says, for example, "I'm full of misery," the most useful response is "What exactly is making you miserable? When did this feeling start? What was going on at the time?"

However, nominalisations can also be used to positive effect. Positive nominalisations such as *happiness, love, creativity, resources, joy, principles, insight, learning, power, awareness, truth, beauty* and *possibilities*, although they may be used by advertisers, gurus and politicians to manipulate people, may also be employed by therapists and counsellors to send clients on a constructive, useful, inner search to help them access positive patterns of behaviour. For instance, saying something like the following can have a powerful therapeutic effect:

"After listening to you, I know that your *unconscious mind* has many *strengths* and *resources* that you can bring to bear on your *situation* which, coupled with your *integrity* and *creativity*, can open up new *possibilities* and bring *satisfaction* and *happiness* to your life once more".

Thus the pattern-matching process can subtly be used to change thoughts and perceptions. Thought patterns *can* be changed directly and consciously of course, provided a person is not overly emotionally aroused. The new thought is fed back into the emotional brain and helps moderate or change any inappropriate pattern-matches that are creating undesired emotional consequences. (For instance, someone who finds it hard to form a relationship with a new partner because of pattern matching to an abusive relationship in the past might be asked to think of 50 ways in which this relationship differs from the previous one.) This means, when people are highly emotionally aroused, the most effective thing to do is to calm down their emotions so that the neocortex can function more intelligently. They can then more easily see all the shades of grey between the emotionally driven black and white frames of reference they are stuck in.

Therapy delivered from the APET model produces faster results and also dispenses with the need for the complex language that cognitive therapists have developed to teach patients how to classify and challenge their thinking. Once people are calmed down and no longer at the prey of heightened emotions, they can be given the information they need, either directly or through metaphor, to help them see their situation from multiple viewpoints. This helps them learn for themselves how calming down enables finer discrimination and a more accurate picture of the world.

The APET model offers a unifying theoretical basis for why any technique that is successful works. For example, with an understanding of the metaphorical pattern-matching function of the brain, and of how our instinctive templates are first programmed in the womb and after birth during REM, we can see how any therapy that directly accesses the REM state – guided imagery for example – can help clients reprogramme unhelpful patterns of responses. Until recently hypnosis (which, as we have explained, involves induction of the REM state) was treated with awe, incredulity or hostility within the psychotherapeutic community. However, as leading exponent, psychiatrist Milton H. Erickson, and others have found, hypnosis is the single most powerful psychotherapeutic tool available to us. It is so powerful precisely because it accesses the state of consciousness in which nature programmes the brain *and can reprogramme it*.[37] (As discussed earlier, of course, this also means that, like any powerful tool, hypnosis can be misused – and frequently is.)

Reframing is another powerful technique, widely recognised as a core skill in effective counselling, that can be put in context through the APET model. A reframe replaces a pattern that is outdated or inappropriate with a richer one that opens us up to new possibilities we hadn't previously realised were there.

All effective therapy involves reframing. The determining factor in a person's happiness is not just what happens to them in life but how they interpret experience, or how they 'frame', or put meaning to, life events. Some 'frames' empower us and some disempower us. When someone unconsciously assumes that their way of perceiving reality is the only way, then a major shift can occur when another view is unexpectedly demonstrated to them. After such a reframe it is virtually impossible to maintain the problem behaviour in the same way.

Panic attacks

As well as providing an organic basis for understanding and integrating the active ingredients within the more potent therapeutic methodologies used today, the APET model also provides a clear theoretical understanding of why certain psychological conditions arise. With this understanding we can look afresh at such debilitating conditions and see how they could be better treated.

A panic attack, for example, is the inappropriate activation of the fight or flight response, the emergency reaction that prepares the body to deal with physical danger. Nowadays most of us are rarely in the presence of life-threatening events and yet that doesn't stop many people experiencing panic attacks. These usually come about as a result of a progressive rising in background stress levels until the point where one more stress – the straw that breaks the camel's back – sets off the alarm reaction, triggering the fight or flight response.

When this first occurs, not surprisingly, people don't understand why their heart is pounding, why they are sweating, why their breathing is accelerated, and so they jump to the alarming conclusion that something must be seriously wrong and that perhaps they are having a heart attack. This causes a further rise in the alarm reaction, a further release of adrenaline, and even more intensified panic symptoms.

When we experience extreme alarm during a panic attack, the brain, naturally enough, desperately scans the environment to find out where the 'threat' to its survival might be. Not surprisingly, many people then make an association with an element in the environment where the panic attack occurs. If it first occurs in a supermarket, for example, an individual may avoid supermarkets in future, even though the panic attack was caused not by the supermarket but by raised stress levels. Once the faulty association has been made, the fight or flight response will continue to fire off every so often, pattern matching to any environment that has similar elements in it to that of the supermarket: a post office, a bank, anywhere with bright lights or crowds or queues. People thus affected may then progressively avoid all these places and gradually the noose of agoraphobia grips them, hindering their interaction with life itself. In the worst cases, they become confined to home, terrified of the outside world.

A combination of relaxation, behavioural therapy and cognitive therapy is useful in treating this condition. Sufferers are taught to calm themselves down and progressively re-engage with life. It can take many sessions of therapy and practice. This whole process, however, is accelerated if we first detraumatise (using the fast phobia cure described on page 284) the memories of the most frightening panic attacks. As a result the brain will cease to pattern match in a destructive way when people enter each new, previously frightening, situation. Once the disabling emotional memories are processed, people can progress more rapidly through the situations that they had previously been avoiding.

Obsessions

Obsessive compulsive disorder (OCD), can take many forms but is most often seen in repeated washing and checking behaviours. Again, often the background trigger is raised stress levels, which may be due to anything from physical illness, a fright, not getting enough sleep to business worries, a relationship breakdown or stress around examinations.[38] Some people have a propensity to develop this disorder in response to raised stress levels.

OCD is a complex neuropsychiatric process characterised by a homogeneous core of three main symptoms:

1. intrusive, forceful and repetitive thoughts, images, or sounds that dwell in the mind without the possibility of rejecting them;

2. imperative needs to perform motor or mental acts;

3. doubt or chronic questioning about major or minor matters.[39]

Sufferers of OCD may be, in effect, responding to posthypnotic suggestions implanted accidentally by environmental factors – they lose track of time and forget how long they have been performing the obsessive behaviour, or whether they even have, and so start all over again. Losing track of time, and amnesia are common hypnotic phenomena.

Clearly, a pattern-match is fired up in the brain and then embedded deeper and deeper by repetition – much as in addiction behaviour. Changing such deeply entrenched patterns is not easy but is possible in many cases and working from the APET model offers multiple ways in which to go about it.

One key step, for example, is to help sufferers take a step back so that they can observe themselves and their behaviour. There are a number of ways this can be done with the help of a therapist. Once the patient's core identity has been separated from the problem and they recognise that *the OCD behaviour is not who they are*, it is possible to stop the behaviour. (Indeed it is possible to effect dramatic recoveries in many conditions by making that distinction very clear to a person.)

Negative ruminations

It has been shown that depression is associated with memory bias – either a better memory for negative events or a poorer memory for positive events and experiences. This has led to the widely accepted theory that the onset of depression somehow facilitates access to negative memories which, once recalled, serve to exacerbate and lengthen the depression.[40] The more that we go back over the stories in our lives, the more we are increasing and programming in the saliency of those patterns. A depressed person who continually resurrects negative life experiences is programming those negative templates into their unconscious mind. Therefore, new stimuli coming into their conscious minds, before ever reaching consciousness, are being matched up and scanned by negative templates to draw out what is negative in those experiences. Perceptions are continuously, subconsciously biased by the negative templates that are programmed in as a result of negative rumination.

In cognitive therapy, people may be asked to challenge their conviction that everything they do is always wrong or hopeless by recalling successes and achievements. But the memory bias and reinforcing of negative patterns make it hard for a depressed person to recall good memories, so it isn't easy for them to generate a more positive attitude to life, however much they are willed to. Therapy based on the APET model, working from the human givens, can take a more diverse and creative approach to shifting unhelpful patterns, particularly through the use of metaphor and story, which impact on the unconscious mind more directly and powerfully than reason.[41] Depression is such an important and fascinating topic we devote the next chapter to it.

Anger disorders

Anger disorders are also accelerating as the rate of environmental change overtaxes many people's ability to adapt. There are a number of physical states that lower the threshold for triggering anger. These include: dementia, physical illness, over-tiredness, hunger, hormonal changes during puberty, pre-menstruation, menopause, birth of a baby, physically craving for an addictive substance such as nicotine, alcohol, caffeine or other drugs, chronic or acute pain, intoxication and sexual frustration.

We all know that a chronically angry person is a stupid person because their higher brain function is inhibited from working by the release of powerful stress hormones from the limbic system. But everyone who is capable of mental concentration and motivated to learn can be taught to control their anger and reduce their stupidity.

There may be a variety of reasons why a person has a problem with inappropriate anger. In the majority of cases, when people lose their temper, it is simply a result of 'the straw that breaks the camel's back' – they are just currently over-stressed. Because of this they see reality in black and white terms, and a small infringement can seem like a huge one. As mentioned, some people develop an addiction to anger. They actually enjoy the feeling of certainty and the emotional high it gives them – they are 'emotional junkies'. In such circumstances, this has to be treated like any other addiction; they have to learn to see how, overall, anger outbursts have more of a destructive effect upon their lives than a constructive one. And they have to be willing to learn how to manage that behaviour responsibly. Sometimes excessive anger is a response to some traumatic life experience, and such individuals would benefit from treatment for post traumatic stress.

In a properly matured human being, anger is a tool in the service of the higher cortex – the observing self. As Aristotle said, "Anyone can become angry – that is easy; but to be angry with the right person, to the right degree, at the right time, for the right purpose and in the right way – that is not easy."

In the 1970s a fashion arose whereby unhappy people were encouraged to 'get their anger out', in a reaction against the controlling tendencies of psychoanalysis. All research on anger management shows, however, that hitting punch bags or pillows, shouting louder and louder and so on, and thereby getting more and more angry whilst doing so, only serve to make a person more unhappy and dysfunctional, even though it appears in the short term as if the exhaustion that all this induces is satisfying. As a therapeutic technique, it was a disaster.[42]

Anger management skills connect far more closely with how the mind/body system works. People can learn to recognise when they are starting to lose their temper, and how to withdraw from an explosive situation with another person before emotion has hijacked the brain. This might take the form of acknowledging the seriousness of the issue but explaining that they are getting too worked up to think straight about it and that they need to be able to address it in a calmer state of mind. Withdrawing from the situation for at least 20 or 30 minutes and doing something calming, such as taking a walk, can give the stress hormones a chance to wash out of the system. In that stage, it is important people do not rehearse the reasons for their excessive emotional response or attempt to justify their anger, as this will just pump it up again. Once calm, it is possible to go back and work at resolving the problem. It is important not to leave the issue unsolved, as that will just leave it to fester and thus further undermine the relationship.

Another important point, which it helps to take on board, is that most arguments are not really about right and wrong. They are really about 'my needs' versus 'your needs'. When we can take that approach in a calm manner it's usually possible to begin negotiating so that both sets of needs are met, or a reasonable compromise is found.

An important skill, which we think young people should be taught as a matter of course, is the use of calming techniques on ourselves. There are times when *everybody* needs to know how to relax. Breathing techniques, such as the 'seven/eleven technique', are invaluable: you breathe in to the count of seven and more slowly breathe out to a count of eleven. When the out breath is kept longer it stimulates the parasympathetic nervous system, the relaxation response. Aerobic exercise can also calm us down. When we are calmed down, we are more able to look at a difficult situation and reframe it.

An essential skill, when on the receiving end of anger, is not to escalate it. Even if receiving an undeserved volume of vitriol, it is not the time to try to reason, because angry individuals are not in a state of mind where they can process a viewpoint that contradicts their own. Arguing with angry people is futile. They need help to calm down because, when angry, they cannot help but see life in a distorted way through their emotional black and white thinking. Their outbursts need not be taken too personally once that is recognised.

Addictions

Most people realise that, if they indulge too heavily in any potentially addictive form of pleasure – whether alcohol, drugs, gambling, shopping or even work, it will interfere with getting other needs met, as addiction usually results in disintegrating relationships, low self-esteem and insecurity created by debt. Young people may often experiment with drugs but, as they mature, form relationships, take on responsibilities, build a family etc., drug use tends to drop off. In other words, there is a natural counterweight to overindulgence in any appetite built in to us. If we over indulge in one pleasure, we lessen the likelihood of other important needs being met, and that provides the motivation to keep any single pleasure from getting out of hand and dominating our lives.

So nature has built this lovely balance into us. But there is a complication: the counterweight must be in place, if tendencies towards addiction are to be thwarted, and that is not always the case. People who are lonely, isolated, involuntarily unemployed, suddenly bereaved, or who, for whatever reason, lack the ability to generate the self-esteem that comes from being involved in work, building a family and involvement in meaningful community activities, are clearly not getting their needs met, and are therefore highly vulnerable to addiction. Many of them lack relationship skills or don't know how to manage their anxiety and stress other than through taking drugs or drink. Some have been traumatised in war or been subject to violent attacks or sexual abuse. Any such cause can damage human beings and make them vulnerable to addiction.

It might seem that this doesn't always apply. What about high achievers who reach a stage in life where they have great wealth, a family and, to all intents and purposes, seem successful, but then become addicts? They are not 'down and outs' or social failures. They are exemplars, however, of the carrot and stick principle we discussed earlier. If they no longer derive pleasure, a healthy, natural reward, from having to stretch themselves to build their career, they may start to try and put pleasure back into their lives by drinking too much or indulging excessively in other pleasures.

The first step in combating an addiction is to help people to recognise that they have one. They must come to recognise that this behaviour is, in the overall economy of their life, causing them more pain than pleasure. This cannot be done by being critical. (Criticising or arguing with an addict only puts them on the defensive and drives them back into their emotional brain and black and white thinking.) They need to be helped to see, in a sympathetic, supportive way how destructive the addiction is in their life, and how it creates an emotional wasteland leading to nowhere except an early grave.

Only when this is seen to be the case, and an undesirable state of affairs, can the next step be taken. Addicts must be helped to build up their self-esteem, so that they can believe it possible to change their lifestyle and rebuild their life. Guided imagery is valuable for helping them engage deeply with this. As their sense of self-empowerment grows, whatever blocks are in the way of getting their needs met more constructively must be removed. This is a problem-solving focus. If it is post traumatic stress that is disabling, they will need to be detraumatised. If it is clinical depression, they will need to be lifted out of it. If they lack social interaction skills, they need to be taught them.

It is also important to keep the attention mechanism in mind when treating addictions. Because all views and beliefs are determined in part by those we interact with, someone who spends much of their time with people who indulge in an addictive lifestyle will inevitably reactivate that mindset in themselves. Because the brain is a pattern-matching organ, any time a person encounters something in the environment that in the past was associated with their addiction, it will automatically reactivate the desire for the substance or behaviour.

The actual chemical need for an addictive substance is usually gone in a matter of days; the body rebalances itself. But the tendency to relapse comes with perceiving a pattern in the environment that recalls the addiction state. There may be a compulsion to complete the pattern – by taking drugs again or whatever.

This means that the ex-addict has literally got to wear the pattern out. When enough time goes by, the brain finds other uses for the neurones involved in that behaviour. Some people achieve this by withdrawing as much as possible from any environment or actions that might activate those patterns. An alcoholic may need to avoid the pub for example. A heroin user would be best advised not to go to places where heroin is used, or mix with people whose main point of connection is their drug use. Otherwise, strong desires will be triggered off again.

Clearly, a part of recovery must involve helping someone meet or spend more time with people who have a healthier attitude towards life. In such company, they will be able to get their needs met in more wholesome ways.

Rituals associated with addiction also need to be avoided, or at least the ex-user must be very conscious and wary of them, so the resolve not to give in is kept strong. For example, if the *last* time you went on holiday you were still a cigarette smoker, you have to be wary that the *next* time you go the pattern-match might trigger off the desire for a cigarette. If you anticipate this, and know it's a temporary thing (part of wearing out old patterns), you don't have to give in. You are fore-armed, and that's the essential thing.

Addiction distorts thought processes, fooling us into thinking that life would be the better for indulging in it. So it is helpful for people to know that most people do not beat an addiction on the first attempt. The skills involved in learning how to overcome addiction take time to build, just as learning to ride a bicycle involves a few tumbles. So, if in the past a man had always got drunk whenever he got angry and, on one occasion, got blotto again, he should be helped to view his lapse as a slip up, not a failure. The therapist's task is to make sure he doesn't give up trying; to help him make good use of the slip up – by seeing that getting drunk didn't actually do anything to solve whatever had made him angry; and to work with him to develop the skills to deal with testing situations more successfully.

So a human givens approach contains essential knowledge for treating addiction. Treatment involves sociological and environmental as well as psychological elements. In summary, to come back from addiction a person first needs help to see what is blocking a better lifestyle, and then help to work out a package of skills and behaviours to enable their needs to be met more effectively – creating the counterweight against relapsing into addiction.

Placebo – nocebo

The placebo response has baffled scientists and puzzled thoughtful human beings since perhaps the dawn of civilisation. It was certainly referred to by Chaucer in his writings. The word comes from *placebo domino*, "I will please the Lord", a term that was associated with travelling friars who demanded money from poor people to say prayers for their dead – in effect, a form of emotional blackmail. For centuries, the word placebo was a term of abuse. But gradually doctors started using it to describe the response whereby some patients recovered from illnesses even when medicine was ineffectual, as if some kind of faith healing had taken place.

One of the functions of modern double-blind trials is to find out whether a medicine is the cause of a person's cure or whether they might have got better because of a doctor's implicit 'suggestion' that a medicine will work. Double-blind means that neither the doctors nor the patients in a trial know who is receiving the active treatment and who the placebo, and somebody neutral hands out the pills. For when doctors know which pill contains the genuine drug, their own beliefs about it somehow transmit to the patients and the patients often improve because of that.

The remarkable thing, however, is that, even with the most stringent double-blind trials, there is still an effect on the control group. A significant number of the control group invariably gets better, even when taking an inert substance rather than an active medicinal ingredient. To be considered effective a new drug must be significantly superior in effect to the placebo response experienced by the control group. (What hasn't been realised till relatively recently, however, is that there is a placebo effect to active medicines too.[43])

Increasingly in recent years, some scientists and clinicians have been asking whether there is any way to harness the placebo response, instead of just dismissing it as an embarrassing finding. For surely the placebo effect must reflect an innate capacity within human beings for self-healing: if we could find a way of tapping into this, we might be able to tap into nature's own way of healing itself. This might open the door to powerful new treatments with no side effects.

Indeed, it *is* possible to tap into the placebo effect. We would suggest that pattern matching – the **P** in APET – is at its basis and can help us understand the mind/body connections involved. Three conditions must be fulfilled before a placebo can work. There must be a pattern that can be matched to, however crudely (we have seen how even just one or two elements of similarity is enough); the treatment must seem plausible enough for the brain to interpret it as capable of bringing about a healing reaction; and the emotions must be engaged – the individual must completely accept that the treatment could work.

So, the placebo, first and foremost, generates a pattern that corresponds to a pattern the brain already knows. Matching to this pattern gives the brain the ability to alter the body's reactions. When a person is offered a pill (dummy or otherwise) to cure a headache, the pattern being matched to is "I've had headaches before and I feel better when

I take a pill/this colour pill/this shape of pill" or whatever.

When the treatment is a novel one, for instance a treatment for cancer, the patient's belief in the plausibility of its working must be stronger, as there is no past success to match to. (The pattern to which the brain must match is one of wellbeing.) It may be sufficient that the patient trusts the doctors and places great store by the fact that they have international reputations or that they successfully treated a family member or friend.

For the placebo effect to work, there must be only one pattern for the brain to try to match to. The pattern must be "This can make me feel better", and there can be no competing patterns, such as "This may work or it may not". For the brain to focus on the one pattern, the emotions must be aroused, creating in effect a trance state of belief and conviction. Expectation, desire for the treatment to work, faith in the doctor and a sense of urgency, for instance, all help arouse the emotions and create the desired focusing of attention. When a credible pattern is focused on with a level of emotional arousal that locks the attention onto the required outcome, the brain then does all it can to pattern match to that result.

Joe tells the tale of his own experience of a placebo response which bears out the above. He once heard, from what he considered a fairly reliable source, that aspirin could stop a hangover. "As I was curious to know whether this could be true, I promised myself that I would try it out when appropriate. But I don't drink to excess very often nowadays (although anybody who knows me knows you don't have to force a drink into my hand!). This meant my frustration levels about satisfying my curiosity were building up the more I was denied an opportunity to put the method to the test. Eventually, however, after a family celebration, I had drunk enough to cause a hangover. So I eagerly took an aspirin and went to bed.

"I woke up the next morning on cloud nine – not a trace of a hangover. I felt as if I were walking on air in a way similar to how I had heard some of my heroin addict patients describe feeling after taking heroin. In fact I suspect that is exactly what I *was* experiencing: the release of my body's own endogenous heroin, namely endorphins."

If we look at the mechanics of what had occurred here we can see a clear illustration of how the placebo response works. First there was a credible theory – that taking an aspirin could prevent a hangover – but there was also a frustration build up: a build up of emotional arousal. So the placebo effect was triggered and Joe woke the next morning after a release of endorphins that made him feel very positive indeed.

However, the story doesn't end there. Joe took an aspirin on another occasion, later, when he thought he might have a hangover. But this time it didn't work! The only difference was that the second time he took the aspirin there was no emotional arousal and Joe's attention was not focused on the outcome.

The emotional arousal and focusing of attention is enormously important. It explains why, for instance, some people who attend accident and emergency departments for crippling headaches respond to placebo tablets.[44] Being in an accident and emergency department is an unusual experience. Just being there sends a powerful message to the emotional brain that there is something seriously wrong, which raises emotional levels and locks attention onto whatever tablet is given. The tablet is a physical metaphor that seeks a pattern-match. The pattern-match provokes an endorphin release that relieves pain.

Other research has shown that, if a placebo is given by injection, it is more effective than if it is given by tablet.[45] This is because an injection is seen as stronger medicine. Also, smaller tablets have been found more powerful than standard tablets, probably because patients are subliminally influenced to believe that they must be receiving a very concentrated essence of the 'medicine'. This unconsciously focuses their attention even more. Such methods give the rituals more credibility.

The placebo effect is an enormously powerful one, as we have seen, but it is definitely not magic. Even when all the conditions are right, as described above, healing cannot occur if, for instance, a cancer is too advanced or the immune system is not strong enough. This, along with any lack of conviction, explains why placebos often do *not* work.

The reverse of the placebo effect also exists. In this, known as the 'nocebo' effect or medical hexing, patients' conditions worsen as a result of doctors unintentionally conveying negative suggestions to which the patients respond. Simple instances might be "I haven't had a patient respond to this treatment yet, but ...", "I don't know much about this treatment personally ...", "Well, it might be worth a try", "This doesn't work for 40 per cent of people". Whenever a doctor focuses a patient's attention on a possible negative outcome, even with a throwaway remark, the emotion the remark arouses in the patient's brain will lock attention onto it and increase the chances of a negative outcome. That is why it is important that doctors are careful with the language they use when giving prognoses or life expectancy projections. In very many cases, their patients may fulfil the predictions that have been suggested to them.

So, to recap, the placebo response is most likely to work when a credible ritual is offered with positive endorsement from the relevant therapist that raises the patient's expectations of improvement or cure. A placebo is an undifferentiated metaphor. Once the instinctive, unconscious, emotional brain has its attention mechanism locked onto a pattern, it does everything it can to try to complete that pattern – to find a match to it.

It has been shown, unsurprisingly, that those who are most susceptible to hypnosis are also most likely to respond to well-delivered placebos. The credible ritual is a metaphor. It can be a physical metaphor like a tablet, injection or procedure, or it can be a mental metaphor, like a phrase, theory or story. Tablets etc. are fairly crude metaphors. The giving of one doesn't convey much guidance about how the patient should use it to mobilise their own immune system. A story, however, especially when delivered while a patient is in the focused attention state of trance can provide a disguised means of giving highly detailed instructions for kick-starting the immune system.

The following is an example of how Ivan used this means to help a depressed woman whose feet were deformed by dozens of painful verrucas. One of the verrucas was as big as a 50p piece and some days she could barely stand with the pain. Over the previous years she had attended chiropodists at different hospitals and received a variety of treatments, even surgery, all to no avail. But, within a few weeks of putting her into a trance and telling her this story, her verrucas had gone and her depression had lifted. Three months later, her feet were completely smooth.

ONCE UPON a time there was a wonderful land ruled over by a wise and popular king. He kept his people safe from enemies and helped them prosper and thus he earned their respect. But, as happens, the king died and his only daughter inherited the kingdom and became queen. At first all went well for she possessed her father's wisdom and worked hard for the good of the people who consequently loved her.

Then calamity struck. Alien barbarians invaded the southern regions of the kingdom and built ugly castles from where they sallied forth, pillaging the surrounding countryside making life unbearable for the people. The young queen didn't know what to do as the invaders drained the lifeblood of her country causing more and more pain and the people lost their spirit.

As the months and years passed the invaders entrenched themselves deeper and deeper and the queen grew more desperate.

One day, an old warrior rode up to her palace and begged an audience. The queen bade him welcome and asked him what he wanted.

"You are a good queen beset by troubles," he said. "And I am here to help you. The troubles come about because, unlike your father, who I knew as a young man, you are not skilled in the arts of war."

"Then what must I do to rid my country of these evil parasites?" the queen asked.

"It is not difficult," said the old warrior. "With your permission, I can do it on your behalf using the tried and tested techniques of siege warfare. But you must give me command of your people to do it."

The queen felt she had nothing to lose and the old warrior set about mobilising her people and turning them into armies, one for each castle. He showed each army how to surround the barbarian castles – lay siege to them – and stressed how important it was that the occupants were prevented from getting any sustenance or nutriment from the surrounding countryside.

"You will soon see," said the old warrior, "that the enemy will either die off in the castles or retreat from whence they came."

And so it was. Soon the land was cleared of the invaders and their ugly castles quickly decayed or were destroyed. Peace and prosperity returned to the kingdom.

The queen thanked the old warrior and rewarded him well and he settled nearby in case she ever needed him again.

The story is clearly a metaphor for the client's problem and for the solution (her immune system needed to "mobilise" itself for a big effort and "lay siege" to the verrucas). She had no conscious recollection of the story after coming out of trance.[46]

Not only does the pattern-matching concept open up an understanding of how the placebo effect works but also, as in the above example, it explains why its conscious use as a psychotherapeutic procedure is often so effective.

Nocebo counselling

Once one understands the APET model it is easy to see why some counselling is ineffective or harmful. Counsellors are often trained to encourage emotionally arousing introspection in their clients about what might be 'causing' their problems. The emotional arousal this produces locks the client's attention on negative patterns of thought and behaviour. This leads, almost inevitably, to a period of negative rumination and the cycle of depression can set in. The process, however unintentional, can, therefore, accurately be characterised as nocebo therapy.

When counsellors encourage people to remember, and get emotional about, negative life experiences – bringing to the fore destructive patterns – they are actually going against nature's inclination to promote survival, health and wellbeing. And that's why some people say they go to see their counsellor feeling miserable and come out feeling suicidal. The essence of good therapy, on the other hand, is placebo therapy – focusing clients' attention on problem solving and solutions.

Metaphor, storytelling and learning

As the brain is fundamentally concerned with matching metaphorical patterns, it follows that this is the most wonderful natural tool for learning. Learning is a process of refining patterns of perception built upon a foundation of both instinctive patterns and learned patterns. All learning is an extension of existing patterns in the student. We are referring here not to learning facts by rote, in effect just storing up a series of bits of information, but to real learning – interacting more effectively with the environment, and developing through experience the ability to discriminate and discern a greater subtlety of the patterns therein and how they connect up with our own inner perceptions.

The way creative breakthroughs are made in science well illustrates this. The breakthrough 'ah hah' experience comes when scientists recognise that a pattern which works in one area of reality can also be applied in another. They take a pattern that explains one phenomenon and use it as a metaphor to explain what is going on in a different phenomenon.

One of the most famous metaphorical insights led to Kekule's discovery of the structure of the benzene ring: one of the most important discoveries in the history of chemistry. He had been trying for years to solve the problem of the molecular structure of benzene. Then one afternoon, as he was puzzling over the problem, he began to doze. He saw atoms gambolling before his eyes. Then he saw larger structures in long rows, twisting and entwining in a snakelike motion, until they looked just like snakes. One of the 'snakes' proceeded to seize its own tail. He awoke with a jolt to realise that the structure of benzene must be a closed ring – a solution suggested to him by the image of the snake swallowing its own tail.

Conveying new, desired patterns in a metaphor or story is perhaps the most effective way of all to refine patterns (although there are other effective methods, such as modelling desired behaviours). Erickson, whom many regard as the most significant clinician and psychotherapist of the twentieth century, was a master storyteller who put this skill to good effect in his work.[47] Often the teachers who most influence pupils' education are those who use anecdotes and stories to make their lessons come alive. In a counselling training context, we ourselves use stories and case histories to illustrate our theoretical principles in order to bring those principles to life. All good communicators use stories for that reason.

If clients are missing some piece of the jigsaw puzzle of life we could offer them a story about another client with a similar problem which shows how *their* behaviour changed, and thus convey the desired new pattern in an indirect way, or we could tell an appropriate traditional story. The world's stories, oral and written, contain a fantastic cornucopia of wonderful patterns which chart the possibilities of understanding ourselves more profoundly and help us engage with the world more fruitfully.

Our colleague Pat Williams, a founder-director of the former College of Storytellers, described how she helped somebody who was struggling with an addiction by telling them the ancient Greek myth about Odysseus who, on his way home to Greece after the battle of Troy, had to pass the island of the sirens. He had been told by the enchantress Circe that all sailors who passed that island were lured to their death on the rocks if they heard the sirens' song. But she had also told him a way to hear the sirens' magical music and survive. She told him to order his sailors to put softened beeswax in their ears, to stop them hearing the singing, and then have them tie him fast to the mast, giving them instructions that, no matter how much he urged or pleaded with them to turn the boat towards the island, they should merely bind him faster and continue on their course, past the island. This was done. When Odysseus heard the sirens' song, he wanted with every cell of his body to go to the island but, because he had forewarned his crew, they ignored his signals to change direction, bound him even more tightly to the mast, and eventually they passed the island. Odysseus was released by the crew, enormously grateful that he had been enabled to survive – and that he had escaped being dragged to his doom.

This powerful metaphorical template, with all its allusions and implications, can be used to show how a drug or addictive experience may be extremely seductive and yet ultimately is destructive. The story also metaphorically sets in place a template for how people can reorganise their internal resources to fight it.

This form of learning can be used if appropriate in conjunction with cognitive behavioural approaches to increase the chances of a successful outcome.

To recap, to help educate clients who are stuck we have to help them understand what is blocking them from getting their needs met. This is done through refining their patterns of perception, helping incorporate these patterns into their own perceptual apparatus and creating a more healthy, outward focus on life. If those patterns are not already active, the job of the counsellor is to help draw them forth, thus providing a stronger and more accurate lens through which the client can perceive reality. Using metaphor is one of the most powerful ways this can be done.

This whole process can be greatly speeded up by using nature's own tool for accelerated learning. This is the state of consciousness characterised by REM sleep, in which, as described in Part I, in the foetus and early months of life, nature lays down the instinctive templates that will later seek out their completion in the environment.[48]

We now know that we can directly access that same cortical organisation through guided imagery. (This state, when entered deeply, is analogous to that of REM sleep.) People can be put into trance by replicating any part of the pattern by which nature triggers the REM state, such as muscle relaxation, inducing rapid eye movements, (as in the 'focus your eyes on my swinging watch' technique and as used in Eye Movement Desensitisation and Reprocessing, [EMDR]), inducing hemispherical switching to the right neocortex by visualisation (a necessary stage of pre-sleep) or by firing off the brain's orientation response (as when a stage hypnotist suddenly pushes down on his subject's shoulder and gives the instruction "Sleep!"). The orientation response focuses attention and is firing continually during dreaming.[49]

The brain absorbs new ideas and information best when in a receptive, open, uncritical trance state. Once patterns have been absorbed and understood, they can be looked at consciously and 'checked out'. In counselling, when we relax people and focus their attention, we have access to some degree to their REM state in which the brain is at its most receptive and able to absorb information uncritically. This is, therefore, the ideal time to offer stories and metaphors to clients' unconscious minds to help them transform their perceptions.

The bigger pattern

Understanding the importance of pattern matching, metaphor and story is fundamental to making teaching more effective and our children more able to develop their full potential in life. Down the ages all good teachers have been great storytellers, but only now do we have a physiological understanding of why it is necessary for them to be so. Research by Dr Robert Ornstein and others shows that, when people are listening to stories, their right hemisphere is very actively engaged in the process. Our left neocortex processes facts and factual information, whereas the right neocortex seems to be involved in creating and revising the 'context' – the bigger pattern – through which facts make sense.[50]

In our technological civilisation we are flooded with factual information from a myriad of sources. But facts on their own don't make us wise. And an excess of facts just raises our stress levels. What makes us wise is fitting facts into a meaningful context, and that is the job of the right neocortex. We, therefore, firmly believe that children need an education that involves history and stories – the patterns that give context and make learning a real experience. It has long been known that children and adults exposed to 'classical' stories (brimming with rich psychological templates) become more flexible in their thought processes, more creative and more intelligent as adults. "Many traditional tales have a surface meaning (perhaps just a socially uplifting one) and a secondary, inner significance, which is rarely glimpsed consciously, but which nevertheless acts powerfully upon our minds. Perhaps, above all, the tale fulfils the function not of escape but of hope. The suspending of ordinary constraints helps people to reclaim optimism and to fuel the imagination with energy for the attainment of goals: whether moral or material."[51]

The quality of stories is important. Our whole culture is saturated with stories – television soap operas, newspapers, magazines, films, plays and popular songs all contain stories about what's going on in people's lives, fictional or otherwise. Our brains crave stories and metaphors. Once a story starts we have to hear it through; the pattern has to be completed. But the stories our brains receive are not just entertainment. They can have a creative or destructive impact on how we understand life and live our lives.

Some metaphors in our culture come from ideas put forward by scientists and spread through the media and educational institutions to the wider population. These can have a powerful effect – creative or destructive. The view that evolution is the story of 'the survival of the fittest', for example, was used by racial supremacists to justify exploitative colonial policies. This evolutionary theory is only a story, not an actual explanation based on facts.

The 'selfish gene' theory is another attempt to supply a metaphor to explain certain biological processes – one that has taken on a devastating life of its own maintaining the forces of pessimism and hopelessness.[52] What the metaphor says to our culture is that 'life is meaningless'. It can be seen as a cultural form of nocebo. Whilst few serious scientists question evolution, the over-emphasis on the selfish gene idea neglects the co-operative principle found throughout nature for furthering survival. This is evidenced between members of the same species and also in symbiotic relationships between different species, and in the huge variety of subtle feedback processes that maintain life in the biosphere.

There is no doubt that stories are powerful. One reason they can have a *positive* effect in influencing behaviour is that, when we give them attention, we actively engage the imaginative side of the mind and go into trance. We open up the part of the brain that can programme in new templates. When children hear a story, the pattern is absorbed into their unconscious minds where it will remain available, awaiting opportunities to interpret and unfold more of reality, until the pattern is completed.

Stories contain the wisdom of the species, because knowledge is metaphorically expressed through them and transmitted orally down the generations.

To demonstrate the levels of meaning and the values that can be extracted from such a story we can look at one which adults could easily dismiss as trivial – the story of the Ugly Duckling.

> ON A FARM a little bird is raised by a duck but feels itself to be very different from all the other ducklings who keep mocking it for being big and ugly. In due course, the ugly duckling becomes so unhappy it decides to run away, leaves the farm and goes in search of his destiny. But every animal it meets laughs at him for being so ugly and he learns that he can ignore them and not get upset by their stupidity. Eventually he finds a little pond where, despite feeling isolated and lonely, he learns to look after himself and survive through the long, cold winter.
>
> As the months pass by, changes happen within him, although he is unaware of this. One day, in early spring, the pond is still and calm, and in the water he sees the reflection of a line of beautiful swans flying high overhead. He wishes with all his heart that he could somehow be with them. The swans call down saying: "Why

don't you join us?" And he said: "How can I, an ugly duckling, fly with beautiful birds like you?" And the swans laugh and say, "But look at your reflection," and the duckling looks at his own reflection in the still pool and realises that he has transformed into a swan. The former ugly duckling is able to join the swans as an equal on their journey.

All children resonate with that story because, at some time, every child feels isolated from their fellows – an outsider who doesn't fit in. There *are* times in life when we feel rejected, when we have to go it alone, when we have got to find the courage to last the course, when our emotional needs are not being properly met. But the template in the story contains more than that. It shows us that, if we approach those times with courage, changes will automatically occur. We can learn from the very deprivations that seem so problematical and, if we persevere and seek out an appropriate environment, our talents and potential can blossom. The story holds out the optimistic prospect that the individual, and perhaps the human species, has somewhere to go; that there is a destiny awaiting us, if we have the courage to seek it, to stretch ourselves and sustain our spirit during troubled times.

Further subtleties include the profound truth, *that we can only see clearly when we are calm*. If the water on the pond had been disturbed the ugly duckling would not have been able to see what he was like. In other words, children hearing this story are given the template that they need to be in a calm emotional state before they can accurately perceive what they actually are.

At an even deeper level, we might draw out the idea that the emotional brain is like an ugly duckling, but, if we are willing to retrain our responses and cultivate and refine our perceptions, we can become more intelligent and raise ourselves up. It's only, as it were, by escaping the world of the ugly duckling that the true potential of the individual can emerge. And the price that has to be paid is that we may have to go against some of the prevailing orthodoxies within society and tread a lonely path for a while.

The patterns in such a rich story stay with us all, like a protective talisman, for the rest of our lives.

A therapeutic metaphor provides a map for the patient, showing them where they are at and what resources they need, and where they can go. It gives them information in a non-threatening way. We all need a map for any endeavour we are about to undertake. We need a sense of form and structure to what we are attempting to achieve. It is surprising, however, how many therapists we meet go into a therapy session *without* a sense of structure, without a 'road map' of what a good therapy session should entail. They may have great ideas and tremendous therapeutic techniques but, unless they know how to apply them at the right time, the results can be as disastrous as taking a wrong turning on a mountain track in the dark.

There is a form, a shape, to a good therapy session – just like a musical composition. It begins with rapport building – the counsellor entering the patient's model of reality. This is done by listening to the patient's story in an empathetic and sympathetic way, and every so often summarising back to the patient our understanding of what we have been told. This is the skill that Carl Rogers called active listening. A better term is 'reflective' listening because you are allowing patients to see themselves *reflected* in your responses to them and, in that reflection, you can begin to reframe their situation slightly. Thus therapy can begin straight away without disrupting the necessary initial unloading of emotion and information. For example, if a woman says in the course of explaining why she has come to therapy, "I am so lonely since I moved here; I have no friends", a good counsellor would reflect back by gently saying, "So you feel sad and lonely and haven't discovered how to make friends in the area yet." (The crucial word is 'yet'.) This is known as a reflective reframe. It accurately reflects back to the patient that you understand how she is feeling but also builds in hope with a reframe that implies things will change for her soon.

This is the first step in a therapy session and, having established rapport, and whilst establishing it, we gather information that is relevant to her therapy. We need to know, for example, where and when the problem occurs, who else is involved, when the problem doesn't occur and so on. We need accurate information in order to build up our understanding about the needs in her life that are not being met, or to see if she is misusing her imagination (worrying) or has been conditioned in an inappropriate way that is stopping her from moving on. As this information is gathered rapport has to be maintained.

The next step is to establish clear goals and make sure both therapist and patient are clear about them. Without goals, therapy can go on forever. The goals, of course, have to be specific and relate to the client's needs because, when their needs are met, the problem will be solved in most cases. The goals may be such things as learning certain social skills and practising them on predetermined occasions, or to take exercise, or learn how to reduce stress levels before going for a job interview. If something is worrying someone, excessively making them depressed and affecting their relationships, then the goal is to lift the depression so that they can connect better to their family, friends and colleagues.

Goals must not be couched in nominalisations. If a patient says, "I just want to be happy", the therapist needs to ask, "What exactly would make you happy? How would you know you were happy?" Clear goals are necessary because the brain needs specific patterns to work upon. Once it has a pattern, it can then endeavour to match that pattern up in the outside world. Our job as therapists is to summon up a new template in the client's imagination that will make this possible.

Goals give a positive focus to the therapy and allow the measurement of progress week by week.

The next step is to work out how to get the client to reach that goal. This is called accessing a strategy. The strategy has to be realistic, one that the counsellor and patient can agree is likely to help them achieve their goal. It would involve a combination of, or all, the elements delineated in the APET model.

During information gathering we would also be accessing resources. That is, finding out what people are good at, what they have achieved in their life, their successes, their qualities, such as a sense of humour, or determination, or examples of when they have been creative. Counsellors need to know about times in clients' lives when they felt good about themselves.

Finally, having developed strategies and accessed resources, we need to talk the patient through situations they need to change to reach their goals. This is called the rehearsal stage and is best done with guided imagery, metaphorical reframes and by helping them vividly conjure up images of themselves coping with their life in more helpful ways and feeling good. By making these patterns vivid, people become compelled to match them up in reality and, providing the goals have been realistic, there is a reasonable chance that they will make changes in the real world. They have the template activated in their mind. They are focused on the 'map' they need to make changes.

This structure is easily remembered by the acronym RIGAAR (**R**apport building, **I**nformation gathering, **G**oal setting, **A**greeing a strategy, **A**ccessing resources, **R**ehearsal).

Of course no one can learn how to do therapy from a book like this – learning only happens in action, when skills are demonstrated and then practised by the student.

To summarise: the APET model is at the heart of human givens therapy. The letters stand for specific processes through which the mind/body system works. These processes are currently being explored by neuroscience and psychology in many direct ways and are not dependent on ideologies.

The **A** is for an activating agent: a stimulus from the environment. The **P** is for the pattern-matching part of the mind, which in turn gives rise to an emotion, **E**, which can produce thoughts, **T**.

But these letters also contain a powerful metaphor that enriches the idea. The first three spell 'ape' and that gives us the idea of an ape telling us what to do.

APE T

So we have this ancient emotional mind that can order us about, and control us: a mixture of primitive instincts and conditioned responses, greeds and selfish desires that, when roused, can cut us off from the richer and more subtle templates, located in the higher cortex and frontal lobes, through which we can experience more of reality than an ape can.

On the other hand, if we emphasise the letters slightly differently, we have 'a pet'.

A PET

As we know, a pet is an animal that was originally wild, but its nature has been constrained – domesticated to serve the needs of a master. This is a co-operative relationship. The pet serves the needs of the master and, in return, the master takes care of the needs of the pet. That is the civilising process we humans have to go through – domesticating the emotional brain, the wild, instinctive creature within us.

So, whilst the individual letters symbolise the way the brain processes information, they also describe the essence of the therapeutic process – helping people to 'master' the mind/body system, particularly the more instinctive, emotional parts of it, and fulfil our human needs and potential.

CHAPTER TEN

A very human vulnerability – depression (and how to lift it)

WITHOUT motivation human beings cannot find meaning in what they do and are left wandering feebly in the joyless grey limbo between a healthy, fulfilling life and insanity.

Why, in ever increasing numbers, are so many people in the grip of this debilitating mental state – one characterised by lack of meaning and motivation, coupled with total exhaustion? Until recently, this has been one of the most perplexing questions in psychology but the new understanding about the role of the REM state that we set out in the first part of this book provides the answer.

Depression is now the number one psychological disorder presenting in the Western world.[1] (In the UK, the *NHS National Service Framework for Mental Health* states that "half of all women and a quarter of all men will be affected by depression at some period during their lives".) Epidemiological studies show that the rate of increase in depression has grown in *all* age groups. It is growing fastest in young people.[2] And suicide rates have increased in all countries, especially among the young.[3] The population born since 1945 has seen depression increase by a factor of nearly ten since their grandparents' time.[4] And even this rate is accelerating. In just four years between 1994 and 1998 the number of people seeking help from their GPs for depression in the UK rose from four million to nine million (although some of this increase may have been due to the de-stigmatising of the condition in the media, encouraging more people to come forward for help).[5]

Furthermore, as countries become westernised, their rates of depression increase. The World Health Organisation (WHO), in its report *The global burden of disease*, estimates that depression will be second only to ischaemic heart disease as a cause of injury and disease worldwide by the year 2020.[6]

Depression is so serious because it is a *strong* emotion. Sustained states of high emotional arousal stop affected individuals from being capable of reflecting on what is really happening to them, seeing their problems in context and setting about solving them creatively. In effect, depression acts as a brake on the development, both of individuals and, when very many people are depressed, of the wider society.

The use of the word 'arousal' may seem odd when linked with depression, but, even though depressed people often look 'flat' and inactive, their blood levels of the stress hormone cortisol are much higher than normal.[7]

Because women are, on average, more in tune with and responsive to their emotional life, higher rates of depression in women are to be expected. And this is what we find. Each year between 2.3 per cent and 3.2 per cent of men are diagnosed as depressed and 4.5–9.3 per cent of women. Thus the rate of depression in women is two to three times higher. This is not simply due to differential reporting but to the different biological, sociological and psychological pressures on women.[8]

If we look at the rate of lifetime occurrences of depression, the same pattern holds. The chance of developing a major depression is one in ten in men and one in four in women. In addition, women on average take 50 per cent longer to recover spontaneously from depression.[9]

As we've seen, all emotions – anger, hate, fear, love, sexual desire and greed (in all its forms) hypnotically lock us into a confined viewpoint – which we refer to as focusing attention.[10] So, a person in the grip of *any* powerful emotion can be said to be locked in an emotionally driven trance state. Depression is no exception.[11]

Our main emotional responses arising from the limbic system (often known as the emotional brain, although the chemicals of emotion pervade all parts of the brain) are connected to the basic survival instincts we share with every other mammal. And it is because they are concerned with survival that they are so powerful and so easily override our reasoning mind, the brain's higher cortex, which, in evolutionary terms, is a comparatively recent development. This means that we must always be prepared for an emotional hijack when the limbic system believes its survival is threatened or its needs are not being met.[12]

A curious aspect of this is that the strong emotions that focus our attention and lock us into a confined, trancelike, viewpoint by focusing our attention, can just as easily be stimulated by the misuse of our imagination as by real events. This is what happens in anxiety, when people worry too much and upset themselves by imagining what might go wrong in some situation, or when a person gets angry by reliving in their mind some injustice they once suffered. Sexual daydreaming also raises arousal levels. The importance of all this for depression will become clear shortly.

Like all emotions, depression is a form of communication conveying a two-way message: outwards, to the people around the emotional person, and inwards, to the individual concerned. Depression's message is, "Something is seriously wrong, I am stuck, I am blocked in my life. I don't know where to go from here."

For most of our existence human beings lived in small, cohesive tribal groups, so when somebody gave out that message, it was readily identified. Living with a depressed person is difficult and everyone knew intuitively that they had to work hard to protect themselves from being sucked into the depressed person's deeply pessimistic and barren world view, devoid of all the stimuli that make life interesting and pleasurable. The group would understand how and why the person was blocked *and be able to do something about it.*

In healthy, traditional, so-called primitive, non-westernised societies – and a few still survive – major clinical depression is almost unknown. Such people live in cohesive communities where they are kept busy with meaningful activity and where practical problems are dealt with quickly. As we have seen, studies of traditional New Guinea tribes and the Amish community (which still tries to live a seventeenth century lifestyle), show that if somebody suffers a crisis, everyone rallies round to help them straight away. There is real community support for individuals, balanced by an understanding that the individual has a responsibility to the community.[13] But depression always increases in third world countries when rising uncertainty caused by political violence, population increase, intense urbanisation, unemployment, food shortages, disease etc., makes them unstable.[14]

Our modern technological society, despite the benefits it brings, is an increasingly complex and stressful culture where more and more people find it difficult to get their emotional needs met. Today a person can send out an emotional message for months, or even years, and nobody around them may actually notice or, if they do, may lack the wisdom to do anything about it.

So, what is different about modern living that might account for the big increase in depression? Here are some suggestions.

Technology and consumerism: In technologically advanced societies, the loosening of social structures has increased the pattern of family and community breakdown. Modern communications technology, in the service of industries that require people endlessly to buy things they don't really need, plays a big role in this. So the media, in a consumerist society, increasingly emphasise the acquisition of material goods and place more emphasis on satisfying the selfish wants and desires of 'me', with a decreasing lack of commitment to other people and wider social responsibilities. This has encouraged much more obsessional preoccupation with the self, with which depression is linked.

It is normal for toddlers to scream "I want it now!" As far as they are concerned they are at the centre of the universe and delayed gratification is not an option. But, in healthy families, as children grow, they are taught to have a more realistic expectation of how things happen. They learn that people have to wait their turn, that success in life is earned, that wants are not the same as needs, that the needs of others should be considered and that they themselves are *not* the centre of the universe. But, in this consumerist age, it suits many vested interests to keep as much of the population as possible behaving like selfish four-year-olds by undermining more healthy developmental processes. Political parties now retain power by manipulating their messages according to the short-term whims of 'focus groups', supposedly sample representatives of the public, instead of by inspiring people with long-term policies and plans that might improve and strengthen society. Politics is now largely reduced to a specialisation of the public relations industry.[15]

"Take the waiting out of wanting" (the same thought that drives psychopaths) was the famous advertising slogan used to launch credit cards in the UK. Television programmes and the advertisements that intersperse them, coupled with corresponding peer group pressure, raise expectations in the population. These expectations stimulate in many a desire for the 'good' life NOW, as if it were a right, undermining the necessity for learning, work and patience in due proportion.

The media also imbue people with simplistic ideas about how we should educate children, what we should wear, how much attention we should receive, what love is and what we should enjoy and be moved by. Because most people are unable to avoid the influences of the entertainment and advertising industries, which constantly assail us, cleverly stimulating our greed for their own profit, there is constant manipulation of the way we live our lives. In other words, we have largely become a new peasantry, a vast international community of peasants. (A peasantry is not, as many might think, impoverished people ruled by rich ones. It is a population that is 'owned', whose beliefs are engineered by propaganda, and whose activities and diversions are largely provided for other people's gain. Throughout history, there have always been plenty of comparatively rich peasants.)

Time pressures: While technology can clearly remove pressures, it can also create new ones. Cars are wonderful inventions, for example, allowing us to keep dry and comfortable as we move all over the land. But spending time stuck in traffic jams is not so wonderful! Since the invention of the mechanical clock we have increasingly segmented days into hours and minutes, and driven ourselves by this artificial measurement. The consequence is that we pack more into the day and organise the way we co-operate with one another more efficiently. This brilliant innovation made industrialisation and modern, organised society possible, but it has also brought many subtle problems with it, not least an increase in time-related stress. It tends to leave, for example, no time for spontaneous relaxation. We, the new peasantry, are now 'sold' leisure packages.

This has more serious consequences than might at first be apparent. When we are driven by the clock we become more intolerant of people who work in a more relaxed timeframe. We also tend to pay less attention to, or ignore altogether, our own, highly evolved and infinitely subtle internal biological clocks – our natural ultradian rhythms.[16] For example, it is quite normal to 'switch off' for 20 minutes every hour and a half as the brain swaps hemispherical dominance from left to right in order to process information, lay down long-term memories and make internal mental and physical repairs. Indeed, we are designed to do this and, whenever we override our natural need for a 20 minute break every 90 minutes or so, it always involves the production of stress hormones to keep us alert. If we continually and inappropriately override this need for regular relaxation, as many do in the modern, target-focused workplace, we become highly stressed, mentally unstable and, eventually, physically ill.[17]

Many people now find it difficult to wind down without the aid of TV, music, drugs or alcohol to change their mood. The ubiquitous presence of TV and computers in homes around the world has many deleterious effects. Over time, when TV is introduced into a community, "both adults and children become less creative in problem solving, less able to persevere at tasks, and less tolerant of unstructured time".[18] Heavy users of TV and computer games report feeling significantly more anxious and less happy than light users. This is because these media employ modern techniques such as cuts, edits, zooming in and panning out, as well as sudden sounds and sudden images, which have the effect of continually alerting the orientation response, and thus keeping attention on the screen.[19] The activity becomes addictive because, once aroused, the pattern of arousal has to be completed – hence the success of soap operas. Increasingly too, watching television and playing computer games restricts the amount of time children spend talking among themselves and with their parents – which steadily retards the development of their social skills.

Another time-related stressor is our heightened expectation for instant solutions to every problem. Enormous amounts of information are now available cheaply and easily through computers and the internet. We are bombarded with news from around the world. 'Crisis' is the watchword. It can seem as though every natural catastrophe, every man-made disaster and cruelty, every political, scientific and social ethical dilemma is paraded before us by news media. But there is no corresponding mental and emotional education in how to discriminate the usefulness and meaning of this information.

There are no solutions to disasters once they have happened. Wars are not tidy problems with neat resolutions. Corruption and injustice require more than a wish that the world were not so. Expectations are seldom realised and when we allow expectations to rage like a fever it is deeply frustrating for people. That life is full of surprises is one of the three certainties. (The other two, as we all know, are death and taxes.)

Expectation and disappointment go hand in hand. We are swept along first by expectation – then by disappointment or surprise. And, once in the disappointed or surprised stage, we quickly forget our earlier expectation. We are not masters of ourselves when swept along like this and, although, being human, expectation and disappointment will always be with us, they are major handicaps that stop us from seeing situations clearly. Hence the growth in cynicism which fuels the creeping feeling that life has no purpose.

Uncertainty: Consider for a moment some of the changes in workplace practices that unsettle us. There is a widely perceived sense of uncertainty and injustice in the world about job stability, which has been generated by technological development and the ease with which capital investment in industry and commerce can move around the world, ruthlessly seeking a better deal. This is often cited as a cause of stress and depression. Certainly, short-term employment contracts have become the norm in professions where one used to consider one could 'have a job for life'. Increasingly, too, redundancy and the lesser likelihood of getting another job, particularly after the age of 40, lowers self-esteem. So too does the growing realisation that the large corporations are more corrupt and unstable than we used to believe, and that the pension fund system that depends on them is proving to be inadequate for retirement needs, increasing financial difficulties and debt. All this creates mental and physical burdens that overwhelm many, as does our increasing taste for unreasonable litigation, where people are encouraged to sue for every minor misfortune or accident, forcing the law to apportion blame and put a price on it. Control over how we work and live is slipping from our grasp – yet a sense of being in control is essential for mental stability and physical health.[20]

However, there is a paradox here. Although we have a need to feel in control, no human being has *ever* known what lies around the corner. We all, in fact, live a transient life whilst pretending that life is permanent. Consequently, being prepared for change is a positive attribute that minimises the risk of suffering stress reactions, anxiety, ill-health and worse when the inevitable changes happen.

Defeatism: A common but largely invisible thread running through current cultures is that we impart to our children, along with all the positive praise and problem-solving skills we like to think we are teaching them, a strong trait of defeatism and negativity. Children quickly emulate their parents' rationalisations for why certain tasks are not attempted; they are 'too tired', or doing such-and-such is not 'worthwhile', or, 'there's no point', or, 'some other day'. This unspoken conditioning is passed on, like some sort of contact disease, alongside other, more positive manifestations of belief and action. The dangers inherent in this have not been widely realised and so nothing is done about it.

Mobility: Travel has never been easier, which in many ways is a huge plus, but we are paying dearly for opening up the world with modern transport. One outcome, which relates directly to depression, is the ease with which it is now possible to move away from our geographical roots and work and live elsewhere. (To be adaptable enough to do this is, of course, a sign of maturity. But many people are not sufficiently mature and mentally stable enough to make the necessary adjustments.) This has contributed to the breakdown of close extended family support in times of trouble.

Relationship breakdown: Research shows that children can be damaged more by the strife leading up to divorce and its subsequent effects than by the death of a parent.[21] For instance, in the UK, children of middle-class parents who were born in 1958 and whose parents divorced before they were 16 were twice as likely to leave school without any qualifications as those whose parents remained married. They showed more behaviour problems in school, were more likely to be unhappy and worried, and were behind their schoolmates at reading and arithmetic. They were also much less likely to go to university or to be in a job when they were 23 years of age. They were four times more likely to live in subsidised social housing and were much more likely to smoke than were other middle-class young adults whose parents had not split up. They were on average also less emotionally stable, left home earlier and themselves divorced or separated more frequently later in life.[22] Such findings are significant because of the rapid increase in broken families we are seeing nowadays, throughout society.

On average, life expectancy is higher, and physical and mental health are much better for mothers, fathers and children in two-parent families. An enormous body of evidence shows that children from stable married families grow up with fewer behavioural and emotional problems, are better socialised and less likely to drift into drugs and criminal behaviour than those who come from one-parent or divorced families. They also appear to make better parents themselves.[23,24,25,26] Despite all the advantages of having both parents, single-parent families are now common, creating a tremendous extra burden on the wider community which has to deal with the social, educational, physical and mental health problems that result.

These are just some of the stressors peculiar to the modern world. But we must not forget that hardship, accident, famine, war and disease have been the common lot of human beings since we appeared on the planet and the majority of people adapt and cope fairly well, whatever the range of pressures. (Many children brought up by a single parent, for example, do well enough, as we know.) This is not too surprising since we have evolved to be adaptable. Nevertheless, whilst the majority cope, even thrive, many do not. The increasing rate of technological and social change is creating a more psychologically disturbed population and the rapid rise in anxiety disorders, depression, addictions and antisocial behaviour illustrates, reflects and compounds this trend.

Depression is not a genetic illness

Because of the massive medicalisation of depression we need to spend a little time showing why depression is not, in fact, a biological disease. The marked increase in the rate of depression revealed in epidemiological studies itself shows that depression cannot be a biological disease carried in our genes. Genes do not change that quickly. Despite the explosion in genetic research and gene mapping, and high hopes of finding a gene for everything, no 'depression gene' has been found, because genes don't work that way.[27,28]

Over the last three decades conclusive evidence has mounted to show that the vast majority of depressions are learned, created by the way we interact with our environment.[29] We know that depression is not an event-driven phenomenon because the majority of people exposed to adverse life circumstances do not develop it. Those who react to events in their lives by getting depressed do so because that is how they have learned to respond to adverse life experiences.

Further support for the environmental learned view of depression comes from the evidence that depression responds well, and often very quickly, to psychotherapeutic interventions that concentrate on stopping negative introspection and helping people get their emotional needs met.[30] Such interventions also greatly reduce the rate of relapse compared to drug treatments based on the biological model. They work precisely because of the human brain's ability to be conditioned by experiences, and *reconditioned*. When depressed people are helped to adapt more effectively to the pressures and uncertainties of modern living by *learning* to respond to adverse life circumstances in better ways, they get better.

That there is a biological *component* to depression is undisputed, since all our emotions are expressed in the language of biochemistry. Also, depression affects our biology by, for example, impairing the proper functioning of our immune system. But the idea that depression is the result of a chemical imbalance in the brain, so disempowering and yet so fervently promoted by self-serving drug manufacturers, is wrong. Although this myth is still confidently told to patients by doctors saturated by drug company propaganda, it is now clear that changes in serotonin levels in the brains of depressed people are a *consequence* of depression, not the *cause* of it. Serotonin levels fluctuate constantly and are directly correlated with the effectiveness with which we all live our lives. Life-enhancing experiences raise serotonin levels at least as effectively as drugs, with no adverse side effects, and more instantaneously.

The criteria for a major depressive episode are well established[31] and treatment approaches have been extensively researched, resulting in clear treatment guidelines.[32] The types of psychological treatment that are effective in lifting depression are brief, short-term therapies that concentrate on problem solving, changing people's attributional style of thinking, focusing their attention away from their emotions and helping them get their needs met by, for example, helping them to improve their relationship skills.[33] The same research clearly shows that the least successful forms of psychotherapy are those operating from psychoanalytical and psychodynamic perspectives – so-called 'insight' counselling, and non-directive, person-centred counselling – all of which tend to encourage emotional introspection and thereby maintain and deepen depression. (The term 'insight' counselling is generally associated with the methods of various psychodynamic schools of therapy but, if they *were* providing insight, they would be more successful than they actually are. *True* insight is an important part of any therapy.[34])

It is also well established that antidepressants can lift the symptoms of clinical depression – completely in a third of those who take them and partially in another third – although they are not nearly as effective in preventing further episodes of depression as the right type of psychotherapy. Antidepressants don't work at all in a third of those who are prescribed them and for many people the side effects are more unpleasant than the depression, so they stop taking them. It takes between four and six weeks for the drugs to exert their maximum effect. There is, as yet, no widely accepted agreement as to why antidepressants sometimes work, although the placebo effect is known to play a part.[35]

Antidepressants like the modern SSRIs, of which Prozac is a member, are very powerful drugs that can cause dizziness, nausea, anxiety, facial and whole body tics, muscle spasms, parkinsonism (symptoms similar to those seen in Parkinson's disease), brain damage, sexual dysfunction, memory loss, neurotoxicity and debilitating withdrawal symptoms that are often mistaken for the original symptoms returning. There is also a direct link between suicide and violent behaviour and their use.[36] They should not be given to children because children's brains are still forming. (Human frontal lobe connections are not fully in place until a person is about 20 years old.[37]) And, because of the common toxic side effects, they should not be prescribed to older people who have any sign of brain deterioration.

St John's wort (Hypericum), the most widely prescribed treatment in Germany for depression, has been shown to be as effective as antidepressants and to have fewer side effects.[38,39] It has also been used to help people with sleep disorders[40] and the physical and mental effects of the menopause.[41] As with antidepressant drugs, until now it has not been known why it works.[42]

Most experts now recommend a combination of medicine and psychotherapy but, since the US treatment guidelines were published,[43] more and more studies show that medication is unnecessary if the depressed person receives *appropriate* help.[44]

Building on all the above information, and considering it from the human givens perspective, it is clear to us why depression occurs and takes the form it does; why some forms of therapy are more effective than others; and how therapists and counsellors can learn to apply the most effective treatment approach in each individual case.

The human givens approach to therapy looks at each person holistically, using an understanding of the psychobiological needs and resources that human beings have evolved over millions of years throughout their animal ancestry to cope with the environment.[45] We look for what is missing in patients' lives and work towards correcting this imbalance so that needs are met. We use a particular blend of the cognitive, behavioural and interpersonal approaches that are proven to be effective, plus other elements such as stimulating the imagination of patients using guided imagery. We also clearly distinguish *needs* from *wants* and build on individuals' inherent resources to add to, and thereby improve, their cognitive, emotional and behavioural skills base where necessary. Therapists and counsellors who learn to work in this way quickly get results that last with most of their patients.

As we have shown, one of the tools nature has given us is the dreaming process through which we metaphorically act out unresolved patterns of autonomic arousal each night so that they are not carried over from one day to the next. This new knowledge about why we dream is the key to understanding the psychobiology of why people can become depressed.

Dreaming and depression

The link between dreaming and depression became clear when we considered the following cluster of research findings in the light of Joe's discoveries about the function of dreams. When depressed people go to sleep, they enter REM sleep (dream sleep) more quickly, have more prolonged and physiologically more intense REM sleep. Although most depressed people sleep less than non-depressed people, they spend a far higher proportion of their overall sleep time dreaming. Depressed people dream excessively. It has been known for some time that, if dream sleep is prevented by waking a depressed patient every time they begin rapid eye movements (REM), severe depression lifts.[46] (Unfortunately the depressed state may return once the person resumes normal sleeping, or may even worsen because of extra compensatory REM sleep, so this is not a reliable treatment method.)

Antidepressant drugs reduce REM sleep.[47,48] So why should a reduction in REM sleep lead to a reduction in depression? The answer lies in the way the brain stimulates itself during REM sleep, a process that involves the PGO spike. As we explained in the chapter on dreams, the PGO spike is the orientation response that draws our attention to changes in the environment, startling changes such as a loud bang or sudden movement, or changes that arouse curiosity – anything that focuses our attention. It first evolved in mammals to activate the flight or fight response to potential danger and is the system which manages the body's responses to stress.

During REM sleep, and just before it starts, there is a massive firing of the orientation response. There has never been a satisfactory explanation for why the eyes dart about during REM sleep, and do so in the womb from about ten weeks after conception, but we suggest that there could be a simple reason: the eyes automatically scan the environment at speed, in response to the firing of the orientation response. The PGO spike is signalling, "something vitally important is happening now", and so the eyes keep on trying to look, darting about in all directions. However, when we are asleep there is no information coming in from the external world. The source of the arousal is internal – the unexpressed emotional expectations from the previous day, major or minor, which are still occupying space in the brain, trapped, as it were, in the autonomic nervous system. As we have shown, the act of dreaming, by metaphorically acting out those unresolved expectations, discharges those arousals and frees the brain to be ready for the concerns of the following day.

But what happens when the emotional arousal level is extreme, as in depressed and anxious people? Hundreds of studies have shown that the fight or flight stress response is hyperactive in such patients.[49] In other words, the morbid and prolonged introspection and self examination, which tends to characterise depressed people, leads to above normal levels of emotional arousal which then need to be discharged during their dreams. In fact, the pressure for emotional discharge caused by excessive emotionally arousing negative introspection is so great that the first REM period of the night occurs much earlier in depressed people, is more prolonged and shows an especially high rate of discharge. This amount of discharge not only reduces the level of arousal in the brain but also actually exhausts it, leaving the person more likely to lack motivation the next day. It is no wonder that so many depressed people say they wake up exhausted from a night's sleep.

In hundreds of interviews and therapy sessions, many of which we have filmed, depressed patients readily talk to us about waking up exhausted and finding it difficult to motivate themselves. The more severe the depression the more exhaustion they experience. As therapists we find talking to depressed patients about their sleep patterns is the quickest way to build rapport with them. They seem to instinctively recognise that we know something about what they are going through. Many of them report waking up early and being unable to get back to sleep, even though exhausted. Since the early hours of the morning are when we have our longest period of dreaming, we can surmise that this early morning awakening is the body's way of preventing any further discharge of arousal caused by excessive self-analysis. In other words, the brain is losing energy so fast it is trying to protect itself by waking early.

So depressed people are tired and lacking in energy when they wake up because their orientation response mechanism is over-worked. It has fired off so much during excessive dream sleep that it is exhausted. And, without this response effectively alerting them to what is happening around them, and enabling them to switch attention from one thing to another, they find it very difficult, and in severe cases impossible, to motivate themselves to do anything.

This explains the common complaint of depressed people: that they feel that 'everything is meaningless ... pointless ... not worth bothering about'. It is a given that, to feel well, fulfilled and mentally healthy, we need a sense of meaning and purpose in our lives. But depressed people no longer have the means to generate such a positive outlook because their attention-switching mechanism is exhausted, leaving them unable to refocus on the bigger picture. It is a closed circle. Although the orientation response gradually recovers as the day goes on, typically the depressed person begins to introspect on that feeling of emptiness, the tiredness, the lack of pleasure and joy or enthusiasm in their lives, and is driven into another intense period of dreaming the following night – piling misery on misery – and becoming even more depressed.

Depression, we are saying, is not a disease; it is a natural response to certain types of emotional introspection that result in excessive dreaming. What is more, there are clear therapeutic implications suggested by this new view of the causal sequence in depression.

The trigger factor for depression is always around emotional needs not being met. It may be some experience of loss: redundancy, failed relationship, divorce, death of a loved one, loss of health, loss of status or a financial setback. All situations where someone feels they have lost, or are losing, control over their lives. If the person tends to be of a pessimistic disposition, this will lead them to excessive negative emotional introspection about the loss, which in turn leads to an excess of emotional arousal discharge through the dream state. In a minority of cases, in a predisposed person, genetic influences may contribute to triggering an excess of negative introspections, though there is no conclusive evidence for this. (When depression runs in families it could simply be caused by conditioning. A defeatist, pessimistic world view is easily passed from one generation to the next, as is the more romantic 'soul in torment' view of depression so common among artistic types who indulge in psychoanalytic explorations of their condition.) But in either case research conclusively shows that the most long-lasting benefit derives from psychological interventions that alleviate the negative introspections, particularly ones that teach depressed people how to do this for themselves. Such interventions are more effective than antidepressants in reducing further episodes of depression.[50]

Why some people get depressed and others don't

So what exactly is a pessimistic disposition? Why do some people get locked into depression while others, with equal or more hardship in their lives, don't? It is, of course, natural from time to time to experience temporary sadness or depression when we feel overwhelmed by stressful events, and that we are losing control. But it is what happens next – how individuals continue to react – that is crucial in the long term. Worrying, deep grief or sadness, like any other form of emotional arousal, forces the brain back into primitive black and white modes of thinking and locks our attention. To the emotional brain everything is either good or bad, right or wrong, safe or dangerous, happy or sad, perfect or irretrievably imperfect. And, when emotional arousal is maintained, it prevents the higher cortex from using its highly evolved ability to tolerate ambiguity and take a wider perspective.

People who are not habitual black and white thinkers can usually 'snap' out of this arousal fairly quickly. However, people who tend towards analysing what has gone wrong in their lives, reviewing the past selectively (picking out the negative aspects), catastrophising every little setback, dreaming up future disasters or engaging in self-blame, tend to stay locked into the state of depression instead of rising above it. This explains something observed for some time – that depressed people habitually adopt a particular way of thinking to explain things that happen to and around them. This is known by cognitive psychologists as their 'attributional style'.[51]

We all have an inbuilt need to make sense of our world and explain to ourselves why things happen the way they do. The type of explanation we give ourselves – our attributional style – is critical and determines whether or not we will get depressed when bad things happen to us. Psychologists have determined three important types of attributional style:

- How *personally* we take events. (Do we tend to blame ourselves for *every* setback rather than considering other possible reasons for something going wrong? If a relationship breaks down, for example, is it always our fault?)

- How *pervasive* we view events to be. (If we lose a job do we think our whole life is ruined or do we view the damage as limited to a short period of time and consider the possibility that other career opportunities may open up?)

- How *permanent* we think an event is. (Do we think a setback will be short lived or go on for ever? If we don't get the house we have set our heart upon, for example, do we say, "Oh well, perhaps something else even better will turn up," or, "I will never be happy again as long as I live"?)

If we take things personally, interpret events as all pervasive or all encompassing and think setbacks last forever, we are candidates for depression. This is because these emotionally driven black and white thinking styles inevitably generate more emotion by repeatedly turning on the fight or flight response that makes us angry (fight) or anxious (flight). In other words, when people catastrophise the 'bad' things that happen to them, magnifying them so that the whole of their life is affected, they are either making themselves feel very hostile or frightening themselves.

What this means, of course, is that they have formed an inner template that says their future is full of pain and misery. They continually match that pattern to painful aspects of their present and past to validate their catastrophic view of their future. This leads to an excessive turning on of the fight or flight response which results in the 'all or nothing' reaction to life events found in all depressed people and explains why depressed people find it difficult to break the whole down into relevant component parts. When thinking is driven by the emotional brain it cannot see the infinite shades of grey between different viewpoints. That is why so many depressed people are perfectionists: if an event they anticipated didn't go totally as planned, for example, it was a disaster; if a relationship isn't perfect, it is terrible. This same tendency makes some depressed people prone to excessive jealousy.

Most things that happen in life have multiple causes. When we are more objective we can see the truth of this and we don't have to blame ourselves unreasonably when things go wrong. But depressed people, because of their emotional arousal, cannot think clearly. That is why they plump for the big, simple-minded, single cause to explain a setback. "Either I am to blame or somebody else is." They either get unreasonably angry with someone else for their difficulties or only ever see themselves as the cause of their difficulties, generating self-blame and low self-esteem. It has not been possible to explain, until now, why antidepressant medication can help relieve chronically hostile feelings. But obviously *any* prolonged emotionally arousing introspection – angry ruminations, worrying, fearful thoughts and feeling helpless as a result of PTSD – can lead to depression. (The background 'noise' of our pessimistic, consumerist society feeds into this personal misery.)

By contrast, healthy people are not driven by these emotional hijacks of the higher cortex. They know how to moderate the assessments that they make as circumstances change, whereas the black and white thinker will often make fixed judgements with lifelong implications. For example, a woman emotionally hurt when her partner left her might decide that she will never embark on a relationship again. She thinks *all* men are untrustworthy, "all men are bastards", so her human need for intimacy is not met and she withdraws into herself.

A person's subjective view of reality is known to be highly correlative with their parents' view of reality. As we've said, this doesn't mean that depression is a genetically transmitted disease; it simply means that we tend to model ourselves on our parents' emotional behaviour and mimic, at least in part, their way of envisioning what is going to happen. Personality research shows that genetics make a 50 per cent contribution to our personality. This means that 50 per cent of our personality is environmentally determined. Good therapy involves working with the relationship between both, helping people use genetic traits (for example, a tendency towards obsessive attention to detail) in a positive rather than a negative way, and helping people change the way they react to, and deal with, their environment and life circumstances.

Because people prone to depression tend to see the difficulties that arise in life as permanent, they become pessimists. It takes considerable and consistent effort on the part of others to resist such a view. A depressed person's cynical pessimism about everything can brainwash people they live or work with, particularly those who are similarly predisposed. As a consequence it can spread like a virus. Whole families become pessimistic and depressed.[52]

A frequently indulged pessimistic view of the future, is a major risk factor for depression. Most people who are clinically depressed don't even go to their GPs because their pessimism convinces them that their situation is hopeless. They may go only because somebody has nagged them into it. This means that, when they *do* go for counselling, it is terribly important that the pessimism – the hopelessness – is challenged in the first session. The whole session should never be given over to history-taking because the patient might not come back, or might even commit suicide, before the next appointment. It must be demonstrated to the patient in the first session that change is possible. This is summed up in the phrase coined by solution focused therapists: "Do something that makes a difference *today*".

Curiously, pessimism is not only a high risk factor for clinical depression; it is also a major risk factor for *all* kinds of illnesses later on in life. It is a bigger determinant, or predictor, of a shortened life-span than any other.[53]

In the treatment of depression we can again see why an important part of any therapist's skill is the ability to calm people's emotions down.[54] Only when they are no longer aroused by the emotion of depression can a patient begin to reason, analyse or imagine different scenarios sufficiently well to perceive that life is complex, that there are multiple reasons for why things happen and that their excessive self-blame, or anger at others, is unrealistic.

People who don't get depressed can see different perspectives to situations – the shades of grey between the extremes of emotionally driven black and white thinking. They have the ability to limit the damage done by a particular negative experience so that they can concentrate on the good parts of their life. They might think, for example, "It's terrible that I've lost this relationship, but other parts of my life are working. I've got a good job. I have a loving family to support me. And, of course, I'm free to get into another relationship again in the future." Or they might say, "It was rotten luck that I had abusive parents – but I didn't choose the bed I was born in. I can see that other parents make a much better job of it than mine did and I'm going to use my experience to do better by *my* children."

Mentally healthy people are flexible thinkers who limit the damage of a setback by *not* globalising. They recognise what is within their control and what is not. They don't get sucked into the illusion that they have *total* control in any situation, nor that they have none at all. This is the opposite of what depressed people do.

When pessimists have a setback, they simplify it by dramatically exaggerating the hopelessness of the situation and the number of diffi-culties they have – catastrophic thinking. They often blame themselves when bad things happen and worry. They emotionally introspect and, consequently, because of the excessive dreaming this causes, feel tired when they wake up and so begin progressively to eliminate all sources of pleasurable stimulation from their lives. Their exhausted state soon means that it becomes too much of an effort for them to go out and socialise, to exercise, make love, keep up their hobbies and interests or celebrate anything. Every time they back out of doing something pleasurable they feel a brief sense of relief and comfort, but never connect this to the fact that a couple of hours later they are even more depressed. And it is the progressive elimination of positive stimulation from their lives that drops them deeper into the black pit of despair.

To recap: depression is an emotion that simplifies (regresses) thinking patterns which, in turn, encourages emotionally arousing introspections that give rise to distorted (excessive amounts of) REM sleep. Dreaming is a prolonged firing of the orientation response and uses up enormous reserves of energy. The excessive dreaming of a depressed person drains the energy they need for normal arousal of attention, leaving them unable to motivate themselves or draw any sense of meaning out of their everyday activities. This is the only explanation for depression that accounts for *all* of the symptoms of severe depression – depressed mood, disturbed sleep, exhaustion, loss of pleasure or interest in usual activities, disturbance of appetite, psychomotor retardation or agitation, loss of energy, feelings of worthlessness and guilt, difficulties in thinking, and recurrent thoughts of death or suicide. In other words, it explains the complete psychobiological cycle of depression.

This is new knowledge. It derives from the human givens and, as one should expect of any new understanding, it explains many other things – including why some treatments work and others don't.

Up until now there has never been a satisfactory explanation for why, when people are given antidepressants, a crude and risky treatment, they nevertheless do work for many people. We can now see that this is because, as mentioned earlier, they all either reduce REM sleep or help correct disordered REM sleep, bringing the sleeping pattern back to normal. The reason there is such a high rate of relapse when people stop taking antidepressant drugs, compared with effective psychotherapy or counselling, is that drugs don't teach people to build a realistic, empowering inner template with which to engage with reality.

The explanation that we have offered also explains why any form of counselling or psychotherapy that *reduces* the amount of emotional introspection a person is doing will help them. And any therapy that encourages and *increases* the amount of emotional introspection they do will harm them. That is why such models as psychodynamic, gestalt, hypno-analytical, person-centred, etc. are contraindicated for treating depressed people: they are focused in the wrong direction. Unfortunately, innumerable people around the world have had depression maintained or more deeply entrenched by well-meaning therapists working from such models, which is why counselling is so often treated with suspicion by the public and is sometimes mocked in the media. (Some American hospitals that employed therapists using these outmoded models are now successfully being sued for large sums of money by the relatives of depressed people because the evidence that these approaches are ineffective, and even harmful, is so strong it stands up in court.[55])

The human givens approach to therapy incorporates therapeutic techniques that have been shown to work effectively, whatever model of therapy they derive from. Anything that works does so because it is in tune with the real needs of a person, and uses their own resources – in other words, is aligned with the givens of human nature. We know, for example, that behaviour therapy works because it guides people back into enjoyable physical activities that take the emotional focus off themselves and re-engage them with the environment, thus pulling them away from their negative introspection. As they take up challenging and interesting activities again, mental and/or physical, this, in turn, stimulates an increase in serotonin levels that helps to regulate their REM sleep.

It is when people's needs are not being met that they are likely to feel stuck and then emotionally introspect about it. When people feel that they are losing control over their lives it is usually because of money problems, unsatisfactory housing, deteriorating health, difficulties at work or school (including bullying), or problems around status, relationships and intimacy. One of the most common reasons for someone sinking into clinical depression is that they are in a deteriorating relationship at home or work which they endlessly introspect about. The resulting depression itself adds to their problems, further destroying relationships because, when family and friends of a depressed person find that they too are beginning to feel depressed, they pull away and emotionally disengage to protect themselves. This further isolates the individual who succumbs to even deeper levels of misery. That is why focusing on improving current relationships is highly beneficial.[56]

Human givens therapists incorporate many interpersonal therapy techniques in their work to improve the quality of people's relationships (by teaching social skills, such as how to ask questions, how to take an interest in other people, how to converse and think about other people's needs etc.). All this helps reduce introspection and normalise sleep patterns. The cycle of depression that is caused by prolonged grieving after bereavement can be broken by getting the bereaved person to re-engage with life. Depression, of course, is also common among people who have highly disabling phobias or who suffer from post traumatic stress disorder (PTSD). Any treatment that successfully detraumatises such people will invariably lift their depression.

Bipolar disorder – manic depression

Severe depression is known as a unipolar affective disorder (from the Latin *affectus* or feeling). It is unipolar because the emotional disturbance takes just one direction – downward into depression. The condition commonly known as manic depression is called by psychiatrists bipolar affective disorder because a sufferer oscillates between highs and lows – periods of mania followed by periods of deep depression.

It is generally agreed that there is a significant genetic contribution to the genesis of manic depression. It occurs with equal frequency in men and women and is usually treated with drugs, particularly lithium, which can help regulate the emotional seesaw that propels the sufferer from mania – extreme excitement and sometimes even violence – to depression – pure inertia and lassitude.

Manic depression occurs in a variety of profiles with some people visiting the depressed pole more frequently, and others spending more time in the manic pole. Some may cycle through both poles with dizzying rapidity; others can spend years at the depressed end before experiencing mania, which is why it can take many years to diagnose accurately. Whilst in the depression phase people, as we have seen, are overusing the REM state, dreaming excessively. In mania, by contrast, people typically do not dream enough – working or playing hard, day and night, with minimal time set aside for sleep and rest because they feel they don't need it. By staying up all night every night they become starved of the vital REM sleep that would reduce the arousal (mania). So arousal levels build and build, till the inevitable point when there is a crash down into excessive REM sleep to make up for the lack ... and the consequent depression.

It is increasingly recognised that self-management of the disorder, combined with medication, is the most effective treatment for the majority of patients.[57] In the depression phase, the psychotherapeutic skills needed to treat depression are apposite. When the manic pole is threatening, it is important for a person to reduce stimulation – cut down on caffeine for example – and apply relaxation techniques. What is especially vital is getting a good night's sleep. However exciting life may seem to an individual during the manic phase, unless they get enough REM sleep they will heighten their arousal levels, accelerating the onset of mania.

Manic depression in many ways highlights the role of black and white thinking in the genesis of depression. In the depressive phase the world is seen from a very black, pessimistic perspective indeed, whilst the opposite is true in the manic phase. Optimism and pessimism are two sides of the same coin. Just as runaway inflation is followed by recession in the world of economics, unbridled optimism is likely to trigger a pessimistic, depressive fallout when the unrealistic dreams turn into the ashes of disappointment.

For whatever reason it arises (and there appears to be a genetic contribution to the condition), the extremes of black and white thinking can be more starkly observed in manic depression. Black and white thinking is, as we have seen, the primitive thinking style of the emotional brain. The neocortex evolved to enable us to refine that dichotomous style of thought so that we can perceive the myriad shades of grey between these two poles and thus chart a more flexible and realistic way through life's difficulties, giving us along the way the bonus of the possibility for ever higher development. Again we can see that the pre-condition for the ability to see and understand the complexity of life, and to navigate our way safely through it, is almost always *less emotional arousal.*

From this understanding we can see that the therapeutic techniques deriving from an understanding of the human givens will be useful in the treatment of bipolar disorder. We have ourselves encountered a number of clients who are now successfully managing their condition using such techniques, without needing drug treatment. But we would wish to emphasise that the majority of sufferers of manic depression are likely to benefit most from a combination of drugs and human givens therapy.

The most effective way to lift depression

With a clearer understanding of what depression is, and what causes it, we can lift it more rapidly. The main focus in treating depression is to lower the emotional arousal and stop the negative introspecting of a patient as quickly as possible, by any psychological means at our disposal. This is done by using whatever methods enable us best to address the unmet needs, or make most use of the innate resources, of the sufferer. We routinely find that using *all* available approaches in one session makes progress much faster. That is why human givens therapy is the most effective treatment for depression, as well as all other emotional disorders.

As outlined in the previous chapter, the human givens therapist, as well as integrating behavioural, cognitive and interpersonal approaches, also uses relaxation to calm the emotions before attempting other interventions, and guided imagery, which stimulates the imaginative faculty to motivate people and help them change, solve problems and get back in control. We can also use humour to reframe situations and demonstrate that life is not a black and white affair. We can encourage people and acknowledge their achievements; inform them; get them to exercise; raise their curiosity and so on. In this way we have a truly organic mind/body approach – which is what human givens therapy is – and can bring about the remission of depression in a fraction of the time that cognitive, behavioural or interpersonal therapy can on their own. Human givens therapists routinely find that they can lift people out of the depressed state in just a handful of sessions, sometimes in one.[58,59] Clients quickly work to reduce negative introspections when it is explained to them that this is the mechanism that is generating their depression.

Sometimes it can be difficult for counsellors, GPs or social workers to see how to apply the approach we are advocating when they have a large case load of clinically depressed patients with huge social problems in their lives – debts, redundancy, no work, illness, disability, family break-up, single parenthood, etc. The key point to remember, when a depressed person's problems seem to be rooted firmly in the environment, is that there is no life situation so dire that others haven't experienced it – and very many manage to cope *without* getting clinically depressed.[60] Clinical depression is an additional layer of suffering for a person in an already difficult situation. (As reported in *The Times*[61], we have demonstrated on film how much can be done in one session for people suffering from multiple problems. Filmed follow-up sessions often even show them looking physically transformed, as well as transformed in motivation and mood.)

We can see the negative impact of depression clearly in the case of people who know that they are dying from cancer. Although far from all patients who know that they are terminally ill become depressed. Very many remain actively engaged with life, perhaps participating in the decisions required in day-to-day family life, looking forward to visits from relatives, organising the disposal of their estate, designing their funeral service, planning special trips and generally setting short-term goals that can be accomplished in the time they have left.

A terminally ill person who is depressed, however, will withdraw from the support of others and frighten themselves with emotional introspections about death and dying and, as a consequence, hasten the process. Negative introspection reduces serotonin levels in the brain. As one of the functions of serotonin is to modulate pain responses, the depressed patient may, as a consequence, experience not only more fear but also more pain. Thus depression is an additional problem to, not a consequence of, highly challenging life circumstances.

When counselling depressed people in difficult life circumstances, it is essential to focus their attention outwards into problem solving. Problems need to be broken down into manageable chunks, and practical ways sought to solve them. This may, for example, involve a counsellor in helping people renegotiate debt repayments or co-ordinate social services, or in showing them how to avail themselves of care relief services. This way, not only do people feel a degree of control over their environmental problems but also the emphasis on problem solving stops them introspecting negatively about their circumstances and thus lowers their arousal levels.

Postnatal depression is often viewed as a special subcategory of depression. But it is caused, just like all other kinds of depression, by emotionally arousing worrying – concerns about coping and about the huge nature of the life change having a baby brings, coupled with inevitably disturbed sleep. As such, it too is best treated in the way we recommend. As very many new mothers feel isolated and inadequate, connecting them with others in the community and building their confidence is vitally important.

Once depression is lifted, some additional psychological repair work may still need to be done. People are often lonely because they don't have the skills for making small talk and have not learned how to make natural, easy contact with other human beings. They may need to practise other social skills or learn how to job hunt, or prepare for a change of career, all of which are possible once the depression is lifted and the person can think again. We should never forget that emotional arousal hijacks our thinking brain and drastically limits our options, not only for thought, but also for action. Once arousal levels are lowered most people can get on with their lives.

But some people seem to get more than their fair share of bad things happening to them. This often happens, not only because they have the pessimistic, emotional black and white view, but because they also have some additional vulnerability. Depression is often accompanied by other conditions and this is called comorbidity (the simultaneous existence of two or more disorders, whether physical or psychological). In depression, these may range from anxiety disorders such as panic attacks and OCD, to medical conditions and personality disorders.

Addictive behaviour is found in some depressed people because, having become depressed, they turn to drugs or alcohol as a way of trying to lift their mood. They then, of course, end up with two problems. All addicts, whether initially depressed or not, eventually become depressed because so many of their needs are unfulfilled.

Panic attacks often present with depression. Counsellors must know how to reassure a sufferer that there is nothing organically wrong and that their symptoms are in fact those of a fear reaction – inappropriate firing of the fight or flight response. Normalising the event and taking the fear out of it will result in them introspecting about it less. Then they should be shown how to bring the anxiety under control by, for example, learning how to stop panic breathing.

The experience of sexual or physical abuse, a serious road accident, or extreme violence, may result in post traumatic stress disorder (PTSD). It will inevitably lead to depression if untreated. This is because traumatised people endlessly introspect about the traumatic event and their subsequent uncontrolled responses to it. This is easily treated as described in the next chapter.

Taking the wrong road

The adverse effects of too much emotionally arousing introspection explain why psychodynamic, 'insight' therapy can often do so much harm. A lady in her early 40s, well dressed, tall and attractive, came to see Joe. She'd been attending various 'insight' therapists for counselling over the past two years and was referred to him by a body therapist whom she had started to consult, in some desperation, to relieve her misery. She said her confidence had completely collapsed to the degree that, were she to meet a friend in the street, even whilst talking to her, she would worry about what kind of an impression she was making and get into a high state of agitation. At work, if she were talking to a customer, she found herself becoming acutely self-conscious, getting tongue-tied and befuddled with them.

As she was quite clear that this problem had been getting worse over the past two years, Joe pointed out that it might not be a coincidence that the more counselling she had the worse her problems seemed to have got. She agreed.

She told Joe that she and her husband had worked hard together and made a great success of their restaurant business. When she had enough money and spare time she decided to "work on herself" and enter counselling to "develop her potential". At that point she was not depressed but, she said, the counselling made her realise that she had had problems all her life. These went back to her childhood and her relationship with her alcoholic father. She felt she had been "in denial" of those painful feelings until the therapy helped her to get in touch with the suppressed pain that was now coming out.

(Now this is a pattern we come across time and time again in clinical practice. Clients attending well-meaning counsellors become emotionally dysfunctional. Using the psychobabble of whatever therapy model they were trained in, the counsellors help their clients to re-experience more and more emotional pain from the past. The more emotionally aroused the clients become, the less they are able to bring rational thought to bear, until they will even accept the twisted logic that *you have to become more dysfunctional before you can get better!*

Such lack of logic would be rejected in any other area of life. Imagine someone going to the doctor with a stomach pain, being given treatment but the pain worsening. On re-examination the doctor says, "I can see what's happening. The treatment is really working. Before you came to see me your immune system was repressing a cancerous growth. It is now no longer repressing it. And, as a result of my treatment, we are making progress, the painful cancer is growing!"

Clearly, that would be utterly absurd. And yet such reasoning is followed, in all innocence, by many counsellors and psychotherapists who tell their clients in advance that they must expect the therapy to be emotionally painful! They then proceed to work in such ways as to fulfil their prophecy, damaging their patients in the process.

By contrast, for a human givens therapist, it is axiomatic that, if the client is emotionally distressed and disturbed, the reason is that their needs are not being met *now*, or that they are misusing the tools that nature gave them to get those needs met, or both. They usually need calming down first, so that they can access their higher cortex, and then some practical coaching in how to improve their life.)

Joe immediately directed the therapy towards finding out what needs were not being fulfilled in this woman's life. He asked her about her children – they seemed to be growing up normally with no more than the usual problems that parents encounter with a young family. She had no money worries. But, when he asked about her relationship with her husband, she readily admitted that this was deteriorating at an alarming rate. Sexual intimacy had stopped. In fact, they had arranged to meet a solicitor the following week to negotiate a separation.

Curiously, this was a subject she didn't even bring up until Joe questioned her. Instead she had been asking whether she could be helped to "get in touch with her past" because there *must* be something there, perhaps in her relationship with her father, and she felt if she could uncover this it would release her from her lack of confidence. In other words, she was asking for more of the same kind of emotionally arousing therapy that had exacerbated her problems.

Perhaps one of the most worrying aspects of this, and similar cases, is that this woman wasn't particularly psychologically troubled prior to going to counselling. In fact, as she and her husband had built their very successful business together, it turned out they didn't have any significant marriage problems either. It was only as the business became more successful and she had more time on her hands that things went wrong. Someone persuaded her to do some work on personal development and she was encouraged to "have counselling to explore her issues". It was in this context that the marital problems seemed to magnify and she began to become emotionally dysfunction-al. To be of use to this woman, Joe had first to undo the effects of the pseudocounselling she had undergone. He lowered her emotional arousal so that her perspective widened and taught her stress control techniques. Then he helped her rebuild her relationship with her husband so that she could get her needs met within what was basically a good and productive marriage.

An avoidable death

Another woman told Joe about the circumstances of her depressed husband's death. She had been deeply worried about his depressed state and felt that he was at risk of suicide. She finally managed to persuade her husband to see his GP, although the husband felt it was pointless to do so. But, having got him to the surgery, all the GP did was change his antidepressant medication. This meant that any benefit he might have been getting from his previous antidepressant would diminish while the new antidepressant would take some weeks to start working.

This is absolutely the wrong way to treat depressed people who are contemplating suicide, as many do. A doctor needs to act there and then to lift the person's mood. Had the GP worked from a human givens perspective he would have known how to challenge the man's attributional style, curb his introspections, create a positive expectancy and buy crucial time by making him promise not to kill himself yet.

The man was obviously highly emotionally aroused and, if the GP had known how to use guided imagery, he could have quickly lowered his arousal level, focused his attention, and taught him how to calm himself down and relax. Then the doctor could have helped him to see his situation more clearly. He could have made positive statements, such as, "Depression is not a permanent state and yours will very probably remit. It does so naturally in the majority of cases." He could have made him laugh or helped him decide on a course of action. He could have reminded him about things that he had achieved in his life and of his proven ability to make changes happen, thus raising his self-esteem. The man would then have left that GP's surgery believing that change was possible, having had it actually demonstrated to him. In twenty minutes, he could have been calmed, reassured and given hope.

But the GP's failure to realise the seriousness of the situation, and the importance of creating hope in his patient, meant that the man went out and hanged himself – the woman lost her husband, and his children lost their father.

Unfortunately, this is happening over and over again because of the mistreatment of depression. Nearly twice as many people commit suicide as die on the roads, and nine times more than that attempt suicide. Although women are two to three times more likely to suffer depression than men are, men are three times more likely to kill themselves. This, again, is due to emotional arousal and the way strong emotion inhibits perceptions and thinking. Women tend to dwell more on their emotions while men tend to go into 'problem solving' mode to deal with difficulties. A man engaged in black and white thinking will tend to see suicide as a solution to a problem. And, because males tend to be more action oriented than females, they are more likely to carry out their 'solution'.

The most sensible way to lower depression and suicide rates is to spread accurate information among the general public about what depression is – an emotion that stimulates black and white thinking and introspection, causing exhaustion because of the excessive dreaming this causes – and train sufficient members of the caring professions in the techniques for lifting it quickly, working from the human givens perspective. These techniques include calming a depressed person down quickly; finding out what needs are not being fulfilled in their life; raising their self-esteem, by drawing their attention vividly to their competencies; identifying and challenging their attributional thinking style; and demonstrating, from the very first session, that change is possible – thus creating a sense of positive expectancy and a belief in, and will to, change.

The following case histories are typical of this approach and show how the use of such skills can be incorporated in counselling sessions.

More casebook examples

The widow: Mary, in her late sixties, was physically robust but her face was etched with grief and despair. Her husband Tom, who had been the mainstay of her life, had died six months earlier. Mary was still tortured by images of his final suffering. She couldn't sleep at night and yet lay on her bed until lunch time because she saw no point in getting up. She was also scared to leave the house because of the panic attacks she had been suffering since Tom's death.

After listening to her story, Joe explained the importance of relaxation and how to control her panic attacks. With guided imagery and progressive muscle relaxation she slowed down her breathing, lines of tension eased from her face and, with eyes closed, she gratefully sank back into the comfort of the armchair. Joe then quietly suggested that she could let go of the image of her husband's final suffering and recall instead happy images of their time together. He gave her time to do this and she clearly enjoyed it. He then reminded her of the many strengths and skills she had developed in raising her large family, now scattered around the world. He also told her that her husband would want her to call upon that strength, and the strength of her relationship with him, to face the new challenges in her life.

When she opened her eyes she and Joe worked out a plan together for what she would do each day, starting with what time she would get up. She said she would like to start baking again so they built that into the plan. Joe explained the importance of aerobic exercise for keeping down her stress levels and lifting depressed feelings. She agreed to resume walking with her neighbour in the evenings, which she had stopped doing since her Tom had died. To ensure that her need for human company would be met Joe also persuaded her to join a social craft group in the town.

Over the next few weeks, her mood lifted dramatically. As she became physically active again she took on more jobs around the house, including some decorating and gardening. Very soon after this her son in America sent her a ticket to join him for a holiday. When she was depressed, he had withdrawn from her and had been reluctant to invite her over. But now that she was focused outward again he was happy to see her, which lifted her spirits still further.

The effect of the human givens approach in this case was rapid and straightforward, as it so often is.

Mary was first helped to bring down her emotional arousal in order to free her to see reality in a more empowering way. Then the meaning of Tom's death and love was reframed into a challenge to her to move on in her life. She was given back a sense of control over her panic attacks. Pleasure and challenge were brought back into her life by resuming walking with friends, baking and decorating. The satisfaction of her needs for attention was shifted from her therapist, to her local community, by getting her to join a local craft group. Finally the lifting of her depression brought her into closer contact with her family again.

The suicide attempt: Judith, a woman in her late twenties, was married with no children and living in rural England.

She came to see Joe following her discharge from hospital after treatment for a twenty-inch diagonal wound across her chest inflicted in her attempted suicide. The stabbing had been so severe that she had been kept in hospital for a week. She had made this attempt on her life because her problems seemed so large and numerous that she could see no other way out.

Judith showed the very common risk factor for depression already referred to: black and white global thinking – the tendency to see the forest but not the individual trees nor the various paths in it. To use another metaphor, if we hold a stone up to our eyes all we can see is the stone. The rest of the world is blotted out as surely as if the stone were as large as a mountain. For a global thinker, the little stone becomes the universe.

The global thinker tends to focus so much on their problems that they can see no way around or through them. All that exists are their problems. They inevitably lose a sense of proportion about their situation. Difficulties become catastrophes. Their imagination piles up the problems one on top of another so that a mountain of misery completely blocks out the wider view. This is exactly the process that led Judith to her desperate act of attempted self-annihilation.

This was her story. She had been unemployed for three years since injuring her back in an accident at work. She was currently waiting for a claim for legal damages to be heard by the courts. Shortly before her attempted suicide, she read in the paper about a person who had lost their injuries claim against their employer and was forced to sell the family home to pay their employer's legal costs. Judith was terrified that if she lost her legal action she and her husband might become homeless too. They were just, in fact, in the process of having a new house built and that was one more thing that troubled Judith ... it had fallen behind schedule. "The builders are taking us to the cleaners", she said. "The house will *never* be finished. The site is a *complete* mess." Again, pessimism and black and white thinking.

Judith also had a phobia about dogs. Her neighbours had a dog and, unless her husband was with her, she was scared to pass their house. This meant that, for much of her time, she was effectively trapped in her own home.

Judith was additionally much troubled by the fact that her sister, whom she was close to, had recently announced, as a result of counselling, that, as a child, she had been sexually abused by their father. Her sister expected and wanted her support. But Judith also had a very close relationship with her father who vehemently denied the abuse. Naturally, her father wanted and expected Judith's support too. She didn't know what to do.

Here we again see black and white thinking at work. Black and white thinking creates a low tolerance for the inevitable ambiguities of life. So much of life is full of unknowns; certainty is the exception. We can't know for sure, for example, that we are choosing the right career, the right partner, the right house, or even the best holiday. In life, we can't always know for sure why what happens, happens. There are too many contributing factors. Someone might say, for example, "Why is my son a drug addict? Is it because I wasn't sufficiently firm with him? Maybe I didn't show him enough love. But then, why isn't my other son a drug addict? I didn't show favouritism to either son. Maybe it's his genes? Or is it the company he keeps? Perhaps it was his disappointment in a love affair that made him vulnerable!" Maybe it was all or none of these reasons.

Black and white thinking demands a definite answer to every ambiguous life situation. Judith's thinking style demanded that she unambiguously support either her father or her sister. But she loved them both so she was paralysed by her continual analytical introspections of the situation.

In the first session with Judith, Joe used about 25 minutes of the session to get her to relax using guided imagery. He then removed her dog phobia (the method will be described in the next chapter) and, whilst she was still relaxed, discussed and reframed the other three main problems she was worrying about. Joe asked her what evidence she had that she was going to lose her court case. She repeated the story in the newspaper.

"That could be a completely different case from yours," he told her. "We must concentrate on the specific evidence. What does your barrister say is the likely outcome of *your* case?"

"Well, he says that I am certain to win since I was injured at work and there are sworn statements from other workers who were witnesses. All that remains to be decided, according to him, is how much in damages I receive."

Joe helped her to see that she was misusing her imagination by creating an improbable negative outcome to her court case. The idea that she was facing the loss of her family home was entirely unreasonable and, because she was relaxed and could think straight, she agreed this was so.

Next the problem of the alleged sexual abuse of her sister by their father was looked at. It was clear that there was no external, validating evidence that abuse had taken place. Judith herself had never seen or experienced such abuse. In such circumstances, the only reasonable course of action was to tolerate the ambiguity of not knowing what, if anything, had actually happened. Her sister's memories might be true, or yet again they might be an artefact – illusory memories – created by the type of counselling that she was receiving. Joe explained that, at present, there was no way of knowing for sure. In any case it wasn't her problem. Her father and sister were going to have to find a way of dealing with it themselves. Judith gave a huge sigh of relief when she realised she didn't have to solve the problem. She could offer her love and support to both family members – at least until more objective evidence became available.

Finally they considered her problem about her new home. What did the architect supervising the building programme have to say? "Well, according to him," she said, "we are only six months behind schedule." Joe joked with her that six months behind schedule was equivalent to twelve months ahead of schedule as far as the average builder was concerned!

When Judith came back the following week she was no longer depressed. Indeed, she had been out on her own and cycled past the house with the dog without experiencing a panic attack. She declared herself baffled by how she could ever have got things so much out of proportion. But we know why. It was due to her attributional style. Her global thinking style, combined with black and white thinking and endless worrying, formed the toxic brew that maintained the emotion of clinical depression and created her suicidal impulses.

The crying woman: Ivan saw Susan some years ago when her husband brought her into his clinic at her GP's suggestion. Her heavy figure oozed misery and seemed to suck the energy out of everyone around her. Speaking with reluctance – it was all such an effort – she described the history of her situation whilst tears slowly ran down her face: eleven years of severe depression, three serious suicide attempts, hospitalisation, psychiatrists, antidepressants that hadn't worked, psychotherapy that made her feel even worse, "if that was possible". And now she was talking again about ending it all. "What is the point of living?"

Following the golden rule of not taking too much history with depressed people but showing the client instead that things can be different *in the first session*, after 30 minutes of listening Ivan set to work. She looked such a picture of despair that, on an impulse, he decided to use humour, an age-old and valuable way to help people see how they are exaggerating things. This need not mean telling jokes or being witty. He simply drew on her own resources and asked her what made her laugh?

Back came the inevitable slow monotone response, "Nothing makes me laugh".

"I don't believe you."

"I never laugh."

"*Everyone* has a sense of humour."

"I have *no* sense of humour. I *never* laugh."

So deep in her depression trance was Susan that he almost believed her, but he carried on anyway and asked her to do an experiment. "Just close your eyes and let your mind go back to the last time you had tears of laughter rolling down your face."

She obediently closed her eyes and Ivan sat back and waited, fingers crossed, while her brain went on a search. Within a few minutes she started to smile. The smiles turned to laughter. Then she started to cry, but this time with tears of laughter! She opened her eyes and splutteringly told of what she had remembered that was so funny. The laughter had dissipated her depression, puncturing a hole in the global blanket of misery she had held fast around her.

For a while at least her brain was working normally and they talked properly. Ivan then asked her what she most regretted about her depression and she said it was the fact that for twelve years, since her "illness", she and her husband had not been on a holiday and she felt this was so unfair on her husband because, when they were young, holidays had meant a lot to them and he still wanted to see more of the world. As, it turned out, so did she.

Ivan called the husband in. He was astonished and pleased to see her smiling and so changed. Whilst in this positive, lively state Ivan got them both to promise, as part of the treatment, to book a holiday straight away to somewhere they really wanted to go but where they had never been before.

Ivan had to see Susan eleven times in all before he was sure she was out of depression. (Coincidentally, once for every year she had been depressed.) At first she would come in and say she was just as bad as before – black and white thinking again – but, by getting her to scale her changing moods and achievements and teaching her how to change her attributional style, she got out of depression for good. Scaling the gradual remission of symptoms is a powerful tool of therapy precisely because it is *not* all or nothing. It is a technique drawn from solution focused brief therapy in which, for instance, a client is asked to place themselves on a scale where 0 means no change in mood and 10 represents a completely positive and optimistic mood. It is a practical and motivating means of monitoring gradual upward changes.

The holiday, of course, gave Susan something outside of herself to focus on. They chose to go to Australia. It brought their relationship back to life: it brought planning, excitement and new experiences into their lives. Part of the reason people can't initiate such activity themselves when they are depressed is that they cannot easily make connections when they are emotionally aroused – the emotional arousal stops them thinking clearly. They just can't see the bigger picture. Ivan has since had several postcards from Susan and her husband from various parts of the world. She is enjoying life again.

* * *

It is now increasingly being recognised that antidepressants are much more dangerous than their promoters had hoped, and that the medical model ideology which maintains that depression is caused by a chemical imbalance in the brain is simplistic. As more and more research shows, the right type of psychotherapy is a much better treatment for sufferers. We hope that help for depressed patients will much improve as more health workers come to understand this and receive improved training in effective counselling techniques. (See Appendix II.)

CHAPTER ELEVEN

Terror in the brain:
overcoming trauma

FEAR IS a natural reaction to danger, a survival signal that switches on the fight or flight response. Sooner or later everyone experiences it. Threatening events frighten all small children and unexpected attacks can temporarily terrify adults – but it is the experience of excessive, or inappropriate, fear of a kind that keeps people on permanent high alert that accounts for a whole range of common mental and behavioural problems. These we are going to explore now. Depression, low self-esteem, psychosis, and a great host of anxiety disorders including post traumatic stress disorder (PTSD) can result from an excessive firing of the fight or flight response. Neuroscience has revealed so much about this that we now understand why the brain's design makes it so vulnerable to extreme fright.

A traumatised creature lives a private hell: hyperalert, terrorised by an invisible mental wound, helplessly in thrall to a powerful emotional memory of a life-threatening event – or series of events – real or imagined. Horrific, violent events can clearly impact on the mind as well as the body to produce such a state, as vividly illustrated in the following description of a Vietnam War veteran's experience:

"I can't get the memories out of my mind! The images come flooding back in vivid detail, triggered by the most inconsequential things, like a door slamming or the smell of stir-fried pork. Last night I went to bed, was having a good sleep for a change. Then ... there was a bolt of crackling thunder. I awoke instantly, frozen in fear. I am right back in Vietnam. My hands are freezing, yet sweat pours from my entire body. I feel each hair on the back of my neck standing on end. I can't catch my breath and my heart is pounding ... The next clap of thunder makes me jump so much that I fall to the floor."[1]

Although originally PTSD was most commonly diagnosed among soldiers, sailors and airmen returning from war zones, current American estimates are that at least eight per cent of the general population ultimately develop it as a result of traumatic experiences, ranging from surviving terrifying natural disasters such as earthquakes, forest fires or avalanches, to car, rail, boat or air accidents, heart attacks, mugging, burning, rape or sexual assault.[2]

We now also realise that people can be vicariously traumatised. Some grandchildren of concentration camp survivors, for example, have subsequently become traumatised by hearing about their grandparents' memories.[3] A female client of Joe's, whose son and his fiancée were horribly burned to death in a tragic car accident, suffered terrifying traumatic flashbacks from her imagined fantasies about what it must have been like to be trapped in a car, burning to death like that.

It is clear from our review of the literature, however, that, though there is now widespread agreement as to what constitutes PTSD, there is still dissension among clinicians about how best to help people who suffer from it.[4] Indeed, critical incident debriefing, the most widely available approach, in which people are usually asked to relive in great detail their terrible experiences, is often found to make the condition worse. The very people whom this technique is designed to help, namely those who are at risk of developing PTSD, are in fact those most likely to be harmed by that process.[5,6,7,8]

Other treatments on offer include pharmacological, behavioural, psychodynamic and cognitive methods, hypnotic techniques including EMDR (eye-movement desensitisation and reprocessing), and various versions of exposure therapy, such as flooding or systematic desensitisation. Many of these approaches may work in the short or long term, but the sheer variety of them, together with the lack of reliability of effect, indicates a failure to understand the psychobiology of traumatic stress reactions. (This is a reflection of a wider problem in psychotherapy and counselling, which still largely works from prescientific models and has yet to incorporate recent discoveries about brain functioning into many commonly practised procedures.[9])

The EMDR technique has been applied to treating PTSD and there is considerable evidence for its usefulness. It was developed by Francine Shapiro, an American psychologist, and involves getting clients to recall traumatic episodes whilst their eyes track the movement of the therapist's hand back and forth in front of them. Several episodes of

tracking the hand movements may be required for a particular traumatic sequence to diminish in its emotional intensity. (Many EMDR
practitioners now use a moving light to automate the process.)

Users of this technique, including Shapiro, admit that they don't
know why it appears to work, although they recognise that there is a
connection with the REM state.[10]

In the light of the organising idea about trauma to be presented in
this chapter it is not difficult to see why this technique often works.
Trauma is encoded by a structure in the limbic system called the
amygdala. Every time someone suffering from PTSD is asked to recall
it, they go so fully back into the memory, into the trance state of the
trauma, that they relive the trauma as if it were happening *now*. Any
process that cures PTSD has to keep the person's awareness focused in
the present so that the higher cortex can reframe the memory as a *past*
event and put it in a realistic perspective.[11]

With the EMDR process the rapid eye movements induced by
following the therapist's moving hand (an ancient hypnotic technique
– remember the old films of hypnotists swinging a pocket watch and
repeating ... "sleep ... sleep") keeps part of the patient's attention
focused on the present whilst allowing another part of their attention
to be engaged by the trauma. In other words, the patient is encouraged
to view the trauma in a disassociated state which automatically lowers
the emotional arousal. The neocortex is then activated and the observing self is able to recode and reframe the event as being in the past
and of only limited relevance and significance to the present. For these
reasons, this somewhat mechanical procedure may often be effective
in treating some cases of trauma.

However, drawing on the APET model, we can not only offer a
better understanding of what PTSD is, we can show why some treatments are more effective than others, and pick the best.

The **A** in the APET model (the A standing for the activating agent,
a stimulus from the environment) in this case is whatever event a
person has experienced or witnessed that involved actual or threatened serious physical harm to them. The **P** in APET stands for pattern
matching – which, in this context, is the process by which the amygdala, the brain's alarm system, seeks to ensure an organism's survival.
It constantly scans the environment for potential threats, comparing

all incoming stimulation, supplied by our various senses, with survival templates – fear memories – to see if they are life threatening or life enhancing. A crackle of twigs or a sudden silence in the forest may trigger the alarm system because previous experience of a crackle or silence has signalled a predator, setting in train an emotional reaction which leads to freezing, fight or flight. The experience is formed into a sensory memory and is passed on to an adjacent organ in the brain called the hippocampus. Here, all of our most recent experiences are stored before they are subsequently transferred to the neocortex.

When a deeply traumatic event occurs, however, the emotional reaction can be so strong that it remains coded in wordless form in the amygdala, permanently retained there as a survival pattern in case it is suddenly needed again in a similar future emergency. (When stress is at a very high level, as in perceived life-threatening moments, the hippocampus is less able to lay down coherent memories and transfer them to the higher cortex.) It is because of the strength of the emotional reaction that the amygdala won't let go of the pattern and the transfer of information across to the hippocampus doesn't take place. Thereafter, whenever that memory is reactivated by something in the environment that in some way 'recalls' the traumatic moment – a certain sound, smell, object or whatever – the amygdala triggers the alarm reaction.[12] This is when PTSD ensues.

About 25 per cent of people exposed to traumatic events develop PTSD, according to American research.[13] Susceptibility depends upon a variety of factors, such as the degree of trauma, and aspects of personality, such as trait anxiety and suggestibility.[14] The amygdala of someone who develops PTSD has literally been imprinted with the pattern of the trauma, which contains all the information surrounding the event.[15] Thereafter, the templates contained in the amygdala, to which all new incoming stimuli are compared, also include a template for that traumatic event. Whenever there is a match, *or a part-match*, the amygdala fires off the alarm reaction, the fight or flight response is activated and, because this all happens at an unconscious level, the person experiences an incomprehensible state of alarm – a strong emotion ... the E in APET.

It is because pattern matching is a metaphorical process – the amygdala is looking for something *like* something else – that people experience flashbacks and other severe alarm reactions when the amygdala spots anything with any similarity to some aspect of a traumatic event. This is why the origin of such reactions can at first seem mysterious. A graphic example of this is provided by the tale of a butcher in the 1920s who began to have 'strange spells': his heart would beat violently, and he would vomit and then lose consciousness. It emerged that these attacks usually followed exposure to certain odours from volatile oils – perfume, lemon oil, banana oil, or ether. The butcher's shop he worked in was frequented by fashionable women, many of whom came heavily perfumed, and, as his doctor described it, "when they would enter the butcher shop ... the patient would become dizzy and lose consciousness". It turned out that, during the Great War of 1914–18, the butcher had had the horribly unpleasant experience of being gassed in the trenches whilst asleep. "The flushing, the rapid pulse, the dizziness and the vomiting," his doctor decided, were "a repetition of the original traumatic event which overtook him in sleep." The man's amygdala was simply pattern matching to *any* strange, strong smell.[16]

In the same way, people who have survived horrific car accidents can have exaggerated alarm reactions to the mere sight of a car, the smell of petrol, or even just the sound of screeching brakes on a television programme. People who have experienced a violent, traumatising sexual attack can later, in a loving relationship, become highly anxious at any form of sexual approach and withdraw from normal sexual intimacy.

We can now see that critical incident debriefing puts a traumatised victim and their counsellor into a double-bind situation. The emotional arousal caused by debriefing 'hijacks' the thinking part of the brain, the T in APET, and prevents the person thinking clearly. And, as we have explained, the more emotionally aroused we are, the less able we are to think straight – as anyone who has ever fallen in love or lost their temper will know. If the counsellor invites the victim to talk about or recall the trauma, hoping to help them set it in context and put it behind them, an emotional charge is set off which inhibits the higher neocortex from functioning. Without input from the neocortex, there is no feedback mechanism available to the brain to detraumatise the memory. Each time an attempt is made to recall the trauma, off goes the alarm, the higher neocortex is inhibited and the traumatic memory is further programmed into the amygdala, thus deepening the trauma in the person's emotional brain.

Sad to say, this is the effect of most counselling for trauma as practised in this country. When counsellors encourage traumatised clients to recreate their memories of the traumatic event, they embed the trauma even more strongly. Fortunately, we can now put forward a more complete understanding of how PTSD develops which explains not only why some people are more at risk of developing PTSD, but also which treatments should work effectively and why.

Freeze, fight or flight

When we are exposed to a sudden and significant stress that we feel may endanger our life, our attention is intensely and instantly fully focused on the source of the threat. Momentarily we freeze, stuck to the ground like mesmerised rabbits. Then, in most people, the fight or flight response is activated. We defend ourselves or run away. But some individuals stay in the freeze response, paralysed, dumb and insensitive to stimuli. This may be especially likely to happen if an escape route is blocked.[17]

In evolutionary terms, freezing was – and is – actually beneficial for many animals. If you suddenly stop moving you become invisible to those predators whose main focus is on movement, and so have a better chance of staying alive.[18] Naturalists watching animals being hunted have noticed that the freezing response occurs an instant *before* the predator makes physical contact with its intended prey. Peter Levine, an international expert on trauma and stress, and holder of a doctorate in medical and biological physics, has vividly described what happens as a cheetah closes in on an impala. "It is almost as if the animal has surrendered to its impending demise. But the fallen impala is not dead. Although on the 'outside' it appears limp and motionless, on the 'inside' its nervous system is still activated from the 70 miles an hour chase. Though barely breathing, the impala's heart is pumping at extreme rates. Its brain and body are being flooded by the same chemicals (for example, adrenaline and cortisol) that helped fuel its attempted escape.

"It is possible that the impala will not be devoured immediately. The mother cheetah may drag its fallen, and apparently dead, prey behind a bush and seek out its cubs who are hiding at a safe distance. Herein lies a short window of opportunity for the impala.

"The temporarily 'frozen' creature has a chance to awaken from its state of shock, shake and tremble in order to discharge the vast amount of energy stored in its nervous system, then, as if nothing had happened, bound away in search of the rest of its herd.

"Another benefit of the frozen (immobility) state is its analgesic nature. If the impala *is* killed, it will be spared the pain of its own demise."[19]

Though it appears that we have separated ourselves from animals like the impala and cheetah, our responses to threat are still biologically formed. They are human givens – innate and instinctive functions of our organism. For the impala, life-threatening situations are an everyday occurrence, so it makes sense that the ability to resolve and complete these episodes is built into their biological systems. Threat, albeit of a different kind, is a relatively common phenomenon for humans as well. Although we are rarely aware of it, we also possess the innate ability to complete and resolve these experiences. From our biology come our responses to threat, and it is also in our biology that the resolution of trauma dwells.

In order to remain healthy, all animals, including humans, must discharge the vast energies mobilised for survival. This discharge completes our activated responses to threat, and allows us to return to a more normal state. In biology, this process is called homoeostasis: the ability of an organism to respond appropriately to any given circumstance, and then return to a baseline of what could be called 'normal' functioning.

In the National Geographic video *Polar Bear Alert*, a frightened bear is shown being run down by a pursuing aeroplane, shot with a tranquilliser dart, surrounded by wildlife biologists, and then tagged. Later, as the massive animal comes out of its state of shock, it begins to quiver and ends up in almost convulsive shaking – its limbs flailing around seemingly out of control. The shaking subsides and the animal is seen to take three long spontaneous breaths that seem to spread through its entire body.

The biologist narrating the film comments that what the bear is doing is shaking off the stress accumulated during its capture. It is pointed out that, if the sequence is looked at again but slowed down in speed, it suddenly becomes clear that the seemingly uncontrolled leg movements are in effect co-ordinated running movements. The animal seems to be completing its 'flight' template, cut short when it was trapped, discharging frozen energy.[20]

Animals and most humans *don't* get traumatised when they can properly discharge their accumulated stress energy by activating the fight or flight response at the time of the event. So the question arises, what is happening in those who *do* develop PTSD?

The answer lies in that other everyday state in which mammals, including humans, become paralysed or frozen – the rapid eye movement (REM) state, the deep trance state we all slip into when we are asleep and dreaming. As we have seen, when we dream, the very same orientation response (the reaction which turns our attention to a sudden unexpected stimulus, such as a loud noise, and freezes our behaviour when awake) fires off while we are sleeping.[21] The orientation response has the same basic function when we are asleep but, as stimuli from the outside world are shut out, it is set off by undischarged emotional arousal patterns from the day before which arise in the brain in the REM state. The orientation response alerts the brain to these patterns which are then discharged by being metaphorically acted out in a dream. The dream thus deactivates the emotional stress.[22]

The very freezing or paralysis of movement that is triggered by the orientation response when something unexpected happens also occurs in the dream state (preventing us from physically acting out our dreams).

We mentioned earlier that it is during the REM state that the foetal and neonatal brain is programmed with its instinctive templates; and that hypnosis is a trance state with many features similar to that of the REM state, often including paralysis. It is when an individual is in this state that new learning can best be programmed. All forms of hypnotic induction work by duplicating part of the REM state programming: for example triggering rapid eye movements can induce a hypnotic state, as can firing the orientation response through shock, or relaxation (which triggers off the pathways to body paralysis in the REM state). Hypnotic inductions are artificial ways of consciously accessing the REM state.[23] This is why hypnosis is such a powerful psychological tool for raising self-esteem, increasing confidence or helping an individual practise new skills or improve their social performance. Hypnosis, then, is the trance state that makes us most receptive to new learning or programming, whether for good or ill, just as the REM state is in the young.

Similarly, in the paralysis of the freeze state during the traumatic event, the amygdala is programmed to retain fear. People 'paralysed' by fear who go on to develop post traumatic stress disorder were in a profound trance during the event, long enough for the horrific experience to be deeply etched into the amygdala, where the survival templates are stored. From then on, whenever the amygdala finds a match or part-match for that experience in the environment, it sets off the alarm reaction. Even just an associated thought or memory coming to mind can do it because the amygdala is unable to distinguish between a thought and sensory information.

We would therefore expect to find that the people most prone to PTSD are those who are also most highly hypnotisable. And this has been shown to be so.[24]

When people have been badly frightened, talking about what happened can be a way of integrating the event and converting it into a normal memory. In such cases, 'talking it out' can be helpful. But for those people at highest risk of developing PTSD, any counselling or critical incident debriefing that gets them in touch with their emotions will, like a posthypnotic suggestion, cue them to relive the trauma, trigger off the emotional reaction, and further embed it.

Creating calm

Effective treatment, by contrast, will involve recoding the traumatic memory as a low arousal memory. Research carried out in their laboratory by Joseph LeDoux and his colleagues shows that when we recall a memory it has to be recoded. That is to say, new proteins have to be synthesised in the amygdala to reconsolidate the memory.[25] If we can find a way, therefore, to get the memory recalled in a low arousal state, it will be recoded as a low arousal memory and the traumatic reaction pattern will be dissolved. To do this, the more objective intelligence of the neocortex must be helped to evaluate the imprint, see that it no longer represents a threat in the here and now, and modify it. Because the more the amygdala is aroused, the more the higher cortex is shut off,[26] keeping the patient in a low arousal state is also key to enabling the neocortex to become involved. This is because communication lines from the neocortex to the emotional brain are much more restricted than communication from the emotional brain to the neocortex.[27] We need to be in a relaxed state for the feedback mechanism to work. Once the information is processed in this way it becomes a normal memory. It will always remain an unpleasant one, but part of normal functioning; not something shadowy that keeps the brain continually on the alert while scanning the environment for danger, and thereby maintaining the person in a state of high arousal.

Furthermore, when the trauma template is released, attention capacity is freed up. People literally become more intelligent again when the data-processing capability of the brain is no longer devoted to scanning input from the environment for a match to a threat.

The history of 20th century military psychiatry is full of examples of doctors and psychiatrists struggling to find ways to help traumatised individuals (the 'shell-shocked' as they were first called) and discover why some individuals seemed more prone to 'crack' under extreme pressure than others.[28] Some had great success, particularly those using hypnosis. This was a common treatment during the First World War when it was widely observed that 'hysterics', as they called them, were highly hypnotisable and open to suggestion (shown by the ease with which they copied one another's symptoms).[29] The following is a description of such work by Dr William Brown, a mathematician and philosopher who took up academic psychology and graduated in medicine. At the outbreak of war he was reader in psychology at London University and a well-known academic expert on hypnosis. He gained practical experience with trauma victims in shell-shock hospitals in England and then went to work at front-line hospitals in France because he believed early treatment was important. About 15 per cent of the cases he dealt with concerned what we would call severe trauma symptoms and PTSD, and for these he used hypnosis.

"The patient would be brought into hospital lying on a stretcher, perhaps dumb, trembling violently, perspiring profusely, his face showing an expression of great terror, his eyes either with a fixed stare or rolling from side to side. When one questioned him and got him to answer in writing he would tell one that he was unable to remember what had happened to him. In some way or other he had been knocked out and had come to find that he was paralysed and unable to speak.

"I interview him alone in my office and tell him in a tone of conviction that I shall restore his speech to him in a few seconds if he will do exactly what I say. I then urge him to lie down upon a couch, close his eyes and think of sleep. I urge him to give himself up to sleep, to let sleep come to him, as it assuredly will. I tell him that he is getting drowsy, his limbs are getting heavy with sleep, all his muscles are relaxed, he is breathing more and more slowly, more and more deeply. Above all, that his eyelids are getting heavy, as heavy as lead, that he feels disinclined to open them however hard he tries. At this stage, which generally supervenes within two or three minutes, he really cannot open his eyes. This is a stage of very light hypnosis quite sufficient for my purposes.

"I now tell him that the moment I put my hand on his forehead he will seem to be back again in the trenches, in the firing line, in the fighting, as the case may be, and will live again through the experiences he had when the shock occurred. This I say in a tone of absolute conviction, as if there is not the slightest shadow of possibility of my words not coming true. I then place my hand on his forehead. He immediately begins to twist and turn on the couch and shouts out in a terror-stricken voice. He talks as he talked at the time when he received the shock. He really does live again through the experiences of that awful time. Sometimes he speaks as if in dialogue, punctuated with intervals of silence corresponding to the remarks of his interlocutor, like a person speaking at the telephone. At other times he indulges in imprecations [cursing and pleading] and soliloquy. In some cases he is able to reply to my questions and give an account of his experiences. In others he cannot do so, but continues to writhe and talk as if he were still in the throes of the actual experience. In every case he speaks and acts as if he were again under the influence of the terrifying emotion. It is as if this emotion had been originally repressed, and the power of speech with it, and is now being worked off and worked out."[30]

After such sessions, the patients would collapse into a profound sleep.

British psychiatrist Dr William Sargant described working with traumatised soldiers during the Second World War. His treatment, like many doctors before him, was to encourage an emotional abreaction because it was often found that sufferers aroused to extremes of terror by hypnosis, drama or drugs would collapse and, on waking, be fully recovered. In 1944, he began using ether to induce abreaction with traumatised soldiers because "ether released a far greater degree of explosive excitement, which made their recital of events extremely poignant or dramatic". Furthermore, "the sudden states of collapse, after emotional outbursts induced by ether, were far more frequent than after those induced by hypnosis or barbiturates.

"Under ether, certain patients could easily be persuaded to relive experiences of terror, anger, or other excitement. Some of them might then collapse from emotional exhaustion and lie motionless for a minute or so, unmoved by ordinary stimuli; and, on coming round, would often burst into a flood of tears and report that their outstanding symptoms had suddenly disappeared. Or they would describe their minds as now freed of the terror aroused by certain obsessive pictures; they could still think of these, if they wished, but without the former hysterical anxiety. When simple excitement at the recital of past experiences did not reach the phase of ... collapse, little or no change or mental improvement might be observed in the patient; if, however, the abreactive treatment was repeated, and drugs were used to increase the amount of emotional stimulation until collapse supervened, sudden improvement could occur."[31]

Sargant also found that, if he couldn't get a description of the traumatic event from his patients, he could invent horrific stories, of soldiers trapped in burning tanks for example, tell them to his patients and this would be sufficient to induce the necessary fear arousal prior to the abreactive collapse. In other words, by pattern matching to *any* terrifying aspect of an event – loud noises, fire, feelings of helplessness etc. – the amygdala's alarm response would fire. As we would expect, an exact match was not required. The importance of this part of Sargant's work is that it showed that even if the surface details of a pattern or a template were different, as long as it was a frightening situation associated with war, it would trigger a state of terror. If this crude pattern-match could be deactivated, the work was done.

Having earlier said that the emotional arousal created during most types of critical incident debriefing can cause harm to those at risk of PTSD, we now appear to be saying that, sometimes, getting people really worked up and emotionally aroused appears to help them to recover. The two statements are not, in fact, at odds because it is *not* the emotional arousal that heals the person. The real active ingredient, as Sargant observed, is the collapse into a totally calm state after exposure to the emotionally arousing stimuli (even if the stimuli are in an individual's imagination). The memory can then be transferred through to, and processed in, the higher cortex. The active ingredient for effective therapy is *calmness*.

The reason, for instance, that exposure therapy can work for severe phobic reactions is that it requires a person to stay in a recreated fear situation until the emotional arousal (usually a terror of dying as a result of exposure to the feared object or circumstance) subsides and calmness follows. Once the person is calm in the face of the threat, the neocortex is released from its emotional shackle and is free to evaluate what has occurred. Having clear evidence that the fear is unwarranted (death didn't ensue), the brain can successfully recode its understanding of the stimulus.

It is only if the person stays in the situation *until the emotional arousal goes down*, however, that exposure therapy works. The danger with exposure therapy is that, if the person cannot handle the highly unpleasant arousal and leaves the situation before they are calm, the trauma will have been programmed in even deeper. This is the problem too with most types of critical incident debriefing. Emotional reliving of the trauma is encouraged and is sufficient to create an emotional charge but not generally to achieve collapse and calm.

Clearly, it is highly painful to re-experience trauma to the point of collapse. The value of the fast trauma/phobia cure technique we are now going to describe is that such terrifying emotional arousal can be bypassed completely because the desired calm state can be created at the outset. It is, therefore, a faster, safer process and more easily tailored to each individual than such techniques as EMDR.

How to cure post traumatic stress disorder

With the understanding of *why* people can suffer long-term traumatisation – the imprint of a life-threatening event is embedded in the amygdala which continually scans the environment, pattern matching to anything similar to elements of that event – we can solve the problem of *how* to remove the imprint and 'convince' the amygdala that the imprinted template is no longer necessary for survival. One of the little acknowledged breakthroughs in psychotherapy in recent times has been the development of an effective and relatively painless way of doing just that.

The technique was first developed by Richard Bandler, one of the co-founders of Neurolinguistic Programming (NLP), after observing and studying films of Milton H. Erickson detraumatising people in hypnosis.[32] The method is variously known as the 'fast phobia cure' (because it is most often used by hypnotherapists for curing phobias), the 'rewind technique' (which is the name preferred by clinical psychologists) and the 'VK dissociation technique' (the V stands for visual and the K for kinaesthetic – feelings) by those who practise NLP.

The version of the technique which is recommended by the European Therapy Studies Institute (ETSI) has been refined to emphasise those elements that we now know are essential in making it effective and to drop aspects that are unnecessary. Clinical experience and research[33] show that it works reliably with almost all cases of post traumatic stress disorder and phobia, but until the publication of our monograph[34] on the subject in 2001 there was no satisfactory published explanation for why it works.

The skills needed to use this trauma resolution method are not difficult to learn, provided that the practitioner has the aptitude and sufficient spare capacity to devote concentrated attention to the traumatised individual they are working with. Many medical and psychiatric professionals have attended one-day training workshops run by MindFields College to learn the technique and have subsequently been able to help severely traumatised people.[35]

The procedure involves relaxing a person very deeply and asking them to imagine themselves in a comfortable and pleasant place of their own choosing. They are then asked to imagine they have a portable television set, with a video and remote control switch. They are asked to imagine themselves watching themselves watching a rerun of the traumatic event on the screen (being doubly dissociated from the event in this way keeps arousal low). Then they imagine 'floating back into themselves' and, from the end of the memory when they know they safely survived the event they quickly go *backwards* through it – 'rewinding' it – and then they 'fast forward' through the memory, working from a time before the event occurred to a time after the event when they had survived it. This is repeated a number of times until the memories produce no trace of emotional arousal. Whilst doing this you can observe rapid eye movements as the brain is being reprogrammed. After doing this, the event ceases to be a traumatic memory. (See Appendix VI for a more detailed description of how to detraumatise someone.)

What this technique achieves, when employed by a competent practitioner, is to take the patterns of traumatic memory held in the limbic system and turn them into ordinary memories held in the higher cortex. This is done by bringing the client's observing self into play while keeping them at a low level of arousal. By removing traumatic memories in this way, the observing self is able to view the troubling pattern of memory and, using the neural connections between the limbic system, where the trauma is 'trapped' or 'imprinted', and the neocortex, reframe it as no longer an active threat to the person.

This is an artificial way of doing what nature does with all learning (another process that is a human given). All of us have memories of events that were emotionally arousing or even life threatening at the time, which we can now look back on and tell an amusing anecdote about. Those memories have moved out of the amygdala's traumatic store, so to speak, into ordinary functioning memory.

Any mechanism that enables a traumatic memory to be turned into an ordinary memory is going to cure phobias and post traumatic stress. But the human givens approach uses the most direct path: keeping the physiological arousal level down so that the neocortex of the observing self can set up the feedback loops necessary to reframe that memory.

When properly applied, the technique will cure phobias, even serious ones, in one session. It is also an excellent way to detraumatise disturbing flashbacks and post traumatic stress symptoms arising from any kind of event perceived as life threatening. But, for people who have a history of abuse, the technique may need to be used over a period of time to deal separately with all the major incidents that the person is still traumatised by.

Fast, non-voyeuristic and safe treatment for trauma

There are three main advantages of the technique. Firstly, it is safe. No harm can come to people by using this technique, whereas, as we have seen, some other talking therapies can embed trauma deeper.

Secondly, it is non-voyeuristic. A person who has been raped, for example, can undergo this treatment without, if they so wish, having to talk to the counsellor about any of the intimate details of the experience. The counsellor doesn't watch the 'film'; the client does. A vivacious young woman came to see Ivan because she was having panic attacks, flashbacks, intrusive thoughts and exhibiting many other distressing symptoms of PTSD. She had been attacked and raped twice, a month apart, by two different men. Both men were caught and convicted. But she was now living in a state of high anxiety and hypervigilance, particularly when in the presence of men who were attracted to her and despite the fact that she hoped for a normal heterosexual relationship. She had changed jobs several times because of her distress. And because of her psychological state she had also seen a clinical psychologist and a counsellor – encounters she had found disturbing, painful and useless. She hated talking about exactly what had happened. Without knowing any more detail about the rapes than you have just read she was detraumatised in one session by using the fast phobia cure technique. When she returned a week later she confirmed that the anxiety had gone. She reported that she had gone straight home after the session, emptied her filing cabinet of all the papers relating to the court case and thrown them in the dustbin "with no emotion at all". Previously, just opening the door of the room where the cabinet was used to make her burst into tears.

Thirdly, the technique is fast. A person traumatised by being in a rail crash, for example, who as a consequence wouldn't use any form of public transport, and didn't even want to leave home, could use buses and trains again immediately after undergoing this process. This was the experience of a survivor of the Paddington rail crash who was treated by a colleague of ours at the request of the Metropolitan Police.

However, it would be quite wrong to say that treatment is always exceptionally quick. When traumas have been endured over a long period of time, although it may be possible to resolve them in a single session, some people will need long-term counselling. This is determined by how much damage was sustained to the personality while the traumatic events were ongoing. Two contrasting case histories illustrate this important point.

A young girl in her middle teens was brought to see Joe. She was suffering from acute anxiety due to having been sexually abused over a number of years by a paedophile lodging in the family home. When she grew older, the perpetrator moved on into another family home in search of younger prey. Only then did the girl tell her mother what had been going on. The mother told the police and the police arrested the paedophile, who confessed to his crimes and is now serving a long prison sentence.

The mother then sent her daughter for 'conventional' counselling where she was encouraged to recall, in great detail, all the episodes of abuse to "get her anger out". Whilst she was in counselling her parents noticed that the young girl was becoming more and more neurotic so they arranged for her to change to another counsellor. But the next counsellor's approach was much the same as the first and, over the next six months, the girl became progressively more neurotic and dysfunctional. At this point, she was brought by her mother to see Joe.

When the girl arrived it was immediately obvious that she didn't actually want to be treated because she felt that this would somehow be disloyal to her current counsellor who she thought was her "best friend in the whole world". (It is interesting, as research has shown,[36] that a person can be damaged by the counselling process and yet feel that the counselling has been positively helpful. The reason for this response is that certain important emotional needs, such as those for attention or friendship, may often be met within a counselling relationship, particularly if the counselling is long term, as all too often it is.)

Joe explained to this young girl that, for his treatment for trauma, she did not have to give him *any* details whatsoever about the abuse. She smiled at once, highly relieved, and visibly relaxed. All she was asked to do was give different code words for her worst memories of the abuse.

She explained that she had been abused in almost every room in the house and that, consequently, she was terrified to be in any room other than her parents' bedroom, where she currently slept because that was the only room in which no abuse had occurred. She gave a code word, such as 'hairbrush', for her worst memory of abuse in her own bedroom, another word for her worst memory in her brother's, and so on for each room in the house. Then, in a single session, they detraumatised key traumatic memories relevant to each room in the house. The young lady went home tired, calm and changed.

When she came back a week later, her mother said that the girl's life had been transformed. She was now sleeping in her own bedroom for the first time since prior to the start of all her counselling. Her parents had placed their house on the market, thinking their daughter could never be happy there again, but she had now told them that she was perfectly comfortable about staying there and that they could take the house off the market. The parents themselves were now also getting along better with each other (all the trauma and stress had previously put them at loggerheads), so the entire family had benefited from that single first session of counselling.

This is an example of a severe degree of trauma, a substantial neurotic reaction, being able to be dealt with quickly. It was possible because the young girl's life was functional outside of the trauma itself. She had a good relationship with her parents; she was doing well in school, and her life had otherwise developed normally, so the trauma was something self-contained which could be resolved quickly.

In other cases, which we might encounter, long-term work is necessary. For example, on another occasion Joe saw a 21-year-old man who had suffered prolonged abuse from his paedophiliac, sadistic father who had sexually tortured and raped all of his children from a very young age on a regular basis. (He is currently serving a prison sentence.) This young man had come from a totally abnormal background and had spent long periods in a zombie-like state. His unnatural upbringing meant that he had not developed normally. The inner templates – human givens – which need appropriate stimuli from the environment to complete themselves were never given the opportunity for fulfilment. He had had no experience of caring parents, loving intimacy, and so on. So, naturally, his reaction patterns were abnormal – severely neurotic or underdeveloped.

In his case it required four years of counselling before his reaction patterns were fully retrained, enabling him to relax and have normal relationships with people, engage with the opposite sex without experiencing undue difficulties, find a meaningful job and become an independent, fully functioning, human being. For the first several months of counselling, several dozen traumatic memories were detraumatised, using the fast phobia technique but, because there were multiple dysfunctions due to his awful history, it was not a complete therapy in and of itself. In cases like that of this young man, a tremendous amount of retraining has to be done to compensate for the unfulfilled patterns which should have been unfolded, and skills which should have been acquired, during childhood and adolescence. The fast phobia technique was an essential part of the therapy, but so was the restructuring and training that took place alongside and after it.

Curing phobias

Phobias are extremely common. Approximately 11 per cent of the population experience a specific phobia at some time in their life.[37] There is a marked gender difference with a lifetime prevalence among women of 15.7 per cent and 6.7 per cent for men.[38] Our, admittedly anecdotal, experience leads us to think that even more people report some degree of phobic response to certain stimuli – the most common of which are spiders, snakes, worms, flying, fear of enclosed spaces, fear of open spaces, fear of crowds and fear of heights. Indeed, as might be expected from what we have explained so far, people can develop a phobic response to *any* situation that has a similarity to situations in which they have previously experienced acute anxiety. People can be phobic of windows if they witnessed something dreadful through a window, of birds if they were ever suddenly frightened by a bird, of grass if they had a panic attack whilst standing on grass, of a particular food if they once almost choked to death whilst eating it, and so on.

The physiology of phobias is much the same as that of post traumatic stress disorder – a pattern (memory template) is imprinted in the amygdala and is trapped there, instead of being transferred to the neocortex. The template may be embedded as the result of a trauma – for example, one woman developed a cat phobia as a child after having kittens thrown at her by other children who thought it hilarious fun when the kittens' claws came out and dug into her chest. But in many cases, children simply learn their phobias from their parents, because children are programmed by nature to learn the fear reactions of their primary carers. If a fearful mother hides in panic under the kitchen table every time there is lightning and a clap of thunder in the neighbourhood, it is not surprising if her children develop a phobia about thunderstorms.

However, when treating a phobia with this technique we don't need to know whether a phobia was caused by a traumatic learning experience or whether it was caused by modelling. This is because the client's only need is to learn how not to be phobic in the presence of that stimulus. All that is important is the deconditioning of the response pattern. It really doesn't matter how the pattern got there.

To decondition the response pattern, we need the client to provide perhaps three or four examples – their most vivid memories – of when they felt fearful in the presence of the phobic stimulus. So, in the case of a phobia of cats, for example, the client is asked to recall three occasions when she felt very scared – a high degree of panic – in the presence of cats. For example: when, as a child, she visited her grandmother whose cat suddenly jumped up onto a garden fence in front of her; when a cat rubbed itself against her legs; and when a cat unexpectedly wandered into her office at work. On all of these three occasions she would have felt extremely and unreasonably scared, with a strong urge to get away from the cat as fast as possible. So we would simply decondition each of those memories after relaxing her and using the fast phobia treatment as described. This is sufficient to detraumatise the response pattern completely.

We then encourage her to imagine, whilst still in the relaxed state, travelling into the future and seeing herself co-existing with the previously phobic stimuli in a normal manner: stroking cats, feeding them, picking them up, etc.

Often, at first, a client doesn't know for sure whether or not their phobic response has gone, so they might still retain a moderate degree of apprehension about their next encounter with the phobic object. To attenuate this reaction we try, if possible, to procure an example of the feared stimulus while clients are still with us so that they can test out their reactions for certain. So, with a cat, one would arrange for a cat to be brought into the room after the technique had been carried out. For an arachnophobic, a spider would, if possible, be caught in a glass jar and be slowly brought towards the client, but with the client always allowed to feel able to say, "Stop". As the client becomes more and more comfortable with the spider getting closer, we would suggest that, within a few minutes, the client will be able to hold the jar containing the spider, look at it closely, then take the jar outside and let the spider free.

Similarly, if someone has a phobia of lifts, we would take them to any nearby building that has a lift and go into it with them. After accompanying the client the first time, we would then let them go up and down on their own to prove to themselves that the phobia is deconditioned. It is, of course, only after the client has encountered the spider, or gone up and down in the lift, that they know that their old reaction pattern has really gone.

The client finds this process exhilarating, not only because they are freed from the inconvenience of their symptoms, but also because their brain, thereafter, literally has more spare capacity once it is not using valuable energy to maintain the phobic template.

Panic attacks and agoraphobia

Therapists working from the human givens perspective use this technique not only for PTSD or phobias, but also in other ways.

Fear of panic attacks is common among people who have experienced one – an understandable reaction since a panic attack is literally a 'dreadful' experience. This fear can easily develop into agoraphobia, where the person is so anxious and afraid of having a panic attack that they won't even leave home.

A panic attack occurs when the fight or flight response, the emergency reaction in the human body which prepares it to deal with physical danger, is inappropriately set off. Since people are rarely in the presence of life-threatening events, and yet still suffer from panic attacks, it is clear that they are mostly triggered by a progressive rising in an individual's background stress levels. There comes a point when one more stress – and it can be quite a small one – becomes the straw that breaks the camel's back. Panic is the result. The person doesn't understand why their heart is pounding, why they are sweating, why their breathing rate is accelerating – all natural reactions to stress – and so jumps to the conclusion that something is seriously wrong (typically that they are having a heart attack), which causes even more alarm and more adrenaline to be released, magnifying the symptoms further.

During this extreme alarm arousal the brain, naturally enough, is scanning the environment to find out what the source of this alarm could be, noting all kinds of accompanying details and coding them in the amygdala for future reference. Not surprisingly then, for many people, the association is with the environment where the panic attack happened. If it happened at the cinema, in future the person will tend to avoid cinemas. But because the panic attack was not caused by the cinema but by raised stress levels, the next time the person feels over stressed, perhaps whilst out shopping, they may experience another panic attack and so start avoiding shops as well – and so on. Progressively, the noose of agoraphobia develops, forming a stranglehold that restricts the person's ability to continue with any normal life.

A combination of relaxation, behavioural and cognitive therapy is a useful treatment modality for this condition: in other words, teaching the person to deal with whatever is raising their stress levels, calm themselves down and progressively re-engage with life. However, this process is rapidly accelerated if the memories of their most frightening panic attacks are detraumatised first. Then the brain won't be pattern matching from the previous panic attack to whatever situation they are going into next. This greatly helps the recovery process.

It is much easier to work with panic attack cases once one understands that the memory templates of past panic attacks have become locked into the emotional brain. Then it is possible to go ahead and do what is necessary to turn them into ordinary memories.

It greatly speeds up recovery for people who have developed agoraphobia, if the pattern matches to environments that disturb them – typically, supermarkets, high streets, schools, tube trains, or any potentially crowded public situation – are defused in this way. They then need help to rehearse imaginatively, in their relaxed REM trance state, entering those environments in a calm manner and going about their business normally. This rehearsal, by giving them a new mental template to match to, helps them more readily re-enter these situations in reality. The usual practice is to establish and agree with the client a hierarchical scale of feared situations and work through them, from least to most feared.

Obsessive compulsive disorder (OCD)

We discussed OCD in an earlier chapter. Obsessions are thoughts, images or impulses that cause marked degrees of anxiety or distress. Compulsions are repetitively carried out behaviours (such as hand washing) or thoughts (such as silently repeating certain phrases or counting things) that follow rigid rules and are performed in an attempt to reduce the distress brought on by the obsessions or as a way of making reparation for intrusive scary thoughts.

But OCD is a very unforgiving master, because the more rituals carried out to appease it, the more the frightening thoughts recur. As with agoraphobia, the noose gets pulled tighter and tighter and the person's area of effective functioning shrinks ever smaller. Every time sufferers carry out a ritual, they reinforce the OCD: just as every time an agoraphobic avoids going out they reinforce their particular fear pattern.

Two to three people in every hundred suffer from OCD.[39] We find that OCD responds well to the fast phobia technique during which the fear of *not* performing the obsessive behaviour is detraumatised (thus making it less frightening), followed by getting the sufferer to rehearse in a dissociated state what it will be like to live *without* performing the abnormal behaviour or having the compulsive thoughts.

As with panic attacks, the triggering factor in OCD seems to be raised stress levels, which may be due to anything from physical illness to a fright, lack of sleep, business worries, relationship breakdown or exam worries. Some people have a propensity to develop this disorder in response to raised stress levels.

Clients are clearly terrified of cutting out their rituals, whether they are washing their hands 50 times in case their son will be killed in an accident in school, or whether they are stacking all their clothes up in a particular order in their bedroom because otherwise they think they will get a terrible disease. The strong emotion aroused locks them into a trance state. (OCD sufferers usually have no sense of time whilst carrying out their rituals, nor often can they remember whether they have carried out the ritual properly or not, resulting in the perceived need to perform it over and over. As we have seen, such time distortion and amnesia are both hypnotic phenomena.)

In their trance the intrusive thought, like a powerful posthypnotic suggestion, instructs the individual that they must perform the behaviour to relieve the fear. This is clearly not rational thinking but just as when, in the REM state, we dream and believe in the reality of the dream, so do the entranced OCD sufferers believe in the reality of the OCD ritual and its consequences. They have no alternative, just as we cannot easily avoid dreaming. The thought of stopping the rituals genuinely frightens them.

One of the key steps in working with OCD – as in effective therapy for any symptomatology – is for the therapist to help the client to separate their core identity from their problem. In this process, by whatever means, the therapist or counsellor helps the sufferer to take a step back into their observing self and recognise that the OCD is not part of who they are (their core sense of self). It is outside them, separate but impinging in unwelcome ways.

Once the person can see themselves as separate from OCD they can recognise and separate out an OCD thought from a normal thought. This is vital: developing the ability to recognise when the OCD is in charge as distinct from when their brain is functioning normally.

Essentially, we want to keep the person in their observing self so that they can observe the OCD and keep their distance from it. Whenever they recognise the OCD thoughts intruding, they must have some form of distraction instantly available to them to pull their attention away from the OCD thought and calm them down.

A useful tactic is to replace the problematic behavioural rituals with less problematic ones and for people to have these harmless rituals prepared in advance so that they can switch into them when they need to distract themselves from the OCD thoughts. The harmless rituals can be anything such as aerobic activity, listening to music, calling a friend on the phone, reading a book of poetry or watching a drama on television – anything that they can immediately engage with as a means of distraction so as to avoid carrying out the rituals that the OCD is commanding them to perform.

As the client learns to avoid, or minimise, carrying out the rituals, a feedback mechanism is set up from the environment, saying, in effect, to the primitive part of the brain affected by the OCD, "Look, these thoughts aren't real ... those imagined bad consequences aren't happening". Once enough of this feedback is received, the OCD thoughts are switched off.

This is where the fast phobia technique can be so useful with OCD. We get the client, in a calm, relaxed and dissociated state, to see themselves on a TV screen, experiencing the frightening thought, but not carrying out the rituals. For instance, they experience, in a dissociated state, the OCD thought instructing them to wash their hands repeatedly, otherwise their son will die, and then watch themselves *not* washing their hands but, instead, doing something entirely different, such as knitting or doing a crossword, with no adverse consequences. Once they have that novel idea in their mind, associated with a relaxed state, they have created a new template that says, in effect, "My son will not die if I don't carry out the rituals – so I can stop doing them".

The following case history illustrates how OCD can be reduced in this way. A man worked in a garage in charge of the spare parts division. His father, at the age of 40, had died of a heart attack. When he himself reached that age he had a panic attack and made the common assumption that it was a heart attack. He went along to his GP who checked him out and told him his heart was absolutely fine. But the raised stress levels triggered off OCD in him. He started to get scary thoughts and developed rituals to appease the thoughts.

Two primary rituals caused him maximum distress. Every day on his way home from work at the garage, the thought would occur to him that he had knocked somebody down, even though he had no awareness of doing so. He imagined someone lying unconscious on the road, bleeding to death as a result of his careless driving. This thought would become so powerful that, by the time he got home, he was in acute anxiety and would have to drive slowly back the whole 30 miles to the garage to check that there had been no accident. This ritual took up a large portion of each evening.

The second ritual that distressed him was caused by the thought, which would occur to him as customers were leaving the garage after work had been done on their cars, that he might have supplied the wrong parts to be fitted. He would visualise the car catching fire and the occupants burning to death. He would experience extreme anxiety, rush out to retrieve the car from the customer and check the new part against the stock just to make sure it was the right one. This, of course, distressed customers and the management of the garage alike.

One useful aspect of working with people with OCD is that, if we give them something to do, they can become quite obsessive about carrying out our instructions, so we can use this compulsive tendency productively to facilitate the treatment. The first intervention with this man was to use guided imagery to help him achieve a deep state of relaxation. Joe got him to imagine himself somewhere really peaceful and safe – the first step in the fast phobia cure. This part of the session was recorded on tape and included the message loud and clear: "Isn't it nice to know that your doctor has thoroughly checked you over and you have a sound, strong, healthy heart?" because that was the worry that had triggered off the OCD in the first place. During that first session Joe also gave the client the instruction that each evening, as soon as he got home, he was to rush into his house, go to his bedroom and sit down and listen to this relaxation tape, rather than drive back to the garage. He reinforced this by encouraging the man to visualise himself, via the fast phobia technique, coming home from work and listening to his tape, with no adverse consequences.

The man did this for a couple of weeks and, as he found that there were no unidentified bodies being discovered on the road between his house and the garage, no hit-and-run stories appearing in the local newspapers, the feedback message from reality got into his brain and the obsessive thought faded away. He was then ready to deal with his next great fear, which centred around handing out spare car parts at the garage.

He was excellent at his job. He knew by heart every spare part the garage had in stock, but this problem of fearing he had supplied the wrong part was overwhelming him. One important counselling principle is that, if a problem is too big to solve in one go, the best thing to do is break it down into smaller chunks and deal with each one.

This is the approach that Joe took. When the thought occurred to the man that the wrong part had been fitted to a car, instead of rushing out and retrieving it to make sure it was the right part – not to check would have left him in such an acute state of anxiety that he would be dysfunctional for the rest of the day – he agreed to alter the ritual. In future, on handing out a spare part, he would write the number of the part in a notebook. Then, after the customer had left with the car, when he felt the anxiety about having given out the wrong part rising, he would go to the stockroom and check the number in his notebook against the stock to make sure the right part had been used. Doing this no longer disrupted the smooth running of the garage and started to moderate his anxiety, making it more tolerable. Again, after a few weeks, the obsessive thought just died away.

Joe saw him on a weekly basis for about six weeks, using the fast phobia technique on each occasion and showing him how to focus his attention outwards and think more positively and constructively, till the OCD was completely eliminated. Well, in truth, there was still one ritual left. He was still listening to the tape compulsively! So, the final step in the therapeutic procedure was to wean him off doing that.

In this case history we can see at work several principles of effective therapy which always work from the human givens: relaxation, enabling the person to go into their observing self; separation of the observing self from the problem; the principle of dissociation in order to facilitate a more realistic template being introduced to the amygdala and to accelerate the development of desired behaviour patterns; the use of imagination; drawing on clients' own resources; breaking down problems so that they can be solved, etc.

Social phobia, fear of job interviews and exams can be helped in much the same way.

The chair's problem

Erickson, who inspired the development of so many of the solution focused approaches to therapy, used a method to cure phobias that was even shorter than the one which we have outlined. He found that it worked with good hypnotic subjects, although he seems not to have recognised that the phobic or traumatised state is always associated with good hypnotic subjects – such disorders are their vulnerability.

Once he had a phobic person sitting in a deeply relaxed trance in a comfortable chair he would ask them to recall what it felt like to be very frightened of whatever their phobia concerned. At the point when they were aroused to a high state of anxiety and very uncomfortable with that anxious feeling, he would ask them if they would like to lose their anxiety. When they nodded their head, he would say something like, "In a moment ... I'm going to ask you to stand up and move to this chair over here ... and to leave your fear behind you in that chair". Because the subject was in a deeply hypnotic state – the REM state, the programming part of the mind – the phobic's brain was receptive enough to take on board that instruction. They would move chairs and leave their phobia in the first chair.[40]

We now know that what Erickson was doing was taking the fear template in the amygdala, the pattern of feeling fear of flying or of cats or of thunder or whatever, and confining its reaction pattern to one stimulus only, namely the chair with which the brain now associates it. Indeed, when subjects came out of trance, Erickson would later ask them to sit down on the first chair again and their strong feeling of fear would instantly return because their amygdala would pattern match to the original template now associated with that specific chair in his office.

Erickson's rapid technique is as effective a cure as going through the fast phobia process we've described here. The difficulty, though, is that one does need great confidence in using hypnotic skills and a deeply hypnotic state in the client in order to effect the restriction of a phobic response pattern to a specific piece of furniture. However, his technique neatly illustrates the mechanics by which post traumatic stress disorder and phobias are developed – a pattern in the amygdala is seeking its counterpart in the environment, seeking something to match up to.

For the sufferer from PTSD, phobic responses, panic or OCD, it doesn't matter how the result is achieved. Whether we remove this pattern from the amygdala with the fast phobia technique and get it processed through the neocortex as an ordinary memory, or change it by restricting the application of the pattern to an innocuous stimulus, as Erickson showed could be done, either way the distressing symptom is reliably disabled and dealt with, and the misery gone.

* * *

Effective counsellors and psychotherapists (there is no meaningful difference between the two titles – both need to be equally competent in relieving patients of psychological/behavioural distress as quickly as possible) require a range of skills that let them operate creatively, in a comprehensive, holistic way, treating each patient as an individual who has unique beliefs, resources and abilities. As we hope we have shown, human givens therapy is a package of skills that brings together all the knowledge and techniques from many different disciplines in the service of relieving distress. We believe that training counsellors and psychotherapists in this approach is the most practical and cost-effective way forward in this hitherto confusing field, for the treatment of all forms of emotional disorder.

However, the implications of our findings go much further than psychotherapy. Teachers and social workers are beginning to realise that the ideas set out in this book have enormous significance for their work (see Appendices III and VII). But it's more useful even than that. The way we think about and plan for change in society, as we try to adapt, would benefit hugely if we all shared a common perception about intrinsic human needs and worked towards ensuring that each of us, our families and the groups we belong to, are getting them met. Then we can concentrate on learning how to leave this place more easily, not grieving, not craving – but free.

A new scientific metaphor: consciousness – more is less

WE HUMAN beings are vulnerable creatures. Indeed, much of this book has focused on how the same biological systems that help us survive can also damage the brain and body when our physical and emotional needs are not met in the world. In this Afterword, by contrast, we are going to draw together some threads laid out in the opening chapter, particularly those about our future evolution and our intrinsic need for meaning. With these we will weave patterns that may seem strange to anyone holding one of the currently more fashionable views about human nature: such as that propounded by some scientists, that we are undistinguished creatures, living ultimately meaningless lives on an ordinary planet, dwarfed by the size of our galaxy – a galaxy which is made up of hundreds of billions of stars and which is itself rendered insignificant by the billions of equally star-rich galaxies in what we now know to be an unimaginably huge universe.

According to this view, since all matter, including all life, derives mainly from four common elements – hydrogen, carbon, oxygen and nitrogen – humankind is "qualitatively no different from the 'lesser' forms of life".[1] Science, it is said, has proved our place in the universal scheme of things to be of no real account and shown that humans are just "a result of blind evolutionary drift."[2] To cap it all, many who hold this view maintain that, since every viewpoint can be deconstructed, no one point of view is more true than any other. Anyone who suggests otherwise is mocked. In consequence, choosing to live a life as a selfish, consumerist hedonist – pursuing pleasure as the highest aim and giving little thought to the morrow – is presumed to be equally as valid a choice as any other.

This widespread nihilistic philosophy ultimately infects every age group and stratum of society and we believe it to be highly destructive. It breeds cynicism and opportunism in politics. It justifies the exploitation of people and the planet in the name of materialistic gratification. It places the supposed 'fact' of meaninglessness in a central position in academic circles and drives people into mind-numbing, life-denying, truth-abandoning tunnel vision in politics, science and religion. We follow it like lambs to the slaughter.

As therapists who work with distressed people and as researchers in the field of mental health, it is clear to us that those who try to explain life in terms of its smallest parts, without connecting and unifying their discoveries with the bigger picture, are helping to undermine our collective mental health. This is because such "destructive reductionism" as neuropsychologist Steven Pinker terms it,[3] creates black and white thinking (a style of thinking also associated with mental disturbance, as we have shown). In black and white thinking, the focus is inwards rather than outwards: thus we can end up believing that 'we are our genes', and that it is genes that are selected,[4] instead of the bodies whose characteristics are determined by an ensemble of genes. When such thinking is harnessed to postmodern 'thought', which also strips out and denies that there is real meaning in what we do, it induces cynical pessimism – a trend in our culture that runs counter to all that we now know about what people need in order to live fulfilled lives.

Concern about these matters, coupled with the knowledge that the need for meaning is a human given, has led us to think more and more deeply about why it should be so. As a result of much questioning, conjecturing and gathering of information from science and other sources, we would now like to put forward a speculative hypothesis – an explanatory organising idea – to show how meaning is a fundamental aspect of all reality.

We are aware that there is a long history of resistance to new theories. Many scientists prefer to sit on the fence endlessly gathering data, but explanations and understanding do not automatically arise out of this process. To be able usefully to discriminate data, one needs a realistic organising hypothesis and we believe that the one we are setting out here could make sense of a mass of data and explain, not only the place of meaning in our lives, but also why and how consciousness might have evolved. We hope therefore, as you read this Afterword, you will temporarily suspend your own beliefs and judgements for a while and let yourself go with the flow of our argument, so that you can absorb it fully and then subject it to critical thought later. We hope merely to interest you in a very different possibility from the currently prevailing sad scenario of meaninglessness outlined above.

The mystery of consciousness

Consciousness, most scientists agree, is the greatest mystery in the universe.[5] In the numerous recent books on consciousness, few authors try to define it or clearly set out its purpose. (There are, however, some notable exceptions, such as psychologist Merlin Donald, who states in his book *A Mind So Rare*: "Consciousness played a causal role in the evolution of the human mind. We are a supremely conscious species; this was the key to our success in the past, and it will continue to be in the future."[6]) For the most part, scientists think they know what consciousness is until they try to articulate it, and then they find that they *can't* explain it. Quite commonly, they claim it to be beyond the human mind to say anything sensible about the subject, because the mind isn't subtle enough to understand itself, and therefore they surmise that consciousness will always remain a mystery.[7] Some scientists, like Daniel Dennett, even trivialise it, regarding it as an epiphenomenon, a by-product of brain activity, which has virtually no influence on mental life and is thus of no consequence.[8] But that argument goes against evolutionary theory which holds that organs and processes which evolve and persist serve a purpose – to help the organism survive; therefore, consciousness must also somehow serve a purpose. But what function or purpose *could* it serve?

This is a particularly acute question in the light of fascinating findings from brain research. The neuroscientist Professor Benjamin Libet and others have shown that the brain processes information taken in through the sense organs and reaches decisions about it *before* presenting that information to consciousness.[9] When brain waves that accompany a decision to act are measured, they are seen to occur a fraction of a second before an individual is aware of having made a decision. In other words, contrary to what had been thought, consciousness is not actually involved in the decision.

What this must mean is that we do not experience reality directly. What we experience is a representation of reality – a *re-presentation* –

we don't experience it in the moment; we experience it shortly after it has occurred. Also, as the brain constantly edits what reaches consciousness from the senses – otherwise we would have information overload – what we experience is just a sample of what actually occurred. Interestingly, this would seem to confirm the observation made by many mystics over the millennia. Humankind, they have said, normally does *not* directly experience reality. When mystics 'enter the moment' totally, as they claim to have done, they report directly experiencing a feeling of immense connection to a greater entity – a feeling, quite different from normal consciousness, which has been described as *undifferentiated unity*. The psychiatrist Arthur Deikman wrote that, "According to mystics, [undifferentiated unity] is an experience in which the usual division between self and the world of objects ceases to exist. The experience is one of supreme bliss, of ultimate fulfilment, but one does not experience it as one would eating an ice cream cone. The person is no longer separated from the experience; the person becomes the experience. Most important of all, undifferentiated unity is not sensory, not a super orgasm; one reaches the experience intuitively. The pure state is temporary, but one who has known it can expand his or her comprehension of life and undergo a personality transformation."[10] Mystics have said there is a science that makes it possible to prepare people to experience the truth directly and that this is the most significant work possible for a human being.

So, we go back to the question: why did consciousness evolve? It must serve some purpose. Some thinkers have had a stab at suggesting one. One theory put forward is that, although the initial decision may not be conscious, consciousness may serve as a second-level corrective by exposing that decision to conscious review. This allows the brain to revise the decision if necessary, giving us greater flexibility in our responses to events. In other words, it is a type of feedback learning mechanism.[11]

Their theory can be explained like this: if, while playing tennis, you managed to return a fast serve, you would have moved to do so *before* you knew whether the ball was coming at you, responding to cues that had not yet reached consciousness. If your return of serve was poor, the ability to become conscious of it afterwards would give you valuable feedback to help you improve that shot next time. The problem with this theory is that, if the brain can make decisions without consciousness, why can't it set up a feedback mechanism to re-evaluate those decisions without consciousness too?

So yet again we are back with the fundamental problem: why is consciousness there at all?

We think the human givens perspective could provide an answer. If we take as our starting point the given that the brain is a metaphorical pattern-matching organ we can see that consciousness is what occurs when an inner template pattern matches up to the stimuli the brain receives through the senses from the outside environment – such as a baby's instinctive response to the human face that we see almost immediately after it's born. It would make sense that, whenever inner and outer patterns match up in this basic reality orientation process, which is a prime function of every brain, a spark of consciousness is released. It is that moment we all recognise when 'the penny drops'. Without this spark, no reality would exist for us. This is because everything we see is a collection of meanings – from a simple object like a glass to a vast panoramic landscape – and the meanings come from this reality orientation process. We have to have had conscious experience of some aspect of what we see for it to mean something to us. For instance, a person who has never encountered a drinking glass before might see it as a hollow, transparent rock; they wouldn't know what it was used for, and it wouldn't call forth associations with water or with social events.

Everything we see is 'mind-externalising'. As the philosopher of science Henri Bortoft once said, "All scientific knowledge is a correlation of *what* is seen with the *way* that it is seen,"[12] and this is as true for ordinary life as it is for science. It is always a relationship that we see. And, for a relationship to be formed, things have to be connected. It is the matching, or connecting, of the inner and outer that is the process that creates consciousness. So, although the brain decides many things prior to consciousness, it can only do so by virtue of the fact that what it is encountering in the world connects up to either an *innate* template (pre-learned instinct) or a *learned* (memorised) template that has passed through consciousness – the glass becomes associated with drinking. Without templates the brain wouldn't be able to register change in the environment or anything that exists.

Why all learning requires consciousness

Viewed from this perspective, all learning requires consciousness. To give a simple example, Ivan's young dog, called Barley, was once let into a garden where chickens were ranging freely. The dog's hunting instinct kicked in and he went after the chickens. He would have killed them but for the fact that the chickens' owner grabbed a stick and went screaming after Barley, thwacking him across his flank, to drive him away from the chickens – and taking him completely by surprise. Up till then, Barley had always associated a raised stick with fun – a game of 'fetch!' But, since the chicken incident, he associates a raised stick, or any similar object, such as a badminton racquet, with chasing chickens and with being struck. His instinctive reactions were recoded in the moment that he became aware of what was happening. Now he instantly cowers at the sight of a raised stick.

We know from experiments carried out in laboratories[13] that if we could measure the readiness potential in Barley's brain while showing him a raised racquet we would see a brain wave, corresponding to the decision to back off, occurring more quickly than a conscious decision could appear in his mind. Clearly, since decisions are made at a level prior to consciousness, the brain can only be basing them on patterns already coded in the brain. Barley had to make new connections in his conscious mind between raised stick, angry shouting, being hit and unloved for a moment, and not chasing chickens because, prior to that learning experience, he had no pattern for such a relationship coded in. His reactions from that time on have become automatic and unconscious – he doesn't chase chickens. Consciousness is not involved any more because he has learned the lesson and the necessary connections are in place.

So consciousness is the 'light' generated by connecting an inner template to an outside pattern: the perceiving of a relationship between this and that. This is what happens when we learn a new skill, like driving a car. At first, because we don't yet 'know', it requires an effort of conscious concentration to remember all the moves involved in changing gear while simultaneously steering, assessing distance, speed and so on. This is stimulating. But, after a while, the brain is coded with those moves, enabling us to change gear in a fraction of the time without even being conscious of it. We drive automatically only once a template for driving has been installed in our unconscious brain *after* driving consciously whilst learning.

Self-consciousness, however, sometimes gets in the way of learning a new skill, as when a trainee athlete's mind is on what people might think if he fails to win, or a young music student cares more about the audience's reaction than the music. This has been quoted as evidence that consciousness impedes learning.[14] What is really happening, however, is that the template for evaluating self-image in social situations has been activated, thus *diverting* consciousness from the task at hand. It is not that consciousness interferes with learning but that conscious attention is being given to the wrong pattern.

It has also been argued that learning can be unconscious. One often cited, so-called illustration of this concerns a professor of psychology who explained to his students that certain reinforcements, applied in the right way at the right time, could shape behaviour, and that pigeons had been taught to play table tennis in exactly that way. The pigeons were given rewards when they carried out actions that approximated all of the movements made in the game. This encouraged them to repeat those actions in the desired order and thus they appeared to be playing table tennis.

But the students were ahead of the professor and, after listening to his lectures, started to shape *his* behaviour. They did this by giving him rapt attention and laughing at his jokes whenever he moved to the right side of the podium. After a while, the professor was directing his entire lecture from that one corner of the platform, totally unaware of what the students had done to him![15]

It is true that the professor was unaware that the students had decided in advance to reinforce aspects of his behaviour so as to manipulate it. But the professor would have been perfectly well aware that, while over at the right of the podium, he received more attention from his students; and hence increasingly chose to stay in that part of the room. So he *was* conscious of what he was learning (that he was getting attention when he stood in a particular spot) but was unaware why it was happening (the students had set him up).

In another experiment intended to support the unconscious learning theory, members of a psychology class were asked by experimenters to compliment girls who wore red. Within a week the university cafeteria was a riot of red clothing. After questioning the girls, the researchers concluded that none of them was aware of being influenced. Clearly though, at the time of being complimented on the red item of clothing, each girl was highly conscious of receiving the compliment. Receiving compliments is always something we are highly conscious of. This conscious experience would increase the probability that the girls would choose to wear red items more frequently. Furthermore, they would be conscious of the increasing popularity of red on the campus as they all wore red more often. This, too, would set up a conscious feedback loop, increasing the probability of red clothing being worn more frequently. What the girls were not conscious of, of course, was that they were being manipulated as part of a psychology experiment by being given insincere feedback (compliments) on their attractiveness when wearing red clothes.[16]

It might be argued that bodily processes of which we are not conscious, such as hair growth or digestion, are also examples of unconscious learning. After all, a baby does not consciously learn to do these things. And none of us were conscious of when they first occurred in our own lives. But we hold that even those complex behaviours must have had an original pattern-match at some point. It is axiomatic that *any* process that functions on an unconscious level in the mind or body must either have passed through an individual's consciousness before mastery; or be the result of chemical codes derived from past conscious pattern-matches in earlier life forms – even as far back as single-celled creatures – and transmitted to us via our genes. (The consciousness of such earlier life forms is sensate consciousness, not self-consciousness.)

The process whereby a new behaviour or characteristic gradually becomes encoded within our genes through natural selection is called genetic assimilation.[17] Consciousness has to have been involved. For instance, Darwin described how, on the Galapagos Islands, he saw finches with different types of beaks. Some had long slender beaks, were tree dwellers and fed on insects. Another species of finch had short, stubby beaks and were ground dwellers, feeding on seeds and cacti. At some point in the distant past, certain finches would have persisted in trying to extract insects from tree bark and others in trying to break off bits of cactus and crack seeds, and this conscious decision would, if continually made over a number of generations, and provided it aided survival, be selected for and lead increasingly to a genetic proclivity for either long or stubby beaks, passed on through their offspring. Thus evolution progresses through consciousness – not blind chance alone.

All learning generates consciousness. The growth of intelligence depends on this. The more we challenge ourselves, the more we learn, the more we can do and the more consciousness we generate. It is when we challenge ourselves that we feel most alive. (When we put what appears to be intelligence into machines, it is merely intelligence 'borrowed' from the people who chose to put it in – not real intelligence and consciousness as some philosophers propose.[18])

But what is it that is so special about inner templates that they can produce consciousness? After all, when a computer matches patterns it doesn't become conscious, so why do living things? To answer this, we must consider the basic structure of reality itself at a point where the psychology of mind and physics meet (as they must). If, as we are suggesting, templates have the potential to produce consciousness when they are pattern matched, they must derive from an aspect of matter that all conscious creatures share.

Clearly a template is not made out of just ordinary matter alone. It must involve an organisation of matter inclusive of special qualities. When we examine consciousness within ourselves, for example, it is our own individual consciousness that we are aware of. This has a uniqueness about it – a sense of 'I'. When I look at a tree it is always *I* that am seeing it. Moreover, when you examine the tree, there is always your 'I am' behind every perception you have of it. *Your* consciousness is always personal to *you*, and *your* individual awareness knows that *you* are a unique window on the universe. So one remarkable quality of consciousness is that everybody has it but it always feels very personal to each one of us.

Consciousness must be matter

Consciousness, then, seems to have this dual aspect to it. There is the 'object' that we are conscious of plus the awareness that it is 'I' and no other who is having this specific experience. The former aspect we will refer to as 'object' consciousness and the latter as 'I am' consciousness. When we look at consciousness from the position of 'I am' consciousness we know that we are separate from the objects of which we are conscious, be they thoughts, emotions, material things, people, etc. Consciousness is behind everything we experience and is unlike anything else in the universe. It has no dimensions and cannot be measured. As Deikman has said, it is somehow *transcendent*.[19] It doesn't have the limitations of ordinary matter.

But, to keep within the laws of science, we must postulate that conscious awareness is made from some kind of matter, albeit a special kind. Physicists have calculated that the material universe started from what they call a *'singularity'* – spacetime folded in on itself, smaller than a grain of sand, yet with an infinite curvature.[20] They have amassed considerable evidence that, 13.7 billion years ago, this singularity exploded in a 'Big Bang'* and set in train the circumstances that gave rise to the complexity of the physical universe, including human beings. So, is there any basis within modern physics for postulating the existence of a special kind of matter of the sort we are suggesting? It would seem that there is. It is widely accepted in physics that there is a vast phenomenon that exhibits the same mysterious, intangible quality as consciousness. It is the stuff that cannot be explained. Physicists call it 'dark matter'.

Dark matter's physical basis is inferred from its gravitational effects, because calculations have shown that galaxies would fly apart unless held together by the gravitational pull of approximately ten times more matter and energy than has been observed. (It is now thought that 96 per cent of matter has not been detected and the rest of the universe consists of 23 per cent dark matter, particles which don't emit any visible radiation, and 73 per cent is dark energy, which appears to be accelerating the expansion of space.[21]) Here is how Sir Martin Rees, the Astronomer Royal and a Royal Society research professor at Cambridge University, describes it: "We now strongly suggest that dark matter cannot consist of anything that is made from ordinary atoms. The favoured view is that it consists of swarms of particles that

---

* Since we are saying that objective matter and subjective matter are *always* present together, the Big Bang theory is not necessary for our idea. We have used it in this presentation of our hypothesis because it is the prevailing model, which most scientists accept holds up and which many new findings support.

have so far escaped detection because they have no electric charge and because they pass straight through ordinary material with barely any interaction."[22] These particles are believed to consist of a type of primordial matter left over from the Big Bang, undetectable by normal instruments.

Our hypothesis, working from psychology back to physics, is in keeping with all this. It is that there are two types of matter: ordinary, atomistic, *objective* matter and another type which is *subjective*. This second type of matter, so infinitely subtle that it permeates everything (because the more subtle something is, the greater its capacity for penetration), accounts for the subjectivity we experience when we are conscious. Subjective matter and objective matter, we suggest, evolved from the singularity: they were once part of the same system and they retain a natural affinity for each other. Wherever there is objective matter, subjective matter is present. And subjective matter is conscious of objective matter.

We need to give this new form of matter a name, in order to talk about it, and so, as the primary characteristic of subjective matter is concerned with relationships, we have called each particle of it a 'relaton' (pronounced 'relate-on' and defined as 'that which is capable of a relationship').

What we are postulating here shouldn't strain the credulity of physicists too much, since many of them subscribe to the 'many worlds' interpretation of quantum theory, which holds that all possibilities are acted out in an infinity of different universes. According to this theory, "there are an infinite number of versions of you, living out an infinite number of different lives in an infinite number of parallel realities".[23]

Some scientists use this notion to get themselves off the hook of the 'anthropic principle' – which is about the incredible range of variable physical factors which must be in place, in exactly the right proportions, for life forms ever to appear. Called the 'multiverse' theory, it posits that there were, and are, zillions of universes, caused by countless Big Bangs, and, purely by fluke, one of them got all the conditions right for life to arise in it. (This is one of two speculations offered to explain how life could have arisen. The other is that the universe is following a design: this implies intelligence, and most scientists reject it out of hand.)

So, although it is hard enough for us to grasp the scale of just one universe, now we are being asked to believe there are *billions* of them being formed every second. Personally, it is beyond our comprehension that life could just be due to chance like this. It is surely far less likely an outcome than the complete works of Shakespeare eventually being produced by the oft-quoted monkey, randomly bashing at the keys of a typewriter. This crazy situation has arisen because scientists, quite rightly, don't want to abandon the scientific quest for knowledge about what the universe is and how it started, and thus leave the field open for religious fundamentalists. The multiverse theory is one escape route from this dilemma.

We are certainly not trying to suggest that there is no randomness involved in evolution. There must always be chance factors involved. A species can be wiped out in a major ecological disaster, for example. But what we *are* suggesting is this: that there was something else in the singularity, besides an infinite density of spacetime that enabled spacetime to be folded in upon itself, something that gave *structure* to spacetime in the singularity. We are suggesting that this was the universal relaton field – a 'field of influence' through which relationships between substances are made possible; a form of subjective matter that manifests itself by connecting things together and giving shape to things. In other words, consciousness was there from the start, unconfined, pervading everything.

We are making a case, in keeping with the laws of science, for evolution not having come about solely by chance. Instead, we suggest, it drew on knowledge and patterns accumulated in the universal relaton field – a material phenomenon of such scope and subtlety that it can only be experienced by human beings momentarily in states of profound intuition. This is our organising idea for how it might have happened.

The relaton field

Our suggestion is that, when the Big Bang occurred, not only was spacetime shattered into the precursors of minuscule particles but the universal relaton field was also shattered and every separate piece of primordial matter took with it a little piece of the relaton field. (In our idea, objective matter and subjective matter are always present together.) Each relaton particle would be capable of a perfect relationship with all others, and have an innate tendency to join up with them in whatever ways presented themselves.

A perfect relationship is analogous to how two drops of water, when they come together, become one. Once joined, the two drops cannot be differentiated: there is a common essence. In this way, relaton fields accompanying particular organisations of matter could join with the relaton fields accompanying other organisations of matter, getting larger and larger all the time. It has been calculated that, following the Big Bang, the first elements to appear were hydrogen and helium particles. The evolution of the elements, when these particles started to coalesce and form gas, was directed by the knowledge, held in the relatons, of what relationships were possible. Then as more and more particles came together and their relaton fields merged, vast 'gas' clouds, stars, planets and galaxies came into being.

Just as the separate pieces of a jigsaw puzzle, when put together, can create a coherent whole picture, so individual particles formed by, and after, the Big Bang retain the potential to create ever more coherent relationships – as the relaton field and the precursors of the particles were once part of a unified whole.

This subjective substance – made up of relatons – would have a variety of characteristics. First, since, like dark matter, it is undetectable, it must be non-atomistic.

Second, it must be capable of relationships, as it was in a relationship with atomistic matter at the time of the Big Bang.

Third, since it is in the nature of relatons to be in relationships, they are always generating consciousness. We previously referred to the two different aspects of consciousness as 'object' consciousness and 'I am' consciousness. The pattern-match between relatons (subjective matter) produces subjective 'I am' consciousness and the pattern-match between relatons and objective matter produces 'object' consciousness. (Even in the singularity itself, a relationship must have existed between relatons and the precursors of objective matter producing 'object' consciousness. Consciousness, as said, was there from the very beginning.) There is an inverse relationship between 'I am' consciousness and 'object' consciousness. Object consciousness necessarily involves separation – disparate objects. The more awareness there is of specific objects, the less awareness of self or 'I am' because of less coherence in the pattern-matching between relatons.

Fourth, since we are capable of being conscious of so many different things, and other species are conscious of things that we are not (think of echo location in bats for instance), relaton particles must, in principle, be capable of forming a relationship with *all* matter.

Fifth, relatons can all relate to each other, so it is in their nature to share knowledge. Knowledge *is* the sharing of relationships (which applies to all matter, not just people); so any relationship is always about shared knowledge.

Sixth, relatons must therefore have the capacity to store knowledge. This would take the form of an impress of patterns (whereas atomistic matter stores most information digitally, in a sequential code such as DNA). The more complex the pattern, the more knowledge is integrated within it and the fewer relatons are required to specify it. (This will be explained fully later.)

Seventh, this matter does not have atomistic matter's limitations of time and space. As the Astronomer Royal says about dark matter, it can flow through us undetected.

So, relationships enable the making of *meaningful* connections. In other words, it becomes clear that the whole is more than the sum of its parts, and the behaviour of the whole cannot be predicted from the characteristics of the parts. This concept is illustrated in the story of the little boy who wanted to understand what made a fly a fly. First he took off one wing, then the other. He then broke off the legs one by one. When he had finished, he couldn't work out where the fly had gone! (The finding of emergent properties is now being studied by many scientists under the rubric of complexity theory.[24])

If the whole were not greater than its parts, there would be no basis for the relaton idea. By this we mean that the whole's properties are not predictable from knowledge of its component parts; e.g. the properties of water, H_2O, are not predictable from knowledge of the properties of oxygen and hydrogen. Nothing can exist without a relaton field and, in accordance with the nature of relatons, each relaton particle has the potential to relate perfectly and completely to all other relatons.

Relatons are capable of organising themselves into any pattern, or template, as long as that template is compatible with the singularity that gave birth to all matter. What are termed the 'laws of nature' are the restrictions placed on atomistic matter, because patterns are not infinitely modifiable. (Thus gravity works according to certain rules and we cannot invent new ones. Nor can we change the speed of light, and so forth.)

Philosophers and scientists have long puzzled over the 'binding problem',[25] the missing link between consciousness and matter. Relatons are that missing link. They facilitate all the relationships that atomistic matter achieves. The relaton template is an essential dimension of any structure in the universe, from subatomic particles to macro particles. It is what enables any relationship to exist – otherwise elementary particles would never have come together, matter would not exist (and neither would we). When particles come together, it is the relatons that pattern match (because they know something of each other – a relationship is always about knowing the 'other'), and enable the generation of a more complex relaton field. An analogy of how this works would be how a magnet organises random iron filings into a pattern.

To recap: when the singularity exploded, each piece of matter had to take a piece of the relaton field with it *because consciousness cannot exist without being in a relationship with matter*. Awareness had to break apart to travel with matter to the ends of the universe. After the explosion, each particle of subjective matter (relaton) was drawn to find a relationship with other particles and driven inexorably to facilitate matter to form ever more complex relationships, beginning with the light elements helium, deuterium and lithium (heavy elements came later). As matter formed more coherent relationships, then relatons too enriched their coherence. It is relatons – 'I' consciousness or the pure unitary sense of existence – that enable material coherence to occur.

'Free' relatons

Every time atomic matter comes into a relationship with other atomic matter, their relaton fields join up. This would have occurred throughout evolution, right from unicellular sea creatures through to fishes, reptiles and mammals. Relaton fields join up, not only when *matter* that they represent integrates with other matter, but even when *ideas* in the human mind become more integrated (such as when space and time became integrated into the scientific idea of 'spacetime').

Whenever, in effect, there is integration and 'two' become 'one', some relatons become 'free' and can be released. The 'free' relatons gravitate naturally towards other free relatons, amalgamating the knowledge they take with them to ultimately enrich the universal relaton field.

The free relatons bring with them a knowledge of the field they have just come from, as well as the capacity to connect with other free relatons and form a relationship field in which that knowledge is shared. But this universal relaton field also continuously needs to relate to matter (otherwise it can't be conscious) and the easiest matter for it to relate to is that from which it has just been separated.

This process is analogous to what was expressed in Bell's theorem. This proved that, when two photons are simultaneously released from an atom and travel in opposite directions, they are still correlated with one another because of their common origin.[26] According to the equations of quantum theory, what happens to one should affect the other, and in a number of experiments this has been proven. For example, it was verified that measuring the properties of one photon simultaneously affects the properties of another photon 10 km away. The two photons, because they were once in a relationship with one another, are still part of the same system – and would remain so, even if they had travelled to different parts of the universe. Thus instantaneous connection, even at vast distance, is not just a mystical understanding but a fundamental property of physics.

So, what happens in the individual relaton fields automatically correlates with what happens in the universal relaton field, developing from the free relatons being released with every new material pattern-match. As each relaton in the universal field carries the impress of the pattern from which it is released, all the relatons joined in the universal relaton field will have knowledge of all the patterns thus far accumulated in the universe. That knowledge will be shared between the relatons now perfectly integrated within the universal relaton field. All patterns coming into being are continually freeing up relatons and adding to the knowledge in the universal relaton field. As Bob Dylan sang, echoing the reported words of Jesus:

"I gaze into the doorway of temptation's angry flame,
And every time I pass that way I always hear my name.

Then onward in my journey I come to understand,
  That every hair is numbered like every grain of sand."[27]

In a very real sense, then, the universal relaton field shares our individual joys, our worries, our pains, our suffering, as well as our discoveries and our learning. This may be what was meant by the cryptic mystical phrase, *as above, so below.* As mystics have said, the parts are known to the whole, and that whole is still evolving with the formation of ever more complex relationships.

Relaton knowledge is never lost. It is conceivable that there were other universes before ours, which collapsed into a singularity and exploded again. While some scientists think our own universe will continue to expand, others claim that the expansion will eventually reverse, in which case it could perhaps collapse once more into a singularity and yet again explode, enabling still more complex matter to emerge. Because relatons keep their knowledge from whatever they have been before, perhaps the process has to be repeated many times to allow even higher life forms to evolve, and thus develop more consciousness.

If knowledge from previous universes had been gathered into the singularity, it would have become available to us in this universe after the Big Bang. This could explain, for instance, the existence of the DNA molecule, believed by Francis Crick, one of the biologists who discovered the double helix structure of DNA, to be far too complex to have evolved spontaneously in the lifetime of Earth. (He has said he believes DNA was brought here in a spaceship.[28]) We think the relaton idea could explain its presence less fancifully. If knowledge of DNA had been in the universal relaton field, our universe couldn't help but develop life.

The universal relaton field must clearly be the most complex relaton field that exists in the universe, since it is the mirror of all relationships in all relatons, connected to all matter. It has a supreme sense of 'I-ness' and it continues to evolve as matter and life itself evolves throughout the universe. It has the most intense subjectivity, the most intense consciousness, that can exist. At this level of organisation it is truth without form. This concept has been described in great detail by poets and mystics from all cultures in all ages. The following is an extract from a lecture delivered over a hundred years ago by Haji

Bahaudin of Bokhara (d. 1900).

> WHEN we say: 'You are a drop of water from an illimitable Sea', we refer both to your present individuality, as a drop, to all your past individualities, as successive drops and waves, and also to the greater bond which unites all these phases with all other drops as well as with the greater Whole. When viewing this Whole, if we do it from the point of view of the grandeur of a Whole Sea, we shall briefly glimpse something of the greatness of the drop in its possible function as a conscious part of that Sea.
>
> In order to know the relationship between the drop and the Sea, we have to cease thinking of what we take to be the interests of the drop.
>
> We can only do this by forgetting what we take ourselves to be, and remembering what we have been in the past, and also remembering what we are at the moment, what we really are; for the relationship with the Sea is only in suspension, it is not severed. It is the suspension which causes us to make strange makeshift assumptions about ourselves, and also to blind us to true reality.[29]*

Mystics describe how it is possible, when greed and emotional arousal is damped down, to tap into this universal relaton field. They have explained that, to have this experience, it is necessary to enter a different state of consciousness from those with which we are all more familiar. As we have explained, normal consciousness is a *re*-presentation of reality, not a direct experience of it. But when someone can actually step into the 'now', as the mystics describe it, their relatons are 'singing in harmony' with the universal relaton field. They directly experience it – experiencing truth without form.

Consciousness has dual aspects. It is Janus faced: looking back and forth, inward and outward. That is why, to engage our highest sense of self, we must engage with objective reality more dispassionately. To help us see this is the function of the Sufi contemplation phrase, *'The phenomenal is the bridge to the real'*.

The more we can engage with objective reality dispassionately – i.e. wanting to see the truth of things as opposed to imposing our own

---

* Bahaudin went on to say that the full meaning of what he was saying would only reach those capable of receiving it, and that unlocking the meaning behind these words requires expert help.

agenda – the more holistically and subtly will we see objective reality. The relatons in our own relaton field will be pattern matching more holistically/subtly and, consequently, will be generating a more coherent sense of self. The more integrated our own relaton field is, the closer we are to contacting the universal relaton field.

To bring together all of the elements needed for just a single living cell to exist and begin to evolve requires an enormous amount of relaton activity. But once it is in existence as a discrete entity, it will need just one relaton template, instead of the many associated with the disparate elements that went into its formation. The more complex something becomes, the fewer relatons are required to specify that complexity. So, the more intelligent a human being is, for instance, the fewer relatons are required to run his or her brain, and the more relatons are available to be released to join the universal relaton field. (Hence the title of this Afterword, *Consciousness: more is less.*)

An analogy of this process could be the way that, when we are first learning something new, large areas of the brain 'light up' (i.e. are involved), but, when we have mastered it, only a tiny part of the brain 'lights up' (the part where the process has been encoded). Another analogy could be the formula discovered by Einstein ($E=mc^2$) that states the equivalence of energy and matter. That formula contains more knowledge, and unites more facts, than a myriad of infinitely more complex formulae that existed prior to Einstein's discovery.

So, the more intelligent we become, the fewer relatons are required, because we are actually becoming closer to 'one'– closer to a coherent pattern. It would follow that, if we were 'completely' intelligent, we would need only one relaton – that expressed in the universal relaton field: the essence of all things.

Consciousness: what we don't yet know

When relatons come together to inform (literally in-form) *atomic* matter there is no consciousness as we would recognise it. However, consciousness exists on a continuum because even inanimate matter has a relaton field. The relaton field of rock, for instance, would enable it to 'know' what is entailed in the formation of rock – a very low level of consciousness which reflects the degree of complexity in, say, granite. But as relaton fields achieve the complexity required to inform living matter, then sentient consciousness comes into being and, eventually, self-consciousness.

Because the templates of living things are infinitely more complex than those of inanimate matter, when the relatons pattern match to something external, the spark of recognition is much more intense, and that is when consciousness as we would recognise it comes about. So, consciousness advances from a level where patterns are so simple that there is no detectable field of consciousness emanating from them, right up to highly complex pattern-matching that produces more and more consciousness.

The templates that guide the instincts of mammals have greater complexity than do those of more primitive creatures, such as fish. But, although mammalian patterns are more complex, the patterns are also necessarily more incomplete, to allow for a greater learning component in the completion of templates. The greater the learning component, the greater the flexibility of response. For example, we all have the template to acquire language but the one we learn is the language spoken in the environment in which we are brought up. Clearly, our language template allows us much more flexibility than the template for language in a bird, which is more rigidly prescribed.

So, the more complex the creature, the more searching it has to do to find the matching patterns to complete its instinctive templates and thereby learn. And the more learning that takes place, the more consciousness is generated. Such consciousness is at its highest in human beings, who do a massive amount of learning in the search to complete patterns. We can see this clearly in young children and probably most of us can recall that sense of real 'aliveness' we felt as a child in our fascination at the world's rich, strange beauty.

Sadly, for many adults as they get older, this process of searching and learning becomes sluggish or stops altogether, and they 'fall asleep' – an apt metaphor often used by poets of East and West for this phenomenon. This was most poignantly expressed by William Wordsworth in his great poem *Intimations of Immortality from Recollections of Early Childhood*, the first stanza of which runs:

> *There was a time when meadow, grove and stream,*
> *The earth, and every common sight,*
> > *To me did seem*

Apparelled in celestial light,
The glory and the freshness of a dream.
It is not now as it hath been of yore;–
Turn whereso'er I may,
  By night or day,
The things which I have seen I now can see no more.[30]

We are all intuitively aware of the significance of complexity. We know that a fly isn't as complex, and does not have the same degree of consciousness, as a mouse, and that a mouse has infinitely less than a monkey. We also know that we have more consciousness than the monkey. We are special precisely because, in our finest moments, we can see multiple connections between things and events, and reflect on and refine those connections. So it is the complexity and density of templates that somehow enable consciousness to be experienced. In other words, although consciousness is present in a fly, it is not concentrated enough to produce self-consciousness. A fly cannot become aware of what it doesn't know. As explained, the *more* complex the pattern a mind can identify (i.e. the more information it integrates), the *fewer* relatons are necessary in the templates within it for generating pattern matching. And, as each *new* significant subtle pattern-match is made, more relatons are freed to join up with the universal relaton field. Intelligence and understanding grow almost exponentially in people who sincerely manage to contain the part of them that consists of selfish wants and conditioning (vividly named the Commanding Self[31] by Sufis) and focus it instead on searching for the truth of reality.

In other words, the more we are stretched and challenged, the more we learn and the more we are refining inner templates, and this in turn increases our consciousness. Many scientists and mystics have spoken about the importance of raising consciousness and of its being a process of gaining knowledge through being challenged and stretched by the activities we carry out in our lives. Albert Einstein, for example, said, "To be sure, it is not the fruits of scientific research that elevate a man and enrich his nature, but the urge to understand, the intellectual work, creative or receptive."[32] Rumi, referring to us all, spoke about a task we have. "You have a duty to perform. Do anything else, do any number of things, occupy yourself fully, and yet, if you do not do this task, all your time will be wasted."[33] The Persian, El-Ghazali, even went so far as to say that this effort supports life to such an extent that it is "... the very force which maintains humanity".[34]

We always have a minimum of consciousness maintaining our reality orientation – our ongoing relationship with the world around us, monitoring where we are, who and what is in our immediate environment, and so on. It is only in the face of uncertainty that consciousness is raised. So any increased consciousness we experience is not about what we know, it is about what we *don't* yet know – what we are learning. This is why we are most conscious in a sudden emergency when we are not on top of a situation that might impinge on our survival. We are in unfamiliar territory, and have to give our full attention to attempting to cope with it. For instance, in the electrifying moment when a man realises his car may be about to crash, he instantly becomes highly conscious because he doesn't know the outcome of the next few seconds. His ability to pattern match becomes key, because the process may contain information vital for his survival. He could die. He reads a massive amount of information from the environment from which his instincts have to make decisions about taking evasive action – the speed of the car, the direction it is moving in, the proximity of other cars or obstacles, the degree to which he should brake and steer and so forth. He must, in a split second of complete concentration, ascertain what he needs to know to best help him avert disaster.

Once a stimulus is familiar to us, has been 'learned', we give it less attention and thus have less consciousness of it. We see this clearly in connection with 'falling in love'. New lovers spend as much time as they can together and are intensely interested in everything about each other, wanting to know as much as possible. In such a state, they are taking in massive amounts of information and are both highly conscious and 'alive'. But as time passes and familiarity creeps in, they typically start to take each other rather more for granted, becoming, as it were, 'saturated' with information. As a consequence, they start to become less conscious of each other – or, as is more usually the case, one becomes less conscious before the other does. The latter would be all too keenly aware of receiving less attention – their lover being less conscious of them. That is the stage when, quite often, rows ensue as one of the lovers tries to force consciousness to rise again.

We are drawn to this state of 'aliveness' and wanting to be closely connected. It is the main reason some people deliberately seek out dangerous activities. But we are not just more conscious in sudden emergencies, risky sports or when falling in love. We also feel more alive when refining our abilities in the practice of a craft or searching for answers to satisfy our curiosity. All these activities involve being stretched. We see this at its most intense in small children, which is why they are so charming when, in their ignorance and excitement about everything, they are so open to the world. In knowing so little but wanting to know and do so much, they are highly conscious. But their excitement, as they ask questions and discover more about the world, is poignant to us as well as charming, for we recall how we too once had that wonder, until the world became more familiar and we began to take it for granted. (Although there always seem to be *some* adults who retain that childlike sense of wonder and enthusiasm for finding things out and who seem to remain more highly conscious, youthful and 'awake' into old age.)

Whatever the circumstances, the more keenly we search for the answers to help us, the more conscious we are. We are more conscious when we are curious and have a problem we want to solve. Once we find an answer, however, the knowledge we have gained becomes unconscious and we want to move on to challenge ourselves further. If we live our lives mechanically, using just what we already know, we are merely standing still or degenerating. Thus people who are not curious and questioning are said to be 'asleep in the world'.[35]

Consciousness and knowledge, then, are infinitely linked and are about *relationships* – the ability to connect to something. Women are, in general, more interested in relationships between people: men more in relationships between ideas and things. The purpose of humankind, as a potentially highly conscious animal, is to know (relate), and the first step in this is to learn how to learn.

Another way of knowing

This way of thinking about consciousness is not only compatible with discoveries made by modern physicists, but is also in tune with what teachers from Eastern wisdom traditions have intuited. Our organising idea reconciles modern science with the intensely metaphorical language used by mystics from many traditions as they tried to express in words what is ultimately irreducible to words. Whereas, in recent centuries, thinkers in our Western culture have put their primary creative effort into understanding *objective* matter using objective material tools, by contrast, Eastern thinkers over the last few thousand years have put their primary effort into understanding *subjective* matter.

Idries Shah, writing about the introduction of scientific method into Europe from Eastern teaching centres, illustrated this distinction between East and West when describing the work in the Middle Ages of Roger Bacon, often considered one of humanity's greatest thinkers. "Roger Bacon was the pioneer of the method of knowledge gained through experience," Shah wrote. "This Franciscan monk learned from Eastern sources that there is a difference between the collection of information and the knowing of things through actual experience. In his *Opus Maius*, written in the middle of the thirteenth century, he says:

> 'There are two modes of knowledge, through argument and experience. Argument brings conclusions and compels us to concede them, but it does not cause certainty nor remove doubts in order that the mind may remain at rest in truth, unless this is provided by experience.'

"This doctrine became known in the West as the scientific method of inductive proceeding, and subsequent Western science is largely based upon it. Modern science, however, instead of accepting the idea that experience was necessary in all branches of human thought, took the word in its sense of 'experiment,' in which the experimenter remained as far as possible outside the experience. Therefore, Bacon, when he wrote these words in 1268, both launched modern science and also transmitted only a portion of the wisdom upon which it could have been based. 'Scientific' thinking has worked continuously and heroically with this partial tradition ever since. And the impairment of the tradition has prevented the scientific researcher from approaching knowledge by means of itself – by 'experience', not merely 'experiment'."[36]

A method of gaining knowledge in this way was rediscovered by Goethe (who also researched Eastern sources) in his scientific work with light and plants. In his experiments, Goethe was able to *directly* perceive qualities from the mental nature of life, qualities overlooked by Newton in his experiments.[37]

In modern times the philosopher of science, Henri Bortoft, has written in depth about the lopsided development of modern scientific consciousness in his book *The Wholeness of Nature*.[38]

"The greatest difficulty in understanding comes from our long-established habit of seeing things in isolation from each other. This is seeing things as objects – the bodily world in which separation, and hence material independence, is the dominant feature. No doubt this viewpoint is one which is encouraged by our own bodily experience of manipulating material bodies. But things are not only objects which can be taken in isolation from one another. In fact they are not *primarily* such 'objects' at all. They only seem to be so when their context is forgotten. What this habit of selectivity overlooks is the way in which things already *belong* together. Because it overlooks this, the analytical mind tries to make things *belong* together in a way which overlooks their belongingness. It tries to put together what already *belongs* together. Thus the intrinsic relatedness is not seen, and instead, external connections are introduced with a view to overcoming separation. But the form of such connections is that they, too, belong to the level of separation. What is really needed here is the cultivation of a new habit, a different quality of attention, which sees things comprehensively instead of selectively.

"When things are seen in their context, so that intrinsic connections are revealed, then the experience we have is that of *understanding*. Understanding something is not the same as explaining it, even though these are often confused. Understanding lies in the opposite direction to explaining. The latter takes the form of replacing a thing with something else. Thus, for example, gas pressure on the walls of the vessel containing it is explained by means of atomic collisions, between gas and wall atoms, and the consequent changes in momenta of the gas atoms. Explanation tends to be reductionistic inasmuch as diverse phenomena are reduced to (explained in terms of) one particular set of phenomena. Thus, for example, in the classical phase of modern physics (i.e., prequantum physics) all the various sensory qualities are reduced to (explained in terms of) mechanical interactions of material particles. Such an explanation evidently takes the form of saying that something is really an instance of another, different thing. Understanding, on the other hand, by seeing something in the context in which it belongs, is the experience of seeing it more fully as itself. Instead of seeing it as an instance of something else, it becomes more fully itself through being seen in its context. Thus, understanding is holistic whereas explanation is analytical.

"The single phenomenon on its own is an abstraction. The aim must be to see the *belongingness* of the phenomena, and so to encounter the phenomena in the mode of wholeness instead of separation. This wholeness, which begins to be experienced through seeing comprehensively, is then recognized as being a higher dimension of the phenomena. It is only on this more comprehensive level that we encounter the concrete phenomenon '... in which the single phenomena become, as it were, one large phenomenon ...'[39] The aim is to enhance seeing so that 'by overcoming the isolation of the single observation, it accomplishes the transition to a higher level of experience'.[40] It is evident that the movement of mind which this entails is the opposite to that entailed in explaining something."

Most people today are unaware that long ago there were people in the East who had accessed what we would regard as very 'modern' knowledge. The term 'psychotherapy' was coined over a thousand years ago by the Persian physician Rhases (Rasi AD 850–923)[41] and there was an awareness of psychological states, psychotherapeutic procedures and the problems caused by indoctrination and conditioning, for example, that our Western culture still hasn't fully digested.[42] Predating Darwin by 700 years, people such as Jalaludin Rumi and his friends were discussing evolution as a fact. They were already aware of the enormous time-span it took for us to evolve from sea creatures to reptiles to mammals and knew that we developed from mammals more primitive than ourselves. They also knew this to be a continuing process and that we are still evolving.[43] Back in the thirteenth century, Ibn el-Arabi stated that modern man was about 40,000 years old, something only realised in the West in the last few decades.[44] Some wrote beautifully about the forces contained in the atom,[45] about relativity[46] and the feasibility of space travel.[47] In different ways they insisted that there is a power in the universe that holds everything together. Operating often in widely different cultures and languages they gave this power many names: Tao, Brahma, Spirit, Cosmos. An increasing number of physicists today are suggesting that a complete description of the universe and our part in it requires the acknowledgement of some unitive force.[48,49,50] When we look at such ancient insights in the light of modern physics, we can see they were not unrelated to atomistic matter, because the objective and subjective *are* connected.

It was only in the twentieth century that Western scientists like Wigner, Schrödinger and Heisenberg realised that there was a subjective element within what they were discovering, but Eastern investigators of subjectivity and consciousness knew about this long ago. They were as much scientists as Western scientists, but they knew the only way to explore subjective matter was with subjective tools. The time has now come for our science and culture to connect and reconcile *objective* matter with the matter of *subjective* consciousness. For that to happen, a bigger organising idea is needed, which is why we are proposing the relaton hypothesis.

Because free relatons are automatically in a perfect relationship with each other, as with the two drops of water when they join together and become one – they remain always and in essence the same. As Tom Stoppard, the great British playwright, wrote, "All the mystery turns out to be this same mystery: the join between things which are distinct and yet continuous, body and mind".[51]

The work of relatons is to organise matter, including us, into specific patterns of existence – relationships – but always with the potential of relating to the greater whole as well, which, in essence, is all relatons unified together. In other words, each one of us has a bundle of relatons holding together the organism that governs our instinctive appetites, from which is derived our sense of 'I'. This is our Commanding Self – normally masked – the greedy core at the heart of us all that has one overarching obsession, its own survival. On occasion, when surprised by an unexpected perception that its interests are under threat, the mask slips and it can be seen as a look of pure self-interest flashing momentarily across a person's face, something totally raw and bestial, for all the world as if they are possessed. (Rather like the startling enactment in a scene in the film of J. R. R. Tolkein's *The*

Fellowship of the Ring where Bilbo, having given it up, unexpectedly sees the ring again and, for a few seconds, becomes like a primitive beast. The very musculature of his face changes, all humanity drains from his eyes, which shine with pure greed.) Once one recognises the Commanding Self as an innate human given it is more easily seen in other people, though it mostly keeps well hidden. It is, however, far more difficult to observe in oneself because, when it 'wakes up', fuelled by strong emotion, it takes over and dominates our perceptions. It is thus a great deceiver because no one likes to think they are like this and we all use every kind of justification to deny that we are. Paradoxically, however, with refinement and learning, it is this same 'I' that has the possibility of being restored to a perfect relationship with the infinity of relatons out in the universal relaton field – in the process, contributing something from our own experience of being intensely material and alive, thus adding to the richness of the universal relaton field, the sum of all knowledge.

This is in accord with all the wisdom traditions which stress that, if our own selfish greeds, obsessions and conditionings are sufficiently reduced, and we gain a measure of control over those emotional arousals that are primarily focused on one's self, instead of on relationships beyond the self, it is possible for our consciousness to start beating in rhythm with a greater reality (the universal relaton field) as when an individual musical instrument harmonises with an orchestra. In other words, as our attachment to the world of objects lessens, our 'I am' consciousness shines brighter and may be able to make contact with the universal relaton field.

Inevitably, much of such teaching went largely misunderstood and, after those communicating this knowledge died, what they taught was often reduced to rituals and mechanically repeated by some of their pupils. But Western scientists are now increasingly recognising that the themes of mystical teachings from different times and cultures, when stripped of cultural accretions, are so constant and so similar in essence that they warrant serious consideration. We too have become convinced that mystics were attempting to express and share some of the concepts we have been discussing, and many religious stories and mythical tales can be seen as metaphorical representations of them.

What, then, is the biological basis for accessing the universal relaton field? There has to be one. If we cannot suggest a plausible answer then it could be said that we might as well think of ourselves as, "transient hairless apes with a genome less complex than a potato's".[52] But, certainly, fundamentalist materialist scientists have made no progress in answering the "hard question"[53] of how and why consciousness evolved.

Back to the REM state

The answer, we believe, lies in developing a better scientific understanding of the mechanics of the REM state. As is clear from much we have written elsewhere in this book, the REM state plays a central role in many aspects of mammalian life. However, this biological fact is not yet appreciated by many scientists, largely because so many of them are specialists unaware of what other scientists have found out. It is in the REM state that our survival instincts, refined over millions of years, are programmed into our mind/body systems. It is therefore intimately concerned with our relationship to reality via the vast accumulation of knowledge passed down through the genome. As we discussed earlier, genes don't encapsulate knowledge; they just encapsulate chemical codes that enable the triggering of appropriate patterns in the relaton template. All the innate knowledge we have, that has been passed on via these genetic codes, is the consequence of consciousness.

The foetus of every type of mammal spends an enormous amount of time in the REM state, drawing into itself the templates it needs to develop and interact with its environment – the directions for further connections, for perception, for the behaviours it will perform after birth. (There is very likely an analogue of this in more primitive life forms, too.*) After birth, those templates are driven to search out corresponding patterns in the environment and pass them through

---

* An example of the REM state in more primitive life-forms comes from research with some of the primitive marsupials, such as the spiny anteater, which shows that the REM state and the slow wave sleep state have not actually been differentiated in them. When they evolved, forty million years before the disappearance of the dinosaurs, their REM state was embedded *within* the slow wave sleep state.[54] Therefore, as we go back down the evolutionary line we would expect to find that the REM state would exist but not be so highly articulated that we would recognise it by the indices we use to detect REM in modern mammals.

consciousness so new learning can take place. That is what makes the world real for an organism – when appropriate feedback from the outside world meshes with an inner template.

The inner templates are accessed via chemical codes – for smell, colour, shape, sound, touch, etc. Information received from the outside world activates these codes, which in turn pattern match to the relevant relaton template, and, to a greater or lesser extent depending on how closely the pattern fits, consciousness is generated. For instance, in the case of the relaton template for 'redness', when consciousness is generated, the redness in the world becomes real to us. And when we see a red that, in our perception of it, is unusual, it demands an even greater degree of attention. The chemical code for redness can be activated by the receipt through the eyes of light from the right wavelength, or, indeed, by an *internal* stimulus that activates the chemical code, such as a memory, a dream or brain damage. We know from physics that redness does not actually exist in the world. Once the chemical code for redness is activated within the brain it stimulates a pattern-match in the appropriate relaton template and causes consciousness of redness.

The REM state is the mechanism that connects us with reality; it is constantly running in the background, searching out at lightning speed the codes needed to match metaphorically to whatever is meaningful in the environment, and thus creating our perception of reality. It is a reality generator, accessing the templates that are the basis of meaning. (This is easily seen when people access memories that evoke strong emotions: rapid eye movements occur even when their eyes are open. We have much evidence of this on film.)

In the dream state, when REM is at its most obviously active and sensory information from the outside world is 'shut off', the templates searching for their completion scan the brain and make metaphorical images from whatever they call up from memory. The dream contains these images and, while we are in it, becomes the reality we are conscious of. This is why the reality in dreams so often feels profoundly richer than waking reality – each particular metaphorical dream image can contain multiple levels of meaning, because the job of the dream is to deactivate emotional arousals and it can do that with several streams of arousals through the same image at the same time (as we saw in the dream of the 'chocolate' aunts described on page 46). Our waking reality is quite different – it is dramatically toned down. It has to be because, if we always saw multiple levels of meaning in everything, we wouldn't be able to make sense of, or operate within, our environment. We would end up totally confused and in a psychotic state. To deal with this problem, the neocortex of the brain, the rational part of our awake mind, inhibits multi-meaning.

(When we are conscious of something while awake, what we actually see is a *parcel* of meanings. Suppose we see a chair. We know that, potentially, we can think about it in many ways: who made it; how old it is; whether we like the look of it; whether it is comfortable, or strong, whether it fits in with the rest of the furniture, and so on. We are capable in our awake state of particularising things into discrete 'boxes' of meanings, so we can pull out whichever meaning is relevant at any given time. We may have many meanings for the concept of lion but, if we see one approaching in the flesh, we had better pull out the meaning that it is life-threatening and we should therefore run. We can't, at that stage, afford multiple meanings about the noble creature. In day-to-day living, consciousness has to be restricted to that which will aid the meeting of our needs in any given situation.)

The REM state does much more than defuse unacted out emotional arousals from the previous day. Like a window, it has many functions, and one is that it can open us up directly to a greater knowledge of reality. We are not the first to suggest this. The anthropologist Weston La Barre, for example, concluded that, "all dissociative 'altered states of consciousness' – hallucination, trance, possession, vision, sensory deprivation, and especially the REM state dream – apart from their cultural context and symbolic content, are essentially the same psychic states found everywhere among mankind; ... shamanism, or direct contact with the supernatural in these states, is the *de facto* source of all revelation, and ultimately of all religions".[55] As we have shown, there is an enormous amount of evidence that throughout the ages some prepared individuals have entered a special state of mind in which knowledge has become available to them. In ancient Egyptian and Greek societies, for instance, resources were invested in building 'sleep temples' to which selected people were invited to stay and be prepared for 'incubating' dreams so that, through their dreams, they could receive enlightenment about matters which concerned them. Our new biological understanding of the REM state may explain why such experiences could be possible. One can be in the REM state and experience a deep sense of being connected up to something vast, alien and yet intimate, and retain individuality. Then, whatever sincere questions are asked, profound, deeply poetical, metaphorical, encyclopaedic and thorough answers arise. Curiously, even while in that state, people are aware of the difficulties they would face if they wanted to share this new knowledge because of its profoundly multifaceted nature. Ibn Ata, for example, talking about this difficulty, said, "We give out strange phrases to ordinary people because our experiences cannot be put in their ordinary phrases. I have known that which cannot be described, through and through, and that which is in it overwhelms all ordinary definition."[56] It's like a television engineer trying to explain how TV works to a caveman.

Learning is the recognition of something we already partly know – i.e. it is available to us once inner templates find completion. As Plato described in the *Meno dialogues*[57], Socrates knew this. He once carried out an experiment with an uneducated slave boy who belonged to his friend Meno. He guided the boy to a spontaneous understanding of a new geometric proposition by asking him questions about a diagram he drew with a stick in the sand in which the geometric relationships could potentially be perceived. At first, the boy confidently thought he knew the answers to the questions. Then, with brilliant logic, Socrates helps the boy let go of his certainty by leading him to recognise his ignorance. Turning to his friend Meno, Socrates says: "Observe, Meno, the stage he has reached on the path of recollection. At the beginning he did not know the side of the square of eight feet. Nor indeed does he know it now, but then he thought he knew it and answered boldly, as was appropriate – he felt no perplexity. Now however he does feel perplexed. Not only does he not know the answer; he doesn't even think he knows."

The boy's perplexity is so great that he goes into a trance, the REM state, numbed as if by a stingray. Socrates points out to Meno that, in his perplexity the boy is now in a better position in relation to what he didn't know. "In fact we have helped him to some extent towards finding out the right answer, for now, not only is he ignorant of it, but he will be quite glad to look for it." In other words, the boy is now ready to learn, to draw something out of the REM state.

Socrates asks Meno, "Do you suppose that he would have attempted to look for, or learn, what he thought he knew (though he did not), before he was thrown into perplexity, became aware of his ignorance, and felt a desire to know?" Meno says, "No." "Then the numbing process was good for him?" "Yes," replies Meno.

"Now notice what, starting from this state of perplexity, he will discover by seeking truth in company with me, though I simply ask him questions without teaching him. Be ready to catch me if I give him any instruction or explanation instead of simply interrogating him on his own opinions."

Without Socrates explaining anything there came a point where, in response to Socrates' questions, the slave boy made the intuitive leap to the answer. How else could that be, asked Socrates, unless at least part of the pattern required for the understanding was in his mind already? "These opinions were somewhere in him were they not?" Meno agreed this seemed so. Then Socrates said a curious thing. "At present these opinions, being newly aroused, have a dreamlike quality ..." This, plus the reference to the numbing effect of being thrown into a state of profound perplexity, clearly shows that Socrates had observed the role of the REM state in learning and knew it was significant. He could not have done this experiment and talked about it like this otherwise.

However, this is a subtle business. It seems we can't 'storm the gates' of the REM state and steal this knowledge. Drug users and cultish 'pseudo-mystics' who delude themselves that they are accessing 'higher states of consciousness', do not generally go on to show greater humanity, wisdom or productivity. This is because, as many great people have pointed out, we can only access truth to the degree that our present understanding enables us to assimilate such knowledge (just as a formula that conveys much knowledge to physicists would mean nothing to non-physicists). There is no way this can be avoided.

Developing consciousness

So, how then do we develop our consciousness, beyond the basic requirements of keeping intact our ability to survive as an organism, interacting with the world, and being effective in it? We must be challenged and stretched ourselves to become more aware of what we don't yet know, just as Meno's slave boy was. To the degree we do that, or it is done to us, we access more refined templates and perceive more subtlety of meaning. That makes us more effective: we can 'read' other people; we can see their true motives more clearly; and, on a higher plane, as we become more in tune with the greater reality – represented ultimately by the universal relaton field – our understanding grows. This helps explain the creative process: how new knowledge comes into being.

When someone sincerely searches for an answer to a question, gathering all the information they can about a problem and seeing it from as many points of view as possible, then creativity, accessed via the REM state, becomes possible. A sincere search for knowledge will initially include looking in books or asking questions of teachers, relatives or friends. But, as inventors well know, they may gather all the available information and still be unable to crack the problem. We cannot integrate new knowledge without going into the REM state, withdrawing consciousness from external perception, daydreaming and making new internal connections that can advance our current knowledge. (The parallel here with effective psychotherapy and counselling practice is clear. To bring about psychological change the REM state has first to generate the possibility in imagination.) This is why inspiration usually comes in those moments when we 'stop trying' and let our imagination roam (i.e. go into the REM state). For this to work, our motivation must come from a need to have the question answered for its own sake – not to gain attention from others or to further our own material gains. Otherwise the question we are asking is, 'how can I get more status?' or, 'how can I get rich?'

A sincere search for knowledge comes from a perception of the level of our current knowledge, and sensing that there is another step forward we are capable of taking. Any increase in knowledge (as opposed to information) that we access must have the effect of altering the patterns through which we make sense of reality. But the more emotionally committed we are to any particular answer, the less likely we are to be able to take that step.

All evolutionary developments must form from patterns of information and knowledge that are ultimately compatible with the original 'singularity', the unified state. As said, that places limitations on what can and cannot evolve. These limitations are the laws of nature and the universe that thoughtful scientists struggle to comprehend. They are givens. Relationships can only evolve in a way that is compatible with these laws – things don't come together randomly – and there is already a predestined order to how things can evolve. Similarly, when people come together to achieve a complex goal the timing must be right, the place must be right and the people must have the right capacity, otherwise the effort is wasted. In setting up a small business, for instance, the people involved must have the right skills, the ability to co-operate, the willingness to accept a period of hardship and struggle before profits ensue, and the necessary range of talents to encompass, for instance, craftsmanship, research, marketing and selling. Even this is not enough. All need to come together at a time when there is a need in the marketplace for the produce of their efforts.

As the universe evolves, we are all contributing to the growing consciousness of the supreme pattern. This is what is meant by the idea of 'service' to something greater than ourselves, echoes of which are found in all religions, and it is perhaps the real task of humankind. Every time we expand our knowledge, every time we match up a template, relatons are released to join the universal relaton field, taking that knowledge with them to add to the pool; thus it is that a more complete pattern for the universe is coming together. This might imply that there is a destiny for the universe – a greater plan – in which humanity has its part to play. Subjective scientists have always insisted that each individual has a 'destiny' that they may, or may not, fulfil. And some have said also that the whole of humankind has a destiny. These are the people who created the great stories of the world, so many of which are about the workings of fate, in which heroes or heroines, after many difficult journeys involving the overcoming of terrible obstacles, somehow meet their destiny and 'achieve their heart's desire'. They also often illustrate how destiny can be altered, or outwitted, depending on choices made. These highly sophisticated tales, by the way they link all the characters and events together in surprising ways that only make sense when a bigger view is revealed, suggest that destiny has its own master plan.

Could it be that destiny is actually a material fact, something which, till now, to Western scientists, has seemed primitive nonsense or, at best, charming folklore? The idea of destiny would make perfect sense if there were templates to connect to – patterns 'out there' available to each of us, arising from a knowledge already gathered from some earlier cycle of the universe, or different part of it. Thus, to 'fulfil one's destiny' might simply mean to become in tune with, or incorporated into, the universal relaton field.

Understanding the centrality of relationships and 'connections' would seem to us to answer the often-asked question: 'How can the world be meaningful with all this suffering taking place in it?' The reason evil can occur is because the pattern of intelligence – the universal relaton field – is itself still evolving. Evil exists because humankind is imperfect. And we are imperfect because the templates we match to have to be incomplete to allow us to learn and adapt.

The second law of thermodynamics, much quoted by chemists and physicists, states that order always tends towards disorder and decay. This process, called entropy, is constantly occurring, stars and galaxies will gradually burn out and the eventual consequence will be 'heat death' – a state in which structure is absent and temperature is uniform throughout the universe. But, as scientists well know, there is an apparent anomaly within that law because, while all that decay is occurring, life is also still evolving, thus bringing greater order, or complexity, into the universe. In our scenario, the overall trend for *less* order in the universe is counteracted by the relaton field, which depends upon *more* order manifesting. This is the universal struggle. The more order the relaton field has, the more it increases rather than decreases. But if the trend towards disorder were to exceed the trend towards order, then relatons would be sucked out from the universal relaton field and split up to accompany each of the countless fragments formed as matter disintegrates.

Just as stars start to burn out and die, so, in effect, do people when too many of their needs are not met. Instead of progressing, they degenerate. Addictions, mental disturbance, pride and selfishness can all serve to undermine people's ability to achieve their potential – and draw relatons out of the universal relaton field to support their chaotic lifestyle. It is a bit like the family that starts off as a close-knit unit and then, for one reason or another, its members start to move apart. Divorce ensues and now, where there was one unit, there are two: two homes to support, two mortgages to pay and, with remarriage, two separate sets of parents/step-parents to relate to and arrange time with perhaps three sets of children. Thus energy is dissipated. All this, however undesirable, requires relaton support, weakening and shrinking the universe, because, as particles of matter separate they have to suck more relatons out of the field to represent the greater number of separate particles that would exist.

So, on the one hand, the supreme pattern of all intelligence, the universal relaton field, is continually *losing* relatons, because things are disintegrating, dying; on the other, to the degree that things are being formed, informed and becoming more integrated, it is *gaining* relatons. And that is a balancing process. There is always the risk that, if more and more disintegration happens, the universal relaton field itself could weaken, and eventually die. In other words, this evolving intelligence of pure awareness, the living pattern in the universe, because it is always in a process of evolution itself, could also be destroyed.

But, we believe, there is an important reason for hope that this will not happen: the existence of complex life in our universe. Life represents a triumph of an infinitely complex ordering of matter. A single living cell, for example, is millions of times more complex, in terms of the ordering of matter, than a star. Since humankind represents the most highly organised complexity of matter within known life forms, at least in this part of the universe, we must be important to the survival of the universe. We possess such an intricate organisation of templates within us that we have the capability of understanding the nature of the universe itself. No other life form that we know of has even started to do that. When we unravel scientific principles and develop the technologies to do so, when we channel our efforts productively, stretch ourselves, learn more, and perfect skills, we are bringing still more order into the universe, and making a huge contribution to the universal relaton field.

Glimpses of the possibilities

The human contribution to the universal relaton field is a two-way process. By damping down our emotions, controlling selfish wants and stretching ourselves, the relatons we free up become part of the universal relaton field (that is the meaning of 'service'). In return, if our orientation is appropriately unselfish, we can draw down knowledge from it. We are saying that knowledge isn't, as empiricists believe, always drawn from outside us; we are also born with innate knowledge and the means to access it, plus, if we go about it the right way, the means to take in more knowledge directly.

In effect, the more relatons are freed up from managing the kinds of daily concerns that sap our energies – our survival needs, anxiety, pride, hostility, greed, and so forth – the more 'spare capacity' is created, which is what enables relatons to resonate with the greater field. Because every relaton (at some level) retains all the knowledge it has ever had – and therefore carries a memory, an intuition, that it was once part of a greater pattern – relatons have the potential to connect with that larger pattern, and achieve moments of true perception. (That is why people with insight into these matters say our most important task is to REMEMBER.) Some relatons will always need to be tied to our living being, managing drives and instincts. They are our 'I', that maintain our life form. But, when there has been spare capacity, the relatons released after bodily death can return to the universal field, still retaining aspects of their 'I', because their patterns will already match up to it. (This might be a material explanation for why, over hundreds of generations and across all cultures, mystics have insisted that human beings can attain permanence: that, in some way, our individual awareness can survive beyond death.) Where there has not been spare capacity, and relatons stay with particles of matter, they still retain their knowledge of what they have been, and thus aspects of their 'I'. These may come together again in some higher life form in another cycle of the universe (if that's the way it works). They therefore still keep the potential of connecting with the universal relaton field.

When we perceive anything, our internal templates (relaton field) are matching up to the relaton field of some other form of matter – there is a temporary sharing of relaton fields. To the degree that you know something about an object then you can potentially receive knowledge about that aspect of the object. To perceive a chair you need to know that a chair is something that you can sit on. As we have said previously, it is always meanings that we perceive. It is our potential relationships with objects that we perceive, not the objects themselves. When we give attention we are sharing our relaton field with the relaton field of some object, person or idea. Since it is the nature of relatons to connect to other relatons, we have an innate drive to do this through the reality orientation process, which is continually maintaining connections to other relaton fields. This even occurs in sleep, hence we seldom fall out of bed, no matter how much we turn or twist. It is this drive that advertisers use, employing all the creativity at their command, to try and make us 'connect' to products and services we don't really need. Once they have tricked us into sharing our relaton field with a product, the tendency is to want to connect up fully by buying it! But this is a low-level activity. People whose emotional needs are being met don't get sucked into shopping frenzies so easily because their relaton fields are otherwise engaged.

Our drive to connect to the richer relaton fields of people is even more intense than our drive to connect to objects, which is why we find so much satisfaction in being part of a group. However this can lead to problems when the prime relaton field we are sharing with the group propounds a prejudiced, narrow perspective on life. This is what happens in cults. The satisfaction of sharing relaton fields with other members of the cult prevents its members accessing wider truths by connecting to patterns that contain more subtle, complex fields, and thus development comes to a halt.

This connecting of relaton fields would explain the seemingly contradictory outcome of experiments in which light can be shown to be a particle *and* a wave, depending on whether the experimenter measures waves or particles – the experimenter's own relaton field can't help but form a relationship with what is being studied and affect the outcome. If an experiment is set up to see if matter can manifest as particles, that potential will be drawn out of matter, because the experimenter's own relaton field is connected to it. Likewise with waves. All relationships are about knowledge – forming a connection and thus increasing understanding – so no scientist can be completely objective.

Of course, matter is neither a wave nor a particle. The act of forming a relationship with it, with one or other possibility in mind, is what draws from it those potentials. Relationship here means having a knowledge of a potential form which matter is capable of taking. The experiment then, properly set up, consummates that potential relationship. The experimental form is perceived by the scientists in his results, i.e. the physical evidence that atomic matter behaves as a wave or a particle. As Edwin Schrödinger said, "The world is a construct of our sensations, perceptions, memories. It is convenient to regard it as existing objectively on its own. But it certainly does not become manifest by its mere existence."[58]

As the universal relaton field evolves, it is gathering into itself all that it is possible for human beings to become (because of its knowledge of all that makes up all human beings in existence). If, through spare capacity, we are enabled to have moments of connection with the universal relaton field, we can gain glimpses of the archetypal human, and aspire towards it. This, perhaps, is what some remarkable people down the ages have achieved.

We think that the concept of the universal relaton field might help reconcile the seemingly opposing perspectives of scientific knowledge and religious belief. For example, it could make sense of such words in the Bible as, "before Abraham was, I am". The relaton field we have conjectured *has* existed from the beginning and its supreme characteristic *is* 'I-consciousness', which is in total subjective harmony with all the particles, waves, relaton fields and intelligence that make up the universe. "Before Abraham was, 'I am'," could thus be a clear scientific statement of the way reality is; the relaton field that existed before all of us existed *is* 'I am'.

Of course this brief sketch of a possible developmental pathway for human consciousness leaves many unanswered questions. But the search for the answers is, we are suggesting, part of what being truly human is all about. We feel that the important human given – the need for meaning – turns self-destructive if not given a positive focus. Meaning arises when we stretch ourselves to make a connection to a bigger pattern, something beyond our own more primitive appetites. It is in the search for truth, combined with service to something greater than ourselves, that human beings find ultimate meaning in their lives. The search for meaning raises consciousness. If therefore we are to continue to fulfil our need for meaning, we must continue to ask questions and refine our ability to unlock the knowledge already within us.

Since ancient times, a knowledge of how to develop human consciousness has been part of the human inheritance and metaphorically expressed, as illustrated by the following traditional tale:

> THERE was once a high country far away where everyone had everything they needed and lived in splendid contentment (because they occupied themselves fully) in palaces and surroundings so beautiful that only the greatest poets could attempt to describe them. It was a wonderful life and the young people there recognised it as such and enjoyed it to the full.
>
> But one day, in one particularly fine royal palace, a young prince of that land was told by his parents that he had to leave and go on a difficult journey to recover a treasure – a pearl – on which their existence depended. "It is a necessary custom. Every young person has to do it," they said. "Only by making this journey, and fulfilling the task we set you, will you achieve the requisite maturity to return, see us all again and help sustain our world. Throughout this trial you must be watchful and make a great effort. We will provision you with treasures enough that you can carry alone, and a special food of small compass, though of illimitable quantity, which will nourish you in your exile, because you mustn't eat of the food of that land. And we will also give you other secret resources, which your guides will explain, and these too will look after you if used properly. The guides will take you down, and then you will be on your own. This cannot be done any other way if you wish to see everyone you love again. Thus it has been ordained from the beginning of time and will be so to the end."
>
> So the prince prepared himself for the journey and set off to a land far below. He travelled in disguise wearing clothes suitable for the country he was to live in, though not befitting his royal birth. When the time came for his guides to leave him on the border, they told him his task was to bring back from that strange country the pearl of inestimable value. But he must be careful, for the pearl was guarded by a dangerous devouring monster.
>
> Alone for the first time in his life, he journeyed westward, making his way down into the new territory. But such was his nature that, wherever he went, he made friends with people and, so beguiling was their company, that he began to eat of their food. And so it was that soon he forgot all about his mission, and even who he was. It was almost as if the air and food of that place had

caused a kind of sleep to fall on him.

For years he lived there, earning a living, keeping out of trouble, following a humble vocation, enjoying himself, quite unaware of what he should be doing.

However, by means familiar to them but unknown to ordinary people, his parents knew of his predicament. They and their friends set to work to release him from the soporific state he had fallen into. A message was sent to him by direct but unfamiliar means, and he was reminded of who he was and what was recorded in his heart. He awoke and found his way to the lair of the monster that guarded the precious pearl. Very carefully, by means of a kind of knowledge that before he did not know he had, he induced a deep slumber in the monster, and was able to take the pearl away. From then on, a kind of light guided him, so that he could retrace his steps up the path down which he had come all those years before.

In almost no time at all he was back home in the land of his parents, to whom he gave the pearl, and everyone rejoiced to see him. But now, thanks to his experiences, he could see that it was a place of even greater splendour and safety than he had ever realised in his youth. And he remembered something odd: that people in the land of his exile had had some inkling of his homeland, especially whenever they talked sincerely of peace.*

It seems that each culture and each generation, whilst making use of its inheritance, has to find its own way to access truth. If this book contains some truth, then the relaton hypothesis implies that we are not the authors of that truth, but to the extent that it contains errors, then that is down to our limitations.

---

* There are several versions of this story from Dervish sources and gnostic traditions including that found in The Acts of Thomas in The Apocryphal New Testament. This is a modern telling.

Appendices

Inducing relaxation
using guided imagery

THERE are three main reasons for using guided imagery and visualisation in counselling. The first is when lowering emotional arousal. The second is when we need to help people rehearse success (new or different behaviours) in their imagination and vividly remember times when things have gone well for them and how good it felt. The third is when we are detraumatising people (see Appendix VI). A knowledge of these skills is fundamental to all good therapy because all processes of behavioural and psychological change involve trance states, which using guided imagery engenders.

The easiest way to learn how to do this is with a relaxation induction. Once rapport is established this is often an appropriate way to end most first sessions of counselling with anxious, depressed or highly stressed people as it gives them immediate evidence that things can be different. We therefore recommend all beginners to practise the classic 'counting down' induction – a form of progressive relaxation of which there are endless variations. For example, as you count down you could ask them to imagine slowly walking down a path into a beautiful garden, or taking steps down a path leading to a peaceful beach where they can unwind. ('Counting down' is, in itself, a metaphor for *going down deeper* into a relaxed state.) Using this technique will give you the confidence to move on with more subtle and powerful techniques later. The process mirrors what happens when we begin to drift off into sleep – the analytical part of our brain switches off and the right brain summons up imagery.

The principles to remember while doing this are:

• **Appear confident and take your time**
It's important that you give a subject who is new to guided imagery as much time as is necessary to experience the trance state. When you talk you should appear confident and knowledgeable. Any doubt, hesitation or lack of confidence will be picked up and you will lose rapport and trust. So always appear confident and take your time. (If you are dealing with someone who might be nervous of hypnosis, call it a relaxation exercise, or yoga, guided imagery or visualisation.)

• **Link your suggestions with the subject's breathing**

Give suggestions for going deeper into trance as the subject breathes out. As you count, each number that you count should be associated with an out breath. You are trying to encourage them to spend longer on the out breath because this stimulates the parasympathetic nervous system, which automatically helps them relax. By telling the subject they can go deeper with each number, indirectly they will be helping themselves to go deeper simply by breathing.

It further develops rapport, and is more hypnotic, if you match your breathing to theirs. (They pick this up subliminally.) You do not have to count with each breath; you may prefer to count every other breath. This will give you the opportunity to intersperse suggestions and encouragement along with the counting. In addition, by counting and pacing your suggestions with the patient's breathing, you will be reinforcing rapport.

• **Use all of the patient's sensory systems**

Because people experience trance with a combination of the visual, auditory and kinaesthetic senses, your induction should have visual, auditory and kinaesthetic inputs. People vary as to which sense they use predominantly in their imagination so you are sure to capture their imagination if you refer to a variety of sensory styles of experience. For example, if an induction consists of a journey, one step at a time, down a path into a beautiful garden, you could ask the subject as they take this journey to *hear* the sound of your voice as they *see* each step in front of them and *feel* each step under their feet and perhaps, you might suggest, even begin to *smell* the beautiful scent of the flowers and herbs growing in the garden (provided that they are not allergic to pollen etc.) and *feel* the warmth of the sun.

Once they reach their special place, you might suggest that they choose to turn to the left or the right or just keep straight on and explore the garden until they find a particular relaxing, private place where they can settle down unobserved and quietly recharge their batteries for a while as they absorb the peace and harmony of their surroundings and perhaps remember other times in their life when they have felt as good.

• **During the induction slow down your voice, lower your pitch and deepen your tone**

Make these changes gradually as the induction progresses, starting the induction in your normal voice then slowly reducing your normal volume, tempo and pitch. At the deepest part of the trance you should have made the maximum alteration in your voice. By changing your voice in this way, you are matching the subject's experience of going deeper into trance. This also helps the subject anchor the trance experience to your voice. In future sessions, you will only need to talk in this special way again and, through pattern matching, the subject will start to go back into trance.

• Bring the subject out of trance by reversing the induction procedure

This principle doesn't apply in every case. But in a counting down induction it reinforces the distinctness of the event to count them back up. So, if you counted from 1 to 20, you would count backwards from 20 to 1. Begin counting backwards still matching the count in time with their out breaths until nearing the end; then begin to break the matching – speed up and bring your tone, pitch and volume gradually back to normal. Whilst counting, say something like, "in a short while, you will find you can open your eyes and be wide awake and fully alert again". This emphasises the change back to an 'awake' state. When the trance is over, thank your subject and ask them to tell you what they experienced.

Effective counselling and psychotherapy: what people should be able to expect from practitioners

THE FOLLOWING check list was prepared by the European Therapy Studies Institute (ETSI) to aid organisations wishing to employ counsellors or psychotherapists (terms which are interchangeable since no meaningful distinction has ever been established between them). It is also widely available to the general public for people seeking help for themselves or members of their families.

There are several reasons why it was felt necessary to produce such a list. Firstly, there is enormous confusion in the field. The differing models on offer (between 400 and 800 depending on whose research you use) mean it is impossible for the public to know what they are letting themselves in for when they go to a counsellor. This profusion of models in itself is indicative that psychotherapy generally is still at a primitive stage of development.

Secondly, much is made by many counsellors, and organisations employing or representing them, about whether or not they are 'accredited', what their academic counselling training is, and whether they have had (or are having) counselling themselves as part of their training. (Some organisations say this is not a requirement; others say it is, yet there is no evidence that having counselling or therapy makes one a better counsellor. In fact in our experience of interviewing hundreds of people who have been through such training, it seems often to be counter-productive.) Research shows that none of these is a good indicator of whether or not a practitioner is likely to be effective. Such preoccupations ignore the main issue which is, 'how effective is this person at helping mentally distressed people?' Indeed, as we and others have shown, some of the most highly trained and 'accredited' people, including doctors and psychiatrists as well as counsellors and psychotherapists – members of all the right organisations – are doing *harm* to the patients they see because they are working from ideologies that originated decades ago. Furthermore, all accrediting bodies are made up of self-serving interest groups promoting restrictive practices that have the effect of stifling development in the field by inhibiting experimentation and the introduction of new ideas.

The aims of any therapy ought to be clear to anyone and the approach taken should employ the latest knowledge available about helping people effectively – in other words, be in tune with reality. This list does much to cut through this confusion by helping people think clearly.

An effective counsellor or psychotherapist:

- understands depression and how to set about lifting it straight away
- can help immediately with anxiety problems including, panic attacks, nightmares, post traumatic stress disorder (PTSD), phobias or other fear-related symptoms
- is prepared to give advice if needed or asked for
- will not use jargon or 'psychobabble'
- will not tell you that therapy is likely to be 'painful' (it only becomes painful if the therapist doesn't know what they are doing)
- will not dwell unduly on the past
- will be supportive when difficult feelings emerge, but will not encourage people to get emotional beyond the normal need to 'let go' of any bottled-up problems
- may assist you to develop your social skills so that your needs for affection, friendship, pleasure, intimacy, connection to the wider community etc. can be better fulfilled
- will help you to draw on your own resources (which may prove greater than you thought)
- will be considerate of the effects of counselling on the people close to you
- may teach you to relax deeply
- may help you think about your problems in new, more empowering ways
- will use a wide range of techniques
- may ask you to do things between sessions
- will take as few sessions as possible
- will increase your self-confidence and independence and make sure you feel better after every consultation.

MindFields College, for which the authors of this book teach, offers seminars, workshops and a diploma course in *effective* psychotherapy from the human givens approach. For information visit: www.mindfields.org.uk or call +44 (0)1323 811440.

Human givens and social work

Social work should be about helping people yet, bogged down in bureaucracy, it has lost its way. Jan Little shows how the human givens approach can put it back on track.

"IT'S performance management, these days." "It's crisis work." "It's case management – we don't actually work with people any more." "It's all paperwork." "It's telling people what they *can't* have."

These were social workers' responses when I asked them, at a training day, how they would define social work. But when I asked them why they had come into social work, they immediately replied, "To help people". And then one added sheepishly, "But wasn't that naïve!"

I *don't* think it was naïve. For me, helping people is still what social work is all about, and unfortunately, under the burden of bureaucracy and paper-work, we've lost sight of the fact that 'helping' is the social work goal.

I am not saying that social work is over-controlled. Indeed, I strongly believe that social work needs to be evidence based and accountable, which inevitably means a certain amount of record keeping. However, tickbox forms completed in duplicate may show we visited a particular family at a particular time and we actually saw the child in question, but they are absolutely no help in determining whether what we did on the visit was in any way effective.

The Department of Health's new Assessment Framework for Children in Need 2000 looked as if it might be a step forward, providing, for the first time, a consistent approach to collating information and assessing families' needs. The framework assesses the child's developmental needs; the carers' ability to parent and the needs of the family arising from poverty, poor hous-ing, and other aspects of environment. All of this information is analysed and provides a sound basis for decision making and action. However, completing the required assessment records entails making tickbox responses and, unfor-tunately, with tickbox tools, there is always the risk of their being misused and completed mechanically. Some social workers feel that completing the assessment records consumes too much time because so much information is required. This is particularly so in areas where the child care team may comprise only a couple of social workers, owing to difficulties in recruiting and retaining staff. We do need a consistent child focused framework for collecting information, but we don't want it failing because of difficulties using it as intended.

The overall emphasis on performance management, monitored by targets and performance indicators etc. serves only to separate social work from its core function: to help. In fact, a problem being masked by the plethora of performance management data is that we aren't at all clear about what we are trying to achieve by them. Performance indicators, such as how many children there are at any one time on the child protection register, are meaningless on their own. Similarly, targets are more likely to concern the completion of work within a certain time scale, rather than meeting a predetermined, highly specific and measurable outcome agreed in each individual case. For instance, all too often the 'goal' in child care is to 'provide support', instead of 'providing support to achieve exactly what and how'.

What needs are not being met?

This is where the human givens approach can be so useful to social work, and I would like to see its adoption widely within it. It encompasses within a very simple framework the diversity of social dilemmas that human beings face: what needs are not being met?

We know that social workers are very often involved in helping people meet their basic physical needs – for sufficient food, for warmth, for a roof over their heads. Similarly, they have a role to play in helping people meet their emotional needs, which, if unmet, lead to stress and distress. It is probably universally accepted that all humans need love, intimacy and self-esteem – but these cannot be handed over on a plate. However, the human givens model identifies other less well recognised emotional needs which can be worked with more directly and which, when fulfilled, automatically increase self esteem and the ability to love and be loved. These givens are the need to *give and receive attention*, the need for *community or connection* (beyond the immediate family), the need for *autonomy or a degree of control*, the need for *purpose or meaning*, and the need for *flow* (utter absorption in a worthwhile activity).

When I say to social workers, "For me, social work is about helping people to get their physical and emotional needs met", they respond at once. It is as if, amid all the rushing about and form filling and working against the clock, they remember "Ah yes! *That's* what I'm supposed to be doing all this for." They can instantly see the relevance of the approach for tackling the problems of the people they work with. A young person just taken into care, for instance, may well resort to negative behaviour in desperation to meet their need for attention (or, if they have been neglected at home, may have resorted to this already). They may well feel all meaning has been stripped from their lives, if they perceive themselves as rejected by their family and cut adrift, and may search to replace it through negative sources such as promiscuous sex, drugs or alcohol. They clearly lose community in the event of their sudden removal from the home where they lived and the connections they have made in their locality. They have no control over what has happened to them. And talents or interests which they previously enjoyed (flow) may somehow fall by the wayside in the transition from home to care.

When an individual's position is viewed in this way, the question becomes "How can we get these needs met more positively, using the resources that the *individual* has?" The answers do not have to be very complicated.

The gymnast

In one care home, Conrad, a young man with mental health problems was discovered to have remarkable gymnastic abilities. That simple discovery and follow-through has led to all five of his emotional needs being met to some extent – and to a diminution of his psychological difficulties. The gymnastics class that he started to attend was in the community, instantly widening his horizons beyond the children's unit where he lived. Quite quickly, he was helping the instructor in class, thus meeting his need for the giving and receiving of attention. As a result of all this, he had purpose in his life, regardless of whatever had happened within his family. And he had flow and a sense of control over his life again.

Angela, a young teenager taken into care, was found to have an ability to play the violin masterfully. It took a long time for this ability to emerge because, in the painful time of her move into care, she had become depressed and unmotivated. Although such an ability may eventually be noted in the records completed for children in care, applying the human givens framework as soon as a young person arrives in care, and keeping it always in mind, enables effective solutions to be reached and set in motion much more quickly. (Conrad and Angela were both truly gifted, but all young people have resources we can use, if we take the time to find them.)

No 'experts' needed

The simplicity of the human givens approach helps overcome social workers' traditional fear that they aren't 'expert' enough to offer counselling. Social work training may cover psychodynamic, humanistic and ecological systems, and cognitive models of assessment and intervention. This may give social workers the impression that any counselling needed should be in-depth and relatively long term. (In fact, this is the last thing that clients may need, as I know from the many young women I've had referred to me to help them 'come to terms with their sexual abuse'. As one young woman put it, "I've talked and talked about how I was sexually abused, and I don't ever want to talk about it again. What I want is help with my life *now*.") So social workers, feeling ill equipped in terms of time and skills, end up getting others to do the direct work – such as counsellors or independent social workers or voluntary organisations – and have even less personal contact with their service users.

But the human givens approach shows how positive results can be achieved in any contact with a service user, however short. For instance, having found out that Angela was a gifted violinist, social workers would need to know how to motivate her to take it up again. With the human givens approach, this might be achieved through the judicious use of techniques such as active listening with a twist ("So you haven't got around to playing again *yet?*) or reframes ("My violin belonged to the old me" – "So the new you has a real talent to draw upon to make you feel happier"), to put a positive slant on a seemingly negative situation. The skill of reframing, along with other crucial skills, such as building rapport quickly, using the imagination constructively instead of destructively and entering an individual's reality, can be learned very quickly within a human givens framework. I also think we could use stories or metaphors much more, to motivate in social work.

Rucksack and rocks

I often tell children, and adults, who are struggling to come to terms with whatever has happened in their family, "I have this theory that we are all born with an invisible rucksack on our back, and parents unintentionally start filling them with rocks as we grow up. Once we are adults and building lives of our own, instead of saying, 'I don't want to wear this anymore; let's take it off', we add our own rocks to the rucksack." I've often had young people tell me that just hearing this enabled them to say, "OK, that was my life with my parents, but I can live my own life now".

Sometimes, referring people to films or books can achieve much, far more quickly than labouring over a troublesome issue. One young woman had been bereaved of her father in a highly traumatic way. Although she was in no way to blame, she felt guilty and responsible. I suggested that she go to see Disney's *The Lion King* (in which the old lion king dies trying to save his son). When she came to see me again, she had done as I suggested, and said calmly, "It wasn't my fault, was it?" The film image had bypassed her resistance to accepting that truth, whereas repeated verbal explorations and reassurances had achieved nothing.

Knitting for charity

The human givens approach works right across the board. It has now been recognised by the Audit Commission, for instance, that, in some local authority areas, the emotional needs of elderly people are being left out of their care plans. The human givens model provides the perfect means for putting them back in: elderly people in residential homes might be fed and warm, but what meaning do they have in their lives? What can we do to help them feel useful and have some control over the way they live? Again, the answers don't have to be complex. They can be as simple as encouraging more able residents to help less able ones; or asking some to knit squares for charity; and others to be in charge of the houseplants. These are practical solutions that don't demand much social worker time but yield such beneficial results.

Help for Simone

The approach can even be used in child protection cases (if a parent's needs can be addressed without detriment to the children). For instance, Simone, a single mother, started to neglect her six young children after her violent partner walked out on her. Social workers had repeatedly told her she needed to clean up her house and get her children to school, otherwise the children would have to be removed. However, they didn't really look at what was stopping Simone. When I reviewed the case with a social worker, it was clear that Simone was isolated and depressed, giving her limited attention to her children's needs and receiving precious little herself. She felt her life was out of control, and that she was a bad mother and had been a bad wife.

The social worker succeeded in getting Simone to see that, if she had the skills to look after her children before her partner left, she still had those skills available to her now. The social worker motivated her to join a parent and toddler group, which enabled Simone to meet other women and start to forge connections with them. Not only has Simone become able to take care of her children properly, but also she is now taking a course in basic computing. She hopes to return to part-time work when the children are all at school.

Creating hope

What is crucial in all this – and integral to the human givens approach – is to convey the message to the people we are helping that we *expect* them to change for the better. When we do social work day in and day out, and see some of the same people on our case list for years on end, it is easy to feel, "This person (or this family) will never change". Subconsciously, people read our expectation of them, and proceed to fulfil it, whatever possibilities they might have had for doing things differently. By concentrating on analysing needs objectively and devising solutions, the human givens approach prevents us from becoming mired in people's moving stories of misery that take away both their hope and our own.

Reducing social worker stress

Because the human givens are about physical and emotional needs that we all have, it works just as well in helping social workers reduce their own stress – and therefore increase their efficacy. In my work counselling social workers suffering from work-related stress, I ask them to look at their own emotional needs and how well they are being met. Ruth, a 30 year old, single, residential social worker at a care home for young people, was one of the first people with whom I tried this approach. She routinely worked long hours and, because the unit was short staffed, ended up working even longer, covering for other people when they were sick. She knew she was feeling increasingly stressed and tired. When she looked at her life, she realised that her needs for giving and receiving attention, community, autonomy and purpose were all met through her work, and her need for flow was not met at all. She was shocked when she realised how much work had taken over her life. She immediately decided to introduce the possibility for flow and to create more balance in how her other emotional needs were met. She has since resumed rowing, which she used to love, and has re-established connections with friends. She is also resolutely refusing to work extra-long hours to cover for others.

She has realised that, when we are stressed and overworked, the first things we drop are the leisure pursuits, the pleasurable activities that we enjoy, and that actually help prevent stress. Deriving all of our emotional needs from the people we work with can create a conflict of interests – on many occasions we need to be able to be emotionally detached. And our generosity in working longer than we should, albeit through a genuine desire to help, may serve only to cover up the cracks in the system and delay the recognition that increased staffing is essential.

Fieldworkers, when they fill out the human givens inventory of needs, can also see why they are feeling lost. Too much work, with lack of clear goals, with too few staff can result in social workers running around responding to crises only. They feel their work has very little meaning or purpose for them (they are not helping people); that they used to have flow (when they carried out direct work with clients) but not any longer; that they cannot give enough attention to service users, so fail to connect with them; that they feel out of control, because they are trying to be in so many places at once.

There is much excellent social work going on, achieved in extremely difficult conditions. However, the human givens approach can help social workers help others more quickly and effectively, thus upping job satisfaction, at the same time as helping them routinely take care of themselves. It is an equalising way of working that says, "We all have needs, and sometimes they just don't get met in the most empowering ways".

The above article, originally entitled 'How to put the heart back into social work' first appeared in Volume 9, No. 4 of the journal *Human Givens*. Jan Little is a freelance trainer and consultant with over 20 years' experience in social work, including 10 in social work management. She has worked for both the statutory and voluntary sectors in social work education, research and development. Although she specialises in children's services, she has also worked in adult services both as a fieldworker and a consultant. She currently provides a counselling service to several local authorities for employees experiencing work related stress.

Human givens and disability

*Disabled people commonly feel patronised, frustrated and excluded.
Mike Hay shows how a human givens approach can help care
professionals meet disabled people's needs.*

"IN OUR view, it is society which disables physically impaired people. Disability is something imposed on top of our impairments by the way we are unnecessarily isolated and excluded from full participation in society ... Thus we define impairment as lacking part of or all of a limb, or having a defective limb, organism or mechanism of the body: and disability as the disadvantage or restriction of activity caused by a contemporary social organisation which takes no or little account of people who have physical impairments and thus excludes them from the mainstream of social activities."[1]

These insightful words were published by the Union of Physically Impaired Against Segregation (UPIAS), a group of British disabled people whose campaigning and lobbying work led to the formation of today's national British Coalition of Disabled People, funded by the Department of Health.

Alas, they penned their words as long ago as 1976 and not a great deal has changed since. Only in the last few weeks, Karen Shook, a wheelchair user and disability service adviser for Parkside Health NHS Trust in London, wrote of disabled people: "Our place in society has traditionally been decided by those other people who 'know what's best for us' – the medical profession, charities, family or the education system. We have 'special needs'. This gives those who are in control of our lives the licence to decide where we should live, how we should be educated, if we can have relationships or if we can marry and have children. Providing for those 'special needs' means being in a separate corner of society, kept away from the mainstream. This is the experience of many disabled people in Britain today.

"I am happy that I am no longer barred from theatres and cinemas for being a 'fire and safety hazard'. I also look forward to the day when I can go to a restaurant for a meal with friends and my visually impaired friends can read the menu in Braille."[2]

UPIAS preceded their statement, at the top of this article, with the phrase, "in our view". It is a pertinent choice of words because the view of disabled people is not often heard, even when we think we are listening. All too often, taking a view leads us to marshal information in such a way as to ignore anything that falls outside our own vision or model. If we are involved in the 'caring' or 'helping' professions, our vision will determine our assessment and treatment/intervention/care plan, laying down for us a set of prescribed outcomes from which we will choose whatever we consider the most applicable for any individual. When vested with authority of rank or role, it is almost inevitable that we bring our 'model' to bear on the person and family we are working with. We can override their perceptions of the world, and, indeed, are often trained to do precisely that. Alternatives will not be taken into account very easily if at all, even if (or sometimes especially if) presented by our client or patient. But it isn't just those with a professional input who suffer from such tunnel vision. It also affects people personally involved in a disabled person's life (perhaps as a partner or close relative), and even very many disabled individuals themselves. Once we adopt a model, consciously or otherwise, we tend to invest in its truth and this in turn reinforces the funnelling of reality into the model – rather like looking down a telescope the wrong way.

To make matters even worse, while we live in a country which is very wealthy, to front-line workers money seems to be continually haemorrhaging out of public life and we are increasingly called upon to 'do more with less'. The public sector calls this 'managing expectations' – a painful euphemism for finding ways of not giving people what they need. By virtue of 'vision' and vicissitude, disabled people are less and less likely to be heard.

Whose problem is it?

The most common 'view' in the world of disability is aggrandised by names such as the clinical/medical or therapeutic model, and concentrates on individual deficit or pathology. It defines how far away from the norm or abnormal the individual is. Disability is seen as internal to the person, and often the particular condition labels and defines the person, as in, "Oh, he's Down's Syndrome." Any possible treatment is offered and, while research concentrates on the aetiology of the disease, the individual is expected to come to terms with their loss (of normality), and learn to fit in. There may be ongoing attempts to help the individual to fit in, through the use of artificial aids or continual medical experimentation and surgery. Sometimes the person sees the latter as helping medical progress. If a cure cannot be found, or attempts to alleviate the condition fail, the individual can be abandoned to their fate with consciences safe – "There is no more we can do for you". If the condition is degenerative, medical maintenance may become increasingly negative, leading to the sort of public debate about quality of life that is played out around us in the media today.

The same clinical approach can be seen at work in social work, and in therapy/counselling settings. The 'problem' is within the individual and the individual must face it. There is little onus placed on wider societal reaction, although some social factors may be acknowledged.

'Angels' and 'eternal children'

Very much linked to the clinical approach is the charity model – the 'common sense' reaction to disabled people. The Elizabethan Poor Law distinguished between the deserving and undeserving poor. This distinction is still to some extent with us today. The charity model imposes moral and value judgements on different conditions or the individuals who 'suffer' them, and then seeks to alleviate the situation. So disabled people may become objects of pity, fascination, fear or disgust. Or they are 'angels', 'special people', or eternal children. These manufactured images raise powerful emotions, especially guilt and sympathy, which are used to raise hard cash. The notion of the disabled person as 'hero' has recently gained currency, where almost superhuman levels of overcoming adversity are encouraged, trumpeted and used to increase donations. Worthy though the aims are, charity work inevitably perpetuates the belief that it is acceptable for an individual to be shunted off by the cash-strapped public sector to beg a charity for money for an expensive mobility aid or piece of communication equipment, rather than a right to it being enshrined within law or public service practice.

Although some charities campaign for social change, charities also principally locate the problem of disability within the individual. Many are cash rich and only a small proportion is run by disabled people themselves.

The traditional or individual approach to disability, whether the clinical or charity variety, usually has a heavy investment in the process of 'loss', developed from studies of bereavement. When I was training as a social worker myself, great weight was placed upon it. According to originator Dr Elisabeth Kubler-Ross, there are stages through which individuals must pass before they can successfully readjust to traumatic circumstances. These stages are shock, denial, anger and depression. The task is to help individuals move through these stages appropriately, ensuring that the individual experiencing loss does indeed move on rather than getting 'stuck' in any one of them, and is probably the dominant mode of emotional or psychological support which is offered to disabled people from the world of counselling. Whilst this journey can be helpful to some individuals, the loss process is facing increasing challenge on a number of fronts. Many people simply do not experience this staged reaction to grief, and there are concerns about counsellors trying to enforce the model by reinterpreting what is said to them in terms of the model and then urging patients to accept it and act in accordance with it. Such a counsellor might declare, "This person is still in denial about having to use a wheelchair. He insists he should be able to get around London as if he were able bodied", entirely failing to see that the person indeed accepts the need for a wheelchair but cannot accept that needing one should be allowed to cut off one's access to large parts of the city.

It is no small wonder, then, that disabled people are suspicious of counselling or therapy or many other services provided by the state. These traditionally centre on the individual's having to come to terms with their particular problem, and take little or no account of the role social factors play in exacerbating disabled people's distress. Young people, for instance, may be referred for counselling because they are perceived as exhibiting 'challenging behaviour' or having an 'anger management problem'. But maybe they are justly angry because their impairments have led to their being excluded from mainstream education, or being unable to take up the career that they had set their hearts on. Maybe it is only the short sight of supposedly non-disabled people which has led to the shutting off of opportunities for those young people, rather than the nature of the impairment itself. We may not even fully realise how frustrated and impotent many disabled people feel, as all too many have been conditioned to be grateful for any service they receive, quietly terrified otherwise of losing their liberty or even their children, if they are viewed as unsafe, or incompetent parents.

Because of the pervasiveness of the belief that disability is the problem of those who are disabled, even disabled people themselves all too frequently internalise this view and imagine that they have no right to further education or a particular job, if the institution cannot cater for their needs. While such a view, in which all onus is on the individual to adapt, is disempowering, the 'social model' of disability is quite the reverse. Developed by disabled people themselves as a reaction against the traditional or individual model, it redefines disability to mean not the functional impairment of an individual but the disability imposed on impaired people by society. Its solutions lie in the

Traditional Model	Social Model
■ problem is the disabled person's impairment	■ problem is how society treats or reacts to people who have an impairment
■ not preventable	
■ solution is to find a cure or to provide care	■ preventable
	■ solution is to stop discrimination
■ person has to fit into society	■ society must become enabling

removal of discriminatory attitudes and barriers and the promotion of 'access' and rights for all disabled people. (See the panel on page 360 for a comparison between the traditional and social models of disability).

Independent living

By shifting one's perspective from the individual to the social model of disability, it becomes possible to see and approach the difficulties faced by disabled people in a far more creative and satisfactory way. This is the step taken by the 'independent living' movement, derived from a set of ideas originated in the 1970s by a group of disabled adults in California who demanded to take charge of their own support. It is now acknowledged by the UK government as well as by disabled people and those working alongside them.

The four principles of independent living state:

• all human life is valuable
• anyone, whatever their impairment, is capable of exerting choices
• people who are disabled by society's reaction to physical, intellectual or sensory impairment and to emotional distress have the right to assert control over their lives
• disabled people have the right to fully participate in society.

Most importantly, just like everyone else, disabled people need to be in charge of their own lives, and to think and speak for themselves without interference from others.

To paraphrase Adolf Ratzka, the founding chair of the European Network on Independent Living, independent living does *not* mean not needing anybody or living in isolation. It simply means that disabled people want the same life opportunities and choices in every day life that their non-disabled family members, neighbours and friends take for granted. That includes growing up in their family home, going to the neighbourhood school, using the neighbourhood bus, getting employment that is in line with their education and abilities, and having equal access to the standard services and establishments of social life, culture and leisure. Such an approach requires a more open minded look at how to provide the opportunities that non-disabled people take for granted, in the same settings in which they enjoy them. Rather than setting up a trampoline class for people with learning difficulties, for instance, why not spend the energy on persuading existing trampoline groups to let people with learning difficulties join. Because of the long history of excluding disabled people, there has been a tendency to seek funds to set up specialist services for those excluded instead of tackling the exclusion itself.

The human givens

Schools of therapy ignore the huge role of the social context in which each individual operates and the influence culture and ideas have in shaping personality and behaviour. Meanwhile, purely social or cultural disciplines ignore internal, psychological issues. The human givens approach bridges the two in a way which leads to powerful and effective interventions in a truly holistic approach to individuals. As this understanding grows, it will challenge the way in which organisations tend to define the needs of people who use their services and the way in which activity is prioritised.

The human givens encompass our emotional needs (such as the needs for intimacy, security, attention, control and meaning in our lives) and the innate resources we have for helping us meet these needs (such as memory, imagination, problem solving skills, self-awareness and complementary thinking styles). As a large 'organising' idea, it provides a coherent form for dealing effectively with the concerns of all human beings, and is particularly pertinent when considering the needs and rights of disabled people. *For disabled people's needs are no different from anyone else's.*

Viewing the issue of disability through the lens of the human givens inevitably throws light not only on the issue but also on the viewer and why we may have adhered to a particular 'model' of disability. For instance, meeting one's own need for status or attention etc may cause an individual to focus on a view of disability which puts the disabled person in the recipient role, grateful for whatever is offered. Someone whose need is to be seen as an expert may consciously or inadvertently behave in a way which overrides the needs of others.

Needs have to be fulfilled in due measure within the overall economy of our mind/body system, and therefore it becomes a matter of meeting all needs in a balanced way, rather than concentrating on just some to the exclusion of others. I am currently working with a group of disabled people and a mix of professionals to see how we can use the human givens in assessment processes, together with the social model, rather than the more traditional approach, which largely looks at what the individual can or can't do from a functional point of view and inevitably focuses on 'deficit', not strengths and aspiration.

What is missing in this person's life?

When an individual's life is not working, the key question from a human givens approach is "What is missing in this person's life"? When we ask this of a disabled person's life, it quickly becomes clear that a great number of basic human needs are unmet. Let us take, for instance, the basic need for security. Disabled people tend to be marginalised economically, and their jobs, if they have any, are insecure. The accommodation they can live in, if they need adaptations or support, is dictated by the housing authorities or the social service departments. Changes in management practice or policy can throw a disabled person's life into instant disarray, by suddenly reassessing and possibly reducing an essential source of funding or aid that enables an individual to hold down a particular job or place in a supported housing scheme or residential placement.

The human need for intimacy is largely disregarded, disabled people being seen by the powers that be as largely non-sexual beings. A local authority may offer to adapt a small downstairs room for a newly disabled woman, totally disregarding the fact that she is also someone's partner. Conversely, the sex lives of disabled people may be regarded as the rightful business of anyone who happens to be passing. (Karen Shook, the disability service adviser for Parkside Health NHS Trust, recalls how, in a supermarket queue, she was asked by a total stranger, "Can you have sex in a wheelchair?" She immediately replied, "Yes, of course, but you have to remember to put the brakes on!"[2])

It is a given that we need both to give and receive attention. All too often disabled people are forced onto the receiving end of (often second rate) attention, having to be grateful for small crumbs, and with little opportunity to give attention to others. Just as commonly, of course, they receive no attention, experiencing only the averted eyes or the question being addressed to the person pushing their wheelchair.

The need to have some degree of control over what happens to us is all too often denied to disabled people. Home helps or carers often turn up when it suits their employer's staff rota, leaving people hungry, uncomfortable or in nightwear till whatever time the helpers can come. There are those who call residential care 'house arrest', when a spell there involves the indignity of being told when to get up, when to wash, when and what to eat, when to go out and when to sleep.

The need for community and to participate in society, which most non-disabled people take for granted, is all too horribly denied very many disabled people. They too would like to make a contribution to society and feel their lives have worth but may well be prevented by a host of barriers, both physical – problems of access to town centres and particular buildings – and psychological – blinkered views on the part of others about what disabled people might or might not be able to do. Given that we meet so many of our needs through community and interaction, the human givens leads us to ask the inevitable question. In what way are disabled people artificially prevented from getting their needs met because of the way in which we organise ourselves and our communities more or less for the convenience of non-disabled people?

Working with the human givens enables us to work with disabled people both on their own 'demons' (some disabled people, just like non-disabled people, really do have difficulty managing anger) and alongside them in a way which enables them to have greater choice and control – and to make the distinction between the two, rather than confuse them. Because the human givens acknowledge common human needs rather than, as historically, separating out disabled people from the rest of 'us', the challenge is how they can have their needs met in a society which seems intent on stopping them! Starting from the human givens puts us alongside disabled people, rather than seeing them as having different needs outside the general mainstream of humanity.

Getting emotional

Those of us who meet disabled people during the course of our work know they are likely to be in a highly emotionally aroused state – usually anger, which is blithely linked to a 'failure to adjust'. High arousal also renders them 'difficult' to work with, so often there is little positive outcome. But using techniques which are in line with the human givens approach offers a means of working with disabled people which is highly satisfactory for all concerned.

We now know, for instance, that strong emotions prevent us from thinking issues through in a way that allows us to make sensible decisions. When we are angry, for example, there are no half-measures: "I am right and you are wrong!" The wider picture, and the fact that very rarely is such a black and white response appropriate, is forgotten in the anger. Anxiety, fear and, crucially, depression are all strong emotions, and put people into a trance, an internal state of locked attention, in which no other view is possible. Failing to calm people down will mean working with people in various degrees of trance where intervention is not likely to succeed, and the failure may be seen as that of the client or service user.

To regain access to our rational faculties, we have to calm down first. This is so for any strong emotion, negative or positive (for instance, elation) – although, in terms of disabled people and their dealings with statutory services, the former is rather more in evidence. There are many simple ways to help people learn to relax. It is certain that, for disabled people who have been strongly aroused for years, simply learning to relax will be a revelation.

And now, the bad news ...

Another critical aspect of focused attention is its effect on how people receive and process information, and what this therefore tells us about how we should communicate shocking or disheartening news. When we are told something shocking, it takes up our whole attention, leaving no room to take in options which need to be carefully thought about. People in a trance state are highly suggestible and so badly phrased negative messages which disabled people absorb in this vulnerable condition will be magnified: "I am sorry; your son will never walk again." "With a mental illness like yours, if I were you, I would seek some kind of menial work." "Forty per cent of these operations fail."

Calming people down helps them to access their 'observing self', which breaks the trance state. The observing self is that part of us which is always outside the content of our experiences, able to observe and analyse them from different viewpoints. Accessing the observing self helps us to process information through the higher cortex, rather than through the more primitive, emotional brain. Standing back from our concerns also enables us to separate them from our core identity. We are not our cancer, our multiple sclerosis, our blindness, our hardness of hearing, our mental illness. This is critical for disabled people who constantly experience being identified or labelled simply as their impairment. This, like any other tyrannical belief, can be internalised, and individuals begin to define themselves as or through their impairment. Learning how to engage the observing self enables individuals to generate or listen to a wider range of options.

Two powerful techniques

One highly effective intervention known by any therapist working from the human givens is the 'fast phobia technique', a painless method of helping individuals overcome severe traumas or phobias. It relies on an understanding of the trance state and enables individuals, when deeply relaxed, to 'fast forward' and 'rewind' through the traumatic experiences, as if watching themselves at one remove on a TV screen. As the impairments of many disabled people have been caused through terrifying accidents or other traumatic events, being able to extinguish any post traumatic stress is highly therapeutic and may also have the effect of lessening some physical pain as well. Some of the lasting trauma suffered by disabled people can also be generated by inconsiderate treatment people have received, or traumatic living conditions at home or in residential care, as children or adults.

Trance can also be used highly positively to help people visualise successful outcomes in their lives and, again, this can be particularly valuable in work with disabled people. Visualisation techniques have proved extremely effective in helping enhance the immune system, control pain and strengthen muscles (imagining flexing muscles has significant effect on muscle power – an extraordinarily powerful resource, therefore, for people with restricted mobility and muscle wasting). We can also use our own virtual reality simulator – our imagination – to rehearse the success of any strategy we desire to put into place. Just as we can misuse this faculty (as in depression), we can also put it to work for us. What we focus on we are more likely to achieve. This is often the missing step in much change planning – people are not helped to buy into the power of their own positive beliefs – and can make the difference between success and failure.

Running a reality check

The human givens approach is as relevant to the individual offering a service as to the individual receiving it. It is crucial, therefore, that service providers take a long look at where they are coming from, in their dealings with disabled people. Tyrannical beliefs about disability are legion! Here are a few of them:

- *impairment is a punishment from God, or because of sins in a past life*
  (This is more embedded in our consciousness than many like to admit. Sometimes parents of a disabled child still feel a sense of punishment, even if not linked to any religious cause.)
- *physical impairment reduces intellectual capacity*
  (How often do you ask directions of the person in the wheelchair, rather than the person pushing?)
- *mentally ill people are inherently dangerous* (This is still a common misconception despite all statistics to the contrary.)
- *people with learning difficulties are angels in disguise* (A seemingly harmless belief, but one which stops people being perceived as fully human, with all the negative consequences that flow from that.)

For every example of disaster and tragedy in a disabled person's life, it is possible to find a similar example of growth and success and achievement. Metaphors of overcoming difficult circumstances, rising above adversity, etc, can be useful to help break established thought patterns, and instil a greater sense of the possible.

But, however uplifting and inspiring such stories may seem, great sensitivity is needed when deciding how or if to repeat them and to whom. We can all too easily end up conveying the message that disabled people should live up to some sort of superhuman model, overcoming extreme adversity and conquering all. Most of us aspire to an 'ordinary life' and that is challenge enough. When disabled people have come together and told managers of long-stay hospitals or residential units just how unpleasantly extraordinary their own existences are – abuse of dignity, grinding boredom, lack of simple life choices – it is often these powerful personal stories which lead agencies to change policy.

We also need to be extremely cautious about making value judgements about the quality of disabled people's lives. Many disabled people say that they would not change their life experiences or their impairments even if they could, often because of what the experience has taught them. Some say they have learned resilience, patience, the value of good relationships, the need for interdependence or how to use humour, to an extent to which they feel they would not otherwise have done. Some who developed impairments suddenly have said that they feel they have become more sensitive and more forgiving people than before. The value some disabled people place on their lives is to do with contribution and purpose – having been able to take up the cause of disability and help others in the process.

Human givens of health and social policy

Just as an understanding and application of the human givens approach helps us to work effectively as individuals with individuals, so it can also help us analyse why some policies work, and point towards better policy planning in the future. Even if all individual issues are dealt with, disabled people remain disabled living in an environment which hinders rather than helps.

We should look again at current policy themes and decide the sorts of policies which need to be developed so that culturally we do not artificially prevent anyone from meeting their own needs. I would suggest, for instance, that the direct payments scheme is absolutely in line with the human givens. In this, individuals are given the money to be spent on needs such as home helps or home carers so that they themselves can employ a personal assistant to come at times and do the activities that suit them, instead of helplessly having to wait until the carer employed by an agency turns up. Conversely, forcing people into residential care or segregated schooling when they don't want to be there, or haven't fully explored all the other options open to them, seems to be working against the entire wisdom of the human givens approach.

It will no doubt be a long haul before disabled people feel fully part of a non-discriminatory society. But when we shift our perspective to focus on the needs of the individual, rather than the needs of the system, it becomes so much easier to see both the wood and the trees – or as some of my disabled colleagues would say, the condition and the person, as labels are for jars!

References

1. *Fundamental Principles of Disability* (1976). UPIAS.
2. Shook, K (2002). Changing attitudes. *Times Chronicle Series*, February 6.

The article featured in Appendix IV was originally entitled 'Disabled by denial' and first appeared in Volume 9, No. 1 of *Human Givens*. Mike Hay is a social services manager and a Fellow of the Human Givens Institute. He has worked alongside disabled people for many years in both hospital and community settings and has managed multidisciplinary teams within learning difficulty and physical and sensory disability services. His current role involves the promotion of the social model and 'independent living' for all disabled people, no matter their age or impairment.

Human givens and physical pain

*Dr Grahame Brown tells how using the human givens approach
has transformed his outcomes with patients suffering from
chronic musculo-skeletal disorders.*

SOME years ago, in my work as a consultant in musculo skeletal disorders, my heart used to sink whenever certain patients shuffled into the NHS cubicle where I held my clinic.

Questions such as "Where are you feeling the pain?" would yield the answer "Everywhere". "How bad is it? When does it hurt most?" "It's always bad. It hurts everywhere." I would retreat behind medical jargon or be brisk in my recommendation that they take more exercise. Hostile looks or responses might ensue. My physical interventions might well go for naught, as they tensed against me and insisted their pain consequently felt worse. I might send them off for yet more investigations. Inevitably they would be back, shuffling morosely into my clinic for yet another consultation which would go nowhere.

Both the patients and I felt hopeless and I knew that could only make matters worse. There is now a major body of research evidence which consistently shows that psychosocial factors strongly predict the outcome in all treatment interventions for musculo-skeletal disorders.[1] For example, in the acute onset of back pain, it is psychological factors which consistently predict outcome at six weeks, six months and 12 months. Such factors include distress; catastrophising; anxiety; depression; blame (seeing the problem as due to something or someone else); personal factors, such as problems at home and problems with the boss (the latter particularly important for work-related disorders); and personal coping strategies, such as resorting to alcohol or drugs.

I knew this, but I frequently wasn't getting anywhere. What was wrong was the way that I was going about the medical interview. Since studying the human givens approach over the last few years, I have consistently been applying it to my medical interviews, and firmly believe that my consultations are now shorter but more effective and that fewer follow up appointments are necessary. I now realise that I can more consistently (but not always!) help people change their attitudes towards pain, whatever the source, and that the way that I relate to them, as their doctor, is key to the achievement of this.

My first priority now is to build rapport with the patient in the short time I have with them. Instead of keeping the head down over the paperwork till a prospective heartsink patient is seated, then greeting them with a tense smile (as all too many doctors do), I now go out into the waiting room to collect patients whenever possible. This gives me the chance to observe in a natural way how they look, how they stand, how they walk and whether they exhibit any 'pain behaviours', such as sighing or limping. I shake them warmly by the hand and begin a conversation on our way to the consulting area. "It's warm today, isn't it? Did you find your way here all right? Transport okay?" By the time we are seated, the patient has already agreed with me several times. This has an important effect on our ensuing relationship – we are already allies, not adversaries – and is an essential element of rapport building which is too often skipped over in the traditional medical model. Next, rather than assuming the patient has come to see me about their pain, I ask *them* what they have come to see me about. Quite often they find this surprising, because they assume that I know all about them from their notes. But even though I will have read their notes, I now assume nothing. I ask open-ended questions that can give me the most information – the facts which are important to *them*.

Barry's back

Fifty year old Barry who works at one of the major car manufacturers in the West Midlands is fairly typical of many of my patients. He was referred to my NHS clinic because he had been off work for nearly 12 months with back pain. Anyone who is off work for 12 months for causes attributed to back pain has a one in four chance of losing their job completely as a result and becoming unemployable. So Barry was at extremely high risk of long term disability. During that 12 month period he had seen his GP, two physiotherapists and a chiropractor for physical treatments, apparently to no avail. At some point his GP had referred him for an X-ray and arthritis in the back had been diagnosed. By the time he saw me, he was exhibiting a high level of disability in terms of daily living activities which he couldn't do.

As he answered my question about why he had come to see me, he mentioned that he had had aches and pain in his back for years but that he had never had to have time off work until a year ago. So I asked him what else had been going on in his life at the time. Within a couple of moments it became clear that Barry, already a widower, had in the course of the previous 18 months experienced an inordinate amount of grief. He had been bereaved of his daughter in tragic circumstances, and also of his grandchild.

When I asked if there were any times when he didn't feel the pain, in the hope of being able to capitalise on such times in his life, he said, "The pain is always there." Other questions revealed that he had enjoyed his job at the factory, particularly the contact with his workmates. He had previously also enjoyed fishing, and going to his club to play snooker. But, arising from the problems with his back, one practitioner after another had advised him, directly or indirectly, to stop doing these activities because they might be harming his back. So, instead of going to work, fishing or going to the club, he would sit at home watching the television. I pointed out that this didn't seem like the kind of thing he would enjoy, as he clearly liked being active. "I know. I can't stand it," he sighed.

I next discovered that his sleep patterns were "absolutely awful" and that they had been awful ever since he had stopped going to work. "So what do you do when you can't sleep?" I asked. "I get up, have a cup of tea or coffee and put the telly on again." "What about your tobacco consumption since you've been off work?" I asked, noticing the heavy nicotine staining on his fingers. "Oh, that's gone up by at least four or five times," he replied.

It was quite obvious that his disabling symptoms of back pain began around the time of the bereavement. Others had made the erroneous assumption that, because he was working in car production, his work was the cause of his pain. The pain was being exacerbated by his lack of sleep, and he had nothing to distract himself from it. His work and pleasures, which had involved satisfying contact with others, had been removed from him.

"Could it be stress?"

After asking him other specific questions about the nature of the disorder which I needed to know as a doctor and being satisfied that these were answered, I physically examined him. As I carefully felt his back, I noticed the characteristic signs of increased muscle tone and tension. When Barry had first mentioned having aches and pains in his back for some years, I had quickly interjected, "As we all do," to normalise his experience – a response I had learned from the human givens approach. Now, while examining him, I again reassured him that all was normal and told him that much of the pain he was experiencing could be caused by the considerable muscle tension which I could feel. He himself then asked, "Could stress be causing this?" And I said, "I think it often does."

At that moment the scales fell from his eyes, and Barry changed in front of me. No one had linked body and mind and life events together for him before because no one he had consulted had asked the questions which would have elicited the connection (as I myself would have failed to do five years ago). He said, "But everybody has been telling me that I've got a serious disorder." So I put his X-rays up on the lightbox for us to look at together and said, "How old did you say you were – 50? Yes, this is normal for everybody of this age. Normal age-related changes. It's like getting those grey hairs on your head."

I suggested that his back was out of proper working order, just like a car engine could be – using the metaphor of a car engine because he worked with cars, and was a 'mechanical' type of man. "We have to tinker around with the engine a little bit to see where the timing is wrong. You've just got some stiff links, and all that bad muscle tension is coming about because you are feeling so low in yourself. Your mood is really low, you've had some terrible things happen in your life, but things can be better." And I added something like, "Oh, the last man I saw from your factory who thought he had a seriously damaged back, he's now back on the job again, and he's really happy."

Taking to task

Barry was clearly ready to take steps to regain control over his life, so I set him some tasks to do before our next meeting. I asked him to cut out tea, coffee and cigarettes after around 5pm, because these would all be affecting his sleeping. I asked him to start walking, just half a mile the first day, a mile the next, and so on, up till about five miles. He agreed to all that. I then said I want him to go back to the pool table and to see his friends again – "It won't damage your back; even if hurts, it's OK". I was emphasising reconnecting him to his social network, because his emotional needs were not being met. He was a man who needed to work, and took great pride in his work, and who, like all of us, needed social contact with other human beings. I also told him that, if he woke in the middle of the night, I wanted him to find the most boring piece of reading matter in the house and not to find a comfortable chair but to stand up reading it. When he felt sleepy he could go back to bed again.

Finally, I said that I planned to get in touch with the occupational health doctor at the factory to book Barry an appointment, with a view to getting him gradually back to work. "What we do in a case like this, we get you back on just one day for the first week, and maybe next week we'll get you on a day and a half, and then two days, and then three days." In this way the mountain he felt he had to climb before being able to work again could be negotiated in manageable steps.

Barry went away seemingly quite confident, although I wasn't sure what the outcome would be. When he returned to my clinic five weeks later, I was staggered. He had hardly any disability in activities connected with daily living. He looked a different man and not only had he cut down on his smoking, he had stopped smoking altogether. The occupational health physician had found him an alternative job, to meet his need to work, and he was now back full time, and also back having a few pints with his friends in the club. He was fishing again too. I said, "Oh, and, by the way, how's your back?" "Well, it's just a bit of an ache now," he answered. "It's reminding you it needs a bit of looking after. Keep on doing just what you're doing," I suggested. And he smiled and said, "Yes, what I've learned from all of this is that the secret is just to keep going." He did not require any pain intervention treatments.

In the circumstances ...

My interviews with Barry were based on what I have learned from the human givens approach to history taking. It is crucial with back pain patients, who make up the majority of my case list and only a small minority of whom have clinically significant pathology, to find out what was happening in their lives when the pain first became severe. Research consistently shows that, particularly for lower back pain, the nature of a person's relationships are a better predictor of back pain than the heaviness of their workload.[2] I always like to ask a person who is attributing their back problem to their work or who is taking a lot of time off from work, "How are things with your boss/line manager/cell leader?" or whomever they report to. If they say they have a good relationship with line management, then they're usually happy at work. If there's a silence when I ask the question or they have a complaint, that's a very important clue to interpersonal problems at work which could be influencing them. A worker at the lower end of the socio-economic hierarchy in an organisation will more likely take time off when stressed or unhappy. It feels easier to attribute difficulties to neck pain, back pain or headaches than to the stress of relationships at work.

The normal X-ray

An important technique in my practice now is that of normalising symptoms. As with Barry, I stress the naturalness of disc degeneration with increasing age. It is extremely rare to find the cause of back pain on an X-ray that you couldn't find by any other means. As a screening process it's almost useless. This has been consistently shown[3] but habits of healthcare practitioners are such that they still tend to reach for the X-ray as the easiest thing to do. Patients expect the X-ray to reveal something. Very often a person is just about coping with their back pain until they see a doctor who requests an X-ray and who announces on the strength of it degenerative changes in the spine or narrow disc spaces or bones rubbing together. These are awful-sounding things for people to hear but essentially they signify just age-related changes. In fact, age-related changes show up on spinal X-rays even in the mid-twenties.

Just recently a man brought in his scan to show me. A surgeon had told him it showed two levels of disc degeneration. "That's very serious, isn't it?" he asked me, with a worried frown. I was able to say that I had just had the privilege of looking after a young woman who had won a gold medal at the Olympics in Sidney. She had four levels of disc degeneration and, yes, her back gave her a little bit of trouble from time to time, but she won a gold medal and she won a gold medal at Atlanta too. Telling a story like that (again a technique learned from the human givens approach) reassures the patient that these things don't have to matter so much.

'Trapped nerves'

Even in cases where there is clear physical pathology, the vocabulary a doctor uses can have a significant impact on a patient's attitude to and response to treatment. A good example of this is sciatica. This is pain resulting from a prolapsed disc, or pressure from a bulging disc on one of the nerve roots in the spine. The pain is usually felt throughout the leg, especially below the knee and goes right down into the foot, often associated with pins and needles sensations or some numbness. It is an excruciating pain to experience and can come on quite suddenly, usually following an episode of back trouble. Sufferers are often terrified, thinking it is really serious. If they believe something serious is happening to their spine, or that they have cancer, or they catastrophise the symptoms, thinking it is the end of their world, they predictably do badly, whatever the management of their condition. One of the most important things I can do when I assess a patient with sciatica is to stress that this is typically a transient episode. I emphasise at the outset that the body has a potential to cure and that well over 90 per cent of cases of sciatica settle quite spontaneously without any surgical treatment intervention, while 50 per cent have completely settled within six weeks.

I make the point of saying that the nerve is swollen, a more accurate description than that denoted by the more commonly used word, 'trapped'. People often have a mistaken belief that, if something is trapped, only surgery will untrap it. But only about two per cent of people with sciatica need *urgent* surgery. I explain that an anti-inflammatory injection, which I am skilled at giving, can calm down the reaction around the nerve, and that it is very soothing. When patients hear that, they can start to relax and, of course, the calmer and more relaxed people are, the less pain they will feel.

Regaining control

It is well known that human beings need to feel a degree of control over their own lives. When we feel helpless, we feel pain more acutely. (This is one of the reasons that patient-controlled analgesia is so successful when used post-operatively, and usually results in a reduction of overall analgesia needed.) Barry, when I first met him, felt he could do nothing to control his pain. This was also the case for Rene, a woman who had been referred to me after diagnosis of repetitive strain injury.

So-called repetitive strain injury (RSI) is an area that I've researched extensively. Sufferers develop non-specific but often incapacitating aches and pains in forearm, shoulder and neck muscles, and relate it to work. But there are almost always psychological factors involved as well. People particularly at risk are those working with display screen equipment, sitting down far longer than the human body was ever designed to sit. When people are tired, under pressure and tense, their shoulders come up, their chins go forward and the spine slumps, putting extra tension on the upper spinal muscles and neck muscles. RSI represents a huge cost to industry in terms of sickness absence, insurance cover and personal injury claims. But, if these cases are dealt with early, it is usually possible to prevent people from becoming chronic sufferers. There is a highly consistent pattern in the presentation of these problems and Rene's case is a good example.

Rene works late

Rene worked as a civil servant and had been experiencing increasing pain around the neck and shoulders and upper limb in the dominant arm, down as far as her forearm, for about nine months. She was starting to take the odd day off work and to become increasingly distressed by her symptoms, responding neither to standard painkillers nor to physiotherapy (which was mainly passive treatments such as ultrasound and heat, directed to where she felt pain). She came into the room looking very anxious and tense, with extremely hunched up shoulders. I gave her a careful physical examination and was soon able to rule out serious nerve root problems or shoulder/joint disorders. But I could quickly identify that she had some very painful muscle tender points (we know them as trigger points) which are a cause of muscle pain. I demonstrated these to her, pressing them to show her where her pain was. I normalised them by explaining that they were related to excessive muscle tension rather than some serious, mysterious disease called RSI, showed her which muscles were shortened and explained how this might have developed because of poor postural habits at work. I also told her that it was very common to start to feel symptoms when under increased mental or emotional strain.

Rene then went on to tell me that she was working too long and too hard and was unable to take breaks. She had a good boss whom she liked very much, and a senior position which she loved working in. But her boss was a bit of a workaholic and Rene, because she was a single person, felt unable to say no to the extra work. Consequently, she had lost control over her working time.

I discovered that she had used to enjoy yoga and keep fit activities in the evenings but, because of the pressure of work building up, she had stopped these activities, staying on at work instead. So important areas of her life were being neglected. We sorted out her posture and I told her that I wanted her to go back to aerobics. She was surprised because she too had been advised to give up physical activity for the sake of her health. But returning to aerobics had a double benefit. Attending the class required her to leave work on time at least twice a week because it started at 7pm. Regaining that element of control then enabled her to start cutting down her working hours to a sensible level. I saw her a year later and she had complete control over her symptoms, with no need for further treatment.

Things can be different

As part of my management of Rene, I showed her that she could feel immediately better by my releasing her trigger points with acupuncture needles and employing a simple physical treatment to mobilise and loosen her neck. Her range of movement was instantly better, making her feel more relaxed and comfortable, and she was able to leave feeling different from when she came in.

A fundamental principle of the human givens approach is that patients must go away feeling better than when they arrived, and more hopeful about the future. One of the ways I now encourage a belief in change is to use an appropriate metaphor. If my patient is a cyclist, I'll talk of stiff joints in terms of stiff links in a bicycle chain which need oiling. I do a treatment to loosen them up and then it is up to the patient to keep the links moving freely. Such metaphors can help convince people that the 'chain' is not broken or snapped; it just needs maintenance and keeping mobile. With technical people, I'll talk of hard disks and software and relays in the spinal cord picking up the wrong messages, and howling in microphones, arising from amplification of sound from wrong signalling, and so forth. Providing a visual and easily understandable image of what is going on in the muscles, nerves and bones helps people to work positively with their condition.

Breaking the cycle of pain

It is often important to help patients understand that there is not necessarily a linear relationship between the onset of symptoms and worsening pain. It is a cycle. It is often unclear whether worries exacerbate pain or pain leads to worry, but the result is that people may focus on their pain, worry about it, consequently have disturbed sleep, become even more susceptible to pain, worry further and gear down their lives so that they become less and less active and increasingly out of condition. Muscles which should be tight, like our stomach muscles, weaken and fatigue more easily. Muscles that should be more relaxed, like our back and neck muscles, become tighter.

The body needs exercise to thrive. I think exercise is a basic human need because, as people gear down and become less fit, so they withdraw from social activities, including work, and become isolated. They are, in effect, suffering a bereavement reaction and very frequently start to become depressed. The more they think about their symptoms and how miserable their life is, the more depressed they become. One of the features of depression is sleep disturbance, and that causes yet more pain. The more pain they feel, the more that reinforces the belief that something serious is wrong, and they gratefully agree to stop doing any enjoyable activities which could worsen their condition further. Fear and avoidance lead into more pain and depression and so the cycle continues.

I stress, as I did with Barry and Rene, how important it is to do what we enjoy doing, and how this will help, not harm. I would never tell anyone to stop exercising altogether, particularly athletes and sporty types. It is very rare for an athlete to need total rest: just relative rest for the affected body part. People get better much more quickly if they can keep doing the activities they enjoy doing and which give their life meaning. I have often had cyclists pedal with one leg and rowers row with one arm. Or I might encourage a different sport, such as cycling, rowing or swimming, while a knee settles down from a running strain. Indeed, trying out a different sport during injury is often what leads to an interest in triathlon events.

The challenge of fibromyalgia

I see many patients diagnosed as suffering from fibromyalgia, an extremely common condition. It has been estimated that up to 20% of patients attending general rheumatology clinics have clinical findings which are consistent with fibromyalgia. There are 10 female sufferers for every one male. *Fibro* means fibrous tissues, *myo* means muscle and *algia* means pain. It is a dustbin term for a condition for which there is no known medical cause – in that sense, very similar to chronic fatigue syndrome. There are essentially three main symptoms: widespread musculo-skeletal pain, symmetrically spread over the whole body from the head to the toes; a feeling of tiredness all the time; and disturbed sleep, often accompanied by vivid dreams. In addition, these unfortunate people often experience irritable bowel, bladder and eye symptoms together with migraine: all typical of dysfunction in the autonomic nervous system. One of the consistent research findings is that sufferers from fibromyalgia have an excess of REM sleep and a deficiency of restorative sleep. Acute fibromyalgia was experimentally induced in a Canadian study in which students were woken up when in non-REM sleep but were allowed to continue REM sleep. After a few days they started to feel aches and pains, and after a couple of weeks they started to feel pain all over the body. As soon as the sleep pattern was corrected, their symptoms disappeared.[4]

We know that growth hormone, thought to help repair tissue strained in the course of everyday life, is released during slow wave restorative sleep. Having too much REM sleep precludes sufficient restorative sleep, and, if we are not getting enough restorative sleep, insufficient tissue healing may take place, leading to widespread pain.

Alas, the condition is not simple to correct when it has become chronic. In normal, non-laboratory conditions, too much REM sleep occurs because of excessive emotionally arousing introspection, arising from worry about oneself, withdrawal from social activities, consequent misery, etc – it is part of the cycle of pain.

Introducing greys

Indeed, patients with fibromyalgia are usually highly emotionally aroused and, before I studied the human givens, I was very confused about how to help them. All I could think of to do was to ask them to take more exercise, these patients do not respond to physical treatments. Usually they say that any physical intervention makes their pain worse. They are classic black and white thinkers who operate in terms of all or nothing. They have pain everywhere, always. Their lives are completely awful; their sleep is always appalling. There are no recollections of the greys, when they felt slightly better, just for a few minutes, when they were persuaded to go down the garden to look at the flowers in bloom; or when they got involved in a gripping book one evening and had a reasonable night's sleep. Because their symptoms are physical, they expect physical treatments, and only physical treatments, to cure their problems.

Using pain scales can be very helpful in breaking down black and white thinking. I ask every patient on each visit how bad their pain is, and I make a note of it. Sometimes they will say that their pain is no better than when they first came to see me, and I can say, "Well that's interesting. It was 8 when I first met you it and now it's right down to 4. So it's 50 per cent better!" Patients are often really surprised, and that helps move them forward.

If I see a fibromyalgia patient within a few years of their 'diagnosis', I have a chance of working successfully with them to open up their receptivity to the mind-body link, reconnect them to their needs, get them involved in more activities and break their illness behaviours. The key, again, is handing back control to the patient. But some people I see have, sadly, suffered from crippling fibromyalgia since childhood, and there is a high possibility of their having suffered either emotional or physical abuse as children. When they say, "I can't cope with the pain," they are using pain as a metaphor for life. Alas, as a musculo-skeletal specialist, I am not in a position to help with their complex emotional needs.

Chronic fatigue syndrome

Although I do not have patients with chronic fatigue syndrome (CFS) referred to me, I've taken a particular interest in the condition for many years, mainly because of good research which has shown that a systematic, gradual incremental increase in aerobic exercise is vital and helps to improve all outcomes for chronic fatigue sufferers. CFS is very similar to, indeed probably the same condition as, 'overtraining syndrome', so well known in endurance athletes. I think chronic fatigue syndrome has also been bedevilled by black and white thinking, both in the sufferers and in the medical profession. The question asked by both is – is it in the body (with a viral biomedical cause) or is it all in the head (emotionally caused)? But clearly there are elements of the physical and the psychological. There are physical manifestations of the disorder and sufferers genuinely feel pain in their muscles, but they are also very often highly stressed, highly emotionally aroused people whose symptoms most often first came on at a time when they were going through difficult life events.

Even more unfortunately, because they are often told by doctors that their physical pain doesn't exist, patients may feel quite damaged by the healthcare system and embark on a mission to find the cause of their problem. If they find a society that supports their own belief about their problem, they develop even more fixed and rigid views about its causation, despite complete lack of objective justification. These entrenched unhelpful attitudes and beliefs then have to be dismantled before any advances can be made.

A realistic set of goals

Just as in psychological therapies, I like to agree realistic goals for my patients to work towards. Before I studied the human givens approach, I used to set goals that were geared to *my* expectations, perhaps demanding amounts of exercise which were inappropriate for certain individuals because of their own negative attitude towards exercise. Now I know better, and work with patients' own goals. I say, "What would you like to be able to do that you can't do at the moment?" Patients always want relief from pain, but that is an absence of something.

I need them to come at that aim from the point of view of something positive which they can do to achieve it. Barry wanted to go fishing, although, still imbued with all the gloom and doom stories he had absorbed from other healthcare professionals (in many cases, relatives and 'friends' also express negative opinions), initially he was doubtful about how sensible that would be. I reframed his belief that fishing might be harmful by telling him at once what an eminently achievable goal resuming fishing would be. We approached it slowly, having him fish for an hour at a time to start with.

Margaret, a woman in her late 60s, could at first think of no other goal than cessation of her pain. I persisted and eventually she told me that she would love to be able to pick up her young grandchildren for a cuddle. This gave us something very positive and practical to work towards. I showed Margaret how to bend properly (from the knee, not the waist), and got her to agree to a programme of walks to build up her strength. A few pain intervention treatments helped her to achieve this goal.

Once a patient has achieved a first goal, they experience the powerful reward of being able to do something they haven't been able to do, often for several years. All I need say then is, "What would you like to do next?" as they are already motivated to move on to another goal.

"Are you saying I'm mad?"

Working from the basis of a mind-body link takes care and diplomacy. Not everyone, as I have indicated, is initially receptive to the idea that there is something *they* could be doing to lessen their pain. People who are black and white thinkers and who are highly aroused when they come for their appointment are quite likely to snap at me, "So you think I need a psychiatrist, do you?" if they are expecting a diagnosis of serious spinal disorder and I'm suggesting tension is playing a part. I used to think that such patients were just difficult people. Now, I understand much better where they are coming from and what makes them respond as they do, and I 'lose' only one or two patients, whereas previously I think I lost quite a few.

I feel enormously empowered, having now at my disposal a range of simple psychological approaches which make such a difference to my patients' physical experience of their problems. I always congratulate patients on every effort that they make, however small. I separate them from their problem, asking questions not about "your painful hip/back/knee" but asking "When is the pain most likely to come along?" so that they can envisage themselves as people also sometimes free from pain. Working in this way is not only more effective and rewarding but I also have more resistance against depression and burnout in myself. People in pain may unintentionally infect with their own misery those who are trying to help them. By ensuring that I have my own needs met, and through my greater understanding of how people experience their pain, I am better able to infect them with my optimism instead.

References

1. Waddell, G (1998). *The back pain revolution.* Churchill Livingstone, Edinburgh. (Pages 85–101; 223–240.)
2. *Guidelines for the management of low back pain at work, evidence review and recommendations 2000.* Faculty of Occupational Medicine, London.
3. Van Tulder, M W, Assendelft, W J J, Koes B W and Bouter L M (1997). Spinal radiographic findings and non-specific low back pain. *Spine*, 22, 427–434.
4. Moldofsky, H, Scarisbrick, P, England, R and Smythe H (1975). Musculoskeletal symptoms and non-REM sleep disturbance in patients with fibrositis syndrome and healthy subjects. *Psychosomatic Medicine*, 371, 341–351.

The above article, originally entitled 'Talking to the person with pain' first appeared in Volume 8, No. 2 of *Human Givens*. Grahame Brown is a physician, holds a post as consultant in orthopaedic and sports medicine at the Royal Orthopaedic Hospital in Birmingham and also has a private practice. Additionally, he is a specialist in occupational health. He has the diplomas of the Scottish Royal Colleges in sport and exercise medicine and the human givens diploma of the European Therapy Studies Institute. He is a Fellow of the Human Givens Institute and an honorary senior lecturer at the University of Birmingham Institute of Occupational Health and School of Sport and Exercise Science.

Human givens and trauma treatment

Counsellors and therapists who use it know that the 'rewind technique' is fast, safe, painless and effective for dealing with trauma. Keith Guy and Nicola Guy have tested it in research.

"THE treatment was like magic." These were the words of a euphoric client after treatment with Keith for symptoms of trauma which had been affecting his life for the past three months. He worked as a gravedigger and had been present during an exhumation. He was plagued by the memory of a dead face grinning at him and of having to handle and walk through a decaying corpse.

"I had started to get nightmares. I didn't sleep very well and I had flashbacks at night. Or, when mowing the grass, something would trigger off the incident," he said. In just one session, using the rewind technique, the panic and anxiety which had dogged him was gone. "I went from not being able to function to functioning. It took the fear and anxiety away."

It is reactions like this, repeated by client after client, that have made us so keen for the rewind treatment to become better known and widely available. Our research study into its effectiveness is, we hope, a first step that will encourage other researchers to test it more rigorously, preferably against other forms of therapy, so that the benefit of rewind can be more forcefully communicated to the thousands of practitioners who need to know about it.

Although Keith had long had an interest in working with trauma and was trained and experienced in using the debriefing model devised by psychologist and former firefighter Jeff Mitchell, it was only when he learned the rewind technique at a MindFields College workshop two years ago that he realised trauma could be treated both quickly and reliably, with the minimum of distress to sufferers.

Debriefing, of which there are now many versions, was designed as a group technique, in which trauma victims were encouraged to talk through their experience and impressions of the trauma, with the debriefer guiding them in their exploration of associated facts, thoughts and feelings. Many elements of the debriefing have repeatedly been called into question, including the tendency to offer it very quickly after a traumatic incident occurred. It is always inappropriate to attempt to debrief people who are highly aroused or distressed. Also, as international trauma expert Noreen Tehrani has pointed

out, group debrief sessions may be harmful to highly imaginative participants, who become traumatised by the visualisation of others' experiences,
and are unlikely to help those with severe trauma reactions.[1] However, just
as worryingly, many debriefers have simply adapted group debrief models for
individual use. The rewind technique, in contrast, does not require people to
go into detail about their experience in order to neutralise its impact and, we
have found, is consistently effective.

How it works

The rewind technique, also known as the fast phobia cure, evolved from the
technique developed by Richard Bandler one of the co-founders of Neurolinguistic Programming (NLP). He called it the VK dissociation technique
(the V stands for visual and the K for kinaesthetic – feelings). The version
recommended by the European Therapy Studies Institute has been refined
and streamlined, as a result of its own research into why and how best it
works.[2] It is highly useful for individuals who, after exposure to traumatic
events, have developed PTSD or lesser forms of the condition. When Keith
began practising the rewind technique with traumatised clients, he found it
consistently effective, almost immediately.

Simply described, the technique works by allowing the traumatised individual, whilst in a safe relaxed state, to reprocess the traumatic memory so
that it becomes stored as an 'ordinary', albeit unpleasant, and non-threatening memory rather than one that continually activates a terror response. This
is achieved by enabling the memory to be shifted in the brain from the amygdala to the neocortex.

The amygdala's role is to alert us to danger and stimulate the body's 'fight
or fight' reaction. Normally, all initial sensations associated with a threatening experience are passed to the amygdala and formed into a sensory
memory, which in turn is passed on to the hippocampus and from there to
the neocortex where it is translated into a verbal or narrative memory and
stored. When an event appears life-threatening, however, there can be sudden
information overload and the sensory memories stay trapped in the amygdala instead of being passed on to, and made sense of by, the neocortex.
While trapped in the amygdala, the trauma memory has no identifiable
meaning. It cannot be described, only re-experienced in some sensory form,
such as panic attacks or flashbacks. The rewind technique allows that
sensory memory to be converted into narrative, and be put into perspective.

Rewind technique? What's that?

We were both so impressed by Keith's initial results when working with the
technique that we were quite stunned to discover rewind is not used routinely

in the UK to treat trauma. We carried out a literature review and found only one research paper, which appeared in the *British Journal of Clinical Psychology* in 1991 and was an account of a very successful use of rewind with traumatised officers in the West Midlands police force.[3] An internet search found only one UK practitioner, a UK-based American GP, Dr David Muss, who is involved in trauma work and was the author of the one research paper we had found. We next telephoned the main trauma hospitals including The Maudsley in South London and various hospitals in the Priory group, which specialise in treating post traumatic stress. None of them was using rewind. Finally, we contacted police forces, fire services and occupational health services in seven counties and none had even heard of it.

It would seem that the European Therapy Studies Institute, through MindFields College, is the only UK body actively promoting and explaining the scientific basis for why it works as part of their training in the rewind

The rewind technique

The rewind technique should be learned and practised under the guidance of an experienced practitioner. It is carried out in a state of deep relaxation, or trance.

Once relaxed, clients are asked to recall or imagine a place where they feel totally safe and at ease. Their relaxed state is then deepened. They are then asked to imagine that, in their special place, they have a TV set and a video player with a remote control facility. Next, they are asked to float to one side of themselves, out of body, and watch themselves watching the screen, without actually seeing the picture. (This is a means of creating significant emotional distance.) Clients next watch themselves watching a 'film' of the traumatic event. The film begins at a point before the trauma occurred and ends at a point at which the trauma is over and they feel safe again. They then float back into their body and imagine pressing the video rewind button, so that they see themselves very quickly going backwards through the trauma, from safe point to safe point. Then they watch the same images, but going forwards very quickly, as if pressing the fast forward button.

All this is repeated back and forth, at a speed dictated by the individual concerned and as many times as needed, till the scenes evoke no emotion. If it is desirable to instil confidence for facing the feared circumstance in the future – for instance, driving a car or using a lift – they are asked to imagine a scenario in which they are doing so, and feeling confident and relaxed. Once accomplished, clients are brought out of trance, and the work of the rewind technique is complete.

Besides being safe, quick, painless and side effect free, the technique has the advantage of being non-voyeuristic. Intimate details do not have to be voiced. It is the client who watches the 'film', not the counsellor. ∎

technique, however still relatively few professionals know about it. As Keith was at the time working for Coventry City Council, offering a counselling service to its employers, and thus had access to very many clients, we decided to conduct a long-term study. Our aim was to establish empirically the efficacy and applicability of rewind, with the intention both of challenging the use of less effective established treatments and promoting the routine use of rewind as a trauma treatment.

Coventry City Council has over 17,000 employees working in a wide range of capacities. They include, for instance, secretaries, managers, refuse collectors, cemetery operatives, social workers, teachers and university staff. Coventry is forward thinking in that it recognises that it is not only problems directly related to work that adversely affect work performance, but problems that spill over from personal life. As a consequence, the counselling service would deal with the whole gamut of life-affecting experience, from bullying, relationship problems and alcohol dependence through to depression, phobias and panic attacks, whatever the causes.

Our study

Thirty people took part in our study (26 women and four men). They comprised all the council's employees who attended for counselling in the two year period between 2000 and 2002, having been diagnosed as suffering from post traumatic stress disorder (PTSD) or partial PTSD. Their ages ranged from 25 to 62, with an average age of 42. They differed widely in terms of jobs and seniority, but teachers accounted for the highest number in any single occupation (13 per cent). Forty three per cent held clerical positions.

Twenty nine people had experienced a single or multiple traumatic event(s) that had continued to impact upon their well being. (Four fulfilled the accepted diagnostic criteria for PTSD,[4] while 25 were experiencing partial symptoms.) Eighteen clients were treated for one trauma, while 11 were treated for two to five traumas. The remaining person had a phobia about heights (thus also a fear of flying) and enclosed spaces such as lifts.

The traumas treated had occurred, in one case, as recently as one month ago and, in another, as long as 46 years ago. Types of trauma included psychological bullying, physical and sexual assaults including rape and sexual abuse, car accidents, muggings, the witnessing of critical incidents, being trapped in lifts and the London Underground, and war experiences (one man was a Falklands veteran). The most common traumas were assaults and muggings.

All participants were asked if they were experiencing difficulties in other aspects of their lives as a result of the trauma or phobia. Almost all reported experiencing problems in at least one area, the three most common being relationships, family or, particularly, work. One man had a history of mental ill health, which included clinical depression; 27 per cent of the women had also experienced depression but the rest had no previous history of mental ill health. Eight per cent reported previous significant physical health problems.

Earlier treatments sought

Seventeen people had sought treatment for their trauma symptoms prior to rewind. Eleven had been prescribed antidepressants and/or sleeping tablets and/or tranquillisers (and two more were offered medication but refused it). Of those who took medication, two found it helpful, and another four found it helpful to some degree but made comments such as, "It did not make me happy"; "It didn't stop the dreams"; "They are only useful for the short term"; and "It was some help".

Eight clients underwent counselling, three of whom found it helpful, although one added that it helped only in the short term and didn't solve the problems being experienced. Three clients said that the counselling they received did not work at all and actually made them feel worse. Two didn't comment. Three clients received psychiatric help, and three sought complementary treatments, which included hypnotherapy, aromatherapy and a herbalist massage. The aromatherapy was perceived as helpful but only in a very limited, short term way. No client was offered rewind by their GP, the psychiatric services or private counsellors they went to.

Each client underwent an assessment session to allow Keith to determine suitability for rewind, to establish rapport and trust, and to explain the purpose of the study and how rewind works. Before having the rewind treatment (see box on page 384) they were asked to rate their wellbeing on a scale of 0 to 50, where 0 is poor and 50 excellent.

The questionnaire

We devised a questionnaire which all of the participants in our study agreed to complete seven to 10 days after treatment, with a final section to be completed between three and six months later. Besides asking the questions which enabled us to find out the information described above, we also asked people to scale from 1 to 10 (where 1 is poor and 10 is excellent) how they had been affected since the trauma, and to scale the level of distress they were experiencing. We asked them to scale their willingness to try rewind; the physical, emotional, social, personal and behavioural effects on them of rewind; and their rating of the technique. We hoped to establish:

- overall success rate of rewind, as measured by clients in terms of their physical, behavioural, emotional, social and personal lives

- success rate correlated to how long ago the trauma had been experienced
- success rate correlated to type of trauma
- success rate correlated to number of traumas experienced
- success rate correlated to the having or not of previous treatment relating to the trauma
- success rate correlated to unrelated problems in client's life
- success rate correlated to client's openness to treatment.

The completed questionnaires were analysed by an independent research company.

The findings are exciting

Forty per cent of clients rated rewind as extremely successful; 53 per cent rated it as successful and seven per cent rated it as acceptable. No one rated the method poor or as a failure.

Prior to rewind, clients on average rated their well being as 12 out of 50. Seven to 10 days after treatment, the average score was 30.3 out of 50. Three to six months later, the average score was 32.2. This represents an improvement of 167.4 per cent on their original ratings.

On a scale of 1–10 (1 is unwilling, 10 is very willing), clients on average scored 9 on willingness to try this type of treatment.

The average level of distress immediately prior to treatment on a 1–10 scale (10 highly distressed) was 6.2.

On a scale of 1–10 (where 10 is excellent), the degree of relaxation induced

"I have finally let go of the fear that gripped me"

EMMY wrote, before rewind: "I remember, 45 years ago, being seven years old and enjoying a day out at the swimming pool. I couldn't swim but I used to love the splashing and the laughter and the picnic lunch after. My brothers, who weren't much older than me but could swim, decided I should learn to swim too. They threw me in the deep end. I can only recall the extreme fear. I remember the gasping. I have a fear not of water but of being under water. I am unable to swim. I am unable to join in the fun with the family, in swimming baths and by the sea. My husband and children all tried to encourage me to learn to swim but I always got extremely panicky."

A week after the rewind treatment, she said, "I can now put my head under water for the first time and I am starting swimming lessons. Three months later, I am more competent in the water. I have fun in the water and I no longer need someone close by me. I am amazed at myself. At 53, I have finally learned to let go of the fear that gripped me, following that fateful day." ∎

by the counsellor (Keith) just prior to treatment was 7.8.

Age, sex, occupation, type of trauma and length of time since trauma was experienced did not affect the efficacy of rewind.

"It's like coming in to the light"

KEN is a 49 year old Falklands veteran who, between March and June 1982, experienced three terrifying events. A missile hit HMS Antelope, but did not immediately explode. Twenty four hours later, it exploded. Ken had to pull bodies out of the water as he was helping to get his colleagues off the ship.

Ken rated his wellbeing, as a result of these events, as 5 out of a possible 50. He described his life before rewind: "I don't go to parties because of the noise. I know the balloons will bang. I pre-empt by ducking under a table. I start to sweat; it's sheer terror for me – it takes me back to the war. I vomit – people think I'm drunk or on drugs. I feel I am back on board; I'm swaying.

"I have lain on the bathroom floor for hours because I feel so physically sick. For days I am on edge, sometimes unable to walk. I avoid sleep because of the nightmares and, after several days, I get hallucinations, I sit in the flat in total darkness for days, curtains drawn. I imagine the bus going by is a jet. The smell of fuel oil, 'burnt pork' makes me feel sick. I'm sweating profusely but I am cold and shaking, in a state of mental confusion.

"I was like a zombie, a robot. I saw my GP in 1983, after leaving the navy. I saw a psychiatrist for a year. It did not help; it was a waste of time. I have no recollection of what they said, apart from being told I was a manic-depressive. Medication did not stop the nightmares. I have been prescribed Valium, Mogadon, antidepressants and I've been given antipsychotic drugs, and they did not help." Seven to 10 days after rewind, he said, "The memories don't seem to bother me anymore. I'm not fearful. I'm unsure – it's like bereavement. I've had 20 years of a wasted life. It's like coming in to the light. I felt jolly, joking and then – but what am I going to 'do with it'? I feel all over the place. I feel like I'm born again at 50."

Three to six months later, he commented, "I feel my face has changed. The light has come on from within; it's a spiritual light. I am more relaxed, more at peace. I think I am content. I have laughed more in the last weeks than the last 20 years. I sleep much better; I eat well; I can relax. I feel much more in control. This has been life changing for me – no more flashbacks or nightmares; it was like a prison sentence. My partner has noticed the difference in me. She likes what she sees." ∎

(Ken has needed ongoing 'adjustment' counselling, as we have termed it. Having lived in hell for more than 20 years, it has been difficult for him to adjust to a 'normal' existence, and he is angry that, through lack of the right treatment, he has had 20 wasted years, not to mention acquiring an unnecessary psychiatric history.)

Seventeen clients needed one session of rewind, 11 clients needed two, and two clients needed three sessions. However, in no case did the same trauma need to be treated twice. All clients with a single trauma needed only one session.

On average, clients needed four rewinds in each session.

In general, the presence of other areas of difficulty in clients' lives did not affect the efficacy of rewind. There were two exceptions: in one case there was an outstanding claim for compensation and in another an outstanding inquest. Outcome from using the technique was probably least satisfactory for these two people.

The client treated for fears of heights, flying and enclosed spaces has fully overcome them. She had been transferred to the 13th floor at work and had previously been planning to resign. She is now not only able to work high up in the building but also to use a lift. She recently flew to India with no difficulty.

Quite evidently, rewind is a consistently successful trauma treatment, with dramatic improvements in clients' wellbeing, self esteem and capacity for a more fulfilling life, sustained over time. It consistently works in one session, although multiple traumas may need additional separate sessions.

Clients were able to clearly understand and measure their own increase in wellbeing and decrease in unwelcome symptoms. The most commonly mentioned effects that rewind had on the clients' lives were:

- increased confidence
- no more flashbacks
- more positive mood
- ability to speak about the trauma
  without triggering alarm or difficulty
- no more fear.

The fact that the treatment was quick, easy and painless was commented on by very many and most said they would recommend the method to others. No other treatment was deemed to equal its success. One client's comment, we think, sums up exactly what rewind aims so successfully to achieve in the treatment of trauma: "I can still recall the picture but it doesn't have the emotional punch. It doesn't hold emotional power any more."

We must profess ourselves unable to understand why rewind is not a routinely available trauma treatment, or indeed cure. The only caveats seem to be that, if there is 'unfinished business' which makes the trauma ongoing (such as compensation claims or, of course, continued abuse), this can overlie a client's ability to move on from trauma.

Back in perspective

It is our sense that trauma is often seen within the mental health profession as a long-term problem, and is perhaps more often misdiagnosed than diagnosed. Some of the symptoms, such as dissociation, hallucinations and intrusive memories, can be mistaken for symptoms of psychosis, and treated accordingly. Also, certain treatments – those which encourage the reliving of the trauma – can deepen it and further embed it. Rewind, however, puts a trauma into perspective very neatly. The treatment takes only a short time, perhaps close to the length of time the incident took to occur – a terrible experience but a tiny part of an entire life. By relocating the traumatic memory from one part of the brain to another – the place where it was meant to end up in the first place, it re-balances the experience within a person's life. Most of the people we work with just want to put their experience into proper perspective, not suffer symptoms any more, and get on with their lives. Rewind is not only powerfully effective in that respect but side effect free. It is also suitable for use with children. We are determined to press for rewind to be recognised and adopted as a first line treatment for trauma symptoms, accessible to all who need it.

References

1. Tehrani, N (1998). Debriefing: a safe way to defuse emotion? *The Therapist*, 5, 3, 24–29.
2. Griffin, J and Tyrrell, I (2001). *The shackled brain: how to release locked-in patterns of trauma*. Human Givens Publishing Ltd.
3. Muss, D (1991). *British Journal of Psychology*, 30, 90–91.
4. *Diagnostic and Statistical Manual of Mental Disorders*, 4th edition (1994). American Psychiatric Association.

The above article, originally entitled 'The fast cure for phobia and trauma: evidence that it works', first appeared in Volume 9, No. 4 of *Human Givens*.

Keith Guy is a qualified social worker and counsellor with many years experience in workplace counselling, both in the public and private sector. He has developed a special interest and expertise in trauma work and, till recently, worked for Coventry City Council Occupational Health as an in-house staff counsellor/trainer and trauma specialist.

Nicola Guy is an experienced social worker and counsellor, also with many years' experience in workplace counselling, in the public and private sectors.

Human givens and education

Teacher trainer Andy Vass shows how knowledge and application of the human givens approach could help hard-pressed teachers reduce stress and improve the climate in class.

WITHIN staffrooms around the country's schools, stress levels are high. At the same time as being understaffed and correspondingly overstretched, teachers are struggling to cope with an increasing workload brought about by a steady flow of new initiatives, rafts of additional targets, a (still) overly prescriptive curriculum which restricts professional autonomy and the incessant quest for higher and higher standards accompanied by endless testing. Set within the context of increasing challenging behaviour from children (a report from Ofsted, the Government's standards watchdog, shows a rise over the last three years in the number of schools "where behaviour is regarded as unacceptable"), and their parents in some cases, the question arises, "Why would anyone want to be a teacher now?"

Why indeed? A report last year from the 'think tank' Demos pointed out that 40 per cent of those who enrol in initial teacher training don't enter the classroom and, more worryingly, that between a third and a half of graduates who actually complete teacher training leave the profession within the first five years. Add these figures to the high age profile of the profession – around 160,000 are due to retire over the next decade – and a potential disaster is looming.

One of the reasons cited by teachers in the Demos report for leaving the profession early was their concern over the limited opportunities for professional autonomy. This is hardly surprising to anyone familiar with the human givens approach, since one of the 'givens' of human nature is the need to feel a sense of autonomy – the opportunity to experience self determination. While teachers experience the process of change as a stream of externally imposed and often badly managed initiatives which they have little opportunity to shape and which do not always reflect the needs of the learners, the challenges facing education will remain unsolved.

Another major reason given for leaving the profession (and this is not just confined to those at the start of their careers) is the high level of stress brought about by the demands of managing increasingly challenging and disruptive behaviour from students, which inhibits the learning process and diminishes the level of job satisfaction.

Complex issues cannot be solved overnight. Clearly, a coherent, long term approach that extends beyond the life of any one parliament, and is not subject to any one political agenda or ideology, is essential. But there is the opportunity to begin to make progress on the second issue (increasing teachers' confidence in the management of children's behaviour) because it can be approached from the perspective of the human givens – the knowledge and evidence that has emerged about how humans learn and the basic needs which, in this context, have to be met if we are to create the most effective climate for both teachers and children to thrive in.

No training in how to connect

For the past five years, in addition to working in schools to support students at risk of exclusion, I have been providing in-service training in behaviour management to schools and local education authorities. I have worked alongside colleagues in modelling skills or leading training sessions in over 500 schools, and the anecdotal but strong evidence I have accumulated is that the stress emerging from difficulties in managing behaviour affects *all* teachers, even the most experienced. However, it is the newly qualified teachers who generally face the sternest challenge with the least preparation and it is these teachers who are leaving the profession early in large numbers.

Over the past two years I have surveyed, within the context of providing additional professional development, all newly qualified teachers in primary and secondary schools in six local education authorities. I wanted to find out how much information and skills training they received in classroom management during the teacher training provided as part of their course rather than during placements in schools. I discovered that the average length of time devoted to the essential skills of connecting to, communicating effectively with and managing the behaviour of children in a positive way was one and a half hours, over the space of a year. When I asked how effective that information was, in the light of actually beginning to teach, an overwhelming majority rated it as either poor or unhelpful.

Thirty years ago, I was given a piece of advice during my own teacher training course which was intended to help me establish my 'control' over my future classes: "Don't smile until Christmas! Show them who is boss from the word go. Start off hard and then ease off when they know who's in charge."

One would have thought that such ridiculous advice would have no part in today's teacher training? Unfortunately, as I learned at a recent workshop attended by over a hundred newly qualified teachers, this approach is still being offered as 'wisdom' to impressionable graduates.

Manage but not control

Teachers cannot *control* the behaviour of children. Effective practitioners *manage* or *influence* the behaviour of their classes. The only point at which individuals can have influence on anyone else is when they have established rapport with them. How connected would a person be if they steadfastly refused to smile at anyone else for three months! Further, since the vast majority of the data processing in the brain attends to non-verbal aspects of communication, what kind of modelling process would a teacher be creating by showing no humour or enjoyment in being in the classroom?

No one would deny that children need clear and unambiguous boundaries set. Not only is this an essential part of meeting other givens such as security and social connection but also helps them to 'belong' to the learning community of the class or school. Smiling, being pleasant, friendly and connecting to children is not incompatible with setting boundaries and saying "No" when necessary. In fact the two things complement each other.

I believe, as do many teachers, that initial teacher training has become obsessively focused on the content of the curriculum to the extent that we commonly talk about 'delivering' the curriculum to children as if it were some kind of commodity. You can deliver milk, mail and newspapers but you can't deliver learning. Teaching and learning occur most naturally and therefore most effectively within human interactions. Ultimately, the quality of those interactions will determine the emotional climate of the classroom and the quality or effectiveness of the learning. If the majority of training relates to *what* people should be teaching as opposed to *how* to create the most effective climate in which to teach it, new teachers begin at a distinct disadvantage. It is not hard to see why many become overwhelmed when confronted with even 'normal' group behaviours, when they have so few skills and strategies to call on.

Indeed, from my survey, it became clear that trainees were most frustrated by tutors' failure to answer satisfactorily when asked questions such as, "What do you do when a child refuses to do what you say?", "How do you stop children from keeping on chatting?" or "What do you do if a child denies doing something naughty, even though you've just seen them do it?" Most often, they were either directed to a book or told that 'it' comes with experience.

However, even many experienced teachers are finding it increasingly tough to manage behaviour – largely because of the loss of autonomy mentioned earlier – and are looking to acquire additional skills. My personal view is that there is a 'knowledge gap' in teaching: a gap I define as the difference between what we now know from recent advances in scientific and psychological knowledge about humans and their behaviour, and what is taught to teachers that subsequently influences their practice in class. The vast majority of teachers in this country are in their late 40s or early 50s, and the knowledge I am talking about wasn't around when they trained. But what we know now, for example, about the significance and influence of language and the role that emotions and, in particular, emotional arousal play in affecting our actions, should be a core component of teacher training.

Serving teachers who trained prior to the availability of this information should have a clear programme of continuing professional development to allow the information and knowledge to be integrated into existing practice and enhance the level of skill they possess.

Attention seeking

Since behaviour in all its manifestations is the way people attempt to get their emotional needs met, an understanding, and application, of the human givens approach has a profound part to play in effective teaching. For any strategy to be effective in managing or influencing the actions of children in class it has to help them meet, as far as possible, the givens with which nature endowed us. It may be helpful to look at a few examples of this.

We know now, for instance, that humans – and more especially children – have a powerful need for attention; that any attention is better than none and that a child will do whatever he or she has to do, in order to meet the need for it. Teachers need to be aware of the equation of attention giving – that it is more constructive to emphasise what children do well than to correct all that they do wrong. On average, there should be five positive comments for every negative one a child receives. There are many ways to give positive attention, including greeting children individually, using their first names and engaging in chit-chat about the football team certain children are known to support or eliciting opinions about the band that is currently number 1 in the charts. Too avid attention seekers can effectively be held in check if teachers acknowledge their need and in effect give them attention by 'ignoring' them: "Who can answer this question? Stuart, I'll come to you after I've asked three other people first." Stuart then knows he will receive attention soon but it is attention for waiting rather than interrupting. The other important aspect is that because the aim is to meet the need for attention in a positive way, it is *preventive*, which is always more effective than having to react to poor behaviour.

The need for attention can be powerfully and productively met when older children are encouraged to help out in classes of younger children. This is particularly effective when children who have behaviour or discipline problems of their own are the ones invited to be 'mentors', thus absorbing the message that they are seen as capable of setting a good example for a younger child and that they possess skills and personal qualities that are valuable and which transcend any behaviour difficulty they may be experiencing at the moment.

Sometimes, creating a project or setting a task that requires a range of skills effectively helps meet the need for attention of those who would normally be frustrated by the demands of a narrowly presented curriculum and looking for less appropriate means of meeting their attention needs. Instead, they work as team members, contributing their particular skills as an organiser or a timekeeper or a recorder or whatever they excel at. Attention then comes from success and cooperation. Such an approach also helps to meet the need for social collaboration.

Ways to create autonomy

When we can recognise the given that people always want some determination over and input into what they do, we can work with this basic need instead of against it. Even though the requirement to follow a narrowly prescribed national curriculum has removed much of the choice from what is taught, teachers can still build some fulfilment of the need for autonomy into the way that they teach. A classic textbook method for teaching the process of photosynthesis, for instance, comprises reading the text, looking at a diagram and then answering set questions to test comprehension. But this provides no opportunity to engage with the learning nor does it afford the chance to embrace different learning preferences. Effective learning requires the learner to do something actively to help process the information and to consider the information from a range of perspectives instead of just receive it. So a teacher could choose instead to provide just the diagram and ask the students to devise from it what they think the text would say, or vice versa; or students could be given the answers to the questions and asked to work out what they think the questions might have been; or they could discuss in groups the eight key points they consider vital to include in any account of photosynthesis. In this way, they come to 'own' their learning. The feeling of autonomy generated by the choices of activity is more likely to engage students and develop in them a sense of flow, which in turn reduces the likelihood of inappropriate behaviour.

Much of the conflict that occurs in classrooms results from so called 'power struggles' which in fact are simply attempts to gain a sense of autonomy or status. Understanding that this too is a given enables teachers to distance themselves from the concept of trying to 'control' situations, which inevitably leads to conflict and failure, and instead to build in the element of choice by means of the language they use in managing behaviour.

Dealing with power struggles

There will be a big difference in the impact of – and therefore the reaction to – each of the following statements:

"Darren, I've told you twice to stop talking. If you do it again then I'll move you over here on your own."

"Darren, the instruction is to work silently. If you choose to keep talking, you'll be choosing to sit on your own over here. If you need my help, let me know. Thanks."

(Try saying them out loud yourself and notice differences in tone of voice and your own likely reaction to being spoken to in these ways.)

Building the language of choice into a teacher's approach provides a clear way of helping children take responsibility for their behaviour. Even 'binds' (questions which appear to be a choice but which effectively bind the person to a particular outcome), often used in therapeutic settings, have their place in the classroom: "Do you want to do the questions before the diagram or after?" "Would you prefer to stay in class and calm down or wait outside the room?"

Choice is vital to the management of a class and teachers can reap enormous benefits in terms of behaviour management if they keep highlighting the fact that children are making choices. If a child who previously had been arguing is now working quietly, the change can be pointed out: "Thanks for choosing to settle down, Azeem." It is a valuable technique for reinforcing good behaviour: "Jenny, how come you chose to search out all this information from the internet and make your project so great?" In human givens terms, such a comment invites children to go into their 'observing selves', the rational, analysing, part of the brain, and reflect on the fact that they themselves make the choices which enable them to achieve whatever it is that they want to achieve.

Emotions make us stupid

One of the most significant pieces of information underpinning the human givens approach is that high levels of emotional arousal make people "functionally stupid" (to quote Joe Griffin's memorable phrase). High levels of emotional arousal lock the brain into one-dimensional thinking and consequently our ability to rationalise and entertain different perspectives is drastically inhibited. When teachers find themselves engaged in power struggles, which by their very nature are emotionally arousing, not only the children but they themselves are less able to see and react responsibly.

For instance, a teacher may challenge a boy who is wandering around the classroom, interrupting others when he should be working, and receives the reply, "I'm only getting a pencil," (said very defensively). If the teacher responds to the tonality and thinly veiled hostility in the voice by saying, "Don't be silly! It doesn't take that long to get a pencil!", rapport between teacher and child is instantly lost because the teacher has failed to see that the child's response was merely an attempt to save face and minimise embarrassment at being caught out and maybe told off in public. Now both teacher and child are emotionally aroused and defensive, each equally keen to save face.

Much more effective is a response which devolves the power, allowing the perpetrator to retain his sense of status by having his actions, or the reasons behind them, validated, yet achieves the desired ends: "Yes, you do need a pencil for this. Now that you have got one, back to work now, thanks. I'll come and check it in a minute." (A teacher may wish to address the rudeness later, and in private, when the emotional heat has subsided.)

As the thinking part of the brain is inhibited when emotions are high, it follows that learning cannot be effective if high levels of conflict or stress exist (often a characteristic of reacting to rather than managing behaviour in class) and therefore all strategies for managing a classroom should have as their first criteria the reduction of emotional arousal.

I hear you

I know from my own contact with many hundreds of new teachers that this is not widely known, let alone explained in training. This means that simple skills such as reflective listening are not taught. Yet reflective listening – the ability to let someone know that their message has been understood – is a core skill in lowering emotional arousal. Without this skill, interactions between people who may not share the same viewpoint are likely to trigger high levels of emotional arousal. How often do children in class feel that the teacher hasn't understood their perspective? How commonly do comments such as "It's not fair!" or "Other people do it too!" punctuate attempts to redirect children to appropriate behaviour?

Reflecting both the child's emotions and the content of what they are saying helps build rapport and lower arousal: "Nadine, I can see you're a bit annoyed because you think I haven't given you a chance for your side of the story. When I've set the class working, then we can talk calmly over there."

Putting it another way

Emotional arousal can also be lowered using the technique of reframing ideas and beliefs – helping a person gain additional, more helpful perspectives on things, when they are stuck in negative thinking. One important element of reframing is to reflect back information with a slight 'twist' that gives a perceived difficulty a transient status: "Mr Smith, I can't do this!" "It's good you chose to ask for help, Jade. Now, which bit can't you do yet?" In this brief exchange, the teacher begins to turn a potentially negative feeling into a positive response as he reframes Jade's comments, firstly as a positive choice ie to seek help, and then begins to reframe the difficulty by the words "bit" (some of it is understood) and "yet" (presupposing that Jade will be able to do the work soon).

The language of influence

An understanding of the subtleties of language and the way in which the brain processes it should be part of every teacher's repertoire. It is a simple truth that everything we say will have an influence over children in our classrooms. We must, therefore, ensure that our words have a positive influence and in as many ways as possible seek to engage human beings' innate resources for helping meet our needs. The vast majority of teachers are hugely committed and want to do their very best for the children they teach. Yet, if one were to eavesdrop into many classroom conversations, a lack of knowledge about presuppositions in language would be evident. Presuppositions are the taking of something for granted in the way that a communication is phrased. Their impact cannot be ignored because they connect with the brain at an unconscious level. Consider, for instance, unhelpful presuppositions: "What have you done now?" (Oh, it's you again); "What else could you add to the picture?" (It isn't good enough); "See, you can behave well when you try!" (You're not useless after all, so why don't you try!)

Conversely, presuppositions can be used powerfully for positive good: "I wonder who'll answer the first question" (somebody will, and it could be you); "Next time you try this, it'll be easier" (there'll be a next time and it will definitely get easier from now on); "How pleased are you with this story?" (the story is pleasing).

Rapport building

Skilled teaching leads to group rapport – when all pupils are in a state of flow, their interest captured and their attitudes relaxed, because they are not fearful of being put on the spot or shouted at or humiliated. In such a state, they are capable of learning and teachers are capable of teaching. A knowledge and understanding of the human givens is not a magical way of achieving this in every case. Many children experience significant psychological difficulties or bring into class patterns established from their experiences outside school that make life extremely challenging for teachers and their peers alike. It is not possible to respond to the needs of absolutely every student at all times within a single classroom and there will always be the need for specialist support and intervention beyond the classroom especially with the present inclusion agenda. However, when teachers feel frustrated or powerless or drawn to confrontation and conflict with students, rapport and therefore influence is lost and no one gets their emotional needs met.

I would argue strongly, from my own experience and the feedback from many hundreds of teachers in all phases of education, that having an increased range of strategies which are compatible with the scientifically validated information on which the human givens approach is based significantly reduces the likelihood of those situations occurring. It also assists us in recognising that it is what we *do* that has the most influence on the climate in our own classrooms.

Spare capacity

Teachers could also benefit enormously from understanding and acting upon the fact that they can only give to others if they also take care of themselves. Nothing will change the fact that teaching is stressful, but there are simple psychological techniques for making it less so. A simple breathing technique – breathing in to the count of 7 and out to the count of 11 – done just before class or at difficult moments – can help lower stress levels instantly. Listening to music between classes, to calm down or liven up, can be helpful. So can engaging with the notion of pattern matching: photos of loved ones or fondly remembered occasions placed on the desk or in a personal organiser can create a lift every time they are looked at. Most importantly, teachers need to learn to take time for themselves – to make some space at break times when they aren't thinking about the job.

They can also usefully apply reframes to their own reflections about their work. Instead of thinking in despair, "I'm not handling 4R/7K/9B at all well!", or "I've messed up my lessons today", simple reframes on the lines of "I haven't got to grips with this class as well as I want to yet" or "I can improve the way I'm teaching such and such tomorrow" could go far to reduce much teacher burnout.

To explore all the areas in which a knowledge and understanding of the human givens can benefit the effectiveness of teachers is beyond the scope of this article. For me, however, the 'organising idea' it represents has provided the evidence for an approach which I have long been teaching and have instinctively known to be right. Quite simply, if as teachers we work in line with the way people naturally function, we will always be more effective, and strategies that are congruent with the human givens will always be the most successful.

The above article, originally entitled 'Teaching that works: using the human givens in the classroom', first appeared in Volume 9, No. 3 of *Human Givens*.

Andy Vass has taught for 27 years and combines work in school with training and consultancy. He has held workshops for over 500 schools and local education authorities, which combine highly practical behaviour management skills with new insights into language and powerful communication. He is a therapist and member of the European Therapy Studies Institute. As well as writing articles for the *Times Educational Supplement*, he is co-author of *Confident Classroom Leadership, Creating Winning Classrooms, Teaching with Influence, Talking Possibilities* and *Strategies to Close the Learning Gap*. He is a consultant to the Department for Education and Skills on a national training programme for behaviour management at primary and secondary phases.

References and notes

PART I – NEW DISCOVERIES ABOUT HUMAN NATURE

Chapter 1 – Seeking completion

1. Ayensu, E. S., Heywood, V. H., Lucas, G. L. and Defilipps, R. A. (1984) *Our Green and Living World*. Cambridge University Press.
2. Llinás, R. R. (2001) *I of the Vortex: from neurons to self*. The MIT Press.
3. Ratey, J. (2001) *A User's Guide to the Brain*. Pantheon Books.
4. Lewis-Williams, D. (2002) *The Mind in the Cave*. Thames & Hudson.
5. Shah, I. (1964) *The Sufis*. Doubleday & Co.
6. Shah, I. (1998) *Knowing How to Know*. The Octagon Press.
7. Deikman, A. J. (1993) *The Wrong Way Home*. Beacon Press.
8. Tyrrell, I. (1993) Exploring the CULT in culture. *The Therapist*, 1, 2, 29–32.
9. Brayfield, C. (2001) What it feels like to be a child with no friends. *Sunday Times*, 8 July.
10. The Mental Health Foundation. (2001) I want to be your friend but I don't know how.
11. Robertson, I. (2000) *Mind Sculpture*. Bantam Press.
12. Csikszentmihalyi, M. (1992) *Flow: the psychology of happiness*. Harper & Row.
13. Auty, G. (2000) *Postmodernism's Assault on Western Culture*. Quadrant.
14. Mithen, S. (1996) *The Prehistory of the Mind*. Thames & Hudson.
15. We would like to thank Peter Silvien for first suggesting to us that the caves were, in effect, schools.

Chapter 2 – Where does human nature come from?

1. Aserinsky, E. and Kleitman, N. (1953) Regularly occurring periods of eye mobility and concomitant phenomena during sleep. *Science*, 118, 273–274.
2. Jouvet, M. and Michel, F. (1959) Corrélations électromyographique du sommeil chez le chat décortiqué et mésencéphalique chronique. *Comptes Rendus de la Société de Biologie*, 154, 422–425.
3. Jouvet, M. (1978) Does a genetic programming of the brain occur during paradoxical sleep? In P. A. Buser and A. Rougel-Buser (Eds.), *Cerebral Correlates of Conscious Experience*. Elsevier, Amsterdam.
4. Karasov, W. H. and Diamond, J. (1985) Digestive adaptations for fuelling the cost of endothermy. *Science*, 228, 202–204.
5. Maclean, P. D. (1982) *Primate Brain Evolution: methods and concepts*. In E. Armstrong and D. Folk (Eds.), Plenum Publishing, 309.
6. Roffwarg, H. P., Muzio, J. and Dement, W. (1966) The ontogenetic development of the human sleep-dream cycle. *Science*, 152, 604–618.
7. Jouvet (1978), op. cit.
8. Jouvet, M. (1977) Neuropharmacology of the sleep waking cycle. In S. D. Iversen, L. L. Iversen and S. H. Snyder (Eds.), *Handbook of Psychopharmacology*, 8, 233–293. Plenum Publishing.
9. Roffwarg, Muzio and Dement, op. cit.
10. Hunt, T. H. (1989) *The Multiplicity of Dreams, Memory, Imagination and Consciousness*, 28–30. Yale University Press.
11. Hobson, J. A. (1989) *Sleep*. Scientific American Library, New York.

12. Tyrrell, I. (1999) Talking to the man who listens to horses: an interview with Monty Roberts. *The Therapist*, 6, 1, 24–28.
13. Walker, S. (1983) *Animal Thought*. Routledge & Kegan Paul.
14. Tattersall, I. (1998). *Becoming Human*. Oxford University Press.
15. Gopnik, A., Meltzoff, A. and Kuhl, P. (1999) *How Babies Think*. Weidenfeld & Nicolson.
16. Lorenz, K. L. (1966) *On Aggression*. Methuen.
17. Manacéïne, M. de (1897) *Sleep*. Walter Scott.
18. Rechtschaffen, A. et al. (1983) Prolonged sleep deprivation in rats. *Science*, 221, 182.
19. Rechtschaffen, A. and Bergmann, B. M. (1995) Sleep deprivation in rats by the disk-over-water method. *Behavioural Brain Research*, 69, 55–63.
20. Hobson, J. A. (1994) *The Chemistry of Conscious States: how the brain changes its mind*. Little, Brown & Company, Canada.

Chapter 3 – The dreaming brain

1. De Becker, R. (1968) *The Understanding of Dreams and their Influence on the History of Man*. Hawthorne, New York.
2. Freud, S. (1953) *The Interpretation of Dreams*. In J Strachey (Ed.), *The Complete Psychological Works of Sigmund Freud*. Hogarth Press.
3. Jung, C. (1965) *Memories, Dreams, Reflections*. Vintage.
4. Hall, C. S. (1953) A cognitive theory of dreams. *Journal of General Psychology*, 49, 277–282.
5. Aserinsky, E. and Kleitman, N. (1953) Regularly occurring periods of eye mobility and concomitant phenomena during sleep. *Science*, 18, 273–274.
6. Dement, W. and Kleitman, N. (1957) Cyclic variations in EEG during sleep and their relation to eye movements, body motility and dreaming. *Electro-encephalography and Clinical Neurophysiology*, 9, 673–690.
7. Foulkes, D. (1985) *Dreaming: a cognitive psychological analysis*. Lawrence Erlbaum Associates.
8. Moruzzi, G. (1963) Active processes in the brainstem during sleep. *Harvey Lectures Series*, 58, 233–297.
9. Hartmann, E. (1967) *The Biology of Dreaming*. C. C. Thomas.
10. Jouvet, M. (1967) *Mechanisms of the states of sleep. A neuro-pharmacological approach*. Presented at the 45th annual meeting of, and published by, the Association for Research in Nervous and Mental Disease, 45, 86–126. New York.
11. Dement, W. (1968) The biological role of REM sleep. In A. Kales (Ed.) (1969), *Sleep: physiology and pathology*. Lippincott.
12. Foulkes, op. cit.
13. Dement, W. (1960) The effect of dream deprivation. *Science*, 131, 1705–1707.
14. Ferguson, J. and Dement, W. (1968). Changes in the intensity of REM sleep with deprivation. *Psychophysiology*, 4, 380.
15. Morrison, A. (1983) A window on the sleeping brain. *Scientific American*, 248, 8694.
16. Morrison, A. and Reiner, P. (1985) *A Dissection of Paradoxical Sleep*. D. J. McGinty.
17. Griffin, J. (1997) *The Origin of Dreams*. The Therapist Ltd (distributed by Human Givens Publishing Ltd).

18. Coran, S. (1996) *Sleep Thieves*. Free Press.
19. Siegel, J. M. et al. (1999) Sleep in the platypus. *Neuroscience*, 91, 392.
20. Dowling, J. (2000) *Harry Potter and the Goblet of Fire*. Bloomsbury.
21. Ornstein, R. (1997) *The Right Mind: making sense of the hemispheres*. Harcourt Brace & Co.
22. Joseph, R. (1996) *Neuropsychiatry, Neuropsychology, and Clinical Neuroscience*. Williams & Wilkins.
23. Winson, J. (2002) The meaning of dreams. *Scientific American*, 12, 1, 54–61.
24. Ellman, S., Antrobus, J. Weinstein, L., Lewin, I. and Singer, J. (1991) *The Mind in Sleep*. John Wiley and Sons.
25. Moffit, A., Krammer, M., and Hoffmann, R. (Eds.) (1993) *The Function of Dreaming*. Albany State University of New York.
26. Ellman, S. J. and Antrobus, J. S. (Eds.) (1991 2nd edition) *The Mind in Sleep*. John Wiley.
27. Jouvet, M. (2001) *The Paradox of Sleep*. MIT Press.
28. Ibid.
29. Ibid.
30. Silveira, R. (1994) Children, television, fear and violence. *The Therapist*, 2, 1, 6–7.
31. Pendergrast, M. (1997) *Victims of Memory*. HarperCollins.

Chapter 4 – The mind entranced: sane and insane

1. *New Scientist* (4 July 1998), 2141.
2. *Science* (1997), 277, 968.
3. Erickson, M. H. and Rossi, E. L. (1976) *Hypnotic Realities*, Irvington Publishers.
4. We are not referring here to animal hypnosis, which is well documented elsewhere, but to experiments that show that, when animals get overexcited and are in a life-threatening situation, they cannot see the obvious way out of their predicament in the same way that they can when they are not emotionally aroused. Spitz, R. (1965) *The First Year of Life*. International Universities Press.
5. Goleman, D. (1996) *Emotional Intelligence: why it can matter more than IQ*. Bloomsbury Publishing, London.
6. Griffin, J. (1997) *The Origin of Dreams*. The Therapist Ltd (distributed by Human Givens Publishing Ltd).
7. Hobson, J. A. (1989) *Sleep*. Scientific American Library, a division of HPHLP, New York.
8. Jouvet, M. (1978) Does a genetic programming of the brain occur during paradoxical sleep? In P.A. Buser and A. Rougel-Buser (Eds.), *Cerebral Correlates of Conscious Experience*. Elsevier, Amsterdam.
9. Yapko, M. (1990) *Trancework: an introduction to the practice of clinical hypnosis*. Brunner/Mazel.
10. Morrison, A. R. (1983) A Window on the Sleeping Brain. *Scientific American*, 248, 86–94.
11. Rossi, E. L. (1993) *The Psychobiology of Mind-Body Healing*. WW Norton.
12. Rossi, E. L. & Nimmons, D. (1991) *The 20 Minute Break*. J. P. Tarcher Inc., Los Angeles.
13. Ibid.
14. Rossi, E. L. (Ed.) (1989). *Collected papers of Milton H Erickson* (vols. I, II, III & IV). Irvington Publishers, New York.

15. Waterfield, R. (2002) *Hidden Depths: the story of hypnosis*. Macmillan.
16. *Science* (1997), art.cit.
17. Robertson, I. (2002) *The Mind's Eye*. Transworld Publishers.
18. Hawkins, P. and Heap, M. (Eds.) (1998) *Hypnosis in Europe*. Whurr.
19. Chester, R. J. (1982) *Hypnotism in the East and West*. Octagon, London.
20. Morrison, op. cit.
21. Hobson, J. A. (1994) *The Chemistry of Conscious States*. Little Brown & Co, Canada.
22. Ibid.
23. Yapko, M. (1992) *Hypnosis and the Treatment of Depressions*. Brunner/Mazel, New York.
24. McGill, O. (1996) *The New Encyclopedia of Stage Hypnotism*. Anglo American Book Company.
25. Griffin, op. cit.
26. Griffin, J. and Tyrrell, I. (Second edition 2002) *Psychotherapy, Counselling and the Human Givens*. Human Givens Publishing Ltd for the European Therapy Studies Institute.
27. Chester, op. cit.
28. Sartorius, N. et al. (1986) Early manifestations and first-contact incidence of schizophrenia in different cultures. *Psychological Medicine*, 16, 909–928.
29. Torrey, F. (1987) Prevalence studies in schizophrenia. *British Journal of Psychiatry*, 150, 598–608.
30. Leff, J. (1992) The international pilot study of schizophrenia: five-year follow-up findings. *Psychological Medicine*, 22, 131–145.
31. Jablensky, A. (1992) Schizophrenia: manifestations, incidence and course in different cultures, a World Health Organization ten-country study. *Psychological Medicine*, supplement 20, 1–95.
32. Chakos, M. H. (1994) Increase in caudate nuclei volumes of first-episode schizophrenic patients taking antipsychotic drugs. American Journal of Psychiatry, 151, 1430–1436; Gur, R. (1998) Subcortical MR1 volumes in neuroleptic-naive and treated patients with schizophrenia. *American Journal of Psychiatry*, 155, 1711–1717.
33. Gur, R. A (1998) Follow-up magnetic resonance imaging study of schizophrenia. *Archives of General Psychiatry*, 55, 145–152.
34. Madsen, A. (1998) Neuroleptics in progressive structural brain abnormalities in psychiatric illness. *Lancet*, 352, 784.
35. Waddington, J. (1998) Mortality in schizophrenia. *British Journal of Psychiatry*, 173, 325–329.
36. Appleby, L. (2000) Sudden unexplained death in psychiatric in-patients. *British Journal of Psychiatry*, 176, 405–406.
37. Whitaker, R. (2002) *Mad in America: bad science, bad medicine, and the enduring mistreatment of the mentally ill*. Perseus Publishing.
38. Tyrrell, I. (2001) *The land of illusion: a filmed interview with a psychotic patient*. MindFields College.
39. Abbot, E. (2001) Letter. *Human Givens*, 8, 4, 47–48.
40. Smith, D. M. (2000) *Moral Geographies*. Edinburgh University Press.
41. Shah, I. (1998) *Knowing How to Know*. Octagon Press.
42. Deikman, A. J. (1982). *The Observing Self*. Beacon Press.
43. Ibid. 95.

PART II – APPRECIATING OUR BIOLOGICAL INHERITANCE

Chapter 5 – The human givens

1. Gopnik, A., Meltzoff, A. and Kuhl, P. (1999) *How Babies Think*. Weidenfeld & Nicolson.
2. Ibid.
3. Ibid.
4. Kagan, J. (1983) *Stress and coping in early development*. In N. Garmezy and M. Rutter (Eds.), Stress, Coping, and Development in Children. McGraw-Hill.
5. Seeman, T. E. and Syme, S. L. (1987) Social networks and coronary heart disease: a comparison of the structure and function of social relations as predictors of disease. *Psychosomatic Medicine*, 49, 4, 341–54.
6. Konner, M. (1991) Universals of behavioural development in relation to brain myelination. In K. R. Gibson and A. C. Petersen (Eds.), *Brain Maturation and Cognitive Development: comparative and cross-cultural perspectives*. Aldine de Gruyter.
7. E.g. Youngblade, L. M. and Belsky, J. (1992) Parent–child antecedents of 5-year-olds' close friendships. *Developmental Psychology*, 28, 700–713.
8. Murray, L. (1997) The effects of infants' behaviour on maternal mental health. *Health Visitor*, 70, 334–335.
9. Thomas, N. (2000) When love is not enough. *The New Therapist*, 7, 3, 16–23.
10. Goleman, D. (1996) *Emotional Intelligence: why it can matter more than IQ*. Bloomsbury Publishing, London.
11. Robertson, I. (1999) *Mind Sculpture: unleashing your brain's potential*. Bantam Books, London. Page 274.
12. Werner, E. and Smith, R. (1992) *Overcoming the Odds: high risk children from birth to adulthood*. Cornell University Press, Ithaca, New York.
13. Hammett, F. S. (1921) Studies in the thyroid apparatus. *American Journal of Physiology*, 56, 196–204.
14. Schanberg, S. M. and Field, T. M. (1987) Sensory deprivation stress and supplemental stimulation in the rat pup and preterm human neonate. *Child Development*, 58, 1431–1437.
15. Robertson, op. cit.
16. Gunter, B. (1999) *Pets and People: the psychology of pet ownership*. Whurr.
17. Reite, M. (1984) Touch, attachment and health. Is there a relationship? In C. Brown (Ed.), *The Many Facets of Touch*. Skillman, New Jersey.
18. Maxwell-Hudson, C. (1999) *Massage*. Dorling Kindersley.
19. Egbert, L. D., Battit, G. E., Welch, C. E. and Bartlett, M. K. (1964) Reduction of postoperative pain by encouragement and instruction of patients. *New England Journal of Medicine*, 270, 825–827.
20. Mayo, E. (1933) *The Human Problems of an Industrial Civilisation*. Macmillan.
21. Daniel, N. (1979) *The Arabs and Medieval Europe*. Longmans.
22. Shah, I. (1978) *Learning How to Learn*. Octagon Press, London.
23. Ibid.
24. Ratey, J. (2001) *A User's Guide to the Brain*. Pantheon Books.
25. Hafen, B. Q., Karren, K. J., Frandsen, K. J. and Smith, N. L. (1996) *Mind/Body Health: the health effects of attitudes, emotions and relationships*. Allyn & Bacon, Boston.

26. Durkheim, E. (1951) *Suicide*. Free Press, New York.

27. Wolf, S. (1992) Predictors of myocardial infarction over a span of 30 years in Roseto, Pennsylvania. *Integrative Physiological and Behavioural Science*, 27, 3, 246–257.

28. Winn, D. (1991) Please don't say that. *Sunday Times Magazine*, 14 July.

29. Lynch, J. (1977) *The Broken Heart: the medical consequences of loneliness*. Basic Books.

30. Dawkins, R. (1978) *The Selfish Gene*. Oxford University Press, Oxford.

31. Margulis, L. and Sagan, D. (1997) *What is Sex?* Simon & Schuster.

32. Behe, M. J. (1996) *Darwin's Black Box*. Simon & Schuster

33. Russel, R. (1993) Report on Effective Psychotherapy: legislative testimony, Hilgarth Press. This report was later endorsed by the American Psychological Association. See also: Hogan, D. B. (1993 edition) *The Regulation of Psychotherapists*, 4 vols. Hillgarth Press.

34. Seligman, M. E. P. In J. Buie (1988) 'Me' decades generate depression: individualism erodes commitment to others. *APA Monitor*, 19, 18.

35. Lane, R. E. (2000) *The Loss of Happiness in Market Democracies*. Yale University Press.

36. Dunbar, R. (1992) Neocortex size as a constraint on group size in primates. *Journal of Human Evolution*, 20, 469–493.

37. Gladwell, M. (2000) *The Tipping Point: how little things can make a big difference*. Little, Brown & Company.

38. House, J., Robbins, C. and Metzner, H. (1982) The association of social relationships and activities with mortality: prospective evidence from the Tecumseh Community Health Study. *American Journal of Epidemiology*, 116, 1, 123–140.

39. Ornstein, R. and Sobel, S. (1989) *Healthy Pleasures*. Addison-Wesley.

40. Depner, C. and Ingersoll-Dayton, B. (1988) Supportive relationships in later life. *Psychology and Aging*, 3, 348–357.

41. McClelland, D. (1989) Motivational factors in health and disease. *American Psychologist*, 44, 4, 675–683.

42. Zeig, J. and Munion, W. (1999) *Milton H. Erickson*. Sage.

43. Suls, J. and Mullen, B. (1981) Life events, perceived control and illness: the role of uncertainty. *Journal of Human Stress*, 7, 30.

44. Cited in Robertson, op.cit.

45. Egbert, Battit, Welch, and Bartlett, op. cit.

46. Seligman, M. (1975) *Helplessness: on depression, development and death*. W. H. Freeman & Co., San Francisco.

47. Erlich, P. and Ornstein, R. (1989) *New World, New Mind*. Doubleday.

48. Egbert, Battit, Welch, and Bartlett, op. cit.

49. Bennett, P. et al. (1999) Affective and social-cognitive predictors of behaviour change following first myocardial infarction. *British Journal of Health Psychology*, 4, 3, 247–256.

50. Rotter, J. (1954) *Social Learning and Clinical Psychology*. Englewood Cliffs, New York.

51. Kendell, K., Saxby, B., Farrow, M. and Naisby, C. (2001) Psychological factors associated with short term recovery from total knee replacement. *British Journal of Health Psychology*, 6, 1, 41–52.

52. Gunter, op. cit.

53. Langer, E. and Rodin, J. (1976) The effects of choice and enhanced personal responsibility for the aged: a field experiment in an institutional setting. *Journal of Personality and Social Psychology*, 34, 191–198.

54. Biderman, A. and Zimmer, H. (1961) *The Manipulation of Human Behaviour*. John Wiley, New York.

55. Winn, D. (1983, 2000) *The Manipulated Mind: brainwashing, conditioning and indoctrination*. Octagon Press, London; Malor Books, Cambridge, Massachusetts.

56. Bordo, S. (1993) *Unbearable weight: feminism, Western culture and the body*. University of California Press, Berkeley.

57. Leichter, H. (1997) Lifestyle correctness and the new secular morality. In A. Brandt and P. Rozin (Eds.), *Morality and Health*. Routledge, London.

Chapter 6 – The gendered brain

1. Colapinto, J. (2000) *As Nature Made Him: the boy who was raised as a girl*. HarperCollins.

2. Shettles, L. (1961) Conception and birth ratios. *Obstetric Gynaecology*, 18, 122–130.

3. Kraemer, S. (2000) The fragile male. *British Medical Journal*, 321, 1609–1612.

4. Tronick, E. and Cohn, J. (1989) Infant-mother face-to-face interaction: age and gender differences in coordination and the occurrence of miscoordination. *Child Development*, 60, 85–92.

5. McClure, E. (2000) A meta-analytic review of sex differences in facial expression processing and their development in infants, children and adolescents. *Psychological Bulletin*, 126, 424–453.

6. Phillips, M. (1999) *The Sex-Change Society: feminised Britain and the neutered male*. Social Market Foundation, London.

7. Kimura, D. (1996) Sex, sexual orientation and sex hormones influence human cognitive function. *Current Opinion in Neurobiology*, 2598.

8. Munro, P. and Govier, E. (1993) Dynamic gender-related differences in dichotic listening performance. *Neuropsychologia*, 61.31, 40, 347–53.

9. Shaywitz, B. A. and Shaywitz, S. E. et al. (1995) Sex differences in the functional organization of the brain for language. *Nature* (16 Feb.), 61.373, 607.

10. Lubinski, D. and Benbow, C. P. (1994) *The Study of Mathematically Precocious Youth: the first three decades of a planned 50 year study of intellectual talent*. Ablex Publishing Corporation.

11. Lubinski, D. A. and Schmidt, D. B. et al. (1996) A 20 year stability analysis of the study of values for intellectually gifted individuals from adolescence to adulthood. *Journal of Applied Psychology*, 81, 4, 443–51.

12. Lubinski, D. and Benbow, C. P. et al. (1995) Stability of vocational interests among the intellectually gifted from adolescence to adulthood: a 15 year longitudinal study. *Journal of Applied Psychology*, 80, 1, 196–200.

13. Lubinski, D. and Benbow, C. P. (1993) Reconceptualizing gender differences in achievement among the gifted. In K. A. Heller (Ed.), *International Handbook for Research on Giftedness and Talent*. Pergamon Press.

14. Tannen, D. (1994) *You Just Don't Understand*. Ballantine Books.

15. Gottman, J. (1998) *Why Marriages Succeed or Fail*. Bloomsbury.

16. Maccoby, E. (1990) Gender and relationships. *American Psychologist*, 45, 4, 513–520.

17. McGuinness, D. (1990) Behavioral tempo in pre-school boys and girls. *Learning and Individual Difference*, 2, 3, 315–325.

18. Holland, P. (2000) Spoiled for a fight: war play in the nursery. *The New Therapist*, 7, 4, 13–17.

19. Connor, K. (1989) Aggression: is it in the eye of the beholder? *Play and Culture*, 2, 213–217.

20. Watson, M. and Peng, Y. (1992) The relation between toy gun play and children's aggressive behaviour. *Early Education and Development*, 3, 4, 370–389.

21. Holland, op. cit.

22. Golombok, S. (2000) *Parenting: what really counts*. Routledge, London.

23. Lee, E. et al. (1991) Androgens, brain functioning and criminality: the neurohormonal foundations of antisociality. In H. Hoffman (Ed.), *Crime in Biological, Social and Moral Contexts*. Prager, New York.

24. Satterfield, J. et al. (1994) Preferential neural processing of attended stimuli in attention deficit hyperactivity disorder and normal boys. *Psychophysiology*, 31, 1–10.

25. Kimura, D. (1999) *Sex and Cognition*. MIT Press.

26. Clare, A. (2000) *On men: masculinity in crisis*. Chatto & Windus, London.

27. Mazur, A. and Booth, A. (1998) Testosterone and dominance in men. *Behavioural and Brain Sciences*, 21, 353–397.

28. Clare, op. cit.

29. Kimura, op.cit.

30. Burne, J. (2001) So you want better results? Try sitting boys next to girls. *The Independent* (education section), 5 April, 2–3.

31. Gender gap examined. News report in *The Psychologist* (2000), 13, 10, 493.

32. Kimura, op. cit.

33. Silverman, E. (1994) The hunter-gatherer theory of spatial sex differences: proximate factors mediating the female advantage in recall of object arrays. *Ethology Sociobiology*, 15, 95–105.

34. Moir, A. and Moir, B. (1998) *Why Men Don't Iron: the real science of gender studies*. HarperCollins.

35. Silverman, op. cit.

36. E.g. Gladue, B. and Bailey, J. (1995) Aggressiveness, competitiveness and human sexual orientation. *Psychoneuroendocrinology*, 20, 5, 475–485.

37. Clare, op. cit.

38. Fromm, E. (1973) *The Anatomy of Human Destructiveness*. Jonathan Cape, London.

39. Clare, op. cit.

40. Phillips, op. cit.

41. Magdol, L., Moffitt, T., Casi, A. and Newman, D. (1997) Gender differences in partner violence in a birth cohort of 21-year-olds. *Journal of Consulting and Clinical Psychology*, 65, 1.

42. Brinkerhoff, M. B. and Lupri, E. (1988) Interspousal Violence. *Canadian Journal of Sociology*, 13, 4.

43. Phillips, op. cit.

44. Tyrrell, I. and Winn, D. (2000) Marginalising men. *The New Therapist*, 7, 2, 24–29.

45. Clare, op. cit.

46. Phillips, op. cit.
47. Tyrrell and Winn, art. cit.
48. Webster, D. (1998) *The Cross-Section Relationship between Unemployment and Lone Parenthood: a multiple regression analysis of 1991 Census data for local authorities in Great Britain.* Glasgow City Housing.

Chapter 7 – The body-linked mind

1. Ader, R. and Cohen, H. (1975) Behaviourally conditioned immunosuppression. *Psychosomatic Medicine*, 37, 333–340.
2. Friedman, H. and Boothby-Kewley, S. (1987) The disease-prone personality: a meta-analytic view. *American Psychologist*, 42.
3. McEwen, B. and Stellar, E. (1993) Stress and metastasis. *Archives of Internal Medicine*, 153.
4. Martin, P. (1997) *The Sickening Mind: brain, behaviour, immunity and disease.* HarperCollins, London.
5. Cohen, S., Doyle, W. and Skoner, D. et al. (1997) Social ties and susceptibility to the common cold. *Journal of the American Medical Association*, 277, 24, 1940–1944.
6. Glaser, R. and Kiecolt-Glaser, J. (1988) Psychological influences on immunity. *American Psychologist*, 43.
7. Kessler, R. (1991) Stressful life events and symptom onset in HIV-1 infection. *American Journal of Psychiatry*, 148, 733.
8. Jones, F. (2000) Translating social support into health. *The Psychologist*, 13, 6, 296.
9. Sklar, L. and Anisman, H. (1979) Stress and coping factors influence tumor growth. *Science*, 205, 513–515.
10. Dubovsky, S. (1997) *Mind Body Deceptions: the psychosomatics of everyday life.* WW Norton, New York, London.
11. Sjodin, I., Svedlund, J., Ottoson, J. and Dotevall, G. (1986) Controlled study of psychotherapy in chronic peptic ulcer disease. *Psychosomatics*, 27, 187–200.
12. Ironson, G. et al. (1992) Effects of anger on left ventricular ejection fraction in coronary heart disease. *American Journal of Cardiology*, 70.
13. Ornstein, R. and Sobel, D. (1989) *Healthy Pleasures.* Addison-Wesley.
14. Cited in Strain, J. (1991) Cost offset from a psychiatric consultation-liaison intervention with elderly hip fracture patients. American Journal of Psychiatry, 148.
15. Burton, H. et al. (1986) The relationship of depression to survival in chronic renal failure. *Psychosomatic Medicine*, March.
16. Bennett, P. (1999) Affective and social-cognitive predictors of behaviour change following first myocardial infarction. *British Journal of Health Psychology*, 4, 3, 247–256.
17. Thornton, E. (1999) Affective status following myocardial infarction can predict long term heart rate variability and blood pressure reactivity. *British Journal of Health Psychology*, 4, 3, 231–236.
18. Carney, R. et al. (1988) Major depressive disorder predicts cardiac events in patients with coronary artery disease. *Psychosomatic Medicine*, 50, 627–33.
19. Helping heart patients take heart. *The New Therapist* (1999), 6, 4, 3.
20. Sobel, D. and Ornstein, R. (1996) *Healthy Mind, Healthy Body Handbook.* DRx, Los Altos.

21. Ostell, A. and Oakland, S. (1999) Absolutist thinking and mental health. *British Journal of Medical Psychology*, 72, 2, 239–250.
22. Robins, L. N., Helzer, J. E., Hesselbrock, M. and Wish, E. (1980) Vietnam veterans three years after Vietnam: how our study changed our view of heroin. In L. Brill and C. Winick (Eds.), *The Yearbook of Substance Use and Abuse*, vol. 2. Human Sciences Press.
23. Peele, S. (1995 edition) *Diseasing of America*. Lexington Books.
24. Faulkner, G. and Biddle, S. (2000) Cited in Why it's time to exercise the mind. *The New Therapist*, 7, 3, 2.

Chapter 8 – Water babies and our distant aquatic past

1. Griffin, J. (1999) Autism: a sea change. *The New Therapist*, 6, 4. 10–16.
2. *What is Autism?* Leaflet published by the National Autistic Society.
3. Dobzhansky, T. (1962) *Mankind Evolving*. Yale University Press.
4. Thorpe, W. H. (1969) *Animal Nature and Human Nature*. Methuen & Co.
5. Tinbergen, E. A. and Tinbergen, N. (1972) Early childhood autism – an ethological approach. Supplements to the *Journal of Comparative Ethology*. Berlin and Hamburg.
6. Jouvet, M. (1978) Does a genetic programming of the brain occur during paradoxical sleep? In P. A. Buser and A. Rougel-Buser (Eds.), *Cerebral Correlates of Conscious Experience*. Elsevier, Amsterdam.
7. Ornitz, E. M. and Ritvo, E. R. (1976) In B. J. Freeman, E. M. Ornitz and P. E. Tanguay (Eds.), *Autism*. Spectrum Books Incorporated, New York.
8. Sinclair, J. (1992). Bridging the gaps: an inside-out view of autism. In E. Schopler and G. B. Mesibov (Eds.), *High-functioning Individuals with Autism*. Plenum, New York.
9. Sachs, O. (1995) *An Anthropologist on Mars: seven paradoxical tales*. Knopf, New York.
10. Ornitz and Ritvo, op. cit.
11. Ibid.
12. Kaufman, D. N. (1970) *To Love is to be Happy with: the miracle of one autistic child*. Souvenir Press, London.
13. Claiborne Park, C. (1965). *The Seige*. Colin and Smythe Ltd, Gerrards Cross.
14. Ibid.
15. Ornitz and Ritvo, op. cit.
16. Ibid.
17. Wing, L. (1971) *Autistic Children: a guide for parents*. Constable, London.
18. Ibid.
19. Bond, J. E. (1979) *Biology of fishes*. W. B. Saunders & Co., Philadelphia, London and Toronto.
20. Furneaux, B. and Roberts, B. (1977) *Autistic Children: teaching, community and research approaches*. Routledge, London and Boston.
21. Kaufman, op. cit.
22. Moy-Thomas. J. A. (1971). (Revised by R. S. Miles) *Palaeozoic Fishes*. Constable.
23. Furneaux and Roberts, op. cit.
24. E.g. Jones, F. H., Simmonds, J. Q. and Frakel, F. (1974) An extinction procedure for eliminating self destructive behavior in a nine-year-old autistic girl. *Journal of Autism and Child Schizophrenia*, 4, 241–250.

25. Ibid.
26. Wing, op. cit.
27. Hermelin, B. and O'Connor, N. (1970) *Psychological Experiments with Autistic Children*. Pergamon Press, Oxford.
28. Wing, op. cit.
29. Schopler, E. (1965) Early infantile autism and receptor processes. *Archives of General Psychiatry*, 13, 323–335.
30. Hermelin and O'Connor, op. cit.
31. Ornitz and Ritvo, op. cit.
32. Bond, op. cit.
33. Thorpe, W. H. (1969) *Animal Nature and Human Nature*. Methuen and Co, London.
34. Bond, op. cit.
35. Kaufman, op. cit.
36. Laski, M. (1961) *Ecstasy: a study of some secular and religious experiences*. Cresset Press, London.
37. Porges, S. W. (1995) Orienting in a defensive world: mammalian modifications of our evolutionary heritage. A polyvagal theory. *Psychophysiology*, 32, 301–318.
38. Porges, S. W. (1997) Emotion: an evolutionary by-product of the neural regulation of the autonomic nervous system. In C. S. Carter, B. Kilpatrick and I. I. Lederhendler (Eds.), The Integrative Neurobiology of Affiliation. *Annals of the New York Academy of Science*, 807, 62–77.
39. Greenspan, S. I. (1997) *The Growth of the Mind*. Addison Wesley.
40. Trevarthen, C., Aitken, K., Papoudi, D. and Robarts, J. (1998). *Children with Autism: diagnosis and interventions to meet their needs*. 2nd edition. Jessica Kingsley, Philadelphia.
41. Ibid.
42. Jacobs, T. (2002) Inside a glass prison. *Human Givens*, 8, 4, 18–21.

PART III – EMOTIONAL HEALTH AND CLEAR THINKING

Chapter 9 – The APET model: the key to effective psychotherapy

1. Whitaker, R. (2002) *Mad in America: bad science, bad medicine, and the enduring mistreatment of the mentally ill*. Perseus Publishing.
2. Dawe, R. M. (1994) *House of Cards: psychology and psychotherapy built on myth*. Simon & Schuster.
3. Dineen, T. (1996) *Manufacturing Victims: what the psychology industry is doing to people*. Robert Davies.
4. "Pulling findings from the trials, it seems that patients referred to counsellors felt themselves better understood and listened to and were more likely to declare themselves satisfied with their treatment but there was no actual difference in patients' ways of coping with their difficulties or their knowledge of what needed to be changed in their lives. There was no difference in social adjustment between those who were counselled and those cared for just by GPs." Counselling in primary care: a systematic review of the research evidence. *British Journal of Guidance and Counselling*. (2000), 28, 2, 215–231.

5. Miller, S. D., Hubble, M. A., and Duncan, B. L. (1995) No more bells and whistles. *Family Therapy Networker*, 19, 2.

6. Robertson, I. (2000) "This trembling web": the brain and beyond. *The New Therapist*, 7, 3, 24–30.

7. Dewdney, A. K. (1997) *Yes we have No Neutrons – a tour through the twists and turns of bad science.* John Wiley & Sons.

8. Webster, R. (1995) *Why Freud was Wrong.* HarperCollins

9. Writing on Behaviourism, Julian Jaynes says: "But the single inherent reason for its success was not its truth, but its programme ... with its promise of reducing all conduct to a handful of reflexes and conditional responses developed from them, and generalising the spinal reflex terminology of stimulus and response and reinforcement to the puzzles of headed behaviour and so seeming to solve them ... In all this there was a heady excitement that is difficult to relate at this remove. Complexity would be made simple, darkness would be made light, and philosophy would be a thing of the past ... off the printed page, behaviourism was only a refusal to talk about consciousness. Nobody really believed he was not conscious, and there was a very real hypocrisy abroad, as those interested in its problems were forcibly excluded from academic psychology." Jaynes, J. (1976) *The Origin of Consciousness in the Breakdown of the Bicameral Mind.* Houghton, Mifflin Co. Boston, page 15.

10. "When I can sensitively understand the feelings which they are expressing, when I am able to accept them as separate persons in their own right, then I find that they tend to move in certain directions. And what are these directions in which they tend to move? The words which I believe are most truly descriptive are words such as positive, constructive, moving towards self-actualization, growing towards maturity, growing towards socialization ... to discover the strongly positive directional tendencies which exist in them, as in all of us, at the deepest levels." *The Carl Rogers Reader* (1990), Constable, London, page 28.

   "In Roger's view (1980) what psychologically troubled people most need is not to be analysed, judged or advised, but simply to be heard – that is, to be truly understood and respected by another human being. Therefore the primary effort of client centred therapists is to apply all other powers of attention, intuition and empathy to the task of grasping what the client is actually feeling." *Abnormal Psychology.* (1988) 5th edition. McGraw-Hill, page 193.

11. Yapko, M. (1992) *Hypnosis and the Treatment of Depressions.* Brunner/Mazel.

12. Mental health promotion in high risk groups. *Effective Health Care* (1997), 3, 3.

13. The following excerpt from a recent book by psychologist Adrian Wells, one of the more innovative and original contributors to cognitive therapy, shows how easily the language of cognitive therapy becomes impenetrable to an outsider and how the process of complexification of theory continues apace. "Schema theory represents a general framework for exploring and conceptualising cognitive behavioural factors in the maintenance of anxiety. However, for cognitive therapy to evolve and for treatment effectiveness to increase, specific models of cognitive-behavioural factors associated with vulnerability and problem maintenance are required. Specific models based on generic schema theory principles have been advanced for panic disorders (Clark, 1985), social phobia (Clark and Wells, 1995) and obsessional problems (Salkovskis, 1985; Wells and Mathews, 1994). These approaches have attempted to integrate schema theory with other psychological concepts considered to be important in specific disorders. The aim in all of these cases is the construction of a model that can be used for individual case conceptualisation for guiding the focus of interventions, and for generating testable model-based hypotheses. Even when specific models are lacking, case conceptualisation and treatments may

be based on operationalising basic constructs of the general theory on a case by case basis." Wells, A. (1997) *Cognitive Therapy on Anxiety Disorders*. John Wiley & Sons, page 14.

14. Yapko, op. cit.

15. Luborsky, L. and Singer, B. (1975) *Comparative Studies of Psychotherapies: is it true that "everyone has one and all must have prizes"?* Basic Books.

16. Danton, W., Antonuccio, D. and DeNelsky, G. (1995) Depression: psychotherapy is the best medicine. *Professional Psychology Research and Practice*, 26, 574.

17. Danton, W., Antonuccio, D. and Rosenthal, Z. (1997). No need to panic. *The Therapist*, 4, 4, 38–41.

18. Roth, A., Fonagy, P. et al. (1996) *What Works for Whom*. The Guildford Press.

19. NHS Centre for Reviews and Dissemination. (2001) *Effectiveness Matters: counselling in primary care*. Vol 5, Issue 2. University of York.

20. Ellis, A. (1971) *Growth through reason: verbatim cases in rational-emotive therapy*. Wiltshire Books.

21. Beck, A. (1976) *Cognitive Therapy and Emotional Disorders*. New American Library.

22. McMullin, R. E. (1986) *Handbook of Cognitive Therapy Techniques*. WW Norton.

23. Zajonc, A. (1995) Catching the Light. Oxford University Press.

24. Goleman, D. (1996) *Emotional Intelligence: why it can matter more than IQ*. Bloomsbury Publishing, London.

25. LeDoux, J. E. (1998) *The Emotional Brain*. Weidenfeld & Nicolson.

26. LeDoux, J. E. (1993) Emotional memory systems in the brain. *Behavioural Brain Research*, 58.

27. Libet, B. (1983) Time of conscious intention to act in relation to onset of cerebral activity (readiness-potential); Part 3: The unconscious initiation of a freely voluntary act. *Brain*, 106, 623–42.

28. Hartmann, T. (2000) *Thom Hartmann's Complete Guide to ADHD*. Underwood Books.

29. Danton, Antonuccio and DeNelsky, op. cit.

30. Danton, Antonuccio and Rosenthal, op. cit.

31. Griffin, J. and Tyrrell, I. (2002) *Psychotherapy, Counselling and the Human Givens*. Human Givens Publishing Ltd for the European Therapy Studies Institute.

32. Johnson, R. (1997) This is not my beautiful wife ... *New Scientist*, 22 March.

33. Ramachandram, V. S. (1998) *Phantoms in the Brain*. Fourth Estate.

34. Robertson, I. (1999) *Mind Sculpture*. Bantam Press. Professor Robertson beautifully described our brains as "vast, trembling webs of neurones ... in flux, continually remoulded, sculpted by the restless energy of the world".

35. Gladwell, M. (2000) *The Tipping Point*. Little, Brown & Company.

36. Grinder, J. and Bandler, R. (1979) *Frogs into Princes*. Real People Press.

37. Battino, R. and South, T. L. (1999) *Ericksonian Approaches*. Crown House Publishing.

38. Yaryura-Tobias, J. A. and Neziroglu, F. (1997) *Biobehavioural Treatment of Obsessive-Compulsive Spectrum Disorders*. WW Norton.

39. Teasdale, J. D. (1988) Cognitive vulnerability to persistent depression. *Cognition and Emotion*, 2, 247–274.

40. Griffin, J. and Tyrrell, I. (2002) *Breaking the Cycle of Depression*. Human Givens Publishing Ltd for the European Therapy Studies Institute.

41. Grinder and Bandler, op. cit.

42. Tavris, C. (1982) *Anger the Misunderstood Emotion.* Simon & Schuster.

43. Dixon, M. and Sweeny, K. (2000) *The Human Effect in Medicine: theory, research and practice.* Radcliffe Medical Press, Abingdon, Oxfordshire.

44. Martin, P. (1997) *The Sickening Mind: brain, behaviour, immunity and disease.* HarperCollins.

45. Ibid.

46. Williams, P. (1998) *Stories that Heal.* (Audiotape) The Therapist Ltd (distributed by Human Givens Publishing Ltd). An account of this case history is given on this audiotape, along with many others.

47. Rosen, S. (Ed). (1982) *My Voice Will Go With You: The teaching tales of Milton H. Erickson.* WW Norton.

48. Griffin, J. (1997) *The Origin of Dreams.* The Therapist Ltd (distributed by Human Givens Publishing Ltd).

49. Griffin, J. and Tyrrell, I. (2001) *Hypnosis and Trance States: a new psycho-biological explanation.* Human Givens Publishing Ltd for European Therapy Studies Institute.

50. Ornstein, R. (1993) *The Roots of the Self.* HarperCollins.

51. Shah, I. (1979) *World Tales.* Allen Lane.

52. Behe, M. J. (1996) *Darwin's Black Box.* Simon & Schuster.

Chapter 10 – A very human vulnerability: depression (and how to lift it)

1. Seligman, M. E. P. (1990) *Learned Optimism.* Pocket Books, New York. After reviewing the data on the rise and rise of depression in Western countries, psychologist Martin Seligman wrote, "We are in the midst of an epidemic of depression, one with consequences that, through suicides, takes as many lives as the AIDS epidemic and is more widespread. Severe depression is ten times more prevalent today than it was fifty years ago. It assaults women twice as often as men, and now it strikes a full decade earlier in life on average than it did a generation ago."

2. Lane, R. E. (2000) *The Loss of Happiness in Market Democracies.* Yale University Press.

3. UNICEF (1993) *The Progress of Nations.* United Nations, 45.

4. Seligman, M. E. P. In J. Buie (1988) 'Me' decades generate depression: individualism erodes commitment to others. *APA Monitor,* 19, 18. "People born after 1945 were ten times more likely to suffer from depression than people born 50 years earlier."

5. *Medical Health Index.* (1999) IMS Health.

6. *The global burden of disease* (1997) World Health Organisation.

7. Nemeroff, C. B. (1998) The neurobiology of depression. *Scientific American,* 278, 6, 28–35.

8. McGrath, E. et al. (1990) *Women and Depression.* American Psychological Association.

9. Ibid.

10. Griffin, J. and Tyrrell, I. (2001) *Hypnosis and Trance States: a new psychobiological explanation.* Human Givens Publishing Ltd for the European Therapy Studies Institute.

11. Ibid.

12. Goleman, D. (1996) *Emotional Intelligence: why it can matter more than IQ.* Bloomsbury Publishing, London.

13. Seligman in J. Buie, op. cit. "On the whole, you do not find much in the way of depression as we know it – suicide, hopelessness, giving up, low self-esteem, passivity and the like – in nonwestern cultures ..."
14. Kleinman, A. (1995) *World Mental Health: Problems and Priorities in Low-Income Countries*. Oxford University Press, New York (for the United Nations).
15. Curtis, A. and Tyrrell, I. (2002) A seething mass of desires: Freud's hold over history. Interview in *Human Givens*, 9, 3, 24–31.
16. Lloyd, D. and Rossi, E. (1992) *High Frequency Biological Rhythms: function of the ultradians*. Springer-Verlag, New York.
17. Rossi, E. and Nimmons, D. (1991) *The 20 Minute Break*. J. P. Tarcher Inc., Los Angeles.
18. Kubey, R. and Csikszentmihalyi, M. (2002) Television addiction is no mere metaphor. *Scientific American*, February, 62–68.
19. Ibid.
20. "Those in low-status jobs with little control over their work got sick and died much more often than those in higher status jobs with more control." Finding from a study of 10,000 London civil servants reported in *Mind Sculpture* by Professor Ian Robertson, Bantam Press (1999).
21. Rutter, M. (1971) Parent-child separation: psychological effects on the children. *Journal of Child Psychology and Psychiatry*, 12, 233–60.
22. Richards, M. et al. (1997) The effects of divorce and separation on mental health in a national UK birth cohort. *Psychological Medicine*, 27, 1121–8.
23. McLanahan, S. and Sandefur, G. (1994) *Growing Up with a Single Parent*. Harvard University Press.
24. Angel, R. and Angel, J. (1993) *Painful Inheritance: health and the new generation of fatherless families*. University of Wisconsin Press.
25. Amato, P. and Booth, A. (1997) *A Generation at Risk*. Harvard University Press.
26. Forehand, R. et al. (1997) Is adolescent adjustment following parental divorce a function of predivorce adjustment? *Journal of Abnormal Child Psychology*.
27. Papermaster, D. (1995) Necessary but insufficient. *Nature Medicine*, 1, 874–5.
28. Le Fanu. J. (1999) *The Rise and Fall of Modern Medicine*. Little, Brown & Company.
29. Yapko, M. D. (1997) *Breaking the Patterns of Depression*. Doubleday.
30. Danton, W. Antonuccio, D. and DeNelsky, G. (1995). Depression: psychotherapy is the best medicine. *Professional Psychology Research and Practice*, 26, 574.
31. *Diagnostic and Statistical Manual of Mental Disorders* (4th Ed.) (1994). American Psychiatric Association, Washington D.C.
32. *Diagnosis, Vol. 2 Treatment Aspect*. United States Public Health Service Agency.
33. Danton, Antonuccio and DeNelsky, op. cit.
34. Of course psychodynamic therapy can, in its early stages, be helpful to some people. We all experience being troubled and worried about things and finding it helpful to talk about our problem with a friend. And, provided the friend is sympathetic, it can create a space wherein we can review what we are worried about and maybe get new perspectives on our problems. And that can be very helpful as long as the conversations are focusing on current problems. It is part of the way we deal with difficulties. But it is when the counselling relationship turns to resurrecting everything that has gone wrong in clients' lives – encouraging them to get emotional about it – that it promotes emotionally arousing introspection and will make people more dysfunctional.

This is the reason why psychodynamic counsellors have such problems around their concept of 'counter transference' where the therapist gets emotionally involved with the client and finds that 'issues' from *their* own past keep coming up all the time. Then they have to go for supervision to talk this through to try and 'understand' it. But the reason this happens is that the therapists themselves have undergone a process of making their own emotional reaction patterns hyper-aroused and easily triggered off, misusing what is, in limited doses, a useful tool.

35. Dubovsky, S. L. (1997) *Mind-Body Deceptions: the psychosomatics of everyday life.* WW Norton & Co.

36. Glenmullen, J. (2000) *Prozac Backlash: overcoming the dangers of Prozac, Zoloft, Paxil, and other antidepressants with safe, effective alternatives.* Simon & Schuster.

37. Robertson, I. (1999) *Mind Sculpture.* Bantam Press.

38. Linde, K., Ramirex, G., Mulrow, C. D., Pauls, A., Weidenhammer, W., Melchart, D. (1996) St John's wort for depression: an overview and meta-analysis of randomized clinical trials. *British Medical Journal,* 313, 253–258.

39. Woelk, H. (2000) Comparison of St John's wort and imipramine for treating depression: randomised controlled trial. *British Medical Journal,* September 2.

40. There are numerous anecdotal references to the effectiveness of St John's wort for insomnia but no scientific studies have been done that we can trace. It is important to remember that sleep difficulties are a cardinal symptom of depression. These difficulties may take the form of having trouble falling asleep, tossing and turning or sleeping fitfully, or waking up too early in the morning. So distressing are such symptoms that they may overwhelm the clinical picture and the depressed person may misdiagnose the condition as insomnia.

41. Grube, B., Walper, A., Wheatley, D. (1999) St. John's wort extract: efficacy for menopausal symptoms of psychological origin. *Advances in Therapy,* 16, 4, 177–186.

42. Rosenthal, N. (1998) *St John's Wort.* Thornsens.

43. *Diagnostic and Statistical Manual of Mental Disorders* (4th Ed.), op. cit.

44. Teasdale, J. D. et al. (2000) Prevention of relapse/recurrence in major clinical depression by mindfulness-based cognitive therapy. *Journal of Consulting and Clinical Psychology,* 68, 4, 615–23.

45. Griffin, J. and Tyrrell, I. (2002) *Psychotherapy, Counselling and the Human Givens.* Human Givens Publishing Ltd for the European Therapy Studies Institute.

46. Vogel, G. W. (1979) *The Function of Sleep.* In Drucker-Collins et al. (Eds.), Academic Press, New York, 233–250.

47. Hobson, J. A. (1994) *The Chemistry of Conscious States.* Little, Brown & Company, Canada.

48. "The efficacy of antidepressant activity, across drugs, is directly related to the capacity of drugs to produce large and sustained reductions of REM sleep." In S. J. Ellman and J. S. Antrobus (Eds.), (1991 2nd edition) *The Mind in Sleep.* John Wiley.

49. Nemeroff, C. B. (1998) The neurobiology of depression. *Scientific American,* 278, 6, 28–35.

50. Danton, Antonuccio and DeNelsky, op. cit.

51. Peterson, C. and Seligman, M. E. P. (1984) Causal explanations as a factor for depression: theory and evidence. *Psychological Review,* 91, 341–74.

52. Yapko, M. D. (1999) *Hand-Me-Down Blues: how to stop depression spreading in families.* Doubleday.

53. Howard Burton et al. (1986) The relationship of depression to survival in chronic renal failure, *Psychosomatic Medicine*.

54. Martin, P. (1997) *The Sickening Mind: brain, behaviour, immunity and disease*. HarperCollins.

55. Dolnick, E. (1998) *Madness on the Couch*. Simon & Schuster.

56. Allen, N. H. P. and Burns, A. (1995) The non-cognitive features of dementia. *Reviews in Clinical Gerontology*, 5, 57–75. "Having a wide range of social roles is known to act as a buffer against the effects of life events that can otherwise lead to depression."

57. Thase, M. E. (2000) Psychopharmacology in conjunction with psychotherapy. In C. R Snyder and R. E. Ingram (Eds.), *Handbook of Psychological Change*. John Wiley & Sons.

58. Woodham, A. (2002) Depressed? Look on the bright side. *The Times*, 6 August.

59. For an example of the client's viewpoint on being helped out of depression quickly with the human givens approach, see On the receiving end ... *The New Therapist* (2000), 7, 2, 22–23.

60. Elwick, L. (1999) A Headache to end all headaches. *The Therapist*, 6, 3, 28–34. This is a poignant description by a woman who, from being healthy and fit, suffered a transpontine infarction resulting in sudden total paralysis and locked-in syndrome. Over several years she found ways to communicate again during which her sense of awareness and intelligence remained undimmed. Throughout this ordeal, doctors said that she did not suffer from clinical depression.

61. Woodham, op. cit.

Chapter 11 – Terror in the brain: overcoming trauma

1. Charney, D. S., Deutch, A. V., Krystal, J. H., Southwick, A. M., and Davis, M. (1993) Psychobiologic mechanisms of post traumatic stress disorder. *Archives of General Psychiatry*, 50, 295–305.

2. Kessler, R. C., Sonnega, A., Bromet, E., Hughes, M., and Nelson, C. B. (1995) Post traumatic stress disorder in the National Comorbidity Survey. *Archives of General Psychiatry*, 52, 1048–1060.

3. Danieli, Y. (1985) The treatment and prevention of long-term effects and intergenerational transmission of victimization. A lesson from Holocaust survivors and their children. In C. R. Figley (Ed.), *Trauma and its Wake*. Brunner/Mazel. 278–294.

4. Nathan P. E. and Gorman, J. M. (Eds.) (1998) *A Guide to Treatments that Work*. Oxford University Press.

5. Wessely, S., Rose, S. and Bisson, J. A. (1999). A systematic review of brief psychological interventions ("debriefing") for the treatment of immediate trauma related symptoms and the prevention of post traumatic stress disorder. In Cochrane Collaboration. *Cochrane Library*, Issue 4, Oxford.

6. Debunking debriefing. *The New Therapist*, 7, 1, 8.

7. Spiegel, D., Hunt, T., and Dondershine, H. E. (1988) Dissociation and hypnotisability in post traumatic stress disorder. *American Journal of Psychiatry*, 145, 301–305.

8. Tehrani, N. (1998) Debriefing: a safe way to defuse emotion? *The Therapist*, 5, 3, 24–29. "If a trauma victim is debriefed in a state of high emotion, the process can increase the arousal to the point of overload, trapping the sensory impressions in the amygdala."

9. Griffin, J. and Tyrrell, I. (2002) *Psychotherapy, Counselling and the Human Givens*. Human Givens Publishing Ltd for the European Therapy Studies Institute.

10. Shapiro, F. and Forrest, M. S. (1997) *EMDR*. Basic Books.

11. Wolinsky, S. (1991) *Trances people live by*. The Bramble Co. Wolinsky gives a clear description of how a person slips into an age-regressed hypnotic trance when they relive a trauma. He developed a technique very similar to Shapiro's, which keeps the patient's awareness focused on the therapist whilst recalling the trauma, thus stopping them from regressing completely into the traumatic memory. His technique also keeps emotional arousal from rising too high, facilitating the reframing and a recoding of the memory by the higher cortex.

12. LeDoux, J. E. (1992). Emotion as memory: anatomical systems underlying indelible neural traces. In S. A. Christensen (Ed.), *Handbook of Emotion and Memory*. Erlbaum, Hillsdale, New Jersey.

13. Wilson, J. P., and Keane, T. M. (1997) *Assessing Psychological Trauma and PTSD*. The Guildford Press.

14. Ibid.

15. Van der Kolk, B. A. (1996) In B. A. Van der Kolk, A. C. McFarlane and L. Weisaeth (Eds.), *Traumatic Stress*. The Guildford Press.

16. Kardiner, A. (1941) *The Traumatic Neuroses of War*. Hoebe, New York.

17. Blanchard, R. J., and Blanchard, D. C. (1989) Antipredator defensive behaviour. *Journal of Comparative Psychology*, 103, 70–82. "If something unexpected occurs – a loud noise or sudden movement – people tend to respond immediately ... stop what they are doing ... orient toward the stimulus, and try to identify its potentiality for actual danger. This happens very quickly, in a reflex-like sequence in which action precedes any voluntary or consciously intentioned behaviour. A poorly localisable or identifiable threat source, such as a sound in the night, may elicit an active immobility so profound that the frightened person can hardly speak or even breathe, i.e. freezing. However, if the danger source has been localised and an avenue for flight or concealment is plausible, the person will probably try to flee or hide."

18. Dixon, A. K. (1998). Ethological strategies for defence in animals and humans: their role in some psychiatric disorders. *British Journal of Medical Psychology*, 71, 417–445.

19. Levine, P. (1998) *Waking the Tiger*. North Atlantic Books.

20. Levine, P. (1998) Blowing off stress. *The Therapist*, 5, 2, 15–20.

21. Morrison, A. R. and Reiner, P. B. (1985) A Dissection of Paradoxical Sleep. In D. J. McGinty, C. Drucken, A. R. Morrison and P. Parmeggiani (Eds.), *Brain Mechanisms of Sleep*. Raven Press, New York, 97–110.

22. Griffin, J. (1997) *The Origin of Dreams*. The Therapist Ltd (distributed by Human Givens Publishing Ltd).

23. Griffin, J. and Tyrrell, I. (2001) *Hypnosis and Trance States: a new psychobiological explanation*. Human Givens Publishing Ltd for the European Therapy Studies Institute.

24. Spiegel, D., Detrick, D. and Frischholz, E. J. (1982) Hypnotizability and psychopathology. *American Journal of Psychiatry*, 139, 431–437.

25. LeDoux, J. (2002) *Synaptic Self*. Macmillan.

26. Ibid.

27. Amaral, D. G., Price, J. L., Pitkanen, A. and Carmichael S. T. (1992). Anatomical organization of the primate amygdaloid complex. In J. P. Aggleton (Ed.), *The amygdala: neurobiological aspects of emotion, memory and mental dysfunction*. Wiley-Liss, New York, 1–66.

28. Shephard, B. (2000) *A War of Nerves: soldiers and psychiatrists 1914–1994*. Jonathan Cape

29. Ibid.

30. Brown. W. (1934) *Psychology and Psychotherapy*. London.
31. Sargant, W. (1957) *Battle for the Mind*. Heinemann.
32. Bandler, R. (1985) *Using Your Brain for a Change*. Real People Press.
33. Guy, K. and Guy, N. (2003) The fast cure for phobia and trauma: evidence that it works. *Human Givens*, 9, 4, 31–35.
34. Griffin, J. and Tyrrell, I. (2001) *The Shackled Brain: how to release locked-in patterns of trauma*. Human Givens Publishing Ltd for the European Therapy Studies Institute.
35. The MindFields College prospectus can be obtained by telephoning 01323 811440 in the UK. Its website is www.mindfields.org.uk
36. Harrington, R. and Harrison, L. (1999) Unproven assumptions about the impact of bereavement on children. *Journal of the Royal Society of Medicine*, 92 (May), 230–32.
37. Kessler, R. C., McGonagle, K. A., Zhao, S. et al. (1994) Lifetime and 12-month prevalence of DSM-III-psychiatric disorders in the United States: results from the National Comorbidity Survey. *Archives of General Psychiatry*, 16, 118–126.
38. Anthony, M. M., and Barlow, D. H. (1996) Specific phobia. In V. E. Caballo and R. M. Turner (Eds.), *International Handbook of Cognitive-behavioural Treatment of Psychiatric Disorders*. Madrid, Siglio XXI.
39. Karno, M., Golding, J. M., Sorenson, S. B., and Burnham, M. A. (1988) The epidemiology of obsessive-compulsive disorder. *Archives of General Psychiatry*, 45, 12, 1094–1099.
40. O'Hanlon, W. H. (1987) *Taproots – Underlying principles of Milton Erickson's therapy and hypnosis*. WW Norton.

AFTERWORD: A new scientific metaphor: consciousness – more is less

1. Gribbon, J. (2002) *Science: a history 1543–2001*. Allen Lane.
2. Gray, J. (2002) *Straw Dogs: thoughts on humans and other animals*. Granta Books.
3. Pinker, S. (2002) *The Blank State: the modern denial of human nature*. Allen Lane.
4. Dawkins, R. (1978) *The Selfish Gene*. Oxford University Press.
5. Carter, R. (2002) *Consciousness*. Weidenfeld & Nicolson.
6. Donald, M. (2001) *A Mind So Rare: the evolution of human consciousness*. WW Norton & Co.
7. Flanagan, O. (1991) *The Science of the Mind*. MIT Press.
8. See Dennett, D. ((1991) *Consciousness Explained*. Little, Brown & Company; Pinker, S. (1997) *How the Mind Works*. WW Norton & Co.
9. Libet, B. (1983) Time of conscious intention to act in relation to onset of cerebral activity (readiness-potential); Part 3: The unconscious initiation of a freely voluntary act. *Brain*, 106, 623–42.
10. Deikman, A. J. (1982). *The Observing Self*. Beacon Press.
11. Frith, C. and Frith, U. (1999) Interacting minds: Biological basis. *Science*, 286, 1692-1695.
12. Bortoft, H. (1996) *The Wholeness of Nature*. Lindisfarne Books.
13. Haggard, P. et al. (1999) On the perceived time of voluntary actions. *British Journal of Psychology*, 90, 291–303; Haggard, P. et al. (1999) On the relations between brain potentials and awareness of movements. *Experimental Brain Research*, 126, 128–33.

14. Jaynes, J. (1982) *Origin of Consciousness in the Breakdown of the Bicameral Mind.* Houghton Mifflin.
15. Ibid.
16. Ibid.
17. Waddington, C. H. (1957) *The Strategy of the Genes.* Allen & Unwin.
18. Chalmers, D. L. (1996) *The Conscious Mind.* Oxford University Press.
19. Deikman, op. cit.
20. Petters, A. O., Levine, H. and Wambsganss. (2001) *Singularity Theory and Gravitational Lensing.* Birkhäuser.
21. Battersby, S. (2003) Cosmic Map. Our Universe in Glorious Detail. (New data from the satelite. Known as Microwave Anisotropy Probe, (MAP) set far beyond the moon to chart the early Universe. *New Scientist.* Vol 177 2382.
22. Rees, M. (1991) *Our Cosmic Habitat.* Weidenfield & Nicholson.
23. Chown, M. (2001) *The Universe Next Door.* Headline Book Publishing.
24. Lewin, J. (1993) *Complexity.* Orion Books.
25. Horgan, J. (1999) *The Undiscovered Mind.* Simon & Schuster.
26. Bell, J. (1987) *Speakable and Unspeakable in Quantum Mechanics.* Cambridge University Press.
27. Dylan, B. (1981) *Every Grain of Sand.* Columbia Records.
28. Drosnin, M. (2002). *The Bible Code 2.* Weidenfeld & Nicolson.
29. Shah, I. (1968) *The Way of the Sufi.* Jonathan Cape.
30. Wordsworth, W. (1888) *The Complete Poetical Works.* Macmillan.
31. Shah, I. (1994) *The Commanding Self.* The Octagon Press.
32. Einstein, A. (1954) *Ideas and Opinions.* Crown.
33. Jalaladin Rumi quoted in Shah (1968), op.cit.
34. See, for example, in El-Ghazali's *Restoration of Religious Sciences,* summarised in *Thinkers of the East,* by Idries Shah. (1971), The Octagon Press.
35. Sanai, H. (d. 1150) *The Walled Garden of Truth.* Translated in 1974 by David Pendlebury. The Octagon Press.
36. Shah, I. (1964) *The Sufis.* The Octagon Press.
37. Zajonc, A. (1995) *Catching the Light.* Oxford University Press.
38. Bortoft, op. cit.
39. Goethe, quoted in Fritz Heinemann, (1934) Goethe's Phenomenological Method. *Philosophy,* 9, 73.
40. Ibid.
41. Peseschtian, N. (1976) *Oriental Stories as Tools of Psychotherapy.* Springer-Verlag.
42. Shah, I. (1968) *The Study of Sufism in the West.* In Shah (1968), op.cit. References to psychotherapy and a psychology of profound sophistication are too numerous to list here.
43. Rumi, J. (13th century) *Mathnavi.* Available in many translations from many publishers.
44. Coates, P. (2002) *Ibn 'Arabî and Modern Thought.* Anqa Publishers, Oxford.
45. Shabistari, M. (13th century) *The Secret Garden.* An English translation is available from Octagon Press.
46. Hujwiri (11th century) *The Revelation of the Veiled.*
47. See, for example, in Nickolson's translation of Diwan-i-Shams-i-Tabriz.
48. Capra, F. (1999 edition) *The Tao of Physics.* Shambhala Publications.

49. Laszlo, E. (1993) *The Creative Cosmos*. Floris Books.
50. Zohar, D. and Marshall, I. (1994) *The Quantum Society*. Bloomsbury.
51. Stoppard, T. (1988) *Hapgood*. Faber & Faber.
52. Book review by Christopher Hart of *Science: A History 1543–2001*, in the *Sunday Telegraph*. 17 November 2002.
53. Chalmers, D. J. (1997) *The Conscious Mind: in search of a fundamental theory*. Oxford University Press.
54. Siegel, J. et al. (2002) *Sleep in Monotremes*. Neurobiology Research, University of Queensland, Brisbane.
55. La Barre, W. (1980) *Culture in Context*. Duke University Press.
56. Shah (1968) op.cit.
57. Translator W. K. C. Guthrie. (1956) *Plato: Protagoras and Meno*. Penguin Books.
58. Schrödinger, E. (1958) *Mind and Matter*. Cambridge University Press.

If you found the ideas presented in this book of interest, you might also like to know about the following:

The quarterly journal of the Human Givens Institute (HGI), *Human Givens: Promoting emotional health and clear thinking,* is the ideal way to keep up with developments arising out of this new school of psychology. It is available by subscription (back issues also available), call +44 (0)1323 811662 for full details or visit: **www.humangivens.com**

For information on training using the human givens approach, visit the MindFields College website at: **www.mindfields.org.uk** or call: +44 (0)1323 811440 to request a prospectus.

If you would like to contact the authors via email you can do so at: info@humangivens.com

Index